THE COMPLETE HANDBOOK OF
PRO FOOTBALL

1989
15th EDITION
THE COMPLETE HANDBOOK OF
PRO FOOTBALL

EDITED BY ZANDER HOLLANDER

AN ASSOCIATED FEATURES BOOK

A SIGNET BOOK

NEW AMERICAN LIBRARY

A DIVISION OF PENGUIN BOOKS USA INC.

ACKNOWLEDGMENTS

The Steelers were coming off a Super Bowl victory over the Vikings. Franco Harris was the game's MVP. Joe Namath refused a $4-million offer to play in the World Football League. Bill Walsh was an assistant coach with the Bengals. It was 1975, the year that also marked the birth of *The Complete Handbook of Pro Football*.

The 1989 season will be conspicuous by the absence of Walsh, after a successful decade as coach of the 49ers; Tom Landry, the legendary Cowboys' leader, and Pete Rozelle, the celebrated outgoing commissioner of the NFL.

For this 15th edition, we also acknowledge the contributions of contributing editor Eric Compton, the writers on the contents page and Rich Rossiter, Kevin Mulroy, Herman Masin, Linda Spain, Dot Gordineer of Libra Graphics, Westchester Book Composition, Elias Sports Bureau, Pete Abitante, Dick Maxwell, Joe Browne, Jim Heffernan and the NFL team publicists.

Zander Hollander

PHOTO CREDITS: Cover—Focus on Sports; back cover— Anthony Neste/Focus on Sports. Inside photos—Ira Golden, Pete Groh, Nancy Hogue, Vic Milton, Mitch Reibel, ABC-TV, CBS-TV, NBC-TV, ESPN, Wide World, UPI, and the NFL and college team photographers.

SIGNET TRADEMARK REG. U.S. PAT. OFF. AND FOREIGN COUNTRIES REGISTERED TRADEMARK—MARCA REGISTRADA
HECHO EN DRESDEN, TN

SIGNET, SIGNET CLASSIC, MENTOR, ONYX, PLUME, MERIDIAN AND NAL BOOKS are published by New American Library, a division of Penguin Books USA, Inc.,
1633 Broadway, New York, New York 10019

First Printing, August, 1989

1 2 3 4 5 6 7 8 9

PRINTED IN THE UNITED STATES OF AMERICA

CONTENTS

Editor's Note: The material herein includes trades and rosters up to the final printing deadline.

Joe Montana readies pass to favorite batterymate...

Greatest Batteries: Dorais-Rockne to Montana-Rice

By JOE GERGEN

Even in redefining the position, in stamping Super Bowl XXIII as his own, Jerry Rice paid homage to the past. While setting a record for yardage and tying a mark for the number of

Joe Gergen, a columnist for Newsday *and* The Sporting News, *never needs a new charge in his batteries.*

...Jerry Rice: MVP of Super Bowl XXIII.

receptions, he evoked the memory of another great player who had used the National Football League's championship game as a stage for his talent. Thirteen years earlier, in the same city, Lynn Swann had become the first receiver to be honored as the Most Valuable Player at the extravaganza.

The quantity of Rice's accomplishments exceeded anything in Super Bowl annals. But it was the quality of the catches on behalf of the San Francisco 49ers that was so impressive, that drew references to the graceful Swann. One play, a leaping grab of a 44-yard pass with Cincinnati cornerback Lewis Billups draped on his back, was a carbon copy of a signature Swann catch against the Dallas Cowboys in Super Bowl X.

Cris Collinsworth instantly made the connection. "I keep going back to that pattern where Billups had him completely covered," said Collinsworth, a fine receiver for the Bengals, "and he made a catch that only Swann could have made, besides Rice." It was a marvelous compliment, one that Rice appreciated.

"Lynn Swann was an idol of mine," Rice said after the game. "It amazed me how he would fly through the air and make catches. I remember one against Dallas. It was the greatest catch I ever saw."

That was precisely the one Collinsworth and others at Joe

Robbie Stadium in Miami had in mind, one they thought would never be repeated. But Rice did a perfectly acceptable imitation of the former Pittsburgh star while creating a few moves of his own, notably the scoring drive he capped by reaching around the pylon to lay the football in the end zone while his body pitched out of bounds. It was the equivalent of Gene Kelly donning a top hat for a tribute to Fred Astaire, then trading it for an umbrella and tap-dancing in the rain.

Of course, Rice couldn't have done it alone. Just as Swann had Terry Bradshaw, the quarterback of four Super Bowl champions, Rice performed at the discretion of Joe Montana. In achieving his third Super Bowl ring in the decade, Montana earned a special niche in pro football history. The Niners' final offensive sequence, a 92-yard march that consumed two minutes, 36 seconds, was a classic.

Knute Rockne was Gus Dorais' catcher at Notre Dame.

"We had them on their eight with three minutes to go," Collinsworth recalled, "and somebody came up to me and said, 'We got 'em now.' I said, 'Have you taken a look at who's quarterbacking?' He's not human."

In leading the Niners down the field to a last-minute touchdown and a 20-16 victory, Montana confirmed Collinsworth's worst fears and enhanced his reputation as the most extraordinary pressure player in the contemporary game. He also proved beyond doubt that he and Rice are among the great batteries ever to play the sport, a passing combination that can stand comparison with the best of all time. In three postseason games culminating with the Super Bowl, they connected 21 times for 409 yards and six touchdowns.

Remarkably, the pair has produced 49 touchdowns in just four seasons, playoff games excluded. Already, the receiver is virtually halfway to the all-time record for TD receptions set by the peerless Don Hutson in an earlier era. Of course, the evolution of the passing game has undergone a rapid acceleration in the last half-century, beginning with Hutson's arrival in the NFL.

Consider that in the formative version of football, batteries were not included. It was a brutal sport based entirely on the concept of power and the results were so horrifying that President Theodore Roosevelt threatened to outlaw it, forcing administrators to open up the game. Thus was the forward pass first allowed in the fall of 1906.

But the rules were so stringent that few teams bothered to practice it. According to the initial regulations, a pass had to cross the line of scrimmage not more than five yards to the left or right of center and couldn't be thrown more than 20 yards. Furthermore, an incompleted pass was treated like a fumble if it hadn't been touched and a pass caught in the end zone was considered a touchback, with the defending team awarded the ball.

A Jerry Rice would not have flourished in such a system. The restraints finally were dropped in 1912 but that in itself wasn't enough to revolutionize the game. The ball still was bloated and difficult to throw. A few college teams in the Midwest experimented with passing attacks but in the East, then the power base of the sports, teams continued to favor strength over finesse.

It was under such conditions that Knute Rockne, who had been elected captain of the 1913 football team at a small Catholic college in Indiana, went to incoming coach Jess Harper in the spring of the year with a request. He said that he and his roommate, Gus Dorais, had summer jobs at a hotel in Cedar Point, Ohio. "We're going to do some special practicing," Rockne said. "Can we take a couple of footballs with us?"

What Rockne had in mind was the implementation of an offense based on the ability to strike through the air. He and Dorais worked on pass patterns, hoping to use them to befuddle national power Army in a game scheduled for West Point on Nov. 1. "Rock kept repeating a phrase," Dorais recalled years later. "'Mobility. Mobility and change of pace. That's what we need. They're not going to know where we're going or when we get there.'"

That's exactly what happened in the historic meeting between Notre Dame and the U.S. Military Academy. The smaller Irish confused the Cadets, striking swiftly from everywhere on the field. Dorais completed an unprecedented 14 passes for 243 yards in the remarkable 35-13 upset. Rockne, only 5-9 and 155 pounds, caught seven passes in the second half alone.

Headlines around the country proclaimed the advent of a new weapon. Army quickly adopted the forward pass and used it to beat archrival Navy. Thirteen years late, football entered the 20th century.

Still, it was a different sport than we know it today. Running backs, operating out of the single wing, continued to dominate the game. And then Don Hutson loped out of Alabama and into a nation's consciousness.

Hutson was a lean receiver who had been timed in 9.7 seconds for the 100-yard dash. But beyond his speed, he had a bewilder-

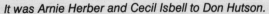

It was Arnie Herber and Cecil Isbell to Don Hutson.

ing variety of fakes and the belief that patterns were something that required constant practice. He reported to the Green Bay Packers in 1935 fresh off a sensational Rose Bowl performance against Stanford.

The Packers already had an exceptional passer in Arnie Herber. If there were any doubt that this was destined to become pro football's first great battery, it was alleviated on the first play from scrimmage in Hutson's first game. The rugged Bears assigned double coverage to Green Bay star Johnny Blood, leaving the slender rookie to the devices of their fastest player, Beattie Feathers. They paid the price when Hutson broke behind his defender and completed an 83-yard touchdown play.

It was a memorable start to a remarkable 11-year career. In that time, Hutson led the NFL in receptions eight times and in touchdown catches nine times. He had at least one reception in 95 consecutive games, a record that lasted for 25 years, was credited with 17 touchdown catches in an 11-game season and in 1945, his final year, he grabbed four scoring passes in a single quarter of a game against Detroit.

All this was the product of hard work as well as natural talent. "For every pass I caught in a game," he once said, "I caught a thousand passes in practice." He also worked with Herber and Packers' coach Curly Lambeau to develop complex patterns that confounded secondaries.

Nor was he adverse to spontaneous invention, such as the time he eluded a Cleveland Rams' defensive back by hooking his arm around the goal post and swinging himself into perfect position to receive a scoring pass. "He was the only man I ever saw," said veteran coach Earl (Greasy) Neale, "who could feint in three different directions at the same time."

In his undersized shoulder pads, the frail-looking receiver was half of two renowned batteries. Herber yielded to Cecil Isbell, a deft passer who threw for 24 touchdowns in 1942, including 17 to Hutson. According to the receiver, Isbell would have joined Herber in the Pro Football Hall of Fame if he hadn't retired prematurely in order to take the coaching postion at Purdue, his alma mater.

"If he stayed around the NFL," Hutson said, "I believe he would have become one of the game's most successful passers, and his name would be all over the record books, and they would talk of him in the same terms they do of Luckman and Baugh."

Isbell was a contemporary both of Sid Luckman, the first great T-formation quarterback, and Sammy Baugh, the nonpareil passer of his era. When Baugh reported to the Washington Redskins in the summer of 1937, head coach Ray Flaherty ordered his best receiver, Wayne Millner, to run a few simple patterns in order to gauge the ability of his celebrated rookie from Texas Christian. "I want you," Flaherty told Baugh, "to hit him square in the eye with the ball."

Baugh nodded but had a second thought as he was calling signals. Pausing momentarily, he yelled to the coach. "Which eye?" he asked. The man wasn't kidding, as the world would soon discover.

With Baugh passing to Millner, the Redskins won the Eastern Division title, then turned back the Bears in the championship game, 28-21. Millner had 11 receptions in that game, including two for touchdowns. The twosome became so closely identified that when Baugh made stage appearances in the offseason, he would conclude the show by throwing passes to Millner, seated in the balcony.

In the ensuing years, the rivalry between the Redskins and Bears would produce some of the most memorable games in NFL history. Among them was the 73-0 rout by Chicago in the 1940 title contest, a game in which Washington's only scoring threat dissolved with Charley Malone's drop of a Baugh pass in the end zone with Washington trailing, 7-0. Naturally, Baugh was asked after the game if the outcome would have been different had Malone made the catch. "Hell, yes," the man said. "The score would have been 73-6."

By then, Luckman, in his second season out of Columbia, had mastered the newfangled T-formation. In his first play as a quarterback the previous year, in a relief role against the Giants at the Polo Grounds, he had completed a long touchdown pass to halfback Bob MacLeod. He confessed later that MacLeod had saved him from an interception, but he didn't need much help thereafter.

With Luckman at the helm, the Monsters of the Midway reached the championship game in four successive seasons, winning three times. Their overall record for those years was 41-6-1. Chicago had all-stars at virtually every position, including end, where Ken Kavanaugh was, in Luckman's words, "an uncanny football player." On Nov. 14, 1943, on the occasion of "Sid Luckman Day" in New York, the Brooklyn native passed for seven touchdowns in a 56-7 romp over the Giants. It's a record that has been equalled but never surpassed.

The Cleveland Browns introduced the next advance in the passing game as they dominated the All-America Conference in the aftermath of World War II. They had an outstanding receiver at each end in Dante Lavelli and Mac Speedie and they occasionally flanked Dub Jones from his halfback position to create extra

Elroy Hirsch caught 'em from Waterfield and Van Brocklin.

pressure on the secondary. It helped that they also had a superb quarterback, Otto Graham.

A basketball standout as well as a football star at Northwestern, Graham emerged as the first master of the sideline pass. "The secret," he said, "is to have the receiver come back. You tell a guy to make a 90-degree cut toward the sideline, but with his momentum he's actually still going downfield. By making the receiver cut back, he has the defender beaten by two steps. The defender is also blocked off by the receiver's body."

Although the Browns pioneered the three-receiver offense, it was the Los Angeles Rams who exploited it fully. They were pro football's first true aerial circus. Not only did they boast two Hall of Fame receivers in Tom Fears and Elroy (Crazylegs) Hirsch but two Hall of Fame quarterbacks, Bob Waterfield and Norm Van Brocklin. For a time, the quarterbacks were platooned by quarters.

In 1950, the Rams amassed an amazing 466 points in 12 games. In successive weeks, they drubbed Baltimore, 70-27, and Detroit, 65-24. "We could score on anyone," said Fears, a great possession receiver who led the NFL in catches with 84.

It was Hirsch, however, who ranked as the most spectacular

Champ Colts: Johnny Unitas to . . . Raymond Berry.

performer on the team. A former halfback with the Chicago Rockets of the AAC, he became pro football's first full-time flankerback with the Rams. Not only did he have great speed but he was virtually unstoppable once he caught the ball, the result of a unique running style he developed as a youngster by constantly faking his way through a grove of pine trees near his Wisconsin home.

"You've heard about the guy who zigged when he should have zagged," Van Brocklin once said. "Well, Roy also has a 'zog' and a couple of variations of 'zug' when he is running at full speed." In 1951, he tied Hutson's record by accounting for 17 TDs on pass receptions. Six of them covered 70 yards or more and the average gain on those plays was 48. "Elroy looks like he's running at full speed but actually he's saving a final burst," Waterfield said. "If I can hang the ball out there, Elroy will run just fast enough to get under it."

Hirsch and Fears teamed beautifully in the championship game that year. With the score tied at 17 midway through the fourth quarter and the Rams bogged down on their 27-yard line, the Browns assigned double coverage to Crazylegs. Van Brocklin coolly looked off his deep threat and passed 73 yards to Fears for the winning touchdown.

The latter part of the decade belonged, unaccountably, to a quarterback who had been cut by his hometown team in Pittsburgh and a receiver with poor eyesight and modest speed. Johnny Unitas and Raymond Berry led the Baltimore Colts to consecutive championships in 1958 and 1959. Theirs was a partnership of precision. No two men ever worked the sidelines more effectively. "The success of a sideline pattern depends on your quarterback," Berry said. "John always had the arm for it."

Joe Namath clicked with Don Maynard and George Sauer.

What Berry brought to the battery was intelligence and a work ethic. He practiced for hours catching underthrown passes, overthrown passes, passes several feet to either side. He wore a helmet and shoulder pads when he practiced, even in the heat of summer, to simulate game conditions. He became the NFL's ultimate first-down receiver, which was never more evident than in the 1958 title game against the Giants, dubbed the "Greatest Game Ever Played." Berry had 12 receptions for 178 yards in the overtime triumph and, when Unitas was driving the Colts to the tying field goal in the waning minutes, it was Berry he went to and Berry who held on.

Following successive championship failures against Baltimore, the Giants acquired Y.A. Tittle from San Francisco, where he had gained a measure of fame for his alley-oop passes to a long-legged, high-jumping receiver named R.C. Owens. In New York, Tittle made the acquaintance of a smooth-striding fellow Texan named Del Shofner and they sparked the Giants to three consecutive appearances in the championship game, all of which they lost.

It was the Packers who dominated the decade. A ground-oriented team whose credo was "run to daylight," they nevertheless had a slick passing combination in choirboy Bart Starr and play-boy Max McGee, an odd couple if ever there was one. It was McGee who starred in the first Super Bowl when, after spending the previous night away from the team hotel in the company of a female companion, he replaced an injured Boyd Dowler on the first series. All the weary McGee did was catch seven passes for 138 yards and two touchdowns.

But his legend as a bachelor paled alongside that of Joe Namath, the antihero quarterback of the New York Jets. Namath had

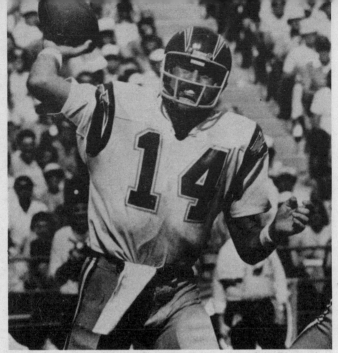

Sparkplugs of the Chargers: Dan Fouts to...

two exceptional receivers in Don Maynard, a lanky whippet, and George Sauer, a sure-handed possession receiver who ran meticulous patterns. "[Sauer] looks like a fast Raymond Berry," said coach Weeb Ewbank, who had guided those championship Baltimore teams. "They both have good moves but it's their determination to do their best that makes them great."

Maynard's speed forced opponents to stretch their defense and Sauer repeatedly took advantage. "Don doesn't run a pattern with the precision of Sauer," Namath said, "but he usually gets where he's supposed to be. He reads defenses so accurately that when I see him raising his hand, I know he's breaking the pattern and I just look for him somewhere else."

It was unconventional Maynard, ol' No. 13 on your program, who starred in the 1968 American Football League championship game but a strained leg muscle made him a doubtful performer in Super Bowl III. Yet, he managed to slip behind the Baltimore defense in an early series and, although Namath's pass sailed just over his fingertips, the Colts were sufficiently jolted to rotate their zone in his direction for the rest of the game. That left Sauer

... *Kellen Winslow, a captivating battery in the '80s.*

room to operate on the left side and the man caught eight passes for 133 yards in the 16-7 victory that remains the most celebrated upset of the modern era.

The San Diego Chargers have been blessed with two of the more productive batteries in recent history, John Hadl to the acrobatic Lance Alworth and Dan Fouts to the spectacular Kellen Winslow. But despite dazzling offensive talent, they never won a championship in the NFL. Similarly, Dan Marino has set records in conjunction with the "Marks Brothers," Mark Clayton and Mark Duper, but the Dolphins have been stymied over the last decade.

Meanwhile, in Dallas, Roger Staubach and Drew Pearson combined to rally the Cowboys to many last-second victories and they even succeeded in winning a championship. Ken Stabler and Fred Biletnikoff were the glue in Oakland's climb to the top. But their success was short-lived compared to that of the Steelers. In a six-year period, Pittsburgh qualified for four Super Bowls and won all four. Bradshaw set career records for touchdown passes (9) and passing yards (932). Swann was credited with three scor-

Super Bowl Steelers did it with Terry Bradshaw and . . .

ing catches, the same number as his equally able teammate on the other flank, John Stallworth.

"Growing up, I used to watch Swann and Stallworth," Rice said.

Now that's he's fully grown, there may not be a better receiver anywhere. Certainly, the battery of Montana to Rice ranks among the finest ever to play the game.

In accepting the Super Bowl MVP award, Rice said, "If it was left up to me, I'd have given it to [Montana]."

Actually, co-awards would have been entirely appropriate. From the time of Dorais and Rockne, there's never been a passer who could do it without a receiver and vice versa.

...prime targets Lynn Swann (88) and John Stallworth.

Bradshaw Blooms
in the Booth

By WENDELL BARNHOUSE

Here was The Big Moment.

As a quarterback who led the Pittsburgh Steelers to four championships in four Super Bowls, Terry Bradshaw knew when to make the big play at the right time. As an NFL analyst for CBS, Bradshaw felt he had learned when to say the right thing at the right time. This was a chance to prove himself in the booth as he had distinguished himself on the field.

It was Dec. 31, 1988. NFC Divisional playoff game in Soldier Field. Philadelphia vs. Chicago. It was a game, an assignment, that Bradshaw and broadcast partner Verne Lundquist had earned. For the 1988 season at least, Lundquist-Bradshaw was 1A to No. 1, Pat Summerall-John Madden. But Bradshaw's big moment on national television was obscured by a meteorological meeting of warm moisture and cold air. Bradshaw worked the biggest game of his life in a fog.

"It was the type of situation, that if you're not any good, you're liable to explode," said CBS producer David Michaels, who watched his telecast fade into the mist. "It was such a joke. We had 12 cameras and if one or two of them were showing anything but fog, we were lucky."

Despite the frustration of not being able to see, Lundquist and Bradshaw kept their cool, their poise and their sense of humor. In essence, they saved the telecast.

At one point, Bradshaw described a hazy reply: "He runs right . . . out of sight." Later, when a player was injured, he said, "You could get hurt in this game and they wouldn't be able to find you. They'd realize you were missing and then send out a search party."

The humor masked the pain and frustration. "It took me two

Wendell Barnhouse writes the TV/radio column and covers college basketball for the Fort Worth Star-Telegram.

A winning team: Verne Lundquist and Terry Bradshaw.

to three days to get over it. I was just so frustrated for Verne and me," Bradshaw said. "We had worked at it and we finally had a playoff game. It's like getting ready for the Super Bowl and they call it off because of bad weather. That was our Super Bowl and we couldn't perform at our best."

Bradshaw thinks viewers and television critics realized the difficult conditions and felt sorry for the announcers. Sympathy or not, Lundquist and Bradshaw were praised for their performance. "Right after the game we had a bunch of phone calls in the press wagon," Bradshaw said. "I was nervous. 'Oh God, they're calling already.' I didn't know what to expect. [CBS Sports executive producer] Ted Shaker came in and said, 'You guys did a helluva job, fantastic.' The CBS people were really happy."

Praise from Shaker was especially welcome. In 1984-85, his first two years with CBS, Bradshaw relied on a Thank-God-I'm-a-country-boy image and style.

"He came in as a bona fide superstar," Lundquist said. "He was a guy with a reputation of having a terrific sense of humor and a larger-than-life personality. He saw himself as an entertainer. He envisioned the booth as a place for entertaining rather than a place for serious analysis of a football game."

When Shaker took over for Terry O'Neil in 1986, he shuffled some of the NFL announcer pairings. Bradshaw and Lundquist were separated and Bradshaw was paired with Tim Ryan.

"Ted Shaker sat down and told me he didn't like the way I did football games," Bradshaw said. "He said, 'I don't want all this silly, all this southern hee-haw stuff.' He said my year with Tim would be a make-or-break year for me."

Concentrating on analyzing the games rather than cracking wise, Bradshaw had a good season with Ryan in 1986, but in 1987 he was paired with Dick Stockton. They were tabbed as that season's "in" team, but the chemistry blew up in their mikes. Before last season, Shaker yielded to heavy politicking from Lundquist and Bradshaw, who wanted a rematch.

"If Shaker hadn't sat me down, I probably would be out of this business by now. People would have run me off, they would have been sick of it," Bradshaw said. "I like doing the games serious. People can never get tired of honest football coverage. If you're a personality, a Dick Vitale, and can't constantly come up with something new, that act can get old. Even John's act, you can only rub some mud so many times, you can only boom, bam, pow so many times. When you're like that, you have to be very creative and that puts a lot of pressure on you. There's no pressure for me to try to be funny."

Early in his television career, Bradshaw said that "if gardened properly, I will grow." Lundquist is one of the best gardeners in the business and Bradshaw is in full bloom. "I'm as good as I can be with Verne," Bradshaw said. "He trusts my judgment and he makes me feel important. He's the guy I fit best with.

"He is a compassionate and sensitive person. He genuinely cares about me. He is extremely intelligent and knowledgeable. I lean on him and listen to him very carefully. He's got great wisdom and for a guy like me who tends to fly off in different directions, he has a very calming effect."

When Bradshaw was named to the Pro Football Hall of Fame this year, he decided to ask Lundquist to be his presenter at induction ceremonies. He popped the proposal to Lundquist after breaking out a bottle of Dom Perignon during a Christmas dinner.

The reigning partners: John Madden and Pat Summerall.

A touched Lundquist admitted to "shedding a tear."

Bradshaw is succeeding where other quarterbacks-turned-analysts have failed. Ex-quarterbacks like Don Meredith and Bob Griese are exceptions to the rule. The list of failures or fizzles includes Joe Namath, Len Dawson, Fran Tarkenton, Roger Staubach, Bart Starr and Johnny Unitas. The reasons are varied.

"A quarterback has to subjugate himself to be the fourth-most important guy on a TV production team behind the producer, the director and the announcer. That's hard to swallow," said producer Michaels, the younger brother of ABC's Al. Bradshaw has learned to blend his considerable personality with a strong work ethic. He has caught the information/reporting bug. He likes to find out the behind-the-scenes information, the good stories and then find the right moment to tell the viewer.

"As I get older and want to accomplish more in this business, I'm becoming more involved in it," said Bradshaw, who earns an estimated $300,000 a year from CBS. He keeps his notes from each game on a home computer and taps the information as needed in the course of the season.

Dan Dierdorff carries weight on Monday Night Football.

"Becoming an analyst is a damned hard discipline to learn," said Michaels, who has been Bradshaw's producer since 1986. "Once Terry realized it was something he couldn't just step into, he set out to learn it. He's one of the those guys who won't settle for mediocrity on any level."

Intelligent analysis comes from knowledge of the game. An analyst who has talked with the offensive coordinator and the quarterback should have a good idea what a team will do when faced with a third-and-four on the opponents' 27.

TV critics have responded to Bradshaw's growth in the booth. "He is much improved," said Steve Fryer of the *Orange County Register.* "He got rid of the 'Aw shucks' attitude and became much more analytical. And he shows a healthy willingness to rip, to go out on a limb with an opinion or a critique."

Rudy Martzke of *USA Today* named Bradshaw as one of his top six analysts for 1988 and the most improved. William Taafe of *Sports Illustrated* wrote that "His twang can be grating, but he's honest and enthusiastic, and dispenses well-reasoned criticism."

Lundquist and Michaels have high praise for Bradshaw's charisma and clout in the NFL lockerrooms.

"He has learned to use the entrée that he has in the lockerroom and on the practice field to glean information from players and coaches and then transfer that information into a broadcast," Lundquist said. "Terry gets as much out of the one-on-one sessions with players and coaches as anyone (including John Madden) we've got working in sports television. He engenders enormous respect because of what he did."

"He is an amazing interviewer," Michaels said. "He can put players at ease. They love to talk to him. It's a amazing what he gets them to tell him. You can sit there with five or six other people in the room, Terry will put his hand on the player's knee and say, 'C'mon, you can tell me.' The guy will forget there's anyone else in the room."

And Bradshaw has even experienced a problem most aggressive journalists face: some players won't talk to him because of something he has said during a telecast. But that doesn't happen very often.

In Week 3 last season, Bradshaw and Lundquist were assigned the Philadelphia-Washington game. They went to Redskins Park for their pregame preparation and Bradshaw asked to talk to nine players. He told the Redskins' public relations men that he wanted a few private minutes with each player. Lundquist was skeptical.

"It was the damndest thing I have ever seen," Lundquist said. "The players would come over and in just five to six minutes he was able to get something that found itself into the broadcast. He was very proud of himself. After it was over, he winked at me and said, 'I told you I could do it.'"

In Week 11, Lundquist and Bradshaw were assigned to work the Tampa Bay-Detroit game—a regional telecast that was going to just four percent of the country, basically the Detroit and

Tampa Bay markets. A nothing game.

"Terry called me and said, 'I know what they're [CBS] doing. They're going to watch us closely to see the kind of job we do.'"

Bradshaw turned a nothing game into a something game. In pregame discussions, with Bradshaw, Tampa Bay quarterback Vinnie Testaverde revealed that he was color blind and was having trouble picking out his receivers. That story line brought national attention to a regional game and telecast and may well have clinched the Fog Bowl playoff assignment for Lundquist and Bradshaw.

The national attention generated by his work in a unique national playoff telecast was just one of the highlights of '88 for Bradshaw. He had been reunited with Lundquist, saw his stock as an announcer soar, been rumored to have a tumor near his heart and been elected to the Pro Football Hall of Fame.

Last October, Bradshaw, 41, experienced chest pains. Preliminary x-rays showed a spot near his heart. KKDA, a Pittsburgh television station that employs Bradshaw as a commentator, broke the story that Bradshaw had a tumor. It took nearly a week for more medical tests and the truth: the spot was just scar tissue from an old injury.

The media attention and coverage should not have come as a surprise to Bradshaw. During his playing career with the Pittsburgh Steelers, he was one of the country's high-profile athletes. From the day he was the first draft pick out of Louisiana Tech in the 1970 NFL draft, Terry Bradshaw has been at center stage. His act has not always been a hit. He struggled with his football career, his analyst career and with his personal life. He has said he has "struggled for everything".

He has described his first marriage (in 1972 to former Miss Teenage America Melissa Babish) as an "immature decision." He says his highly publicized marriage to international skating JoJo Starbuck was a case of unrequited love. But now Bradshaw is a happy camper. Bradshaw married Charla Hopkins on Feb. 15, 1986. Marriage No. 3 was helped along by the Lundquists because Nancy Lundquist helped Terry and Charla get back together after they had endured an on-again, off-again relationship.

"This one has happiness and contentment," Bradshaw said. "That happens when you bring two people together who are happy with themselves and each other." The Bradshaw family (Rachel is two and Charla was due to give birth to a second child in July) lives in the Roanoke-Keller-Westlake area, 40 minutes to the northwest of downtown Dallas, 20 minutes from Fort Worth and 15 minutes from D/FW airport.

"All you need to see is him rolling around on the floor with

Ex-Redskin Joe Theismann makes his mark at ESPN.

Merlin Olsen and Dick Enberg: NBC's veteran combo.

his baby daughter," Lundquist said. "I wish everybody could see him like that. Terry has a soft side. I've been around enough superstars and most of 'em aren't any fun."

During the offseason Bradshaw keeps busy by making a dozen or so speaking appearances a month, mostly to major corporations. His audiences range from groups of 60 to 7,000. As with his football and television careers, Bradshaw got off to a slow start as a public speaker. In 1984, he was booked to speak to a group the day after former president Gerald Ford had spoken there. Bradshaw had to agree to forfeit his honorarium if his speech was not a hit.

"But I got my fee," Bradshaw said. "I had a reputation for not being very smart. What are you gonna do about it? People have to take a chance on you. When you meet people for the first time, they have an image, an impression of you. My image started with some writers in Pittsburgh who thought I was dumb, stupid."

Bradshaw is well aware of the power of the press. He became the butt of joking insults fired his way by Dallas linebacker Thomas "Hollywood" Henderson during Super Bowl XIII week. Henderson's most quoted line was "Bradshaw is so dumb that he couldn't spell cat if you spotted him the 'c' and the 'a.' Last season, a writer in Buffalo wrote that Jim Kelly was a smart version of Terry Bradshaw.

"Everybody thinks I'm an idiot. That's fine. That's just life," Bradshaw said. "When it first started, I hated it. The only way to handle that is to go out and win."

Before teaming up again with Lundquist last season, Bradshaw said he wasn't worried about the competition to be No. 2 at CBS behind Summerall and Madden. Now he has a different perspective. He likens his situation to being a backup quarterback who knows he can play and wants to start.

"[Joe] Theisman's at ESPN, [Dan] Dierdorf's at ABC, [Merlin] Olsen's at NBC and Madden's at CBS. They are your No. 1s. I happen to think I'm ahead of some of those guys. It's my sixth year. I won't be satisfied until I'm a No. 1 analyst. I'm giving myself three more hard-working years to make it happen.

"That doesn't mean I'm going to cause any problems . . . and I don't want John's job. It's the competitive juices. I'm confident and I know I'm good. Like my football career, after my fifth or sixth year I knew I was good. If I didn't feel that way, it would go against everything I've been taught."

The Eagles' Reggie White is No. 1 in the sack world.

REGGIE WHITE
AND
THE SACK PACK

By RAY DIDINGER

Anyone who watches pro football knows about the sack. A 285-pound defensive lineman, breathing fire, wraps his mitts around the opposing team's quarterback and—whump—slams him.

Loss of yardage.

Loss of down.

Sometimes, loss of quarterback.

That's the sack and it is what every NFL defensive lineman and linebacker lives for.

Sacks made Mark Gastineau dance, they made Lawrence Taylor rich and they made Howie Long famous. Sacks are what separate the stars from the grunts in the trenches. Grab enough quarterbacks and some of that glamor is bound to rub off on you.

Next to the touchdown, the sack is probably the most exciting play in football. The fans can see it coming, even if the quarterback cannot. It brings the crowd to its feet. Look, here comes the blitz. L. T. has a clear shot. Get him, get him . . . Oooooh, what a hit.

Try to think of another play that stirs such emotion. Try to think of another play that makes such a powerful statement.

Webster's unabridged dictionary defines the sack as "the pillaging or plundering of a captured town or city by its conquerors . . . Hence, to ruin through despoliation."

The term was created for the likes of Attila the Hun. Today, it is applied to one-man armies such as Reggie White, the Philadelphia Eagles' 6-5, 295-pound defensive end who led the NFL in sacks each of the past two seasons. He, too, pillages, plunders and ruins through despoliation.

In the process, White also helps the Eagles win. Last year, he was a driving force in the team's 10-6 finish and its first NFC East Division title since 1980. White now has 70 sacks in 57 regular-season NFL games, astounding numbers when you consider he faces double and triple-team blocks on every play.

Philadelphia head coach Buddy Ryan calls White "the best defensive player I've ever been around." High praise considering Ryan coached three Super Bowl teams and worked with the likes of Alan Page and Carl Eller at Minnesota and Dan Hampton, Richard Dent and Mike Singletary at Chicago.

"They were all great athletes," Ryan said, "but Reggie is bigger and faster than any of them. Eller was 6-6 and 245 and ran the 40 in 4.6. Reggie is 50 pounds heavier and just as fast. Reggie is as fast as [Lawrence] Taylor and Taylor is a linebacker. They just don't make people like Reggie. He's got the whole package."

Like a quarterback, Ray Didinger keeps an eye on the sack pack as a sports columnist on the Philadelphia Daily News.

Sacks and the Giants' Lawrence Taylor are synonymous.

Just how important is the sack?

Bill Walsh says that "a good pass rush late in the game is the key to NFL football." He should know, having won three Super Bowls in San Francisco before stepping down as head coach.

Ryan's much-copied "46" defense is built around the pass rush. It helped win a Super Bowl for Chicago in 1986 and it enabled the Eagles to finish second in NFL takeaways last season. The idea is to create pressure, force the other team to make mistakes.

And it all starts with heat on the quarterback.

The Buffalo Bills went from last place (1985) to first (1988) in the AFC East when defensive end Bruce Smith and linebacker Cornelius Bennett bolstered the pass rush. Last season, Smith and Bennett accounted for almost half of the Bills' 46 sacks and the team finished 12-4, their best regular-season mark since 1964.

The Los Angeles Rams improved from 6-9 in 1987 to 10-6 last year when they adopted a variation of the "46" defense—two down linemen and five linebackers in passing situations. The Rams led the NFL with 56 sacks (up from 38 in 1987) and designated blitzer Kevin Greene had $16\frac{1}{2}$ sacks, second only to White's

The Rams' Deacon Jones inspired sack stats.

league-high 18.

Everyone is arming themselves with pass-rushers. Ever since Taylor made his huge impact with the New York Giants, NFL teams have looked for linebackers who could rush like defensive ends. Atlanta made Aundray Bruce the No. 1 selection in last year's draft. Bennett was the second player selected (behind QB Vinny Testerverde) in 1987. That's the trend.

The bend-but-don't-break defense is out.

The attacking defense is in.

"The game today is won on big plays," Ryan said, "and your chances for making a big play on defense are much better if you're aggressive. That's what makes Reggie so great. He can turn a game around with two or three plays. Not too many defensive players have that kind of ability...to just take over a game."

White has done that on several occasions since joining the Eagles in 1985 after a brief tour with Memphis of the USFL.

In the 1987 opener, White sent Jay Schroeder, then Washington's starting quarterback, to the sidelines with a bruised shoulder on the first series. Doug Williams came on in relief and White

As a Jet, Mark Gastineau created the sack dance.

promptly wrestled a ball from his grasp and ran 70 yards for a touchdown.

Last season, the Eagles were trailing a critical November game against the Giants, 17-10, in the fourth quarter. The Giants were marching toward what could have been a killer touchdown when White leveled quarterback Phil Simms with a clean but jarring hit.

Simms left the game with a bruised shoulder and his backup, Jeff Hostetler, took over. Hostetler could not move the ball at all and the Eagles came back to win in overtime, 23-17. White's hit on Simms turned an almost certain loss into a win.

The Eagles went to Dallas on the final week of the season needing a victory to clinch their first playoff spot in seven years. White took over the game, sacking Cowboy quarterback Steve Pelluer four times and demoralizing the Dallas offensive line. The Eagles won easily, 23-7.

"That was an awesome performance," a newsman said after the game.

"That's Reggie," Ryan replied.

Defensive linemen have been mauling NFL quarterbacks for years, but it wasn't until the late '60s that the statisticians thought much about it. For awhile, the plays were lumped in with yards lost rushing. In the '60s, the league added a new team category: opponents tackled attempting passes. Still, no one thought about keeping it as an individual stat until David "Deacon" Jones came along.

Jones was a Hall of Fame defensive end who played 11 seasons with the Los Angeles Rams, two with San Diego and one with Washington. At 6-5 and 250 pounds, blessed with extraordinary quickness, Jones brought a new and dynamic quality to defense. He also brought a new term: the sack.

The Deacon forever changed the way people watched—and talked about—the pass rush.

"I was in the right place at the right time," said Jones, now manager of a computer firm in Santa Monica. "I came along just when teams were looking for that kind of [quicker] guy to rush the passer. It was like this is what I was born to do.

"When I was getting three or four quarterbacks a week, but it wasn't an official statistic and it didn't have a name, I said, 'I have to think of a word. Something short so it can fit in a headline.' That's when I came up with 'sack.'

"I looked it up and it meant to crush, to destroy, to devestate. I said, 'Yeah, that's what I do to quarterbacks. I SACK 'em. I put the fear of God in them.'"

The press loved the term and it gained immediate acceptance around the NFL. The Rams credited Jones with 26 sacks in 1967 and 28 the following year. However, the league didn't recognize individual sacks as an official statistic until 1982.

There was a feeling the sack might not be a fair stat since the player who actually makes the sack might not always be the one who makes the play. Quite often, the first rusher chases the quarterback into the arms of a straggler who makes the tackle and gets all the credit.

But virtually all NFL numbers are skewed in some way. Defensive backs get full credit for their interceptions even though the quarterback's arm may have been hit by a rusher. So the argument that sacks were somehow invalid as an individual stat never made a whole lot of sense.

Besides, the fans wanted to keep score on L.T., Gastineau and company.

So in 1982, sacks became an official league stat and Gastineau set the recognized single-season record of 22 sacks in 1984. White came within one sack of tying Gastineau's mark in 1987 despite playing just 12 games due to the NFL strike. If Deacon Jones gets credit for naming the sack, then Gastineau should get credit for choreography. The 6-5, 270-pound former New York Jets' star celebrated each sack with a fist-pumping, hippity-hop dance that some folks loved and others hated.

Over the years, other pass-rushers have copied Gastineau's act or come up with a version of their own. In Buffalo, Smith and Bennett do something called the Fred Sanford. After each sack, they put their hands on their chests and stagger around in a mock heart attack ala comedian Redd Foxx in the TV show "Sanford and Son." Again, the reviews are mixed.

"I don't go for that stuff," Deacon Jones said. "It's a waste of energy. You're better off saving your strength for the next snap, that's where it counts. To me, it's just another indication that today's players think as individuals. They do these dances to call attention to themselves. I liked making a name for myself, but I was a team player. My No. 1 goal each week was to help my team win. I don't think these guys feel that way. I see a lot of 'me, me, me' out there."

Norm Willey agrees. Willey was a 6-2, 240-pound defensive end with the Eagles from 1950 through 1957. He was one of the first great pass-rushers along with Gino Marchetti (Baltimore), Len Ford (Cleveland), Andy Robustelli (Giants) and Ed Sprinkle (Chicago).

No one was counting sacks in those days and it's too bad. Willey (nicknamed "Wildman" by his Eagle teammates) figures

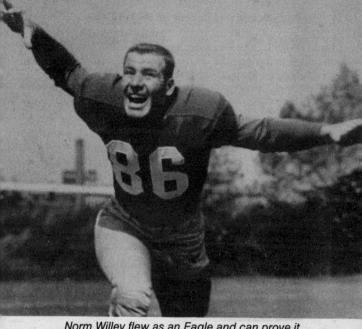

Norm Willey flew as an Eagle and can prove it.

he averaged 30 sacks a year in a 12-game season. Willey had 15 sacks in one 1955 game against the Giants. That's almost as many sacks as Lawrence Taylor had all last season ($15\frac{1}{2}$).

Willey still has the newspaper clipping to prove he isn't making this up. It does seem rather farfetched—15 sacks in a single game. But there it is, pressed carefully in Willey's scrapbook. The story says New York quarterback Charlie Conerly got so disgusted, he finally walked off the field in the second half.

"I didn't think it was that big a deal," said Willey, 61, now a physical education teacher at Pennsville (N.J.) High School. "I knew I was having a good game, but I wasn't counting how many tackles I had. Back then, you just played. It wasn't all this show biz like it is today.

"I got the (NFL) Player of the Week award, which was nice. The papers wrote it up, then it was forgotten. There wasn't the focus on defense that there is now. We didn't have 'sacks' and we didn't have guys doing backflips everytime they made a tackle. That Gastineau . . . he was the worst."

Willey still works for the Eagles on game day, lining up the visiting team for player introductions and helping with security on the sidelines. He has enjoyed watching Reggie White emerge as his All-Pro successor at defensive end.

"Reggie is the best today, without a doubt," Willey said. "He has everything—the size, the power, the speed."

Yeah, but will White ever get 15 sacks in a single game?

"It will be tough with the way they let offensive linemen use their hands today," Willey said. "The rules really favor the offense. But this guy [White] is so good, really, anything is possible."

Reggie White stands out for other reasons, reasons that have little to do with football.

At 27, White has been a licensed Baptist minister for 10 years. Football may be his livlihood, but religion is his passion. He considers it his source of strength, his purpose and his real life's work. His football career is merely setting the stage.

White dedicated his life to the Lord while he was attending Howard High School in his native Chattanooga, Tenn. He claims it was a natural evolution. He was raised by his grandmother after his parents moved away with the military. His grandmother was a deeply religious woman who enjoyed reading the bible. Young Reggie found peace there, too.

Today, White preaches in churches across the country. His nickname is "The Minister of Defense" and he takes it seriously. He refuses to be involved in the NFL's Lineman of the Year award because it is sponsored by a beer company. He doesn't care about the cash involved. He feels the principle is more important.

White truly believes the Good Lord blessed him with special athletic gifts and it is up to him to use those gifts to do the Lord's work. One way he can do that is to play pro football and prove that it is possible to be both a macho guy and a Christian.

The other way is to use his football platform to spread Christ's name. His postgame interviews are sprinkled with religious references. It annoys him terribly when reporters edit those remarks out of their stories.

"That's the message I want to get across," White says. "That's me."

This might seem a curious crossbreeding: football and religion. Some people wonder if there isn't a basic conflict here: a preacher man bashing people around on the football field. In other words, what's a good Christian doing leading the NFL in sacks?

"There's nothing wrong with the game if it's played fairly and with respect," White said. "It's physical but it doesn't have to be vicious. I don't try to hurt anyone. If I get a shot at a quarterback, I take it but it's always within the rules. To take a cheap shot would go against everything I stand for. Most of what goes on out there is within the rules. People might not think that but it's true.

"I know there are some people who don't understand me but there's nothing I can do about that. My junior year at Tennessee, I was hurt and didn't play that well. People said, 'Oh, he's a Christian. He's not tough enough to play this game.'

"My senior year I played well and people said, 'He can't be a Christian. Look at him. He's too mean.' After awhile, you just give up trying to please other people and you do what you feel is right.

"I know who I am and I know what the Lord has in mind for me. That's all that matters. And I think if people really watch me and listen to what I say, they'll understand."

It is easy to see the influence White has on his Eagle teammates. Every time tailback Keith Byars or wide receiver Cris Carter score a touchdown, they kneel in the end zone and offer a prayer of thanks. Quarterback Randall Cunningham and flanker Ron Johnson join them.

White has not twisted any arms to get his message across— indeed, most of the players were active Christians before they joined the Eagles—but his presence has given the team a quiet spiritual focus. He conducts a weekly Bible reading at his South Jersey home attended by a dozen teammates.

"I don't go around the lockerroom preaching and telling guys how to live their lives," White said. "Accepting Christ is a personal decision. The most I'll do is invite a player to attend a bible reading. If he wants to come, fine. If he doesn't, that's fine, too. There's no pressure."

Two years ago, White invited Carter to a Bible reading. The former Ohio State star accepted and the next day he told White he was turning his life over to Christ. Carter says it was the best decision he ever made.

"Our society is crying out for role models," White said. "That's what I'm doing now. I'm trying to be the best role model I can be, both on and off the field."

But all is not sweetness and light with Reggie and Eagle management, in particular Patrick Forte, his former agent, now an assistant to the team president. White filed a law suit in March against Forte, charging him with breach of contract, negligence and breach of fiduciary duty.

Bengal Boomer and the Southpaw Syndrome

By JACK BRENNAN

Boomer Esiason is left-handed.

Quite possibly you already know that. Quite possibly you don't care. Researchers estimate there are 500 million left-handed people in the world.

But Norman Julius Esiason, the limelight-loving quarterback of the Cincinnati Bengals, cares very much about being left-handed. He knows that left-handed passers have been a remarkably rare breed in pro football—in far smaller proportion than their 10 percent of the general population.

Sure, Boomer allows, he is scarred like all left-handers, having lived 28 years under the yoke of a righties-dominated world.

"I remember always having to search for that one left-handed desk in the classroom," Esiason says, "Every now and then, I'd have to sit next to the ugliest girl in school because the only left-handed desk was there.

"All right-handers think left-handers are handicapped," he adds. "We as left-handers have one of the hardest jobs in the world, trying to teach right-handers that we can do everything they can do."

But clearly these are hurts left in the past. This flamboyant Bengal from East Islip, N.Y., broke all the real or imagined bonds of left-handers last season, winning the NFL Most Valuable Player award while leading the Bengals into the Super Bowl from the worst previous-season finish for a Super Bowl team (4-11) in history.

Jack Brennan of the Cincinnati Post *has been covering the Bengals since 1984, the year that Boomer Esiason was a rookie quarterback and Sam Wyche a rookie head coach.*

Boomer Esiason loves being a lefty.

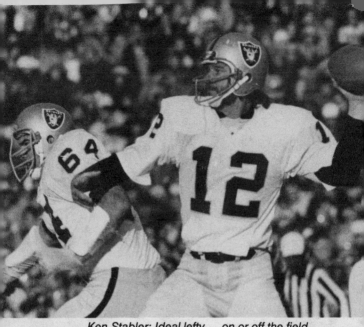

Ken Stabler: Ideal lefty . . . on or off the field.

He joined ex-Raider Ken Stabler in what had been a one-man club—left-handed quarterbacks with an arguable claim to NFL greatness—and like any executive trying to market a product in a competitive world, he sees big dividends in being different.

"For me, being left-handed is great," Esiason says. "I look different on the field, I play different, I think different. The whole aura of being left-handed, to me, is fun. I wouldn't have it any other way."

The idea of being right-handed would no be more appealing to Esiason than the prospect of dumping Grecian Formula on his beach-boy blond hair.

"I've said many times that there are probably 100 guys my size with dark hair and dark eyes, and they're right-handed," he says. "If I was one of those guys, it would be very easy to get lost in the sauce. There's really only one who's my size, my looks and left-handed, and that's me.

"It's one way, in such a team sport as football, that I really am an individual, and to be considered one of the best at my position just makes it feel that much better."

To make his the perfect story, one ought to be able to say that Esiason overcame tremendous obstacles to reach his current plateau. One ought to be able to cite reasons why left-handers generally don't make good quarterbacks, and to explain how Esiason became the exception to the rule.

Once past Stabler and himself, after all, the historian is hard-pressed to produce a list of the Top 10 lefties in pro football history. There really are only six who ever became established performers, the other four being Frankie Albert (San Francisco, 1946-52), Bobby Douglass (Chicago, 1969-75; San Diego, 1975; New Orleans, 1976-77; Green Bay, 1978), Jim Zorn, Seattle, 1976-84; Green Bay, 1985), and Steve Young (Tampa Bay, 1985-86; San Francisco, 1987-present).

After that, the southpaw list dwindles with the likes of Jim Del Gaizo (Miami, 1972; Green Bay, 1973; N.Y. Giants, 1974); Terry Baker, (L.A. Rams, 1963-65), David Humm (Oakland, 1975-79; Buffalo, 1980; Baltimore, 1981-82; L.A. Raiders, 1983-84) and Allie Sherman (Philadelphia-Pittsburgh, 1943; Philadelphia, 1944-47).

Unlike baseball, which has sound logistical reasons why left-handers should not play catcher or shortstop, football has no apparent theory on its southpaw quarterback syndrome. It seems to be more a statistical oddity than anything else.

"I couldn't give you an answer," says Bengal coach Sam Wyche, a former right-handed quarterback. "I never gave it much thought when we drafted Boomer [in 1984], other than to realize that we would run rollout plays to the left instead of the right.

"To me, that's really about the only other major difference when it comes to coaching a left-handed quarterback. We're still predominantly a right-handed team—we run more formations with the tight end on the right side, like most teams—and when Boomer is in the pocket, he throws as well to the left as to the right.

"I can't," Wyche concludes, "see any reason why anyone would discriminate against left-handed quarterbacks."

Some have contended that because left-handed passers put a rotation on the ball that is opposite to a right-hander's rotation, their throws are hard to catch.

"It's definitely a spin in reverse," says Allie Sherman, the left-hander who is much more known for his coaching (N.Y. Giants, 1961-68) than for his short-lived playing career. "If a receiver finds himself suddenly in a game with a left-hander, he has to glom onto that ball and concentrate a lot more. He's got to make sure he follows the ball all the way into his hands."

But Sherman agrees that a left-hander's pass is not inherently harder to catch; just different. "If a coach can get a man who throws the ball strongly and with accuracy . . . hell, what's the difference?" he says. "I don't think coaches have anything against that."

And Esiason, for his part, says he rarely has experienced even a mild complaint from receivers about the way his passes spin. "The only problems I've had have related to the amount of heat I put on the ball," he says. "When I first came to the Bengals, some of the guys said I threw it too hard.

"But no one has ever said it was spinning the wrong way, or the ball came out of my arm differently, or that it looked strange in the pocket. I think too much is made of that. A receiver is one of the finest athletes on the field, and most of the guys in the NFL can catch it whether it's a knuckleball or coming end-over-end, or whatever. I've also been in the Pro Bowl, throwing to guys I don't practice with, and nobody said a thing."

And so, Esiason goes right on finding things he likes about being left-handed. He delights in the idea that left-handers are a maverick breed, born to flaunt society's rules and not care who cares.

Stabler, of course, fit that role perfectly.

"Kenny was more of a pocket passer than I am," Esiason says. "In terms of style, I really related more to Bert Jones as an idol. But Kenny had a reputation as a gambler and just generally a wild guy. I remember some of the plays he pulled, like the one where he fumbled on purpose and the Raiders would up getting the winning touchdown."

But Esiason draws the line of left-handed comparisons at Douglass, the former Bear who is regarded as one of the great all-time flakes.

"He was a maniac; there was a real, true left-hander," Esiason says. "He had the spirit of a linebacker. I'm not talking tough like Jim Kelly [Buffalo], I'm talking of a guy who loved to try to run right over linebackers.

"Cris Collinsworth said my first year here that I was throwing wild-high passes like Bobby Douglass, and I said, 'No, please, don't compare me with that nut.' But left-handers have a reputation for having a certain amount of personality handed to them, and I think I'm like that."

Certainly, Esiason had his share of controversial and confrontational moments en route to his 1988 MVP season. In college at Maryland, he participated in a publicized feud with Duke's Ben Bennett over who was the best passer in the Atlantic Coast Conference. Does it matter who was No. 1 now? And coming out of college, Esiason blasted all 28 NFL teams for bypassing him in the first round of the 1984 draft. The outspoken 38th pick has dramatically made his point.

Bobby Douglass shook 'em up as a swinging southpaw.

In 1987, he was undoubtedly the most abused professional athlete in Cincinnati, angering fans with a militant pro-strike attitude while the Bengals stumbled to a 4-11 finish in the interrupted season. At one point during the 24-day players' strike, Esiason said that leading his team through the unrest was more important to him "than a Super Bowl ring."

Eventually, Esiason did admit to club management in the spring of 1988 that his union activities hurt his quarterbacking, and he promised to concentrate solely on football during the 1988 season.

The fruits of that decision were spectacularly evident last season when he joined Dan Marino as the only quarterbacks ever to lead their conference in passing for every week of a season—and Esiason quickly became once again a very popular player.

Jim Zorn was a Seattle portsider for nine years.

But he isn't about to permanently adopt a right-hander's personality. Though he and Wyche made great strides last year in patching up what had been a stormy relationship, Boomer still can't resist an occasional public tweak of Wyche's nose.

"Sam's the coach and I'm the player," begins one of Esiason's favorite lines. "Whatever he says, I do . . . unless I disagree with it."

Contrasting himself with Ken Anderson, the precision Bengals' passing machine of the '70s and early '80s, Esiason says: "Kenny is like . . . like a nice shade of blue. You see it, you like it, and that's great. Myself, I'm flaming red. Sometimes I'm not sure Cincinnati is ever going to get used to me."

A Miami writer noted last season that "Cincinnati looks upon Esiason with a stepmother's scolding glance, a mixture of fondness and disapproval."

But Cincinnatians are as prone as anyone to joining the bandwagon of a winner, and providing Esiason can prove in training camp that he has shaken a sore shoulder that hampered him late last season, he could be seen as the most valuable quarterbacking commodity in the NFL.

"I know I still have a good eight years left in me," says Esiason, who has finished among the NFL's top seven passers in three of the last four seasons. "I haven't won a Super Bowl yet, but I've only been there once, and other than that, I don't know what I can do.

"I've learned a lot in five years, and I know where I stand. It doesn't matter to me any more what some magazine says about me. Only a few players in the league have been fortunate enough to win some of the awards I won last year, and even though I realize I'm only able to do that with my teammates, I feel I'm in a certain class of athlete who has accomplished something."

Esiason, who makes his off-season home in Cincinnati with wife Cheryl, has displayed to NFL fans a great arm, excellent scrambling ability, improving accuracy and an unfailing knack for being a leader on the field. Though Bengal fans decried that strong pro-union stand in 1987, his teammates loved him for it, especially since he lost more salary money than any of them.

"We were mostly a running team for the last part of last season," says wide receiver Collinsworth, "but don't think for even a minute that Boomer isn't *The Man* for this team. I think it's true that all real leaders have to do something above and beyond the call of duty to make people see them that way, and that's exactly what happened with the way Boomer led us through the strike. In the long run, that ended up being good for our football team."

Most Bengal fans also have come to realize that Esiason's flair

49er Steve Young: Only active lefty besides Boomer.

for getting noticed can be a major plus toward the goal of keeping their small-market team in the national headlines.

Because he is so much more outspoken and media-friendly than San Francisco's Joe Montana, the postseason endorsement and appearance derby made Esiason look like the winning quarterback in Super Bowl XXIII, not the loser.

He played himself in a guest role on the soap opera, "All My Children," appeared on game shows, did an "It's Fantastic" plug the NBA and was able to pick and choose from numerous endorsement opportunities.

"Obviously, I lost the Disney World thing to Joe," Esiason says, referring to the now-traditional perk for the Super Bowl winning quarterback. "But I saw the Disney people on our sidelines during the fourth quarter. They went scurrying across to the San Francisco side at the end, but I think they really wanted me to be the one to do it.

"When a company signs a deal with an athlete, it's almost as if it is at the mercy of the athlete . . . depending on his performance, on and off the field, and that can be tough. But one thing I tell all the companies—when you sign me to a deal, you're getting somebody who won't be charged with DWI, who won't get suspended for drugs, and who will stand up for loyalty to teammates and family. Plus, you'll also have somebody who says his piece, adds excitement to himself and is not a dud."

Esiason also promises that the 1989 season will not be a dud for the Bengals, and he has more than his own talent and charisma to bolster that prediction. Since the 1970 merger, every Super Bowl loser but one has at least made the playoffs the following season. Denver broke the string in 1988, missing the playoffs after two straight blowouts in the Super Bowl.

"It took me a full week to get over the feeling of losing because we came so close," he said of the 20-16 loss to San Francisco, dubbed by commissioner Pete Rozelle as the best game in Super Bowl history. "There were so many things that all of us could have done to win that game, and you have to think about that. But we didn't get blown out—we still got a little honor back for the AFC—and it was extra special because of all the bad things we went through in 1987.

"I know it's hard to repeat as a conference champion, but I think things will go well for us. For sure, it's easier for a team that has lost the Super Bowl to get back in the game than it is for the team that won. I think we wouldn't have been worth a damn this year if we had won the game, and I know that's something the 49ers will have a hard time dealing with."

And if the Bengals make it back to the Super Bowl, Esiason will have another chance to break a Super Bowl record—Longest TD pass by a lefty (one yard, Ken Stabler, Super Bowl XI).

INSIDE THE NFC

By GEORGE WILLIS

PREDICTED ORDER OF FINISH

EAST	CENTRAL	WEST
Washington	Minnesota	L.A. Rams
N. Y. Giants	Chicago	San Francisco
Philadelphia	Tampa Bay	New Orleans
Dallas	Green Bay	Atlanta
Phoenix	Detroit	

NFC Champion: Minnesota

The San Francisco 49ers might well be the team of the decade, but there's little question the NFC is the conference of the '80s, having won five consecutive Super Bowls and seven of the last 10.

Though no team has won back-to-back NFL championships since the 1979 AFC Steelers, NFC teams have maintained their recent dominance with physical defenses combined with offenses that feature solid running games and a big-play passing threat, (i.e. Super Bowl XXIII winner San Francisco and XXII champ Washington).

Heading into '89, at least seven teams feature those elements in their attack. If tackle Steve Wallace returns from his broken leg, the only key player missing from the 49ers' Super Bowl team is retiring center Randy Cross. And, of course, Bill Walsh is gone—to the front office—replaced by defensive guru George Seifert as the club seeks its fourth straight NFC West title.

The 49ers will get a sturdy challenge from the Rams, who

---

gets his kicks as beat man on the New York Giants

started fast last year before fading. A maturing Jim Everett has a capable receiving corps to complement the Rams' strong running game.

The Saints just missed qualifying for the playoffs despite sharing the division title. They could contend again if their running game accelerates. Atlanta likely will finish in the cellar again, but should be improved and capable of being a spoiler.

The NFC East could be the conference's most competitive division. The defending champion Eagles didn't do much during the offseason to improve, but they still have quarterback Randall Cunningham and defensive end Reggie White, perhaps the two best in the league at their positions.

The Redskins, smarting after not making the playoffs last year, have improved their running game by acquiring Gerald Riggs and Earnest Byner. Doug Williams and Mark Rypien may be the best one-two quarterback tandem in the league.

The Giants haven't been to a playoff game since winning Super Bowl XXI, and if the offensive line doesn't stabilize, they won't make it again this year. A Monday Night season opener at Washington promises to be a difficult beginning. The Cardinals' season rests on a shaky foundation, the fragile legs of quarterback Neil Lomax.

In the NFC Central, Chicago and Minnesota will battle it out again. This time, the quarterback situations are reversed. Wade Wilson is the solid No. 1 at Minnesota, but the Bears' spot is up for grabs.

Tampa Bay, with its young players gaining experience, could provide some positive moments, but don't expect more than one or two upsets. Ditto for Green Bay and Detroit. Despite the Packers' influx of free agents and rookie tackle Tony Mandarich, they're still building for the future. So are the Lions, who drafted Heisman Trophy winner Barry Sanders and will play their first full season under coach Wayne Fontes.

Who'll make the postseason party? Washington, Minnesota and the Rams will be the division winners, with San Francisco and Chicago qualifying as wild-cards. The Vikings and Redskins will meet in the NFC championship game in the Metrodome, with Minnesota earning the trip to New Orleans.

ATLANTA FALCONS

TEAM DIRECTORY: Chairman: Rankin Smith Sr.; Pres.; Rankin Smith Jr.; VP: Taylor Smith; Dir. Pub. Rel.: Charlie Taylor; Head Coach: Marion Campbell. Home field: Atlanta Stadium (59, 643). Colors: Red, black, silver and white.

SCOUTING REPORT

OFFENSE: The Falcons (5-11) showed some improvement in 1988, but still need to improve in all phases of the game to be a

Rushing and receiving, John Settle resounded with a bang.

consistent winner. The biggest need offensively is to keep quarterback Chris Miller healthy. He missed four games in midseason with a sore ankle.

Other injuries crippled the offense, too. Tight end Alex Higdon went out early with torn knee ligaments, the offensive line had a variety of ailments and wide receiver Stacy Bailey missed some time in midseason with a bad shoulder.

The good news is that John Settle is a bona fide big-time back who can carry a team. The addition of tight end Shawn Collins, 27th draft pick, will help. The Falcons' offensive production ranked 13th in the NFC and 25th overall last year, but should improve if Miller and company stays healthy.

DEFENSE: After recording a league-low 17 sacks in 1987, the Falcons had 30 sacks last year. After struggling early, No. 1 pick Aundray Bruce got comfortable with his pass-rush responsibilities and became a dominating linebacker. He should be even better this year. If fellow second-year man Marcus Cotton can stay healthy, the Falcons' linebacking corps will be formidable.

The Falcons must improve their run defense, which allowed 144.9 yards per game, the most of any NFC team. Cornerback Scott Case is the leader of a secondary that now has No. 5 overall draft pick Deion ("Neion Deion," "Prime Time") Sanders.

KICKING GAME: The punt-cover team finished second-best in the NFL, yielding 5.8 per return, and punt returner Lew Barnes finished fifth in the NFC with a 9.4 average.

Punter Rick Donnelly was ranked third in the NFL with a 35.7 net and second in the NFL with 27 punts inside the 20-yard line. Placekicker Greg Davis tied a club record with a 52-yard field goal and made nine kicks over 40 yards.

THE ROOKIES: The secondary got a big boost with the addition of Sanders, the colorful Florida State product who has already begun his pro career—as an outfielder in the New York Yankee farm system. Ralph Norwood, a 6-6, 273-pound tackle from LSU, will add size and youth to the offensive line. Running back Keith Jones of Illinois could replace Gerald Riggs, who went to the Redskins.

OUTLOOK: The Falcons would hope to finish around .500 this year and may do it if their key players can remain healthy. The overriding question is whether owner Rankin Smith will get the Georgia Dome he seeks or move the team elsewhere.

FALCONS VETERAN ROSTER

HEAD COACH—Marion Campbell. Assistant Coaches—Tom Brasher, Fred Bruney, Scott Campbell, Chuck Clausen, Steve Crosby, Rod Dowhower, Foge Fazio, Jim Hanifan, Claude Humphrey, Tim Jorgensen, Jimmy Raye.

No.	Name	Pos.	Ht.	Wt.	NFL Exp.	College
82	Bailey, Stacey	WR	6-0	157	8	San Jose State
71	Baldinger, Gary	NT	6-3	265	4	Wake Forest
85	Barnes, Lew	WR	5-8	163	3	Oregon
5	Benyola, George	K	5-10	185	2	Louisiana Tech
97	Boyle, Jim	T	6-5	285	3	Tulane
63	Brotzki, Bob	T	6-5	275	4	Syracuse
98	Brown, Greg	DE	6-5	265	9	Kansas State
93	Bruce, Aundray	LB	6-5	245	2	Auburn
77	Bryan, Rick	DE	6-4	265	6	Oklahoma
23	Butler, Bobby	CB	5-11	175	9	Florida State
10	Campbell, Scott	QB	6-0	195	5	Purdue
68	Carlson, Mark	T	6-6	295	2	Southern Connecticut
25	Case, Scott	CB	6-0	176	6	Oklahoma
75	Casillas, Tony	NT	6-3	280	4	Oklahoma
74	Clayton, Stan	TG	6-3	265	2	Penn State
20	Cooper, Evan	CB-S	5-11	194	6	Michigan
51	Cotton, Marcus	LB	6-3	225	2	Southern California
	Craig, Paco	WR	5-10	170	2	UCLA
22	Dimry, Charles	CB-S	6-0	175	2	Nevada-Las Vegas
86	Dixon, Floyd	WR	5-9	170	4	Stephen F. Austin
3	Donnelly, Rick	P	6-0	190	5	Wyoming
64	Dukes, Jamie	G	6-1	278	4	Florida State
48	Flowers, Kenny	RB	6-0	210	2	Clemson
79	Fralic, Bill	T-G	6-5	280	5	Pittsburgh
76	Gann, Mike	DE	6-5	275	5	Notre Dame
41	Gordon, Tim	S	6-0	188	3	Tulsa
99	Green, Tim	LB	6-2	245	4	Syracuse
26	Griffin, Keith	RB	5-8	185	6	Miami
73	Harvey, James	G	6-3	265	2	Jackson State
81	Haynes, Michael	WR	6-0	180	2	Northern Arizona
80	Heller, Ron	TE	6-3	235	3	Oregon State
89	Hester, Jessie	WR	5-11	170	5	Florida State
88	Higdon, Alex	TE	6-5	247	2	Ohio State
69	Hoover, Houston	T	6-2	285	2	Jackson State
78	Kenn, Mike	T	6-7	277	12	Michigan
33	Lang, Gene	RB	5-10	206	6	Louisiana State
87	Lee, Danzell	TE	6-2	237	3	Lamar
94	Martin, Charles	NT	6-4	280	6	Livingston
6	McFadden, Paul	K	5-11	166	6	Youngstown State
7	Millen, Hugh	QB	6-5	216	2	Washington
12	Miller, Chris	QB	6-2	195	3	Oregon
84	Milling, James	WR	5-9	156	2	Maryland
34	Moore, Robert	S	5-11	190	4	Northwest Louisiana
67	Oswald, Paul	G	6-4	275	2	Kansas
49	Primus, James	RB	5-11	196	2	UCLA
59	Rade, John	LB	6-1	240	7	Boise State
55	Radloff, Wayne	C	6-5	277	5	Georgia
95	Reid, Michael	LB	6-2	226	3	Wisconsin
42	Riggs, Gerald	RB	6-1	232	8	Arizona State
66	Robison, Tommy	G	6-4	290	2	Texas A&M
61	Scully, John	G	6-6	270	9	Notre Dame
44	Settle, John	RB	5-9	207	3	Appalachian State
37	Shelley, Elbert	S	5-11	180	3	Arkansas State
24	Taylor, Kitrick	WR-KR	5-10	190	2	Washington State
72	Thomas, John	T	6-4	290	2	Toledo
58	Tuggle, Jessie	LB	5-11	225	3	Valdosta State
54	Williams, Joel	LB	6-1	227	11	Wisconsin-LaCrosse

TOP DRAFT CHOICES

Rd.	Name	Sel. No.	Pos.	Ht.	Wt.	College
1	Sanders, Deion	5	DB	5-11	185	Florida State
1	Collins, Shawn	27	WR	6-3	215	Northern Arizona
2	Norwood, Ralph	38	T	6-6	273	LSU
3	Jones, Keith	62	RB	6-1	210	Illinois
6	Sadowski, Troy	145	TE	6-5	243	Georgia

FALCON PROFILES

CHRIS MILLER 24 6-2 195   Quarterback

Emerged as the leader the Falcons thought he'd be when they picked him with the 13th selection in the first round of the 1987 draft ...Makes Falcons a much more dangerous team when he's in the lineup... Has played 16 games in two seasons...Falcons were 5-6 in games Miller started and finished in 1988 ... Completed 184 of 351 passes for 2,133 yards and 11 TDs...Passing yardage was most by a Falcon quarterback since Steve Bartkowski in 1984...Quarterback rating of 67.3 was 11th-highest in the NFC...Rushed 31 times for 138 yards...Was intercepted 12 times...Threw for three TDs against Eagles Oct. 30...Rewrote record books at Oregon, where he passed for 6,681 yards and became the first Pac-10 quarterback since Jim Plunkett to earn all-conference honors in back-to-back seasons...A shortstop in baseball, he was drafted by the Blue Jays in 1983 and later drafted by the Mariners in 1985...Played one year in the minors...Born Aug. 9, 1965, in Pomona, Cal....Earned $350,000 last year.

JOHN SETTLE 24 5-9 207   Running Back

One of the great success stories of 1988...A second-year free agent who moved into starting lineup when Gerald Riggs went down with knee injury...Responded by collecting 1,594 total yards (fourth-best in the NFL)...Earned trip to Pro Bowl...Rushed 232 times for 1,024 yards and seven TDs...Was first free-agent running back since 1970 NFL merger to gain more than 1,000 yards in a single season...Caught team-high 68 passes for 570 yards and one TD...Longest run was 62-yarder against New Orleans Sept. 11...Caught team season-high 10 passes against San Diego Nov. 13...A four-year starter at Appalachian State, where he set multiple school records...Born June 2, 1965, in Reidsville, N.C....Earned $105,000 last year.

SCOTT CASE 27 6-0 176   Cornerback

Earned first trip to Pro Bowl of five-year career... Led NFL and set club record with 10 interceptions... Seemed to always be in the right place at the right time... Has 19 interceptions during his career to rank sixth on Falcons' all-time list... Had 65 tackles, one sack and one forced fumble... Had two interceptions against Packers Nov. 6 and Bucs Nov. 27... A second-round pick in 1984 out of Oklahoma... Had school-record eight interceptions during senior year as Sooner ... Also played at Northeastern Oklahoma Junior College... Born May 17, 1962, in Waynoka, Okla.... Has a ranch near Jay, Okla.... Earned $325,000 last year.

BILL FRALIC 26 6-5 280   Guard

A dominant force on offensive line... Recognized by peers as one of the top guards in football... Earned third trip to Pro Bowl after helping Falcons produce fifth-best rushing offense in the NFC... Missed final two games after undergoing knee injury... Second player taken in 1985 draft, out of Pittsburgh ... Was selected NFL Rookie of the Year by *Sports Illustrated*... His jersey at Pitt was retired... Participated in Wrestlemania II in April 1986. Was 12th of 20 wrestlers to be thrown over the top rope... An avid weightlifter... Born Oct. 31, 1962, in Pittsburgh... Earned $350,000 last year.

AUNDRAY BRUCE 23 6-5 245   Linebacker

Responded to pressures of being the first overall pick in 1988 draft with a solid performance in rookie season... Got off to rocky start missing 3½ weeks of training camp with sprained knee, but answered bell for all 16 regular-season games... Gathered six sacks to lead team and all NFL rookie linebackers... Collected two sacks against Raiders Nov. 20 ... Had 70 total tackles, nine quarterback hurries and six passes deflected... Also had two interceptions and one fumble recovery... Had stellar career at Auburn... Born April 30, 1966, in Montgomery, Ala.... Is 13th of 14 children... Earned $1.9 million last year.

MARCUS COTTON 23 6-3 225   Linebacker

Teams with Aundray Bruce to give Falcons two outstanding prospects at linebacker... When not nagged by injuries, he showed great potential... Collected five sacks and forced one fumble... Credited with three quarterback hurries and defensed two passes... Missed 2½ games early in the season with ankle sprain... Injured a knee in Week 9 and underwent arthroscopic surgery for cartilage damage... Should be 100 percent for training camp... Doubts still linger about practice habits and durability... Could become a great player with more dedication... Was a second-round draft pick in 1987 after being projected as a possible first-rounder heading into senior year at Southern Cal... Born Aug. 11, 1966, in Los Angeles... Earned $445,000 last year.

TONY CASILLAS 25 6-3 280   Nose Tackle

Bounced back from personal problems during offseason and training camp to start in all 16 regular-season games... Totaled 107 tackles and two quarterback sacks... Forced three fumbles... Has 290 tackles during three-year career... Improves each season... Often occupies blockers, freeing linebackers to make tackles... Played in front of Brian Bosworth at Oklahoma... Earned Lombardi Trophy during senior season, awarded best lineman in the country... Has degree in communications... Was No. 2 overall pick in 1986 draft... Born Oct. 26, 1963, in Tulsa, Okla.... Earned $250,000 last year.

MIKE KENN 33 6-7 277   Tackle

Wise veteran who is steadying influence on young team... Still very capable... Had good season in 1988... Voted as alternate to Pro Bowl... Has played in 158 games during 11-year career. Ranks second on club all-time list behind Jeff Van Note, who played 246 from 1969-86... Has not missed a game because of injury in nine of previous 11 seasons... Has started 158 of a possible 165 games . . . Selected to five Pro Bowls . . . Was 13th player selected in 1978 draft . . . Played at Michigan . . . Born Feb. 9, 1956, in Evanston, Ill . . . Is a gourmet cook . . . Earned $390,000 last year.

STACEY BAILEY 29 6-1 157   Wide Receiver

Missed six games with shoulder injury aggravated against Giants Oct. 23 . . . Caught just 17 balls on the season, but they went for 437 yards for a whopping 25.7 yards per catch that was second-highest average in NFC among players with at least five receptions . . . Scored two TDs, including season-long 68-yard reception against Dallas Sept. 25 . . . Nicknamed "Spoon" . . . Born Feb. 10, 1960, in San Rafael, Cal. . . . Training dogs as hobby . . . A third-round draft in 1982 out of San Jose State . . . Earned $250,000 last year.

COACH MARION CAMPBELL:

The Falcons showed improvement in his second year as the team's head coach with 5-11 record after a 3-12 mark in 1987 . . . Highlight was 34-17 victory against eventual Super Bowl-champion 49ers in San Francisco . . . Team could have done better in 1988 had it not been plagued by injuries . . . Considered one of the best defensive minds in the league . . . Has 28 years of professional coaching experience . . . Served as Falcons' defensive coordinator before replacing Dan Henning . . . Started his coaching career as line coach of the AFL Boston Patriots . . . Was defensive line coach with Vikings 1964-66 and worked for the Rams from 1967-68 . . . Was defensive coordinator at Atlanta before serving as head coach from 1974-76 . . . Went to Super Bowl in 1980 as Eagles' defensive coordinator . . . Became Eagles' head coach in 1983, but fired in 1985 . . . Born May 25, 1929, in Chester, S.C. . . . Was All-SEC defensive lineman at Georgia and played for the 49ers in 1954 and 1955 and Eagles from 1956-61 . . . A two-time Pro Bowl selection.

Young Chris Miller gives Falcons hope at quarterback.

GREATEST COACH

In their 23 years of existence, the Atlanta Falcons have celebrated a division championship just once—in 1980, when the
Falcons posted a 12-4 record under coach Leeman Bennett. Included in that season was a nine-game winning streak that made
Atlantans proud.

But 1980 wasn't Bennett's only success story. During his six
years there, the Falcons had only two losing seasons; three times
they finished second in the NFC West.

Bennett, at 46-41, remains the only Falcon coach to have a
winning record. He went on to coach at Tampa Bay for two
seasons.

INDIVIDUAL FALCON RECORDS
Rushing

Most Yards Game:	202	Gerald Riggs, vs New Orleans, 1984
Season:	1,719	Gerald Riggs, 1985
Career:	6,631	Gerald Riggs, 1982-88

Passing

Most TD Passes Game:	4	Randy Johnson, vs Chicago, 1969
	4	Steve Bartkowski, vs New Orleans, 1980
	4	Steve Bartkowski, vs St. Louis, 1981
Season:	31	Steve Bartkowski, 1980
Career:	149	Steve Bartkowski, 1975-85

Receiving

Most TD Passes Game:	3	Lynn Cain, vs Oakland, 1979
	3	Alfred Jenkins, vs New Orleans, 1981
	3	William Andrews, vs Denver, 1982
	3	William Andrews, vs Green Bay, 1983
	3	Lynn Cain, vs L.A. Rams, 1984
	3	Gerald Riggs, vs. L.A. Rams, 1985
Season:	13	Alfred Jenkins, 1981
Career:	40	Alfred Jenkins, 1975-83

Scoring

Most Points Game:	18	Lynn Cain, vs Oakland, 1979
	18	Alfred Jenkins, vs New Orleans, 1981
	18	William Andrews, vs Denver, 1982
	18	William Andrews, vs Green Bay, 1983
	18	Lynn Cain, vs L.A. Rams, 1984
	18	Gerald Riggs, vs L.A. Rams, 1985
Season:	114	Mick Luckhurst, 1981
Career:	558	Mick Luckhurst 1981-87
Most TDs Game:	3	Shared by Lynn Cain, Alfred Jenkins, William Andrews and Gerald Riggs
Season:	13	Alfred Jenkins, 1981
	13	Gerald Riggs, 1984
Career:	48	Gerald Riggs 1982-88

CHICAGO BEARS

TEAM DIRECTORY: Chairman: Edward B. McCaskey; Pres.: Michael B. McCaskey; VP-Player Personnel: Bill Tobin; Dir. Adm.: Tim LeFevour; Dir. Finance: Ted Phillips; Dir. Marketing and Communications: Ken Valdiserri; Pub. Rel. Dir.: Bryan Harlan; Head Coach: Mike Ditka. Home field: Soldier Field (66,946). Colors: Orange, navy blue and white.

SCOUTING REPORT

OFFENSE: For the first time since the Super Bowl Shuffle video, Jim McMahon begins the season without clearly being No. 1 quarterback. Mike Tomczak erased some of Mike Ditka's doubts about his ability by performing well during a four-game

Neal Anderson took great strides toward filling Payton gap.

stretch late in the year when McMahon was injured. And after losing to the 49ers in the NFC championship game, perhaps McMahon's magical powers are diminishing. Even Jim Harbaugh can't be counted out. He had an excellent performance against Detroit Dec. 11.

Neal Anderson eased the anxiety over the retirement of Walter Payton with 1,106 rushing yards, but the fullback spot is wide-open. The receiving corps isn't outstanding, but Dennis McKinnon and Ron Morris are capable of providing the big play.

DEFENSE: Wilber Marshall who? Many thought losing the All-Pro linebacker to the Redskins would leave a huge hole in the Bears' defense, but it didn't. Six players started games at Marshall's old position and there was no noticeable dropoff. Chicago (12-4) finished No. 1 against the run, allowing 82.9 yards per game, and No. 2 overall (272.5). Linebacker Mike Singletary can't play much better than he did last year, when he earned NFL Defensive Player of the Year honors.

There are questions, though. Defensive end Richard Dent is coming back from a broken leg. This could be an opportunity for defensive end Trace Armstrong, the 27th draft pick. William Perry returns from a broken arm and the usual weight problems. The defensive line is aging with Dan Hampton and Steve McMichael. Cornerback Donnell Woolford, the Bears' first choice, is an important addition.

KICKING GAME: There are little or no concerns here. Placekicker Kevin Butler has missed just one of his last 32 field goals inside the 40 and punter Bryan Wagner was second in the NFC with a 41.5 average. Return specialists McKinnon (punts) and Dennis Gentry (kickoffs) can break one at any moment.

THE ROOKIES: Clemson's Woolford could start at left cornerback; he's aggressive and solid on man-to-man coverage. Florida's Armstrong, the second first-round pick, is a Dan Hampton clone who could make William Perry expendable. Second-round pick John Roper of Texas A&M will lend immediate help at linebacker.

OUTLOOK: It's tough to bet against the Bears. They've played in three NFC championship games in the last five years and have won five straight NFC Central titles. As long as their defense continues to dominate games the way it has in the late '80s, there's every reason to think they'll be among the league's best teams in 1989.

BEARS VETERAN ROSTER

HEAD COACH—Mike Ditka. Assistant Coaches—Jim Dooley, Ed Hughes, Steve Kazor, Greg Landry, Jim LaRue, John Levra, Dave McGinnis, Johnny Roland, Dick Stanfel, Vince Tobin.

No.	Name	Pos.	Ht.	Wt.	NFL Exp.	College
54	Adickes, John	C	6-3	264	3	Baylor
35	Anderson, Neal	RB	5-11	210	4	Florida
79	Becker, Kurt	G	6-5	269	8	Michigan
62	Bortz, Mark	G	6-6	272	7	Iowa
86	Boso, Cap	TE	6-3	240	3	Illinois
6	Butler, Kevin	K	6-1	195	5	Georgia
94	Chapura, Dick	DT	6-3	275	3	Missouri
74	Covert, Jim	T	6-4	278	7	Pittsburgh
82	Davis, Wendell	WR	5-11	188	2	Louisiana State
95	Dent, Richard	DE	6-5	270	7	Tennessee State
37	Douglass, Maurice	CB-S	5-11	200	4	Kentucky
22	Duerson, Dave	S	6-1	203	7	Notre Dame
23	Gayle, Shaun	S	5-11	194	6	Ohio State
29	Gentry, Dennis	WR	5-8	180	8	Baylor
99	Hampton, Dan	DE	6-5	270	11	Arkansas
4	Harbaugh, Jim	QB	6-3	204	3	Michigan
63	Hilgenberg, Jay	C	6-3	265	9	Iowa
24	Jackson, Vestee	CB	6-0	186	4	Washington
92	Johnson, Troy	LB	6-0	236	2	Oklahoma
53	Jones, Dante	LB	6-1	236	2	Oklahoma
88	Kozlowski, Glen	WR	6-1	205	3	Brigham Young
44	Krumm, Todd	S	6-0	189	2	Michigan State
43	Lynch, Lorenzo	CB-S	5-9	199	2	Cal State-Sacramento
85	McKinnon, Dennis	WR	6-1	177	6	Florida State
9	McMahon, Jim	QB	6-1	190	8	Brigham Young
76	McMichael, Steve	DT	6-2	260	10	Texas
84	Morris, Ron	WR	6-1	195	3	Southern Methodist
51	Morrissey, Jim	LB	6-3	227	5	Michigan State
25	Muster, Brad	RB	6-3	231	2	Stanford
72	Perry, William	DT	6-2	320	5	Clemson
52	Pruitt, Mickey	LB-S	6-1	206	2	Colorado
59	Rivera, Ron	LB	6-3	240	6	California
20	Sanders, Thomas	RB	5-11	203	5	Texas A&M
75	Shannon, John	DT	6-3	269	2	Kentucky
50	Singletary, Mike	LB	6-0	228	9	Baylor
97	Smith, Sean	DT	6-4	290	2	Grambling
32	Stinson, Lemuel	CB-S	5-9	159	2	Texas Tech
26	Suhey, Matt	RB	5-11	213	10	Penn State
49	Tate, David	CB-S	6-0	177	2	Colorado
57	Thayer, Tom	G	6-4	270	5	Notre Dame
80	Thornton, James	TE	6-2	242	2	Cal State-Fullerton
18	Tomczak, Mike	QB	6-1	198	5	Ohio State
78	Van Horne, Keith	T	6-6	283	9	Southern California
73	Wojciechowski, John	G	6-4	270	3	Michigan State

TOP DRAFT CHOICES

Rd.	Name	Sel. No.	Pos.	Ht.	Wt.	College
1	Woolford, Donnell	11	DB	5-9	185	Clemson
1	Armstrong, Trace	12	DE	6-3	260	Florida
2	Roper, John	36	LB	6-1	230	Texas A&M
2	Zawatson, Dave	54	T	6-4	275	California
3	Fontenot, Jerry	65	G	6-3	270	Texas A&M

BEAR PROFILES

NEAL ANDERSON 25 5-11 210   Running Back

Had outstanding season despite the pressure of replacing retired all-time great Walter Payton . . . Earned first trip to Pro Bowl as a reserve in 1987 . . . Finished as the team's leading rusher for second straight year with 1,106 yards on 249 carries . . . Fifth player in Bear history to rush for 1,000 yards in a season and is the first Bear other than Payton to rush for 1,000 since Gale Sayers in 1967 . . . Also caught 39 passes for 371 yards . . . Was NFC's fourth-leading rusher . . . Scored 12 touchdowns to tie for second in NFC . . . A first-round selection (27th overall) in 1986 out of the University of Florida . . . Was the school's all-time leading rusher (3,234 yards) . . . Born Aug. 4, 1964, in Graceville, Fla. . . . Earned $235,000 last year.

KEVIN BUTLER 27 6-1 195   Kicker

Led the Bears in scoring (82 points) for the fourth straight season and now ranks fifth in club history with 431 points . . . Has made 31 of his last 32 field goals inside the 40 and has connected on 14 of his last 15 overall . . . Made 15 of 19 field goals in 1988 after missing three of first four attempts . . . Made 12 of 13 inside the 40 . . . Longest FG was 45-yarder against Minnesota Dec. 19 . . . Converted 37 of 38 PATs . . . Jim McMahon's favorite teammate . . . A fourth-round selection out of Georgia in 1985 . . . Born July 24, 1962, in Savannah, Ga. . . . Earned $280,000 last year.

MIKE SINGLETARY 30 6-0 228   Linebacker

Continues to be mainstay of Bears' talented defensive unit . . . Voted Associated Press NFL Defensive Player of the Year . . . Earned same honor following 1985 season . . . Led Bears with a career-high 170 tackles . . . Earned sixth straight Pro Bowl appearance . . . Only Walter Payton (9) has been to more Pro Bowls in Bear history . . . Had one sack and recovered one fumble . . . A second-round draft choice out of Baylor in 1981 . . . Was Southwest Conference Player of the Year in 1979 and 1980 . . . Born Oct. 9, 1958, in Houston . . . Has 407 tackles in last three seasons...Well worth the $825,000 he earned last year.

JIM McMAHON 30 6-1 190   Quarterback

Rebel quarterback who has had trouble living up to legendary status gained during Bears' Super Bowl run in 1985...Started the first nine games last year before suffering a sprained knee at New England...Led the club in most pass categories—attempts (192), completions (114), yards (1,346) and rating (76.0)...Was 7-2 as a starter in 1988 and is 46-15 in his career as a starter during the regular season...Had surgery Jan. 13 to repair patella tendon in right knee...Earned $750,000 last year...Will be seriously challenged by Mike Tomczak for starting job this year...A first-round draft pick out of Brigham Young in 1982...Born Aug. 21, 1959, in Jersey City, N.J.

DAVE DUERSON 28 6-1 203   Safety

A steady veteran who makes few mistakes... Finished second on the team behind Mike Singletary with 105 tackles...Earned fourth consecutive trip to Pro Bowl...Defensed six passes...Forced two fumbles and collected one sack...Had two interceptions...A third-round draft pick out of Notre Dame in 1983...Set school record with 256 return yards on 12 career interceptions...Voted 1987 Travelers Man of the Year for numerous off-field contributions to community...Plays all brass instruments...Born Nov. 28, 1960, in Muncie, Ind....Earned $375,000 last year.

RICHARD DENT 28 6-5 260   Defensive End

Many felt Bears lost best chance to go to Super Bowl when Dent broke his leg against Green Bay at Soldier Field Nov. 27...Had been one of the most dominant ends in the league to that point...Collected 10½ sacks and 61 tackles...Has 70 sacks in 70 games over the last five seasons...Had bizarre encounter with NFL regarding the league's substance-abuse policy. Refused to take an unannounced drug test, then took the case to court when the NFL tried to suspend him. Case was settled out of court...One of the best finds in Bear history . . . An eighth-round draft pick from Tennessee State, where he set school record with 39 sacks . . . Born Dec. 13, 1960, in Atlanta . . . Earned $600,000 last year.

DENNIS McKINNON 28 6-1 177   Wide Receiver

Stepped in as the Bears' top receiver following trade of Willie Gault to Raiders . . . Led Bears in receiving with career highs in receptions (45) and yards (704) . . . Catch total was the most by a Bear wide receiver since James Scott's 50 in 1977 . . . Averaged 15.6 yards per catch . . . Longest was 76-yard TD reception . . . Bears are 18-1 in games he has caught a TD pass . . . Also returned 34 punts for 277 yards . . . Made team as free agent in 1983 because of special-teams play . . . Returned punt a club-record 94 yards for TD in Monday Night game against Giants Sept. 14, 1987 . . . Played at Florida State . . . Has degree in criminology . . . Born Aug. 22, 1961, in Quitman, Ga. . . . Earned $345,000 last year.

DAN HAMPTON 32 6-5 270   Defensive End

Seems to get better with age . . . Did not make fifth Pro Bowl, but had credentials worthy of consideration . . . Had fine year in 1988, collecting 9½ sacks . . . Tied with Steve McMichael and Ron Rivera with 88 tackles to rank third on team . . . Was dominating force along defensive line, especially before injury to Richard Dent . . . Loves to win . . . Was visibly angry at loss to 49ers in NFC championship . . . Has been a fixture since being selected in first round (4th choice overall) of 1979 draft . . . Was Southwest Conference Defensive Player of the Year during senior year at Arkansas . . . Born Jan. 19, 1957, in Oklahoma City, Okla. . . . Earned $775,000 last year.

JAY HILGENBERG 30 6-3 265   Center

The picture of durability . . . Has played in every game (117) since joining the team in 1981 . . . Has a consecutive-start streak of 84 games . . . Had solid season anchoring offensive line . . . Earned fourth straight Pro Bowl appearance as a starter . . . Helped block for rushing game, which ranked third in the NFL with 2,319 yards on the ground . . . Extremely strong against nose tackles, but is agile enough to pull and lead block on off-tackle runs... Brother Joel plays for Saints... Avid outdoorsman... Signed with Bears as free agent in 1981 after standout career at Iowa... Born March 21, 1959, in Iowa City, Iowa... Earned $525,000 last year.

STEVE McMICHAEL 31 6-2 260   **Defensive Tackle**

Had a career-high and team-high 11½ sacks, marking the first time since 1983 that Richard Dent failed to lead the club in sacks... Sack total tied for seventh in the NFC and NFL... Enters 1989 with the longest consecutive-start streak at 85 games... Hasn't missed a game in five seasons... Biggest surprise of year was his missing the Pro Bowl... Recorded 88 tackles, tying Dan Hampton and Ron Rivera for third on team ... Recovered two fumbles... 1980 third-round selection by Patriots but was cut... Signed with Bears as free agent in 1981... Played at Texas... Born Oct. 17, 1957, in Houston... Earned $500,000 last year.

COACH MIKE DITKA:

Last year he became the first tight end to be inducted into the Pro Football Hall of Fame... Was named 1988 Associated Press and *Football News* NFL Coach of the Year after leading Bears to fifth straight NFC Central title and NFC-leading 12-4 record... Also won Coach of the Year honors in 1985 when Bears won the Super Bowl... Outspoken leader... Suffered a mild heart attack Nov. 2. Returned to work one week later and was back on sideline after missing only one game... Cooled temperament after attack. Ceased screaming at players, officials and reporters... Served as special-teams and receivers coach with Cowboys from 1973-81 ... Was All-American at Pitt (tight end, linebacker, punter) and played 12 years for the Bears, Eagles and Cowboys... Born Oct. 13, 1939, in Carnegie, Pa.

GREATEST COACH

Affectionately known as "Papa Bear," George S. Halas was the Bears' founder and head coach for 40 years. He died in 1983 at the age of 88, but he lives on as a sports legend.

The son of a Czechoslovak tailor, he was a baseball and football star at the University of Illinois, played end for the Bears for nearly a decade and even got to play right field for the New York Yankees—19 games in 1919.

He built an incredible coaching mark of 326-151-30 that easily ranks him No. 1 among the NFL all-time winningest coaches. His Bears won six NFL titles, including the awesome 73-0 trouncing of the Washington Redskins in 1940. He was chosen as a charter member of the Pro Hall of Fame.

INDIVIDUAL BEAR RECORDS

Rushing

Most Yards Game:	275	Walter Payton, vs Minnesota, 1977
Season:	1,852	Walter Payton, 1977
Career:	16,726	Walter Payton, 1975-87

Passing

Most TD Passes Game:	7	Sid Luckman, vs N.Y. Giants, 1943
Season:	28	Sid Luckman, 1943
Career:	137	Sid Luckman, 1939-50

Receiving

Most TD Passes Game:	4	Harlon Hill, vs San Francisco, 1954
	4	Mike Ditka, vs Los Angeles, 1963
Season:	13	Dick Gordon, 1970
	13	Ken Kavanaugh, 1947
Career:	50	Ken Kavanaugh, 1940-41, 1945-50

Scoring

Most Points Game:	36	Gale Sayers, vs San Francisco, 1965
Season:	144	Kevin Butler, 1985
Career:	750	Walter Payton, 1975-87
Most TDs Game:	6	Gale Sayers, vs San Francisco, 1965
Season:	22	Gale Sayers, 1965
Career:	125	Walter Payton, 1975-87

DALLAS COWBOYS

TEAM DIRECTORY: Owner/Pres./GM: Jerry Jones; VP-Pro Personnel: Bob Ackles; Pub. Rel. Dir.: Greg Aiello. Head Coach: Jimmy Johnson. Home field: Texas Stadium (65,024). Colors: Royal blue, metallic blue and white.

SCOUTING REPORT

OFFENSE: The new leadership of owner Jerry Jones and coach Jimmy Johnson banks on Troy Aikman as the Cowboys' future, but expect Steve Pelluer to open the year as the starting quarterback. It may be Pelluer's last chance to prove himself as a credible signal-caller. He has been inconsistent throughout his career, looking brilliant one week and mistake-prone the next. Danny White continues to hang on but will likely be the odd man out for Dallas (3-13 last year).

Cowboys bank on $11-million rookie Troy Aikman.

With the unstable play at quarterback, most of the offense revolved around All-Pro running back Herschel Walker, who averaged 4.2 yards on 361 carries (runnerup to the Colts' Eric Dickerson) and 9.5 yards on 53 receptions.

The wide-receiving duo of Michael Irvin and Ray Alexander is young and talented and the offensive line is in decent shape except for center, where Tom Rafferty is nearing the end of his career.

DEFENSE: Without changes, the Cowboys' defensive line could be a sore spot. Jim Jeffcoat isn't intimidating, Ed Jones is long past his prime, Danny Noonan seems injury-prone and Kevin Brooks hasn't played to his potential. The Flex Defense has been junked, a move that pleased many of the younger players who felt constrained. Veterans Garry Cobb and Eugene Lockhart are solid linebackers, but some young talent needs to emerge at starting and backup roles.

Robert Williams took his lumps early last year at cornerback, but continued to improve and should work effectively opposite veteran Everson Walls. Strong safety Bill Bates is a battering ram, but questionable on coverage.

KICKING GAME: Placekicker Roger Ruzek missed training camp in a contract dispute and struggled most of 1988. He should bounce back and have a good 1989. Mike Saxon can punt for a decent average and is excellent at placing the ball inside the 20. Darryl Clack averaged 21.6 yards per kickoff return, the third-highest average in the NFC.

THE ROOKIES: UCLA's Aikman was coveted from the start, but the Cowboys won't press him into service. Second-round pick Daryl Johnston of Syracuse will be a blocking fullback for Walker. Mark Stepnoski, a third-rounder from Pittsburgh, is a highly-touted guard who is quicker than most of the Cowboys' current linemen. Tony Tolbert, a fourth-rounder from UTEP, may be moved from linebacker to defensive end.

OUTLOOK: The Jerry Jones/Jimmy Johnson Era begins amid skeptics still smarting over the way Tom Landry was fired. The only way to soothe those hard feelings is to win football games, something the players think they can do under Johnson, who has said all the right things. The last-place schedule should help, but being in one of the league's tougher divisions won't.

COWBOYS VETERAN ROSTER

HEAD COACH—Jimmy Johnson. Assistant Coaches—Hubbard Alexander, Neill Armstrong, Joe Brodsky, Dave Campo, Butch Davis, Alan Lowry, Dick Nolan, Jerry Rhome, David Shula, Dave Wannstedt, Bob Ward, Tony Wise.

No.	Name	Pos.	Ht.	Wt.	NFL Exp.	College
36	Albritton, Vince	S	6-2	210	6	Washington
87	Alexander, Ray	WR	6-4	190	3	Florida A&M
82	Barksdale, Rod	WR	6-1	192	3	Arizona
40	Bates, Bill	S	6-1	199	7	Tennessee
99	Brooks, Kevin	DT-DE	6-6	273	5	Michigan
27	Burbage, Cornell	CB-S	5-10	189	3	Kentucky
57	Burton, Ron	LB	6-1	245	3	North Carolina
85	Chandler, Thornton	TE	6-5	245	4	Alabama
42	Clack, Darryl	RB	5-10	218	4	Arizona State
22	Clark, Kevin	CB-S	5-10	185	3	San Jose State
59	Cobb, Garry	LB	6-2	230	11	Southern California
—	Coyle, Eric	C	6-3	260	2	Colorado
55	DeOssie, Steve	LB	6-2	245	6	Boston College
26	Downs, Michael	S	6-3	204	9	Rice
44	Dykes, Sean	CB	5-9	178	2	Bowling Green
81	Edwards, Kelvin	WR	6-2	204	4	Liberty
85	Folsom, Steve	TE	6-5	240	5	Utah
46	Fowler, Todd	RB	6-3	221	6	Stephen F. Austin
38	Francis, Ron	CB	5-9	201	3	Baylor
80	Gay, Everett	WR	6-2	209	2	Texas
66	Gogan, Kevin	T	6-7	306	3	Washington
45	Hendrix, Manny	CB-S	5-10	178	4	Utah
20	Horton, Ray	CB-S	5-11	190	7	Washington
52	Hurd, Jeff	LB	6-2	245	2	Kansas State
88	Irvin, Michael	WR	6-2	198	2	Miami
53	Jax, Garth	LB	6-2	225	4	Florida State
77	Jeffcoat, Jim	DE	6-5	263	7	Arizona State
90	Jones, Anthony	TE	6-3	248	6	Wichita State
72	Jones, Ed	DE	6-9	273	15	Tennessee State
68	Ker, Crawford	G	6-3	285	5	Florida
56	Lockhart, Eugene	LB	6-2	230	6	Houston
67	Marrone, Doug	T-G	6-5	295	2	Syracuse
83	Martin, Kelvin	WR	5-9	13	3	Boston College
20	Miller, Solomon	WR	6-3	176	3	Utah State
58	Naposki, Eric	LB	6-2	230	2	Connecticut
30	Newsome, Timmy	RB	6-1	237	10	Winston-Salem State
67	Newton, Nate	G	6-3	317	4	Florida A&M
73	Noonan, Danny	DT	6-4	282	3	Nebraska
51	Norton, Ken	LB	6-2	236	2	UCLA
31	Owens, Billy	S	6-1	207	2	Pittsburgh
16	Pelluer, Steve	QB	6-4	208	6	Washington
60	Petersmarck, Brett	T-G	6-4	275	2	Eastern Michigan
64	Rafferty, Tom	C	6-3	262	14	Penn State
50	Rohrer, Jeff	LB	6-2	227	7	Yale
9	Ruzek, Roger	K	6-1	195	3	Weber State
39	Sargent, Broderick	RB	5-11	215	3	Baylor
4	Saxon, Mike	P	6-3	188	5	San Diego State
10	Secules, Scott	QB	6-3	219	2	Virginia
93	Sileo, Dan	DT	6-2	291	3	Miami
79	Smith, Daryle	T	6-5	276	3	Tennessee
25	Tautalatasi, Junior	RB	5-11	208	4	Washington State
63	Titensor, Glen	G	6-4	270	8	Brigham Young
71	Tuinel, Mark	C	6-5	283	7	Hawaii
95	Walen, Mark	DT-DE	6-5	267	3	UCLA
34	Walker, Herschel	RB	6-1	223	4	Georgia
24	Walls, Everson	CB	6-1	193	9	Grambling
65	White, Bob	C	6-5	273	3	Rhode Island
11	White, Danny	T	6-3	197	14	Arizona State
78	Widell, Dave	T	6-6	300	2	Boston College
23	Williams, Robert	CB	5-10	186	3	Baylor
76	Zimmerman, Jeff	G	6-3	313	2	Florida

TOP DRAFT CHOICES

Rd.	Name	Sel. No.	Pos.	Ht.	Wt.	College
1	Aikman, Troy	1	QB	6-4	220	UCLA
2	Johnston, Daryl	39	RB	6-1	235	Syracuse
3	Stepnoski, Mark	57	G	6-2	270	Pittsburgh
3	Weston, Rhondy	68	DE	6-4	275	Florida
4	Tolbert, Tony	85	LB	6-6	230	UTEP

COWBOY PROFILES

HERSCHEL WALKER 27 6-1 223   **Running Back**

While the Cowboys may have floundered as a team, Walker did nothing to hurt his reputation as one of football's best backs...Led NFC in rushing with 1,502 yards and was third in the NFL in total yards from scrimmage with 2,019...Rushed an NFC-high 361 times for 4.2 yards per carry and five TDs...Was team's second-leading receiver with 53 catches for 505 yards and two TDs...Earned second trip to Pro Bowl ...Signed with Cowboys as free agent Aug. 13, 1986, after leading the USFL in rushing in 1983 and 1985 as a member of New Jersey Generals...Was league MVP in 1985...Gained 7,046 total yards and scored 61 TDs during three seasons in USFL...Won Heisman Trophy in 1982 after stellar career at Georgia, where he rushed for 5,259 yards...Born March 3, 1962, in Wrightsville, Ga....Earned $1.8 million last year.

RAY ALEXANDER 27 6-4 190   **Wide Receiver**

Stepped in and did admirable job at a position where Cowboys lacked depth...Finished the season as team's leader in receptions (54), receiving yardage (788) and TD receptions (six) ...Signed with Dallas in 1987 after two seasons in the Canadian Football League... Broke his left wrist in training camp and spent the '87 on injured reserve...A product of Florida A&M...Finished second in the CFL in receiving yards (1,590) and third in catches (88) while playing for Calgary in 1986...Caught eight passes for 132 yards and one TD in eight games with Denver in 1984...Born Jan. 8, 1962, in Miami... Earned $132,000 last year.

EVERSON WALLS 29 6-1 193   **Cornerback**

Steady veteran whose lofty reputation has forced opposing quarterbacks to throw in another direction...Shared team lead in interceptions with two...Was ninth on squad with 61 tackles...Has all the skills of a top-rated defensive back; he's a quick-thinker who recovers quickly and has good instincts...Is second on club's all-time list of interceptions with 44 (Mel Renfro leads with 52)...Has played in four Pro

Bowls... Correctly predicted winner of all nine playoff games last season while serving as radio commentator... Joined team as free agent out of Grambling in 1981 and set club record with 11 interceptions that season... Born Dec. 28, 1959, in Dallas... Earned $500,000 last year.

DANNY NOONAN 24 6-4 282   Defensive Tackle

Established himself as the club's starting right defensive tackle... Shared team lead in sacks with Garry Cobb, each collecting 7½... Was fifth on team in tackles with 84... Had one interception... Was Cowboys' No. 1 pick and 12th overall choice out of Nebraska in 1987 ... Affectionately called "Schwarzenegger" or "Danny the Barbarian" by teammates... Is the Cowboys' strongest player, able to bench-press over 505 pounds ... A consensus All-American in 1986, anchoring Huskers' second-ranked defense in the nation... Born July 14, 1965, in Lincoln, Neb., six miles from UN campus... Earned $225,000 last year.

JIM JEFFCOAT 28 6-5 263   Defensive End

Capable veteran on Cowboys' defensive line ... Had solid season in 1988, collecting 6½ sacks... Was sixth on the club in tackles with 80... Led team in forced fumbles with 3½ ... A hard worker who gives his best at everything... Has 51 sacks over the last five seasons, more than any other Cowboy... Set club record in 1985, sacking Redskin quarterback Joe Theismann five times... Had a career-high 14 sacks in 1984... Has returned two pass interceptions and one fumble for touchdowns... A first-round draft pick out of Arizona State in 1983... Born April 1, 1961, in Cliffwood, N.J.... Comes from a family of six children... Earned $236,000 last year.

BILL BATES 28 6-1 199   Safety

Has not cooled his relentless hard-hitting style even after six seasons... Led team in tackles for first time in his career with 124 total stops, 85 solo... Intercepted one pass and credited with a half-sack... Defensed six passes and recovered one fumble... Was second on team in special-team tackles with 22... Another example of Cowboys' tradition of developing free agents... Signed with Cowboys in 1983 and made the club largely on special-teams play... Made Pro Bowl squad in 1984 as a special-teamer... Was four-year starter at Tennessee... Born June 6, 1961, in Knoxville, Tenn.... Avid in charity work, particularly with United Way and Special Olympics... Earned $245,000 last year.

GARRY COBB 32 6-2 230   Linebacker

Signed as a free agent last season after being released by the Eagles... Proved a valuable acquisition... A steady, dependable and intelligent linebacker... Was third on the team with 104 total tackles... Shared team lead in sacks with 7½, a career high... Recovered one fumble and forced another... Originally a ninth-round draft choice of the Cowboys in 1979, but was waived late in preseason... Signed with Lions as free agent... Played six seasons (1979-84) in Detroit... Acquired by Eagles before 1985 season in exchange for Wilbert Montgomery... Enjoyed outstanding career at Southern Cal, where he helped Trojans win two national championships... Also played baseball (center field) at USC and was offered contracts by the Angels and Cubs... Born March 16, 1957, in Carthage, N.C.... Has degree in sociology... Earned $315,000 last year.

STEVE PELLUER 27 6-4 208   Quarterback

When most of the offseason was spent talking about using the No. 1 to draft a player at his position, there was reason to feel insecure and frustrated... Pelluer was all that in 1988 as he failed to establish himself as the Cowboys' No. 1 quarterback... And with the arrival of No. 1, Troy Aikman, there's little question of who will eventually be No. 1... Last year, Pelluer was often inconsistent and at times very erratic... Nearly doubled his career totals by completing 245 of 435 passes for 3,139 yards and 17 TDs... Guilty of 19 interceptions... QB rating of 73.9 was ninth-best in the NFC... Was sacked 21 times ... Pulled in favor of Kevin Sweeney during second half against Giants Nov. 6... Did not start following week... A fifth-round draft pick in 1984 out of Washington, where he finished as the Huskies' second all-time passer with 4,603 yards... Born July 29, 1962, in Yakima, Wash.... Earned $302,000 last year.

MICHAEL IRVIN 23 6-2 198   Wide Receiver

Exciting young player who showed great potential before being slowed late in the year by an ankle injury... Was the No. 1 draft choice out of Miami in 1988, the 11th pick overall and the Cowboys' highest draft pick since Tony Dorsett was taken with the second pick in 1977... Finished the year as the club's fourth-leading receiver with 32 catches for 654 yards and five TDs... Averaged 20.4 yards per catch... Caught winning pass in Miami's 1988 national championship victory over Oklahoma in Orange Bowl... Broke career receiving records at Miami for catches (143), yards (2,423) and TDs (26) ... Born March 5, 1966, in Ft. Lauderdale, Fla.... Grew up in family of 17 children... Earned $965,523 last year.

EUGENE LOCKHART 28 6-2 230   Linebacker

An intense player who was a consistent, solid performer in 1988... Ranked second on the team with 121 total tackles, including 72 solo ... Forced two fumbles during the season... Did not record a sack for first time in his career... Recovered from broken fibula in right leg against Atlanta Dec. 6, 1987... Should push for All-Pro honors this season ... A sixth-round draft pick out of Houston in 1984, he became first rookie ever to start at middle linebacker for Cowboys when veteran Bob Breunig was sidelined with a back injury that season... Has 450 tackles over the last four seasons... Born March 8, 1961, in Crockett, Tex.... Earned $315,000 last year.

COACH JIMMY JOHNSON: The personal choice of new owner and former college roommate Jerry Jones to replace legendary Tom Landry and lead the Cowboys back to respectability...

Enters first NFL job with loads of collegiate credentials and a 10-year contract... Compiled a 52-9 record during five seasons at the University of Miami, winning a national championship in 1987 with a 12-0 record... From 1985 through last season, Miami put together the fifth longest regular-season winning streak in NCAA history with 36 straight victories ... Was a defensive tackle on Arkansas' 1964 national-championship team ... Began coaching career at Louisiana Tech ... Also coached at Wichita State, Iowa State and Oklahoma before returning to Arkansas as defensive coordinator from 1973-76 ... Coached at Pittsburgh for two years before assuming head-coaching duties at Oklahoma State, where he compiled a 29-25-3 record in five seasons ... Moved to Miami in 1984 ... Overall collegiate coaching record is 81-34-3, with 3-4 mark in bowl games ... Born July 16, 1943, in Port Arthur, Tex.

GREATEST COACH

Despite the stunning manner in which he was fired during the offseason, the legacy of Tom Landry will long be remembered in Dallas and the NFL.

From 1966-85, Landry guided the Cowboys to 20 consecutive winning seasons, 18 playoff appearances and five Super Bowls. The Cowboys won Super Bowls VI and XII.

His 29 consecutive years as head coach ties Curly Lambeau's record set with the Green Bay Packers from 1921-49 and Landry ranks third among the NFL's top 10 all-time winningest coaches with a record of 270-178-6.

An All-Pro defensive back with the Giants in 1954, Landry was named the Cowboys' head coach in 1960 and brought many innovations to the game, including the flex defense and the rebirth of the shotgun offense.

INDIVIDUAL COWBOY RECORDS
Rushing

Most Yards Game:	206	Tony Dorsett, vs Philadelphia, 1978	
Season:	1,646	Tony Dorsett, 1981	
Career:	12,036	Tony Dorsett, 1977-87	

Passing

Most TD Passes Game:	5	Eddie LeBaron, vs Pittsburgh, 1962
	5	Don Meredith, vs N.Y. Giants, 1966
	5	Don Meredith, vs Philadelphia, 1966
	5	Don Meredith, vs Philadelphia, 1968
	5	Craig Morton, vs Philadelphia, 1969
	5	Craig Morton, vs Houston, 1970
	5	Danny White, vs N.Y. Giants, 1983
Season:	29	Danny White, 1983
Career:	154	Danny White, 1976-87

Receiving

Most TD Passes Game:	4	Bob Hayes, vs Houston, 1970
Season:	14	Frank Clarke, 1962
Career:	71	Bob Hayes, 1965-74

Scoring

Most Points Game:	24	Dan Reeves, vs Atlanta, 1967
	24	Bob Hayes, vs Houston, 1970
	24	Calvin Hill, vs Buffalo, 1971
	24	Duane Thomas, vs St. Louis, 1971
Season:	123	Rafael Septien, 1983
Career:	874	Rafael Septien, 1978-86
Most TDs Game:	4	Dan Reeves, vs Atlanta, 1967
	4	Bob Hayes, vs Houston, 1970
	4	Calvin Hill, vs Buffalo, 1971
	4	Duane Thomas, vs St. Louis, 1971
Season:	16	Dan Reeves, 1966
Career:	86	Tony Dorsett, 1977-87

DETROIT LIONS

TEAM DIRECTORY: Pres.: William Clay Ford; Exec. VP/GM: Russ Thomas; Dir. Football Operations/Head Coach: Wayne Fontes; Dir. Pub. Rel.: Bill Keenist. Home field: Pontiac Silverdome (80,500). Colors: Honolulu blue and silver.

SCOUTING REPORT

OFFENSE: The Lions (4-12) ranked 28th—dead-last—in the NFL in total offense last year. But Wayne Fontes, starting his first full season, hopes to change that with the new "Stretch" offense, which is devised to stretch defenses into covering the entire field. The scheme will incorporate much of the "Run 'n' Shoot" made popular in the USFL by current Lions' offensive coordinator Mouse Davis. The question is, do the Lions have the personnel for such an offense?

Quarterback Chuck Long was disappointing last year and had elbow surgery in February. Garry James (3.0 average on 182 carries, five TDs) and James Jones (3.3 on 96 carries and without a TD in the last two seasons) do not suggest offensive might. That's why the Lions are hoping for big things from Heisman Trophy winner Barry Sanders, the running back who was third overall in the draft.

The only true threat among the receivers is Pete Mandley, who averaged 14 yards on 44 receptions, with five TDs. The offensive line consistently broke down.

DEFENSE: The Lions can boast of one of the league's most talented young linebacking corps. Outside linebacker Mike Cofer made the Pro Bowl, rookie Chris Spielman set a club record with 153 tackles and George Jamison did a respectable job when Jimmy Williams went down with an injury.

But outside of nose tackle Jerry Ball, there is little intimidating about the defensive line. The secondary also needs help as 1988 top pick Bennie Blades, a free safety, is the only player with Pro Bowl potential. Cornerbacks Jerry Holmes and Bruce McNorton are inconsistent and vulnerable to deep passes.

KICKING GAME: Placekicker Eddie Murray and punter Jim Arnold provide the Lions with a strong kicking game. Mandley averaged 7.8 yards on 37 punt returns, so the Lions needed help there. They should get it up from ex-Saint Mel Gray, whose 12.2-yard average on 25 punt returns was second-highest in the league.

Whatever their problems, Lions can count on Pete Mandley.

THE ROOKIES: Christmas came early in the form of Oklahoma State's Sanders, who should lend instant punch to the running game. Southern Cal quarterback Rodney Peete was disappointed with his Round 6 selection, but not the team. He throws well on the move and should be perfect for the Lions' offense. Virginia second-round pick John Ford is a rock-solid 200-pound receiver who could push for playing time.

OUTLOOK: Fontes' motto is "Restore the Roar," but he might settle for a loud growl. In the last three years, the Lions haven't beaten a team that finished the year with a winning record. But there is hope in Motown. The Lions showed more fire under Fontes, who went 2-3 as interim coach. The most crucial task is to create an offense that can produce more points than the defense will give up.

LIONS VETERAN ROSTER

HEAD COACH—Wayne Fontes. Assistant Coaches—Don Clemons, Darrel Davis, Frank Gansz, June Jones, Dave Levy, Billie Matthews, Dick Modzelewski, Mike Murphy, Herb Paterra, Charlie Sanders, Jerry Wampfler, Woody Widenhofer.

No.	Name	Pos.	Ht.	Wt.	NFL Exp.	College
65	Andolsek, Eric	G	6-2	277	2	Louisiana State
6	Arnold, Jim	P	6-3	211	7	Vanderbilt
68	Baack, Steve	NT	6-4	265	5	Oregon
97	Baldwin, Steve	NT	6-4	270	5	Tulsa
93	Ball, Jerry	NT	6-1	292	3	Southern Methodist
61	Barrows, Scott	G-C	6-3	280	4	West Virginia
25	Bernard, Karl	RB	5-11	205	2	SW Louisiana
36	Blades, Bennie	CB-S	6-1	218	2	Miami
75	Brown, Lomas	T	6-4	275	5	Florida
44	Carter, Pat	TE	6-4	250	2	Florida State
91	Caston, Toby	LB	6-1	240	3	Louisiana State
89	Chadwick, Jeff	WR	6-3	190	7	Grand Valley State
45	Cherry, Raphel	S	6-0	190	4	Hawaii
2	Clark, Robert	WR	5-11	175	2	North Carolina Central
55	Cofer, Michael	LB	6-5	245	7	Tennessee
67	Dallafior, Ken	G	6-4	278	5	Minnesota
41	Edmonds, Bobby Joe	RB-KR	5-11	186	4	Arkansas
77	Ferguson, Keith	DE	6-5	260	9	Ohio State
14	Gagliano, Bob	QB	6-3	205	2	Utah State
69	Gambol, Chris	T	6-6	303	2	Iowa
98	Gibson, Dennis	LB	6-2	240	3	Iowa State
53	Glover, Kevin	C-G	6-2	275	5	Maryland
23	Gray, Mel	RB-KR	5-9	166	4	Purdue
62	Green, Curtis	DE-NT	6-3	270	9	Alabama State
34	Griffin, James	S	6-2	203	7	Middle Tenn. State
71	Hamilton, Steve	DE-DT	6-4	270	5	East Carolina
12	Hilger, Rusty	QB	6-4	205	5	Oklahoma State
17	Hipple, Eric	QB	6-1	211	9	Utah State
43	Holmes, Jerry	CB	6-2	175	8	West Virginia
33	James, Garry	RB	5-10	214	4	Louisiana State
58	Jamison, George	LB	6-1	226	3	Cincinnati
30	Jones, James	RB	6-2	229	7	Florida
90	Jones, Victor	LB	6-2	245	2	Virginia Tech
99	Kab, Vyto	TE	6-5	240	6	Penn State
83	Lee, Gary	WR-KR	6-1	201	3	Georgia Tech
80	Lewis, Mark	TE	6-2	250	3	Texas A&M
50	Lockett, Danny	LB	6-2	250	2	Arizona
16	Long, Chuck	QB	6-4	211	4	Iowa
82	Mandley, Pete	WR-KR	5-10	191	6	Northern Arizona
29	McNorton, Bruce	CB	5-11	175	8	Georgetown, Ky.
74	Milinichik, Joe	G-T	6-5	275	3	North Carolina State
31	Mitchell, Devon	S	6-1	194	3	Iowa
42	Morris, Randall	RB	6-0	200	6	Tennessee
52	Mott, Steve	C	6-3	265	7	Alabama
3	Murray, Eddie	K	5-10	175	10	Tulane
86	Nichols, Mark	WR	6-2	208	7	San Jose State
49	Paige, Tony	RB	5-10	235	6	Virginia Tech
26	Painter, Carl	RB	5-9	185	2	Hampton Institute
51	Robinson, Shelton	LB	6-2	236	8	North Carolina
60	Rogers, Reggie	DE	6-6	280	3	Washington
47	Roundtree, Ray	WR	6-0	182	2	Penn State
84	Rubick, Rob	TE	6-3	234	8	Grand Valley State
73	Salem, Harvey	T-G	6-6	285	7	California
64	Sanders, Eric	T-G	6-7	280	9	Nevada-Reno
72	Singer, Curt	T	6-5	279	3	Tennessee
54	Spielman, Chris	LB	6-0	234	2	Ohio State
81	Starring, Stephen	WR	5-10	172	7	McNeese State
21	Tullis, Willie	CB	5-11	195	9	Troy State
35	White, William	CB	5-10	191	2	Ohio State
76	Williams, Eric	DE	6-4	280	6	Washington State
59	Williams, Jimmy	LB	6-3	230	8	Nebraska
38	Williams, Scott	RB	6-2	234	4	Georgia
21	Woolfolk, Butch	RB	6-1	212	8	Michigan

TOP DRAFT CHOICES

Rd.	Name	Sel. No.	Pos.	Ht.	Wt.	College
1	Sanders, Barry	3	RB	5-8	196	Oklahoma State
2	Ford, John	30	WR	6-2	200	Virginia
3	Utley, Mike	59	G	6-6	295	Washington State
4	Crockett, Ray	86	DB	5-9	180	Baylor
5	Pete, Lawrence	115	DT	6-1	280	Nebraska

LION PROFILES

JIM ARNOLD 28 6-3 211   Punter

Earned second consecutive trip to Pro Bowl ...Led NFC punters with 42.4-yard average ...Net average of 35.9 also was conference high...Longest was 69-yarder at Green Bay Nov. 20, a career best...Landed 22 punts inside the 20...Punted a club-record 97 times ...A fifth-round selection by Kansas City in 1983...Led league in punting in 1984... Signed with Lions as free agent in 1986...Set NFL record in 1987 with net average of 39.6...Led nation in punting during senior year at Vanderbilt with 45.8 average...Has degree in sociology...Born Jan. 31, 1961, in Dalton, Ga....Earned $160,000 last year.

CHRIS SPIELMAN 23 6-0 234   Linebacker

Second-round draft pick in 1988 who had sensational rookie year...Set team record with 153 total tackles, eclipsing the old mark of 148 set by Ken Fantetti in 1981...Had team season-high of 16 tackles at Minnesota Nov. 6...Had 10 or more tackles on six occasions...Was Lions' only 1988 draft choice to start in all 16 games...An intense competitor who loves to hit...Won Lombardi Award as a senior at Ohio State...Had 546 career tackles as a Buckeye...Born Oct. 11, 1965, in Canton, Ohio...Earned $450,000 last year.

MICHAEL COFER 29 6-5 245   Linebacker

Beginning to be recognized as one of the top linebackers in the league...Earned first trip to Pro Bowl of six-year career after posting a career-high 12 sacks, the most ever by a Detroit linebacker...Sack total was sixth-highest in the NFC...Had 75 total tackles, second-most of his career...Forced three fumbles and recovered two...Often lines up in down position to rush the passer...Always gives all-out effort...Has been clocked under 4.5 in 40-yard dash...A third-round draft choice in 1983 out of Tennessee...Born April 7, 1960, in Knoxville, Tenn....Earned $260,000 last year.

GARRY JAMES 25 5-10 214   Running Back

Became the first back other than James Jones to lead the Lions in rushing since 1984... Accounted for 934 total yards... Rushed for 552 yards on a career-high 182 carries... Caught a career-high 39 passes for 382 yards and two TDs... Had a career-high eight catches against Tampa Bay Nov. 13... Was second on the team in scoring with 42 points ... Best rushing day came in season-opener against Falcons: 24 carries for 96 yards and one TD... A second-round draft pick in 1986... Gained 688 yards during rookie season... Part of famed Dalton-James gang at LSU, where he and Dalton Hilliard (now with Saints) accounted for more career rushing and receiving yards (8,394) than any backfield tandem in Southeastern Conference history... Born Sept. 4, 1963, in Gretna, La.... Earned $180,000 last year.

BENNIE BLADES 22 6-1 216   Free Safety

First-round draft pick in 1988 who showed tremendous potential in initial NFL season... Was fifth on the team in tackles with 102... Only member of secondary to have at least one sack, interception and fumble recovery... Tied for team lead in fumble recoveries with four... Had two interceptions and forced three fumbles... Was third overall pick, the Lions' highest draft position since 1980... Was consensus All-American for Miami Hurricanes... Co-winner (with Bengals' Rickey Dixon) of 1987 Jim Thorpe Award given to nation's outstanding defensive back... Concluded collegiate career as school's all-time leader in interceptions with 19... Born Sept. 3, 1966, in Ft. Lauderdale, Fla.... Earned $1,078,480 last year.

PETE MANDLEY 28 5-9 191   Wide Receiver

Led Lions in receiving for second straight season... Caught 44 passes for 617 yards and four touchdowns... His 56-yard catch against Chicago Oct. 9 was longest of career and the team's longest last season... Set personal best with 37 punt returns for 287 yards... Ranks first on Lions' all-time list with 143 career punt returns... Also leads in career punt-return yardage with 1,360... Second-round draft choice out of

Northern Arizona in 1984...Attended same high school as Dallas quarterback Danny White (Westwood High, Mesa, Ariz.) ...Born July 29, 1961, in Mesa...Earned $267,000 last year.

CHUCK LONG 26 6-4 211   Quarterback

Suffered strained knee ligament against Bears Oct. 9 and missed six weeks before coming back for short-lived appearance against Minnesota Thanksgiving Day...Did not see action in final three games...Rusty Hilger handled quarterback duties after backup Eric Hipple went down with a broken ankle... Long completed just 75 of 141 passes for 1,558 yards and seven TDs...Best outing came in 22-14 loss to Saints Sept. 18, when he completed 20 of 33 for 274 yards and two TDs...Remains future of franchise despite disappointing season...Completed 55.8 percent of his passes for 2,598 yards in 1987...First-round draft choice out of Iowa in 1986...Born Feb. 18, 1963, in Norman, Okla...Was Heisman Trophy runnerup to Bo Jackson in 1985...Earned $275,000 last year.

EDDIE MURRAY 33 5-10 175   Kicker

One of the league's most reliable kickers... Tied an NFL record previously set by Redskins' Mark Moseley in 1982 for field-goal accuracy with 95.24 percent (20 of 21)... Added to career marks in points (847), PATs (271) and field goals (192)...Posted 82 points to lead Lions in scoring for the ninth straight year...Kicked four field goals against Green Bay Nov. 20...Longest field goal was 48 yards at Minnesota Nov. 6...A seventh-round draft pick in 1980... Born Aug. 29, 1956, in Halifax, Nova Scotia...Outstanding racquetball player...Earned $195,000 last year.

ERIC WILLIAMS 27 6-4 280   Defensive End

A five-year veteran who spent the last two seasons at defensive end after playing nose tackle in 1985 and 1986...His 6½ sacks equaled a personal best...Had two sacks at Kansas City Oct. 23...Collected 43 tackles ...Defensed four passes and caused three fumbles...Born Feb. 24, 1962, in Stockton, Cal....Was collegiate teammate of Vikings'

Keith Millard at Washington State . . . Third-round draft pick in 1984 . . . Father Roy played with Lions and 49ers from 1958-64 . . . Earned $275,000 last year.

JAMES JONES 28 6-2 229   **Running Back**

Will try to bounce back from two consecutive subpar seasons . . . Rushed for 314 yards on 96 carries . . . Did not score rushing touchdown for second straight season . . . Caught 29 passes for 259 yards and no TDs . . . Was placed on inactive list for Sept. 3 game against Atlanta with rib injury . . . Also missed Oct. 30 game against Giants with stomach muscle problem . . . Had best day against Rams when he rushed for 32 yards on 12 carries and caught two passes for 48 yards . . . First-round draft choice out of Florida in 1983, the 13th player selected overall . . . Born March 21, 1961, in Pompano Beach, Fla. . . . One of 10 children . . . Earned $270,000 last year.

COACH WAYNE FONTES: Was named the club's 17th head

coach on Dec. 22, 1988 . . . Served as interim head coach the final five weeks of the season after firing of Darryl Rogers . . . Was 2-3 during interim period . . . Signed three-year contract . . . Spent four seasons as Lions' defensive coordinator following nine-year stint with Tampa Bay . . . Was Bucs' defensive coordinator in 1982 when team led the NFC in defense . . . A former defensive back with New York Jets (1963-64) . . . Holds Jets' record for the longest interception return, 83 yards . . . Played football and baseball at Michigan State . . . Coached at Dayton (1968), Iowa (1969-71) and Southern Cal (1972-75) . . . Born Feb. 2, 1940, in Canton, Ohio . . . Brother Len is former secondary coach with Giants.

GREATEST COACH

Raymond "Buddy" Parker coached the Lions from 1951-56, chalking up a record of 47-23-2 and transforming the Lions from a mediocre sideshow to an NFL championship team. Prior to his arrival, the Lions had enjoyed just two winning campaigns in 11 seasons.

In Parker's first season as head coach the Lions went 7-4-1. The following year, 1952, they won their first NFL title since 1935, beating the powerful Browns, 17-7, in the first of three straight title games between the two teams.

The Lions beat the Browns again, 17-16, in 1953 for their second title. But the Browns bounced back to win the '54 title game, 56-10, snapping a string of eight consecutive losses to Detroit.

INDIVIDUAL LION RECORDS

Rushing

Most Yards Game:	198	Bob Hoernschemeyer, vs N.Y. Yanks, 1950
Season:	1,437	Billy Sims, 1981
Career:	5,106	Billy Sims, 1980-84

Passing

Most TD Passes Game:	5	Gary Danielson, vs Minnesota, 1978
Season	26	Bobby Layne, 1951
Career:	118	Bobby Layne, 1950-58

Receiving

Most TD Passes Game:	4	Cloyce Box, vs Baltimore, 1950
Season:	15	Cloyce Box, 1952
Career:	35	Terry Barr, 1957-65

Scoring

Most Points Game:	24	Cloyce Box, vs Baltimore, 1950
Season:	128	Doak Walker, 1950
Career:	847	Eddie Murray, 1980-88
Most TDs Game:	4	Cloyce Box, vs Baltimore, 1950
Season:	16	Billy Sims, 1980
Career:	47	Billy Sims, 1980-84

GREEN BAY PACKERS

TEAM DIRECTORY: Chairman: Dominic Olejiniczak; Pres.: Bob Harlan; Sec.: Peter Platten III; Exec. VP-Football Operations: Tom Braatz; Exec. Dir. Pub. Rel.: Lee Remmel; Head Coach: Lindy Infante. Home fields: Lambeau Field (56,926) and County Stadium, Milwaukee (55,976). Colors: Green and gold.

SCOUTING REPORT

OFFENSE: There's potential in this Packer team, as evidenced by their two-game sweep over the Vikings last season. But if the Pack (4-12) is ever going to really come back, the offense must first find a consistent quarterback who can put points on the board. Don Majkowski and Randy Wright split time last year and neither was especially efficient.

Packers tabbed Michigan State OT Tony Mandarich No.2.

During one six-week stretch, the Packers totaled 39 points and were shut out three times. The running game remains suspect after finishing 13th in the NFC last year, and Brent Fullwood (4.8 average on 101 attempts, with seven TDs) has yet to prove he can carry the full load.

Second-year wide receiver Sterling Sharpe (14.4 average on 55 receptions) is among the Packers' best offensive weapons. And he and the other receivers can only benefit from the drafting of offensive tackle Tony Mandarich, No. 2 in the draft and the one who will help get the quarterbacks more time to throw.

DEFENSE: Linebacker Tim Harris is a budding star at pass-rushing, but Green Bay is in need of some tough people up front to stop the run. The Packers allowed 132 yards-a-game rushing last year, the 13th-highest figure in the NFC. Bob Nelson and Blaise Winter will battle for the job at nose tackle, where three different players started last year.

Strong safety Mark Murphy is a solid player but the secondary as a whole is aging and slow. Second-year man Shawn Patterson should push for more playing time at defensive end, where Alphonso Carreker and Robert Brown combined for only half a sack in the first 15 games.

KICKING GAME: The Packers used three different kickers without much success. Things got so bad that a Milwaukee radio station auditioned kickers in the County Stadium parking lot. Overall, the Packers made 13 of 25 field goals. Punter Don Bracken will be pushed in camp by Maury Buford, who averaged 41.3 yards per punt with the Giants last year.

THE ROOKIES: Michigan State's Mandarich is considered among the best linemen ever to come out of the draft and will be an immediate starter. Defensive end Matt Brock of Oregon has good quickness out of the blocks and should help the Packers' pass rush. Anthony Dilweg of Duke will get a long look at quarterback.

OUTLOOK: The last-place schedule can't hurt the Packers, who have won just 10 non-strike games in the last three seasons. But unless a quarterback emerges who can run Infante's offense, the Packers will likely struggle again. Infante's honeymoon may already be over. The smallest crowd in 28 years (44,327) saw the final home game at County Stadium in Milwaukee.

PACKERS VETERAN ROSTER

HEAD COACH—Lindy Infante. Assistant Coaches—Greg Blache, Hank Bullough, Joe Clark, Charlie Davis, Buddy Gels, Dick Jauron, Virgil Knight, Dick Moseley, Willie Peete, Howard Tippett.

No.	Name	Pos.	Ht.	Wt.	NFL Exp.	College
59	Anderson, John	LB	6-3	228	12	Michigan
67	Ard, Billy	G	6-3	270	9	Wake Forest
69	Bartlett, Doug	NT	6-2	257	2	Northern Illinois
6	Beecher, Willie	K	5-11	175	2	Utah State
40	Bland, Carl	WR	5-11	182	6	Virginia Union
82	Bolton, Scott	WR	6-0	188	2	Auburn
61	Boyarsky, Jerry	NT	6-3	290	8	Pittsburgh
17	Bracken, Don	P	6-1	211	5	Michigan
32	Brown, Dave	CB-S	6-1	197	15	Michigan
93	Brown, Robert	DE	6-2	267	8	Virginia Tech
9	Buford, Maury	P	6-1	191	7	Texas Tech
51	Bush, Blair	C	6-3	272	12	Washington
63	Campen, James	C	6-3	270	3	Tulane
58	Cannon, Mark	C	6-3	258	6	Texas-Arlington
30	Carruth, Paul Ott	RB	6-1	220	4	Alabama
26	Cecil, Chuck	S	6-0	184	2	Arizona
60	Croston, David	T	6-5	280	2	Iowa
72	Cupp, Keith	C	6-6	300	2	Findlay College
56	Dent, Burnell	LB	6-1	236	4	Tulane
80	Didier, Clint	TE	6-5	240	8	Portland State
99	Dorsey, John	LB	6-2	243	6	Connecticut
85	Epps, Phillip	WR	5-10	165	8	Texas Christian
21	Fullwood, Brent	RB	5-11	209	3	Auburn
23	Greene, Tiger	CB-S	6-0	194	5	Western Carolina
35	Haddix, Michael	RB	6-2	227	7	Mississippi State
74	Haley, Darryl	T	6-5	265	7	Utah
65	Hallstrom, Ron	G	6-6	290	8	Iowa
41	Harris, Darryl	RB	5-10	178	2	Arizona State
97	Harris, Tim	LB	6-5	245	4	Memphis State
50	Holland, Johnny	LB	6-2	225	3	Texas A&M
25	Howard, Bobby	RB	6-0	220	3	Indiana
53	Howard, Todd	LB	6-2	244	3	Texas A&M
92	Inglis, Tim	LB	6-3	237	3	Toledo
24	Jakes, Van	CB-S	6-0	190	6	Kent State
38	Jefferson, Norman	CB-S	5-10	183	2	Louisiana State
26	Keel, Mark	TE	6-4	245	2	Arizona
94	Kellar, Scott	NT	6-3	265	3	Northern Illinois
81	Kemp, Perry	WR	5-11	170	3	California (Pa.)
10	Kiel, Blair	QB-P	6-0	214	5	Notre Dame
22	Lee, Mark	CB-S	5-11	189	10	Washington
7	Majkowski, Don	QB	6-2	207	3	Virginia
34	Mason, Larry	RB	5-11	205	3	Troy St.
98	Matthews, Aubrey	WR	5-7	165	4	Delta State
98	Moore, Brent	LB	6-5	242	2	Southern California
57	Moran, Rich	C-G	6-2	275	5	San Diego State
37	Murphy, Mark	S	6-2	201	8	West Liberty
79	Nelson, Bob	NT	6-4	275	3	Miami
91	Noble, Brian	LB	6-3	252	5	Arizona State
43	Novoselsky, Brent	TE	6-3	232	2	Pennsylvania
96	Patterson, Shawn	NT-DE	6-5	270	2	Arizona State
28	Pitts, Ron	CB-S	5-10	175	4	UCLA
75	Ruettgers, Ken	T	6-5	280	5	Southern California
83	Scott, Patrick	WR	5-10	170	3	Grambling
84	Sharpe, Sterling	WR-KR	5-11	202	2	South Carolina
19	Smith, Jeff	RB	5-9	205	5	Nebraska
89	Spagnola, John	TE	6-4	242	10	Yale
87	Stanley, Walter	WR-KR	5-9	179	5	Mesa College
54	Stephen, Scott	LB	6-2	232	3	Arizona State
29	Stills, Ken	CB-S	5-10	186	5	Wisconsin
49	Sutton, Mickey	CB	5-9	172	4	Montana
70	Uecker, Keith	G-T	6-5	284	7	Auburn
73	Veingrad, Alan	T-G	6-5	277	3	East Texas State
52	Weddington, Mike	LB	6-4	245	4	Oklahoma
86	West, Ed	TE	6-1	243	6	Auburn
48	Wilkins, Gary	TE	6-2	235	3	Georgia Tech
90	Williams, Toby	NT	6-4	75	7	Nebraska
68	Winter, Blaise	DE-DT	6-3	275	5	Syracuse
33	Woodside, Keith	RB	5-11	203	3	Texas A&M
16	Wright, Randy	QB	6-2	203	6	Wisconsin

TOP DRAFT CHOICES

Rd.	Name	Sel. No.	Pos.	Ht.	Wt.	College
1	Mandarich, Tony	2	T	6-5	315	Michigan State
3	Brock, Matt	58	DE	6-4	270	Oregon
3	Dilweg, Anthony	74	QB	6-3	215	Duke
4	Affholter, Eric	110	WR	5-11	180	USC
5	Query, Jeff	165	WR	5-11	165	Millikin

PACKER PROFILES

TIM HARRIS 24 6-6 245   Linebacker

Was shining star of Packers' defensive unit ... Totaled 13½ sacks to rank fifth in the NFL ... Has 28 sacks during three-year career ... Shared team lead with 111 total tackles ... Deflected two passes, forced two fumbles and tied NFL record with two safeties in a season ... Had once-in-a-lifetime game against Vikings Oct. 16. Sacked Wade Wilson for safety and also returned a blocked punt 10 yards for a touchdown ... Wilson also was victim of Harris' second safety in Dec. 11 rematch. Packers won both meetings with Vikings ... Talkative, exuberant, sometimes more vocal than coaches would like ... A Memphis State product taken in the fourth round of 1986 draft ... Can also play defensive end ... Named team's Rookie of the Year in 1986 ... Born Sept. 10, 1964, in Birmingham, Ala. ... Due for hefty raise after earning $130,000 last year in final year of a three-year contract.

MARK MURPHY 31 6-2 201   Strong Safety

Had outstanding season, leading the team in interceptions (5) and sharing lead in tackles (111) ... Tied linebacker Tim Harris in total stops, but had a team-high 86 unassisted tackles ... His five interceptions were a career-high; he had just six in previous seven seasons ... Also led team in fumble recoveries with four ... Sat out 1986 because of stress fracture in his left foot ... Signed with Packers as free agent in 1980 out of West Liberty State in Pennsylvania ... Born April 22, 1958, in Canton, Ohio ... Has degree in business administration ... Earned $260,000 last season.

BRENT FULLWOOD 25 5-11 209   Running Back

Showed signs of brilliance Packers expected from him when they made him their first-round draft choice in 1987. But, as in his rookie season, injuries curtailed his production ... Started just 10 games and put on inactive list for two others because of injuries ... Still wound up as club's leading rusher with 483 yards on 101 carries ... Also led team in scoring with 48 points on eight TDs (seven rushing) ... Was team's top kickoff-return man, averaging 20 yards on 21 returns ... Had the Packers' only 100-yard rushing day of the season and first of his career, gaining 118 yards on 14 carries against New England Oct. 9 ... Born Oct. 10, 1963, in Kissimmee, Fla. ... Was a unanimous All-American at Auburn after leading SEC in rushing with 1,391 yards ... Set a national record in high school by returning three kickoffs for touchdowns in one game ... Earned $250,000 last year.

DON MAJKOWSKI 25 6-2 207   Quarterback

Made nine starts, most of any Packer quarterback, but split most of his time with Randy Wright ... Led team in passing, completing 178 of 336 for 2,119 yards and 9 TDs, 11 INTs ... Best outing was at Detroit Dec. 4 when he hit 30 of 43 passes for 327 yards and one TD ... Had 255-yard day at Phoenix Dec. 18 ... Was sacked six times at Buffalo Oct. 30 and five times against Colts Nov. 13 ... Still needs grooming but could be Packers' QB of the future ... A 10th-round draft choice in 1987 out of Virginia. Was school's all-time leading passer and total offense leader ... Grandfather pitched in New York-Penn League, throwing two perfect games ... Name is pronounced Mah-kow-skee ... Earned $260,000 last year.

STERLING SHARPE 24 5-11 202   Wide Receiver

Looks like Packers found a keeper when they drafted Sharpe with their first-round pick in 1988 ... Led team in receptions and receiving yardage, catching 55 balls for 791 yards ... Had trouble finding end zone, scoring just one TD ... Was not helped by the shuttling of quarterbacks, but showed great promise ... Best outing came against Bears Sept. 25, when he caught seven passes for 137 yards. Caught season-long pass of 51 yards in that game ... Caught eight passes for 124 yards against Detroit Nov. 20 ... Was also a heralded punt-returner at University of South Carolina, but returned only nine punts for 48 yards for Packers ... An excellent route runner with flair for the dramatic ... Born April 6, 1965, in Glennville, Ga. ... Had 2,444 receiving yards as collegian ... Earned $1.25 million last year.

BILLY ARD 30 6-3 270   Guard

One of 20 players and three Giants the Packers acquired during unprotected free-agent signing period...A proven veteran who should instantly improve Packers' line...Except for knee injury in 1984 that sidelined him for one game, Ard would have had a string of 111 consecutive games at left guard for Giants... Was part of offensive line that helped Giants win Super Bowl XXI...Was bothered by calf injury in 1988... Very quotable player who gives good insight into pro game...A devotee of an offseason weight program...One of the Giants' best finds as an eighth-round draft pick in 1981 out of Wake Forest...Born March 12, 1959, in East Orange, N.J....Earned $300,000 last year.

JOHNNY HOLLAND 24 6-2 225   Linebacker

Entrenched himself as a starter at right inside linebacker...Finished third on the team with 108 total tackles...Defensed six passes and forced three fumbles, recovering one... Started 13 games, missing three others with injuries...Was runaway choice for Packer Rookie of the Year in 1987...Has superior body control and excellent quickness...A second-round draft choice out of Texas A&M...Nicknamed "Mr. Anywhere" because of his ability to be where the ball is... Began college career as a quarterback...Born March 11, 1965, in Hempstead, Tex....Earned $167,000 last year.

DAVID BROWN 36 6-1 197   Cornerback

Has played in 113 consecutive games, including 82 during part of an 11 year-career with Seahawks...A smart, experienced pro... Had three interceptions in 1988 for a career total of 56 to remain NFL active career leader in that category...Collected 37 tackles and credited with three passes defensed...When he left Seattle, he ranked second on the club's all-time lists of games played (159) and games started (159), trailing Steve Largent...Was a first-round pick of the Steelers in 1975 out of Michigan...Joined Seahawks in expansion draft in 1976...Named in 1983 to all-time team for second 50 years of Michigan football...Born Jan. 16, 1953, in Akron, Ohio... Earned $390,000 last year.

ED WEST 28 6-1 243   Tight End

Has been a consistent and reliable performer since making the Packers' roster as a rookie free agent in 1984 . . . Had the most productive year of his career in 1988, catching 30 passes for 276 yards and a team-high three touchdowns . . . Clearly prospered under the offensive system of Lindy Infante . . . Always known as a terrific blocker, but now is displaying consistent pass-catching skills . . . Had six receptions for 59 yards against Tampa Bay Oct. 2 and three receptions for 63 yards against New England Oct. 9 . . . In 1987, caught 19 passes for 261 yards and one TD . . . Has started 27 of 28 games over last two seasons . . . Was a three-year starter at Auburn . . . Born Aug. 2, 1961, in Colbert County, Ala. . . . Earned $195,800 last year.

SHAWN PATTERSON 24 6-5 270   Defensive End

Young defensive lineman who could find spot in starting lineup during his sophomore season . . . A good technique player with excellent speed (4.7 in the 40) for his size . . . Had 42 tackles last year . . . Credited with five sacks, one forced fumble and one recovered fumble . . . Spent most of the season at right defensive end . . . Packers were surprised he lasted until the second round . . . Was first-team All-Pac 10 at Arizona State . . . Played mostly defensive tackle in college, where he recorded 190 tackles during his four-year career . . . Described as "a complete football player" by head coach Lindy Infante . . . Earned $391,000 in 1988.

COACH LINDY INFANTE: It wasn't a stunning debut for the new Green Bay coach last year—4-12 as compared with the 5-9-1 Packers in '87 . . . But they did sweep the Vikings in the season series and Infante's influence was significant . . . Green Bay set a team record for most passes attempted (582) and completed (319) and there's some promising young talent aboard . . . Known as one of football's best offensive minds . . . Was Browns' offensive coordinator for two years before replacing Forrest Gregg . . . Served two years

Ubiquitous and conspicuous is young LB Tim Harris.

as head coach of Jacksonville Bulls of USFL ... Was Bengals' quarterback/receivers coach before that ... Began coaching career in 1965 at Miami Senior High School, then moved to the University of Florida in 1966-71 ... Was Memphis State offensive coordinator from 1972-73 and at Tulane in 1976 ... Joined Giants' offensive staff in 1977 ... An All-SEC defensive back at Florida ... Drafted by Browns in 12th-round in 1963, but opted to play for Hamilton of Canadian Football League ... Born May 27, 1940, in Miami.

GREATEST COACH

While there were many number great athletes who starred for the Packers during their glory years of the 60s, the most famous star of all was coach Vince Lombardi. Immediately upon his arrival in 1959, he began transforming the sleepy Wisconsin town of Green Bay into Titletown, U.S.A.

Using an authoritative, disciplined approach, Lombardi guided the Packers to five NFL championships in seven years (1961-62, 1965-67), a feat without precedent in pro football history. His 1966 and '67 teams won the first two Super Bowls.

The Packers won nine of 10 playoff games under Lombardi and compiled a 98-30-4 record. He was enshrined in the Pro Football Hall of Fame in 1971. Fittingly, the Super Bowl trophy is named in his honor.

INDIVIDUAL PACKER RECORDS

Rushing

Most Yards Game:	186	Jim Taylor, vs N.Y. Giants, 1961
Season:	1,474	Jim Taylor, 1962
Career:	8,207	Jim Taylor, 1958-66

Passing

Most TD Passes Game:	5	Cecil Isbell, vs Cleveland, 1942
	5	Don Horn, vs St. Louis, 1969
	5	Lynn Dickey, vs New Orleans, 1981
	5	Lynn Dickey, vs Houston, 1983
Season:	32	Lynn Dickey, 1983
Career:	152	Bart Starr, 1956-71

Receiving

Most TD Passes Game:	4	Don Hutson, vs Detroit, 1945
Season:	17	Don Hutson, 1943
Career:	99	Don Hutson, 1935-45

Scoring

Most Points Game:	33	Paul Hornung, vs Baltimore, 1961
Season:	176	Paul Hornung, 1960
Career:	823	Don Hutson, 1935-45
Most TDs Game:	5	Paul Hornung, vs Baltimore, 1961
Season:	19	Jim Taylor, 1962
Career:	105	Don Hutson, 1935-45

LOS ANGELES RAMS

TEAM DIRECTORY: Pres.: Georgia Frontiere; VP-Finance: John Shaw; VP-Media and Community Rel.: Marshall Klein; Dir. Operations: Dick Beam; Adm. Football Operations: Jack Faulkner; Dir. Player Personnel: John Math; Dir. Marketing: Pete Donovan; Dir. Pub. Rel.: John Oswald; Head Coach: John Robinson. Home field: Anaheim Stadium (69,007). Colors: Royal blue, gold and white.

SCOUTING REPORT

OFFENSE: Coach John Robinson shifted most of the offensive emphasis away from the running game and onto the passing arm of quarterback Jim Everett, who set career marks for passes attempted, completed, passing yardage and touchdown passes. Everett is the primary reason the Rams' passing game was the

Jim Everett joined elite list with five TD flips in a game.

league's third-best after finishing last or next to last the previous four years.

Entering his fourth season, Everett should hit his prime this year. It doesn't hurt him to have the NFC's top receiver in 1988, Henry Ellard, and speed-burner Aaron Cox.

The Rams' running attack is still capable of dominating a game. Greg Bell rushed for 1,212 yards and scored 108 points. Gaston Green, a first-round bust last year, should get the chance to redeem himself. And a new entry is 1989 first-rounder Cleveland Gary.

The offensive line, featuring guard Tom Newberry, center Doug Smith and tackle Jackie Slater, is one of football's best.

DEFENSE: The Rams wanted a more potent pass rush when they created the Eagle defense, which features up to six linebackers, and it worked even better than expected. With basically the same personnel that had 38 sacks in all of 1987, the Rams got 36 sacks in the first six games last year and totaled an NFL-high 56 for the season.

Linebacker Kevin Greene led with 16½ sacks, but Gary Jeter (11½) was left unprotected and signed with New England.

Linebackers Carl Ekern and Mike Wilcher also are coming off good years and the Rams made defensive end Bill Hawkins their first draft pick. Defensive backs Johnnie Johnson and LeRoy Irvin are experienced veterans.

KICKING GAME: Mike Lansford became the club's all-time leading scorer last year, but hit the uprights on consecutive field-goal attempts in a 35-24 loss to Denver. Dale Hatcher took over the punting duties from Rich Camarillo and averaged 39.6.

THE ROOKIES: Miami's Hawkins should develop into a solid player on a line hurt by free agency. A graduate student in finance, he should have little trouble picking up the Rams' complex defensive schemes. Gary, his college teammate, is an all-purpose back who should emerge as a third-down specialist.

OUTLOOK: The Rams were sitting pretty at 7-2 before a winless November. The slide to 10-6 wrecked the team's momentum and sent it stumbling into the playoffs. Still, the Rams should be a confident group heading into 1989. If Everett continues his development and the Eagle defense continues to baffle offenses, expect Robinson's bunch to contend again.

RAMS VETERAN ROSTER

HEAD COACH—John Robinson. Assistant Coaches—Larry Brooks, Dick Coury, Artie Gigantino, Marv Goux, Gil Haskell, Hudson Houck, Steve Shafer, Fritz Shurmur, Norval Turner, Fred Whittingham, Ernie Zampese.

No.	Name	Pos.	Ht.	Wt.	NFL Exp.	College
83	Anderson, Willie	WR	6-0	169	2	UCLA
42	Bell, Greg	RB	5-10	210	6	Notre Dame
92	Brown, Richard	LB	6-3	240	2	San Diego State
89	Brown, Ron	WR	5-11	181	6	Arizona State
84	Cox, Aaron	WR	5-10	174	2	Arizona State
72	Cox, Robert	T	6-5	270	3	UCLA
94	Darby, Byron	DE	6-4	260	7	Southern California
57	Davis, Wayne	LB	6-1	213	3	Alabama
39	Delphino, Robert	RB	6-0	205	2	Missouri
62	Diaz-Infante, David	C	6-2	280	2	San Jose State
80	Ellard, Henry	WR	5-11	180	7	Fresno State
11	Everett, Jim	QB	6-5	214	4	Purdue
51	Faryniarz, Brett	LB	6-3	225	2	San Diego State
25	Gray, Jerry	CB	6-0	185	5	Texas
30	Green, Gaston	RB	5-10	189	2	UCLA
91	Greene, Kevin	LB	6-3	238	5	Auburn
5	Hatcher, Dale	P	6-2	211	6	Clemson
9	Herrmann, Mark	QB	6-4	186	9	Purdue
28	Hicks, Clifford	CB	5-10	188	3	Oregon
81	Holohan, Pete	TE	6-4	232	9	Notre Dame
47	Irvin, LeRoy	CB	5-11	184	10	Kansas
59	Jerue, Mark	LB	6-3	234	7	Washington
86	Johnson, Damone	TE	6-4	230	4	Cal Poly-SLO
52	Kelm, Larry	LB	6-4	226	3	Texas A&M
1	Lansford, Mike	K	6-0	190	8	Washington
67	Love, Duval	G	6-3	280	5	UCLA
90	McDonald, Mike	LB	6-1	235	5	Southern California
24	McGee, Buford	RB	6-0	206	6	Mississippi
98	Miller, Shawn	DE	6-4	255	6	Utah State
66	Newberry, Tom	G	6-2	281	4	Wisconsin-LaCrosse
26	Newman, Anthony	CB	6-0	199	2	Oregon
22	Newsome, Vince	S	6-1	183	7	Washington
58	Owens, Mel	LB	6-2	224	9	Michigan
75	Pankey, Irv	T	6-5	267	9	Penn State
93	Reed, Doug	DE	6-3	250	6	San Diego State
78	Slater, Jackie	T	6-4	280	14	Jackson State
61	Slaton, Tony	C-G	6-3	265	6	Southern California
56	Smith, Doug	C	6-3	260	12	Bowling Green
23	Stewart, Michael	S	5-11	195	3	Fresno State
53	Strickland, Fred	LB	6-2	224	2	Purdue
37	Washington, James	S	6-1	191	2	UCLA
33	White, Charles	RB	5-10	193	9	Southern California
54	Wilcher, Mike	LB	6-3	240	7	North Carolina
99	Wright, Alvin	NT	6-2	256	4	Jacksonville State

TOP DRAFT CHOICES

Rd.	Name	Sel. No.	Pos.	Ht.	Wt.	College
1	Hawkins, Bill	21	DE	6-6	260	Miami
1	Gary, Cleveland	26	RB	6-0	230	Miami
2	Stams, Frank	44	LB	6-2	230	Notre Dame
2	Smith, Brian	48	LB	6-6	245	Auburn
2	Henley, Darryl	53	CB	5-8	165	UCLA

RAM PROFILES

GREG BELL 27 5-11 210   **Running Back**

Had most productive season of five-year career, rushing for 1,212 yards on 288 carries ...Third-leading rusher in NFC...Also rushed for 1,000 yards (1,100 with Buffalo) in 1984...Led NFL with 18 touchdowns (16 rushing) and 108 points...TD total was second on Rams' all-time list, behind Eric Dickerson's 20 in 1983...Best day was 155 yards on 21 carries against Atlanta Oct. 9...Had 1,336 total yards from scrimmage to rank seventh in NFC...Came to Rams from Buffalo as part of Dickerson deal with Indianapolis Oct. 31, 1987...A Notre Dame grad who set a school record with a long-jump of 24-6...Born Aug. 1, 1962, in Columbus, Ohio ...1988 salary: $300,000.

HENRY ELLARD 28 5-11 180   **Wide Receiver**

Established himself as one of the top receivers in the league...Led the NFL in reception yardage with 1,414 on 86 catches (second in NFL)...Selected to Pro Bowl after going in 1984 as a punt returner...His 86 catches broke club record of 84 set by Tom Fears in 1950...Caught at least six passes in nine different games and had career-high 10 TD catches...Has led the team in pass-receiving for five straight seasons...Surpassed 100 yards receiving in four games...Best day was 11 catches for 167 yards at Denver Nov. 27...Returned 17 punts for 199 yards...A second-round draft choice out of Fresno State in 1983...Born July 21, 1961, in Fresno, Cal....1988 salary: $375,000.

JIM EVERETT 26 6-5 214   **Quarterback**

Began to show the potential Rams anticipated when they gave up two players, two first-round draft choices and a fifth-rounder to get him from Houston in 1986...Set Rams' single-season passing mark of 3,964 yards... Broke club records for most completions (308) and attempts (517) in a season...His 31 TD passes led NFL and set club record...First Ram quarterback to start all 16 games since 1983...Quarterback rating of 89.2 was second in the NFC and fourth-best in the NFL... Passed for 377 yards in losing effort at Philadelphia Nov. 6... Had five 300-yard passing days during the year... Led nation in total offense during senior year at Purdue... Born Jan. 3, 1963, in Emporia, Kan.... Attended El Dorado High School in Albuquerque, N.M.... 1988 salary: $400,000.

AARON COX 24 5-10 174 — Wide Receiver

First-round draft choice in 1988 who paid immediate dividends... An excellent route runner with speed (4.39 in the 40) and leaping ability... Caught 28 passes for 590 yards and five TDs... Averaged a healthy 21.1 yards per reception... Caught at least one pass in every game except two... Longest reception was 69-yarder for a touchdown against Giants Sept. 25... First career touchdown was 54-yarder against Raiders Sept. 18... Caught 126 passes for 2,480 yards during four-year career at Arizona State... Born March 13, 1965, in Los Angeles... 1988 salary: $772,500.

JACKIE SLATER 35 6-4 280 — Tackle

Senior member of Rams who serves as offensive team captain... Voted to fourth straight Pro Bowl and fifth in last six seasons... Sixth on club's all-time list in games played with 178... Tied with LB Carl Ekern for most seasons played (13)... Selected NFLPA-NFC Offensive Lineman of the Year for the second straight season by NFC defensive linemen and linebackers... Big, powerful and intense competitor... A third-round draft choice in 1976... Played at Jackson State, where he was first recipient of Walter Payton Physical Fitness Award... Born May 27, 1954, in Jackson, Miss.... 1988 salary: $500,000.

MIKE LANSFORD 31 6-0 190 — Kicker

One of most consistent kickers in the NFL... Set a career high with 117 points... Reached 100-point plateau for third time in his career ... Has 582 points during seven-year career, a Rams record... Converted on 45 of 48 PATs and 24 of 32 FGs... Surpassed Bob Waterfield (1945-52) as the Rams' all-time leading scorer... Converted four of five field goals in

12-10 win over Saints Oct. 30...Is 120-for-163 in career field goals...Signed with team as free agent in 1982...Born July 29, 1958, in Monterey Park, Cal....Kicked at Pasadena City College for two years, then transferred to Washington...Made 73 consecutive extra points for Huskies...1988 salary: $195,000.

TOM NEWBERRY 26 6-2 281   Guard

Regarded as a dominant force in the offensive line...Started for NFC in Pro Bowl...Rapid development allowed the Rams to include Kent Hill in deal for Jim Everett in 1986...Has started every game but one during three-year career...In 1988, he ended 34-day holdout by returning to club on Aug. 24...A second-round draft pick in 1986...Excellent athlete who has run the 40 in 4.68...Has 34-inch vertical leap and can bench-press 460 lbs. and squat 740...Born Oct. 20, 1962, in Onalaska, Wis....Won four bouts in college "Tough Man" contest in 1985...Earned first-team NAIA All-America honors at Wisconsin-LaCrosse...1988 salary: $350,000.

DOUG SMITH 32 6-3 260   Center

One of the league's outstanding centers...Selected to play in fifth straight Pro Bowl...Earned spot on team in 1978 as free agent and will go down as one of club's all-time linemen...Calls offensive-line signals...Has started 120 of 140 games as a Ram...Missed most of 1979 and 1980 seasons with knee injury...Born Nov. 25, 1956, in Columbus, Ohio...Has played every position on offensive line except left tackle...Was a four-year letterman at Bowling Green, where he earned degree in education...Frequent speaker for the Fellowship of Christian Athletes...1988 salary: $300,000.

KEVIN GREENE 27 6-3 238   Linebacker

Former backup player who entrenched himself in starting lineup early in season and enjoyed super year...Led team with 16½ sacks to rank second in NFL behind Eagles' Reggie White (18)...Benefited from Rams' use of five linebackers in "Eagle" defense...Had three sacks at Atlanta Oct. 9 and three sacks in wild-card loss at Minnesota...Finished year with 51 tackles . . . Was third on team with eight passes defensed . . . A fifth-round draft pick in 1985 . . . Has played linebacker and defensive end . . . Was a walk-on at Auburn, where he earned starting role and led team with 11 sacks as a senior . . . Has a degree in criminal justice . . . Spent six years of youth in Germany, where father was stationed . . . 1988 salary: $225,000.

JERRY GRAY 26 6-0 185   Cornerback

Earned third straight trip to Pro Bowl in third full season as a starter . . . A gifted athlete with great instincts and quickness . . . Plays the run well . . . Finished second on team in total tackles with 63 . . . Tied for second in interceptions with three . . . Returned interception 47 yards for first career touchdown against Green Bay Sept. 4 . . . Credited with 13 passes defensed to tie LeRoy Irvin for team lead . . . Born Dec. 16, 1962, in Lubbock, Tex. . . . Was two-time consensus All-American at University of Texas, where he played safety . . . A first-round selection (21st overall) in 1985 draft . . . 1988 salary: $200,000.

COACH JOHN ROBINSON:

Guided Rams back to playoffs after missing postseason party in 1987 . . . It was the fifth time in six seasons under Robinson that Rams have made playoffs . . . The 10-6 record marked fifth time in six seasons Rams have compiled 10 or more wins . . . Holds club record for coaching victories with 58 . . . Also has served most seasons as Rams' coach at six . . . Joined Rams in 1983 after posting 67-14-2 record at USC . . . Started as Oregon assistant in 1960 . . . Was an assistant at USC for three years before joining John Madden at Oakland in 1974 . . . Born July 25, 1935, at Dale City, Cal. . . . Has pro record of 58-43 . . . Earned degree at Oregon, where he played end for the Ducks.

GREATEST COACH

Chuck Knox began formulating his reputation as one of the league's most successful head coaches in 1973. That year he took over a declining Rams' franchise and immediately turned it into a winner.

During Knox's five-year tenure with the club, the Rams won five consecutive division championships and reached the NFC championship game in 1974, '75 and '76. He was named the NFL Coach of the Year in 1973, an award he would win three more times with other clubs.

Knox remains the winningest coach in Ram history with a 57-20-1 record for a winning percentage of .760. After leaving the Rams, he spent five years at Buffalo before moving to Seattle, where he is currently head coach.

INDIVIDUAL RAM RECORDS

Rushing

Most Yards Game:	248	Eric Dickerson, vs Dallas, 1985
Season:	2,105	Eric Dickerson, 1984
Career:	7,245	Eric Dickerson, 1983-87

Passing

Most TD Passes Game:	5	Bob Waterfield, vs N.Y. Bulldogs, 1949
	5	Norm Van Brocklin, vs Detroit, 1950
	5	Norm Van Brocklin, vs N.Y. Yanks, 1951
	5	Roman Gabriel, vs Cleveland, 1965
	5	Vince Ferragamo, vs New Orleans, 1980
	5	Vince Ferragamo, vs San Francisco, 1983
	5	Jim Everett, vs N.Y. Giants, 1988
Season:	31	Jim Everett, 1988
Career:	154	Roman Gabriel, 1962-72

Receiving

Most TD Passes Game:	4	Bob Shaw, vs Washington, 1949
	4	Elroy Hirsch, vs N.Y. Yanks, 1951
	4	Harold Jackson, vs Dallas, 1973
Season:	17	Elroy Hirsch, 1951
Career:	53	Elroy Hirsch, 1949-57

Scoring

Most Points Game:	24	Elroy Hirsch, vs N.Y. Yanks, 1951
	24	Bob Shaw, vs Washington, 1949
	24	Harold Jackson, vs Dallas, 1973
Season:	130	David Ray, 1973
Career:	582	Mike Lansford, 1982-88
Most TDs Game:	4	Elroy Hirsch, vs N.Y. Yanks, 1951
	4	Bob Shaw, vs Washington, 1949
	4	Harold Jackson, vs Dallas, 1973
Season:	20	Eric Dickerson, 1983
Career:	58	Eric Dickerson, 1983-87

MINNESOTA VIKINGS

TEAM DIRECTORY: Chairman: John Skoglurd; Pres.: Wheelock Whitney; Exec. VP/GM: Mike Lynn; Dir. Administration: Harley Peterson; Dir. Football Operations: Jerry Reichow; Dir. Pub. Rel.: Merrill Swanson; Head Coach: Jerry Burns. Home field: Hubert H. Humphrey Metrodome (63,000). Colors: Purple, white and gold.

SCOUTING REPORT

OFFENSE: There shouldn't be any quarterback controversies in Minneapolis this year. Wade Wilson is coming off an outstanding season in which he was the NFC's top-rated quarterback (91.5). His main target, wide receiver Anthony Carter, is a game-breaker and tight end Steve Jordan is fearless over the middle.

The running game, the only offensive weak spot, will have to produce more than its 1988 average of 113 yards per game. Darrin Nelson gained just 380 yards and his rushing average (3.4) was a five-year low. D.J. Dozier, the No. 1 pick in 1987, gained just 167 yards.

All-Pro tackle Gary Zimmerman and 1988 top pick, guard Randall McDaniel, key a formidable offensive line that allowed just 37 sacks in an 11-5 season.

DEFENSE: This was the NFL's best unit in 1988, allowing just 255.7 yards per game. Overall, the Vikings were fifth against the rush and second against the pass.

There are more stars here than at a Lakers' game. Tackle Keith Millard, end Chris Doleman, safety Joey Browner, linebacker Scott Studwell and cornerback Carl Lee all made the Pro Bowl. Others such as linebacker Jesse Solomon and nose tackle Henry Thomas had impressive credentials.

The unit set club record for interceptions (36) and interception returns for TDs (five). It also led the league in takeaways with 53.

KICKING GAME: Placekicker Chuck Nelson was 0-for-2 in field-goal attempts during five weeks in October, but he converted 11 straight during one stretch and missed just five of 25 during the year. Punter Bucky Scribner averaged 40.3. Punt-returner Leo Lewis and kickoff-return man Darryl Harris ranked fifth in the NFC in their respective categories.

Chris Doleman is a powerhouse in NFL's No. 1 defense.

THE ROOKIES: Wake Forest linebacker David Braxton excels on pass coverage but needs to polish his open-field tackling. Darryl Ingram of California is a pass-catching tight end and good blocker. John Hunter of BYU and Jeff Mickel of Eastern Washington will add depth to the offensive line.

OUTLOOK: As good as the Vikings were in 1988, they should get better. They're still smarting at not winning the division title due to a pair of costly losses to Green Bay. The Vikings are among the league's youngest teams, with more than 30 players having five years or less experience. With their defensive talent and Wilson and Carter on offense, the Vikings should make a serious challenge for a berth in Super Bowl XXIV.

VIKINGS VETERAN ROSTER

HEAD COACH—Jerry Burns. Assistant Coaches—Tom Batta, Jerry Brown, John Brunner, Pete Carroll, Monte Kiffin, John Michels, Floyd Peters, Dick Rehbein, Bob Schnelker, Paul Wiggin.

No.	Name	Pos.	Ht.	Wt.	NFL Exp.	College
89	Allen, Anthony	WR	5-11	182	4	Washington
46	Anderson, Alfred	RB	6-1	219	6	Baylor
50	Berry, Ray	LB	6-2	230	3	Baylor
47	Browner, Joey	CB-S	6-2	212	7	Southern California
81	Carter, Anthony	WR	5-11	175	5	Michigan
37	Curtis, Travis	S	5-10	180	2	West Virginia
56	Doleman, Chris	DE	6-5	250	5	Pittsburgh
42	Dozier, D.J.	RB	6-0	198	3	Penn State
27	Edwards, Brad	S	6-1	198	2	South Carolina
31	Fenney, Rick	RB	6-1	240	3	Washington
62	Foote, Chris	C	6-4	265	8	Southern California
29	Fullington, Darrell	S	6-1	183	2	Miami
16	Gannon, Rich	QB	6-3	197	3	Delaware
74	Greer, Curtis	DE	6-4	258	9	Michigan
80	Gustafson, Jim	WR	6-1	181	4	St. Thomas
82	Hilton, Carl	TE	6-3	232	4	Houston
30	Holt, Issiac	CB	6-1	197	5	Alcorn State
51	Howard, David	LB	6-2	228	5	Long Beach State
72	Huffman, David	G	6-6	283	10	Notre Dame
76	Irwin, Tim	T	6-6	289	9	Tennessee
84	Jones, Hassan	WR	6-0	195	4	Florida State
83	Jordan, Steve	TE	6-4	230	9	Brown
69	Kalis, Todd	G	6-5	269	2	Arizona State
9	Kramer, Tommy	QB	6-2	207	13	Rice
39	Lee, Carl	CB	5-11	183	7	Marshall
87	Lewis, Leo	WR	5-8	171	9	Missouri
63	Lowdermilk, Kirk	C	6-3	263	5	Ohio State
79	Martin, Doug	DE	6-3	270	10	Washington
26	McMillian, Audrey	CB	6-0	190	4	Houston
64	McDaniel, Randall	G	6-3	268	2	Arizona State
57	Merriweather, Mike	LB	6-2	221	7	Pacific
75	Millard, Keith	DT	6-5	262	5	Washington State
1	Nelson, Chuck	K	5-11	172	6	Washington
20	Nelson, Darrin	RB	5-9	183	8	Stanford
96	Newton, Tim	DT	6-0	283	5	Florida
99	Noga, Al	DT	6-1	245	2	Hawaii
52	Rasmussen, Randy	C-G	6-1	254	6	Minnesota
36	Rice, Allen	RB	5-10	203	6	Baylor
60	Rodenhaser, Mark	C	6-5	252	2	Illinois State
48	Rutland, Reggie	S	6-1	195	3	Georgia Tech
13	Scribner, Bucky	P	6-0	205	5	Kansas
25	Smith, Daryl	CB	5-9	185	2	North Alabama
54	Solomon, Jesse	LB	6-0	232	4	Florida State
94	Strauthers, Thomas	DE	6-4	265	5	Jackson State
55	Studwell, Scott	LB	6-2	230	13	Illinois
97	Thomas, Henry	NT	6-2	268	3	Louisiana State
11	Wilson, Wade	QB	6-3	203	9	East Texas State
65	Zimmerman, Gary	T	6-6	284	4	Oregon

TOP DRAFT CHOICES

Rd.	Name	Sel. No.	Pos.	Ht.	Wt.	College
2	Braxton, David	52	LB	6-1	230	Wake Forest
3	Hunter, John	80	OT	6-7	290	BYU
4	Ingram, Darryl	108	TE	6-3	230	California
6	Mickel, Jeff	163	T	6-6	282	Eastern Washington
7	Roland, Benji	191	DT	6-3	270	Auburn

VIKING PROFILES

WADE WILSON 30 6-3 203   Quarterback

Established himself as the Vikings' No. 1 quarterback with outstanding season...QB rating of 91.5 led the NFC and was third in NFL...Voted starter in Pro Bowl...Completed NFC-high 61.4 percent of passes for 2,746 yards and 15 TDs...Also rushed for 136 yards and two TDs...Great scrambler and very durable...Was 7-3 as starter in regular season and 1-1 in playoffs...Ranks No. 3 on Vikings' all-time list of touchdown passes thrown with 45...An eighth-round draft pick in 1981...Was NAIA All-American at East Texas State...Born Feb. 1, 1959, in Greenville, Tex....Enjoys waterskiing and golf...Earned $250,000 last year.

JOEY BROWNER 29 6-2 212   Safety

Regarded as one of the top players at his position...Always around the football...Had five interceptions during regular season and three in two playoff games...Had never intercepted a pass in playoffs until last season...Was third on team in tackles with 117...Has 743 tackles in six-year career...Earned fourth consecutive Pro Bowl appearance...Born May 15, 1960, in Warren, Ohio...A USC product, he was first defensive back ever taken by Vikings in the first round (1983)...A blackbelt in Kenpo...Wife Valeria is international model...Earned $300,000 last year.

ANTHONY CARTER 28 5-11 175   Wide Receiver

Set club record with 1,225 receiving yards...Yardage total ranked third in NFC...Had 72 receptions and six TDs...Caught seven passes for 147 yards (21.0 average) in playoffs...Set three NFL single-game playoff records after '87 season: most reception yards (227 vs. 49ers); most punt return yards (143 vs. Saints), and longest punt return (84 yards vs. Saints)...Joined NFL in 1985 after playing three years in the USFL for Michigan Panthers and Oakland Invaders...Had All-American career at Michigan, where he started four years and set records for receptions (161), reception yards (3,076) and touchdowns (37)... Vikings acquired his rights from Miami, which drafted him in the 12th round in 1983... Born Sept. 17, 1960, in Riviera Beach, Fla.... Earned $225,000 last year.

CHRIS DOLEMAN 27 6-5 250   **Defensive End**

Voted Miller Lite Lineman of the Year after sharing team-lead in sacks with eight... Donated $25,000 award to homeless of Minneapolis... Has emerged as a dominant force on talented Viking defensive line... Quick, agile and strong... Earned second straight Pro Bowl selection... Seventh on team in tackles with 58... Forced two fumbles... First-round draft choice (fourth overall) out of Pittsburgh in 1985... Has been starter all three seasons... Born Oct. 16, 1961, in Indianapolis, Ind.... Played on Vikings' charity basketball team during the offseason... Had 19 sacks in last two seasons... Earned $275,000 last year.

STEVE JORDAN 28 6-4 230   **Tight End**

Voted to third consecutive Pro Bowl after finishing second on club with 57 receptions for 756 yards and a career-high five TDs... Averaged 13.3 yards per reception... Caught four passes for 63 yards during playoffs... Ranks fourth on Vikings' all-time list in reception yards with 3,568... Leader among Viking tight ends in career receptions with 274... Has enjoyed four straight exceptional seasons... Seventh-round choice out of Brown in 1982... Has a degree in civil engineering... Born Jan. 10, 1961, in Phoenix... Hobbies include reading, art and theater.

JESSE SOLOMON 25 6-0 232   **Linebacker**

Underrated player who is just beginning to emerge from the shadows of more famous teammates... Led team in tackles with 121 during the regular season... Had 2½ sacks and four interceptions... Forced one fumble and recovered two... Returned one interception 78 yards for a touchdown... Missed both playoff games with a knee injury that required offseason surgery... Should be at full strength this year... A

great find after being taken in the 12th round of the 1986 draft
... Played at Florida State after transferring from North Madison
(Fla.) Junior College ... Born Nov. 14, 1963, in Madison, Fla.
... Earned $200,000 last year.

KEITH MILLARD 27 6-5 262   Defensive Tackle

Earned first trip to Pro Bowl ... Rapidly
emerging as one of the top interior defensive
linemen in the league ... Tough, hard-nosed,
determined ... Won't quit ... Was fourth on
team in tackles with 86 and shared sack lead
with Chris Doleman at eight ... Also forced
two fumbles and recovered two ... Had 13
tackles in two playoff games ... Was first-
round pick of Vikings in 1984 (13th overall), but signed with
Jacksonville Bulls of USFL ... Joined Vikings in 1985 ...
Washington State product ... Earned $247,000 last year ... Born
March 18, 1962, in Pleasonton, Cal.

CARL LEE 28 5-11 183   Defensive Back

Gained confidence in second year at cornerback after playing free safety for most of his
career ... Led squad in interceptions with
eight, returned two for touchdowns, including
one of 58 yards ... Voted to first Pro Bowl ...
Supports run well ... Was sixth on team in
tackles with 61 ... Recovered one fumble ...
A proud example for Vikings' scouting
department ... Was 35th defensive back and 186th player chosen
when taken in the seventh round of 1983 draft ... Attended Marshall University, where he was a four-year starter ... Born April
6, 1961, in South Charleston, W.Va. ... Earned $175,000 last
year.

SCOTT STUDWELL 35 6-2 230   Linebacker

Ironman of Vikings' defensive unit ... One of
the most respected players in the NFL ...
Entering 13th season ... Has been a starter
since 1980 ... Voted to Pro Bowl last year
after leading team in tackles with 123 ...
Forced two fumbles and recovered two ...
Collected one sack ... Led team with 15
tackles during playoffs ... Has 1,702 career
tackles ... Led team in tackles for six consecutive years through
1985 ... Played at Illinois, where he broke Dick Butkus' season

record with 177 tackles as a senior . . . A ninth-round draft pick in 1977 . . . A member of Vikings' 25th anniversary team selected by fans in 1985 . . . Earned $300,000 last year . . . Born Aug. 27, 1954, in Evansville, Ind.

GARY ZIMMERMAN 27 6-6 284   Tackle

Former USFL player who has reached star status in the NFL . . . Big, strong, with impeccable pass-blocking skills . . . Earned second straight trip to Pro Bowl after anchoring an offensive line that helped Vikings produce a team-record 406 points . . . Teams with rookie guard Randall McDaniel to give Vikings a solid left side . . . Signed with the Vikings in May, 1986, after club acquired his rights in two-part trade with Giants . . . Played two seasons with Los Angeles Express of USFL . . . Was Giants' first-round pick (third overall), in 1984 supplemental draft . . . Played at Oregon, where he earned finance degree . . . Born Dec. 13, 1961, in Fullerton, Cal. . . . A certified pilot. . . . Earned $650,000 last year.

COACH JERRY BURNS: "Losing the 49ers game means the

failure to fulfill a dream," Burns said following his team's elimination in the divisional playoff. "Now we've got to start all over again." . . . Burns has been anything but a failure in his three years as head coach, as his 28-19 record will attest . . . Well-liked by his players and staff . . . Helped build the No. 1-ranked defense in the NFL . . . Served as Vikings' assistant head coach and offensive coordinator from 1968-85 . . . Played quarterback at Michigan . . . Served as backfield coach at Hawaii in 1951 and Whittier in '52 . . . Coached a year of high-school ball in Detroit before a 12-year stretch (1954-65) at Iowa (last five as head coach) as Hawkeyes won two Big 10 titles . . . Left for Green Bay under Vince Lombardi, then moved to Vikings . . . Credited with originating one-back offense . . . Born Jan. 24, 1927, in Detroit.

GREATEST COACH

Had it not been for his illustrious coaching career, Bud Grant might have been best known as the answer to this trivia question:

What athlete in 1950 played on the NBA champion Minneapolis Lakers and was a first-round draft choice of the Philadelphia Eagles?

Instead, Grant is hailed for his 18 seasons as the Vikings' head coach. During that time, he guided the team to a regular-season record of 158-96-5 to rank seventh among the league's all-time winningest coaches.

Under Grant, the Vikings made the playoffs 12 times, winning the NFC championship four times. The Vikings, however, were 0-4 in Super Bowl appearances.

INDIVIDUAL VIKING RECORDS

Rushing

Most Yards Game:	200	Chuck Foreman, vs Philadelphia, 1976
Season:	1,155	Chuck Foreman, 1976
Career:	5,879	Chuck Foreman, 1973-79

Passing

Most TD Passes Game:	7	Joe Kapp, vs Baltimore, 1969
Season:	26	Tommy Kramer, 1981
Career	239	Francis Tarkenton, 1961-66, 1972-78

Receiving

Most TD Passes Game:	4	Ahmad Rashad, vs San Francisco, 1979
Season:	11	Jerry Reichow, 1961
Career:	50	Sammy White, 1976-85

Scoring

Most Points Game:	24	Chuck Foreman, vs Buffalo, 1975
	24	Ahmad Rashad, vs San Francisco, 1979
Season:	132	Chuck Foreman, 1975
Career:	1,365	Fred Cox, 1963-77
Most TDs Game:	4	Chuck Foreman, vs Buffalo, 1975
	4	Ahmad Rashad, vs San Francisco, 1979
Season:	22	Chuck Foreman, 1975
Career:	76	Bill Brown, 1962-74

NEW ORLEANS SAINTS

TEAM DIRECTORY: Owner: Tom Benson; Pres./GM: Jim Finks; VP-Administration: Jim Miller; Bus. Mgr./Controller: Bruce Broussard; Dir. Media Rel.: Rusty Kasmiersky; Head Coach: Jim Mora. Home field: Superdome (69,551). Colors: Old gold, black and white.

SCOUTING REPORT

OFFENSE: Wide receiver Eric Martin was the Saints' most dependable offensive weapon in 1988, finishing as the NFC's second-leading pass catcher with 85 receptions for 1,083 yards. But their running game, considered the team's strength, was sluggish, ranking 11th in the NFL.

Vet WR Eric Martin earned first trip to the Pro Bowl.

Running back Craig "Ironhead" Heyward and receiver Brett Perriman, the club's top two draft picks in 1988, were expected to make significant contributions but didn't.

Quarterback Bobby Hebert is not spectacular but efficient at operating the short-passing game. His longest completion went for just 40 yards and the Saints may look for the long pass more often this year.

DEFENSE: In 1987, turnovers were a big factor in the Saints' success as they finished with a plus-20 giveaway-takeaway ratio, including a league-high 30 interceptions. But last year, they finished even in giveaways and takeaways at 32 and the interceptions dropped to 17. Their sacks also fell from 47 to 31.

Inconsistency was the main problem. One week the Saints allowed the Giants 14 yards rushing; the following week they gave up more than 200 to the Vikings. The linebacking corps of Rickey Jackson, Sam Mills, Vaughan Johnson and Pat Swilling could be the best in football. But improvements need to be made in the pass rush and pass coverage.

KICKING GAME: The Saints lost talented return specialist Mel Gray to free agency. But the kicking duties remain in the capable legs of Morten Andersen and punter Brian Hansen. Andersen, the most accurate kicker in NFL history, will try to rebound from the worst season of his career last year, when he set a personal record for misses (10) in a season. Hansen was the NFC's sixth-leading punter with a 40.5 average.

THE ROOKIES: Top pick Wayne Martin of Arkansas is a highly-regarded defensive end who should help the Saints' crumbling defensive line. Help for the secondary should come from either No. 2 pick Robert Massey of N.C. Central, No. 3 Kim Phillips of North Texas State or No. 4 Michael Mayers of LSU.

OUTLOOK: The Saints go marching into 1989 with something they've never felt before: disappointment despite a winning season. Actually, they're miffed at being eliminated by the NFL playoff formula, despite a 10-6 record that earned a share of the NFC West title.

Coach Jim Mora perhaps summed it up best when he said, "When you go 10-6 and you're one win out of the playoffs or one win out of the division championship, you're not all that bad a football team." The Saints should make a good run for it in 1989.

SAINTS VETERAN ROSTER

HEAD COACH—Jim Mora. Assistant Coaches—Paul Boudreau, Dom Capers, Vic Fangio, Joe Marciano, Russell Paternostro, John Pease, Steve Sidwell, Jim Skipper, Carl Smith, Steve Walters.

No.	Name	Pos.	Ht.	Wt.	NFL Exp.	College
7	Andersen, Morton	K	6-2	200	8	Michigan State
28	Atkins, Gene	CB-S	6-1	200	3	Florida A&M
76	Board, Dwaine	DE	6-5	248	10	North Carolina A&T
85	Brenner, Hoby	TE	6-4	240	9	Southern California
67	Brock, Stan	T	6-6	292	10	Colorado
75	Clark, Bruce	DE	6-3	275	8	Penn State
41	Cook, Toi	S	5-11	188	3	Stanford
72	Dombrowski, Jim	T	6-5	295	4	Virginia
95	Dumbauld, Jonathan	DE	6-4	259	3	Kentucky
63	Edelman, Brad	G	6-6	270	8	Missouri
52	Forde, Brian	LB	6-2	225	2	Washington State
11	Fourcade, John	QB	6-1	208	3	Mississippi
97	Geathers, James	DE	6-7	290	5	Wichita State
27	Gibson, Antonio	S	6-3	204	4	Cincinnati
77	Gilbert, Daren	T	6-6	295	5	Cal State-Fullerton
74	Gregory, Ted	NT	6-1	260	2	Syracuse
10	Hansen, Brian	P	6-3	209	6	Sioux Falls
92	Haynes, James	LB	6-2	233	6	Miss. Valley
3	Hebert, Bobby	QB	6-4	215	5	NW Louisiana
34	Heyward, Craig	RB	6-0	251	2	Pittsburgh
61	Hilgenberg, Joel	C-G	6-2	252	6	Iowa
87	Hill, Lonzell	WR	5-11	189	3	Washington
21	Hilliard, Dalton	RB	5-8	204	4	Louisiana State
57	Jackson, Rickey	LB	6-2	239	9	Pittsburgh
53	Johnson, Vaughn	LB	6-3	245	4	North Carolina State
90	Johnson, Walter	LB	6-0	240	3	Louisiana Tech
93	Johnson, Will	LB	6-4	228	2	Northeast Louisiana
23	Jordan, Buford	RB	6-0	223	4	McNeese State
55	Kohlbrand, Joe	LB	6-4	242	5	Miami
60	Korte, Steve	C	6-2	260	7	Arkansas
24	Mack, Milton	CB	5-11	182	3	Alcorn State
84	Martin, Eric	WR	6-1	195	5	Louisiana State
39	Maxie, Brett	S	6-2	194	5	Texas Southern
36	Mayes, Rueben	RB	5-11	201	4	Washington State
51	Mills, Sam	LB	5-9	225	4	Montclair State
80	Perriman, Brett	WR	5-9	175	2	Miami
83	Scales, Greg	TE	6-4	253	2	Wake Forest
56	Swilling, Pat	LB	6-3	242	4	Georgia Tech
69	Swoopes, Patrick	NT	6-4	280	2	Mississippi State
82	Tice, John	TE	6-5	249	7	Maryland
54	Toles, Alvin	LB	6-1	227	5	Tennessee
65	Trapilo, Steve	G	6-5	281	3	Boston College
78	Walker, Jeff	T	6-4	289	3	Memphis State
73	Warren, Frank	DE	6-4	290	9	Auburn
44	Waymer, Dave	CB	6-1	188	10	Notre Dame
94	Wilks, Jim	DE	6-5	266	9	San Diego State
18	Wilson, Dave	QB	6-3	206	8	Illinois

TOP DRAFT CHOICES

Rd.	Name	Sel. No.	Pos.	Ht.	Wt.	College
1	Martin, Wayne	19	DE	6-5	275	Arkansas
2	Massey, Robert	46	DB	5-10	180	N.C. Central
3	Phillips, Kim	79	DB	5-9	185	North Texas State
4	Mayes, Michael	106	S	5-10	180	LSU
5	Haverdink, Kevin	133	OT	6-6	275	Western Michigan

SAINT PROFILES

ERIC MARTIN 27 6-1 195   Wide Receiver

Established himself as one of the top receivers in the NFL... Earned first trip to Pro Bowl ... Compiled the most spectacular year of his career with 85 catches for 1,083 yards, both club records... Was second among NFC receivers in receptions behind Henry Ellard of Rams (86)... Tied for team lead with seven TD receptions... Caught season-high 10 passes for 146 yards against Washington Nov. 6... Had season-long, 40-yard TD reception against Denver Nov. 20... Doesn't have great speed but runs tight patterns... Ended career at LSU as SEC's all-time career leader in receiving yardage... Holds school record with 100-yard kick return... Seventh-round draft pick in 1985... Born Nov. 8, 1961, in Van Vleck, Tex.... Earned $180,000 last year.

SAM MILLS 30 5-9 225   Linebacker

Named starter for NFC defense in his second Pro Bowl... Missed final game of the season because of injury, but finished second on the team with 100 total tackles... Tied for team lead in recovered fumbles with three... League's shortest linebacker, but doesn't give an inch on the run... Aggressive, quick and intelligent... Has played for Jim Mora three seasons in the USFL and three seasons with Saints... Division II All-American at Montclair State in 1980... Originally signed with Browns as free agent in 1981, but was released... Born June 3, 1959, in Neptune, N.J.... Earned $229,000 last year.

MORTEN ANDERSEN 29 6-2 200   Kicker

Voted to Pro Bowl for fourth consecutive year, despite an average season considering his lofty standards... Hit 26 of 36 field goals and 32 of 33 PATs... Made 20 of 24 field goals inside the 40-yard line... Longest field goal was 51-yarder against Raiders Oct. 23... Had 110 points to rank third in the NFC in scoring. It was his fourth consecutive 100-point season

...Ranks as the NFL's most accurate kicker of all time at 78.2 percent...Has scored in 78 straight games, also a club record ...Speaks six languages...Born Aug. 19, 1960, in Struer, Denmark...Was fourth-round draft choice in 1982 out of Michigan State...Earned $325,000 last year.

BOBBY HEBERT 29 6-4 215   Quarterback

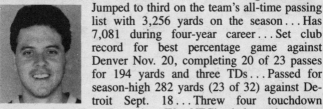

Jumped to third on the team's all-time passing list with 3,256 yards on the season...Has 7,081 during four-year career...Set club record for best percentage game against Denver Nov. 20, completing 20 of 23 passes for 194 yards and three TDs...Passed for season-high 282 yards (23 of 32) against Detroit Sept. 18...Threw four touchdown passes against 49ers Sept. 4...Was NFC's sixth-rated quarterback at 79.3...Not spectacular, but efficient...Played three seasons in USFL, leading Michigan Panthers to title in 1983... Born Aug. 19, 1960, in Galliano, La....A product of Northwestern Louisiana State...Signed with Saints as free agent in 1985...Earned $550,000 last year.

RUEBEN MAYES 26 5-11 201   Running Back

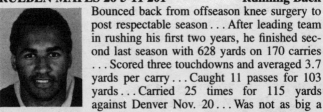

Bounced back from offseason knee surgery to post respectable season...After leading team in rushing his first two years, he finished second last season with 628 yards on 170 carries ...Scored three touchdowns and averaged 3.7 yards per carry...Caught 11 passes for 103 yards...Carried 25 times for 115 yards against Denver Nov. 20...Was not as big a factor in offense as in previous years...Tore knee ligaments in wild-card playoff game against Minnesota Jan. 3, 1988. Was operated on two days later...Rushed for 2,270 yards in first two seasons...A third-round draft pick in 1986...Holds every rushing record in Washington State history...Born June 16, 1963, in North Battleford, Saskatchewan...Earned $190,000 last year.

DALTON HILLIARD 25 5-8 204   Running Back

Led Saints in rushing yardage for first time in his career . . . Carried 204 times for 823 yards, a 4.0 average . . . Had first-ever 100-yard rushing game as a pro, totaling 127 yards on 25 carries during final regular-season game against Atlanta Dec. 18 . . . Was team's third-leading receiver with 66 receptions for 703 yards and one TD . . . Returned six kickoffs for 111 yards . . . A second-round pick out of nearby LSU in 1986 . . . Ended collegiate career ranked third on all-time SEC rushing list behind Herschel Walker and Bo Jackson . . . Born Jan. 21, 1964, in Patterson, La. . . . Earned $220,000 last year.

VAUGHAN JOHNSON 27 6-3 245   Linebacker

Recorded 108 stops to lead Saints in total tackles for second straight season, but didn't make Pro Bowl . . . Also had two sacks, one interception and seven passes defensed . . . A tenacious inside linebacker who loves leveling the big hit . . . Had 86 tackles in 1987 to lead team . . . Played with USFL Jacksonville Bulls in 1984-85 . . . Had 154 tackles in 1984 . . . A No. 1 pick by Saints in 1984 supplemental draft . . . Signed in 1986 . . . Attended North Carolina State . . . Spends offseason working in family construction firm . . . Born March 4, 1962, in Morehead City, N.C. . . . Earned $290,000 last year.

RICKEY JACKSON 31 6-2 239   Linebacker

Another key contributor in what might be the best linebacking corps in the NFL . . . Was third on team in tackles with 90 . . . Shared with Pat Swilling team lead with seven sacks . . . Collected one interception . . . Forced two fumbles . . . Credited with five passes defensed . . . Holds club record for most consecutive starts with 117 . . . Hardest hitter on punishing defense . . . Went to Pro Bowl from 1983-86 . . . A second-round draft choice in 1981 . . . Played defensive end at Pitt along with Hugh Green . . . Part of Pitt senior class that had 19 players drafted into the NFL . . . Born March 20, 1958, in Pahokee, Fla. . . . Earned $600,000 last year.

JIM DOMBROWSKI 25 6-6 295   Tackle

Improving young offensive lineman who figures to be a force for years . . . Spent 1987 getting on-the-job training after missing majority of rookie season with broken bone in his foot . . . Was more comfortable in 1988, helping the Saints produce the NFC's third-best rushing offense . . . Should improve technically and physically after spending offseason working out at Saints' practice facility . . . A No. 1 draft choice in 1986 . . . Was first offensive lineman and sixth player picked overall . . . A consensus All-American at Virginia . . . Holds degree in biology . . . Born Oct. 9, 1963, in Williamsville, N.Y. . . . Earned $250,000.

COACH JIM MORA: Proved Saints were for real by guiding

team to second consecutive winning season . . . At 10-6, Saints finished in three-way tie for the NFC West championship, but were eliminated systematically from the division crown and the playoffs by NFL's tie-breaker system . . . Opened year winning seven of first eight games, but lost five of last eight . . . Ingredients remain to contend for division crown this year . . . He's 29-19 in three years with Saints . . . Coached Philadelphia Stars to two USFL championships . . . Played tight end and defensive end at Occidental College, where he roomed with Jack Kemp, the quarterback who would go on to the Buffalo Bills, Congress and now George Bush's cabinet . . . Was head coach at his alma mater and an assistant at Stanford, Colorado, UCLA and Washington before taking assistant roles at Seattle and New England . . . Born May 24, 1935, in Glendale, Cal.

GREATEST COACH

He has been in New Orleans for just three seasons, but it's not premature to call Jim Mora the franchise's greatest coach. After all, he's done what such formidable predecessors as Hank Stram, Bum Phillips and Dick Nolan could not do: lead the Saints to a winning season and playoff berth. This happened in 1987 when they posted a 12-3 record.

Expectations for this once laughable franchise have grown so high that last year's 10-6 mark was a bit of a disappointment, despite being only the Saints' second winning campaign ever in their 22-year history. Thus far, Mora has compiled a 29-18 record in his three years in the NFL. It's a good record that figures to get better.

Rickey Jackson shoots for landing on the Moon.

INDIVIDUAL SAINT RECORDS

Rushing

Most Yards Game:	206	George Rogers, vs St. Louis, 1983
Season:	1,674	George Rogers, 1981
Career:	4,267	George Rogers, 1981-84

Passing

Most TD Passes Game:	6	Billy Kilmer, vs St. Louis, 1969
Season:	23	Archie Manning, 1980
Career:	155	Archie Manning, 1971-81

Receiving

Most TD Passes Game:	3	Dan Abramowicz, vs San Francisco, 1971
Season:	9	Henry Childs, 1977
Career:	37	Dan Abramowicz, 1967-72

Scoring

Most Points Game:	18	Walt Roberts, vs Philadelphia, 1967
	18	Dan Abramowicz, vs San Francisco, 1971
	18	Archie Manning, vs Chicago, 1977
	18	Chuck Muncie, vs San Francisco, 1979
	18	George Rogers, vs Los Angeles, 1981
	18	Wayne Wilson, vs Atlanta, 1982
Season:	121	Morten Andersen, 1987
Career:	646	Morten Andersen, 1982-88
Most TDs Game:	3	Walt Roberts, vs Philadelphia, 1967
	3	Dan Abramowicz, vs San Francisco, 1971
	3	Archie Manning, vs Chicago, 1977
	3	Chuck Muncie, vs San Francisco, 1979
	3	George Rogers, vs Los Angeles, 1981
	3	Wayne Wilson, vs Atlanta, 1982
Season:	13	George Rogers, 1981
Career:	37	Dan Abramowicz, 1967-72

NEW YORK GIANTS

TEAM DIRECTORY: Pres.: Wellington Mara; VP/Treasurer: Timothy Mara; VP/GM: George Young; Dir. Pro Personnel: Tom Boisture; Dir. Pub. Rel.: Ed Croke; Head Coach: Bill Parcells. Home field: Giants Stadium (76,891). Colors: Blue, red and white.

SCOUTING REPORT

OFFENSE: The Giants' offense struggled all season behind a young, inconsistent offensive line that allowed 60 sacks and blocked for just 3.4 yards per rush. The '89 unit should look like this: Doug Riesenberg at right tackle, replacing Karl Nelson, who will miss the season following a recurrence of cancer; 1988 No. 1 pick Eric Moore at right guard, veteran Bart Oates at center,

With skills undiminished, Phil Simms rounds out a decade.

second-year man John Elliott at left guard and William Roberts at left tackle.

Running back Joe Morris bounced back from a disappointing 1987 to gain 1,083 yards, but George Adams was a non-factor in the team's 10-6 campaign.

Phil Simms is 33, but remains one of the best quarterbacks in the league. His numbers, 3,359 yards passing and a 21-11 touchdown-to-interception ratio, were remarkable considering the problems up front. Tight end Mark Bavaro, if healthy, should bounce back from a subpar season. The club remains stocked with talented young receivers in Stephen Baker, Mark Ingram and Odessa Turner.

DEFENSE: The big question is at inside linebacker, where future Hall of Famer Harry Carson has retired. Pepper Johnson and Gary Reasons will man the inside positions, but both had trouble covering running backs on pass patterns and aren't as tough against the run as Carson was.

Outside linebacker Carl Banks has a lot to make up for after a dismal showing and Lawrence Taylor remains a terror on the field but must control his off-the-field problems.

The Giants are solid at cornerback with Mark Collins and Sheldon White, who could challenge Perry Williams on the right side. Veteran safeties Kenny Hill and Terry Kinard struggled early last season and will be a prime target for opposing quarterbacks.

KICKING GAME: Placekicker Paul McFadden and punter Maury Buford saved the Giants last year when Raul Allegre and Sean Landeta went down with injuries. But McFadden (Falcons) and Buford (Packers) are gone. The Giants haven't returned a punt or kickoff for a touchdown since 1978.

THE ROOKIES: Deja-Moo. Top two picks Brian Williams of Minnesota and Bob Kratch of Iowa added almost 600 pounds to an already-beefy list of offensive linemen. Both will be tried at left guard, with Williams moving to center when Oates decides to make law his career. Greg Jackson of LSU will be groomed at safety, where Hill and Kinard are aging.

OUTLOOK: Much will depend on how quickly the young offensive line finds cohesiveness. A more imaginative offensive scheme may be needed now that the defense can no longer win games on its own.

GIANTS VETERAN ROSTER

HEAD COACH—Bill Parcells. Assistant Coaches—Bill Belichick, Tom Coughlin, Romeo Crennel, Ron Erhardt, Len Fontes, Al Groh, Ray Handley, Fred Hoaglin, Lamar Leachman, Johnny Parker, Mike Pope, Mike Sweatman.

No.	Name	Pos.	Ht.	Wt.	NFL Exp.	College
33	Adams, George	RB	6-1	225	5	Kentucky
2	Allegre, Raul	K	5-10	167	7	Texas
79	Althoff, Jim	NT	6-3	278	2	Winona State
24	Anderson, Ottis	RB	6-2	225	11	Miami
85	Baker, Stephen	WR	5-8	165	3	Fresno State
58	Banks, Carl	LB	6-4	235	6	Michigan State
88	Baty, Greg	TE	6-5	240	3	Stanford
89	Bavaro, Mark	TE	6-4	245	5	Notre Dame
64	Burt, Jim	NT	6-1	260	8	Miami
44	Carthon, Maurice	RB	6-1	225	5	Arkansas State
25	Collins, Mark	CB	5-10	190	4	Cal State-Fullerton
98	Cooks, Johnie	LB	6-4	251	2	Mississippi State
38	Cox, Greg	S	6-0	223	2	San Jose State
77	Dorsey, Eric	DE	6-5	280	4	Notre Dame
76	Elliot, John	T	6-7	305	2	Michigan
28	Flynn, Tom	S	6-0	195	6	Pittsburgh
37	Haddix, Wayne	CB	6-1	203	3	Liberty
48	Hill, Kenny	S	6-0	195	9	Yale
15	Hostetler, Jeff	QB	6-3	212	6	West Virginia
74	Howard, Erik	NT	6-4	268	4	Washington State
82	Ingram, Mark	WR	5-10	188	3	Michigan State
68	Johnson, Damian	T	6-5	290	4	Kansas State
52	Johnson, Thomas	LB	6-3	248	4	Ohio State
43	Kinard, Terry	S	6-1	200	7	Clemson
90	Lambrecht, Mike	NT-DE	6-1	275	3	St. Cloud State
5	Landeta, Sean	P	6-0	200	5	Towson State
86	Manuel, Lionel	WR	5-11	180	6	Pacific
70	Marshall, Leonard	DE	6-3	285	7	Louisiana State
80	McConkey, Phil	WR	5-10	170	6	Navy
60	Moore, Eric	T	6-5	290	2	Indiana
20	Morris, Joe	RB	5-7	195	8	Syracuse
84	Mowatt, Zeke	TE	6-3	240	6	Florida State
65	Oates, Bart	C	6-3	265	5	Brigham Young
55	Reasons, Gary	LB	6-4	234	6	NW Louisiana
72	Riesenberg, Doug	T	6-5	275	4	California
66	Roberts, William	T	6-5	280	5	Ohio State
81	Robinson, Stacy	WR	5-11	186	5	North Dakota State
22	Rouson, Lee	RB	6-1	222	5	Colorado
17	Rutledge, Jeff	QB	6-1	195	11	Alabama
51	Shaw, Rickey	LB	6-4	240	2	Oklahoma State
11	Simms, Phil	QB	6-3	215	11	Morehead State
56	Taylor, Lawrence	LB	6-3	243	9	North Carolina
21	Thompson, Reyna	CB	6-0	193	4	Baylor
83	Turner, Odessa	WR	6-3	205	3	NW Louisiana
73	Washington, John	DE	6-4	275	4	Oklahoma State
27	Welch, Herb	CB-S	5-11	180	5	UCLA
36	White, Adrian	S	6-0	200	3	Florida
71	White, Robb	DE	6-4	270	2	South Dakota
39	White, Sheldon	CB-S	5-11	188	2	Miami, Ohio
23	Williams, Perry	CB	6-2	203	6	North Carolina State
69	Winters, Frank	C	6-3	280	3	Western Illinois

TOP DRAFT CHOICES

Rd.	Name	Sel. No.	Pos.	Ht.	Wt.	College
1	Williams, Brian	18	C	6-5	295	Minnesota
3	Kratch, Bob	64	G	6-3	285	Iowa
3	Jackson, Greg	78	S	6-0	200	LSU
4	Tillman, Lewis	93	RB	5-11	190	Jackson State
4	Henke, Brad	105	DT	6-3	270	Arizona

GIANT PROFILES

LIONEL MANUEL 27 5-11 180   Wide Receiver

Avoided injury bug in 1988 and had best season of five-year career, with more than 1,000 yards receiving for first time (65 receptions for 1,029 yards)...Played in all 16 games for first time during his career as a starter...Best game came in Week 3 at Dallas with nine receptions for 142 yards...Accelerates out of cuts faster than most receivers, making him dangerous on 17- to 20-yard in-cuts...Was seventh-round draft pick out of Pacific in 1984...An accomplished musician, he sang and played drums in L.A.-based rock band. Also plays guitar and synthesizer...Born April 13, 1962, in Los Angeles...Among Giants' protected free agents heading into this season...1988 salary: $225,000.

JOE MORRIS 28 5-7 195   Running Back

Overcame injuries and personnel changes along the offensive line to rush for 1,083 yards, fifth-highest in the NFC...It was third 1,000-yard season in last four years...Rushed 307 times for 3.5 average and scored five TDs...Had three 100-yard rushing days ...Best was 140-yard effort against Chiefs on Dec. 11...Set all-time rushing records at Syracuse, surpassing marks of Jim Brown, Larry Csonka and Floyd Little...Was Giants' second-round draft choice in 1982 ...Younger brother Jamie is running back with the Redskins... 1988 salary: $500,000...Born Sept. 16, 1960, in Fort Bragg, N.C....Father Earl was career man in U.S. Army.

BART OATES 30 6-3 265   Center

Mainstay of offensive line and only remaining member of 1986 line that led team to Super Bowl XXI...Handled every snap during 16-game season after yielding punt and placekick snaps to Joe Fields...Has started 58 of 60 games since joining Giants in 1985...Joined club as free agent after played for Philadelphia/Baltimore Stars of USFL for three seasons...Played in three straight USFL title games...Was Stars' second-round selection after stellar career at BYU, where he received accounting degree...Is now attending Seton Hall Law School during offseason...Born Dec. 16, 1958, in Mesa, Ariz....1988 salary: $250,000.

PHIL SIMMS 33 6-3 215   Quarterback

Was the most consistent offensive performer throughout the season...Passed for 3,359 yards and 21 TDs...Rating of 82.1 was down from previous season due to changes along the offensive line and inconsistent running game ...Still managed to complete 54.9 percent of his passes with just 11 interceptions...Had three 300-yard passing days, including season high of 324 yards at Philadelphia Oct. 10...Missed one game (Nov. 27 at New Orleans) with bruised shoulder...Was MVP of Super Bowl XXI after setting Super Bowl record with 88 percent completions (22 of 25) for 268 yards and three TDs...Born Nov. 3, 1955, in Springfield, Ky...Was first-round draft pick out of Morehead State in 1979...Seven-handicap golfer... 1988 salary: $750,000.

LAWRENCE TAYLOR 30 6-3 243   Linebacker

Missed first four weeks of the season after being suspended for failing a preseason drug test...Came back to lead team in sacks with 15½ and earn eighth consecutive trip to Pro Bowl...A fierce competitor who played with painful muscle tear in chest during critical midseason stretch...Recorded three sacks against Detroit Oct. 16 and at New Orleans Nov. 27...Finished fourth on team in tackles with 73. Forced team-high five fumbles...League MVP in 1986 after amassing 20½ sacks...Was second overall pick out of North Carolina in 1981...Born Feb. 4, 1959, in Williamsburg, Va....Avid golfer who is popular on pro-am circuit...Was to earn $1 million in base salary in 1988 but lost $250,000 because of suspension.

MARK BAVARO 26 6-4 245   Tight End

Struggled through disappointing 1988 after posting back-to-back All-Pro seasons... Caught 53 passes for 673 yards and four TDs ... Missed nearly all of training camp in contract holdout. Signed multi-year deal prior to last preseason game... Was plagued by toe, shoulder and knee injuries that led to dropped passes early in the year... Caught nine passes for 148 yards against Eagles Oct. 10 for only 100-yard receiving day... Finished second on team in receptions to Lionel Manuel ... Saw streak of 28 games with at least one reception end against Falcons Oct. 23... Still considered one of the premier tight ends in the league... A reliable blocker when healthy... Product of Notre Dame who somehow lasted until fourth round of 1985 draft... Born April 23, 1963, in Winthrop, Mass.... 1988 salary: $700,000.

MARK COLLINS 25 5-10 190   Cornerback

Showed steady improvement in third pro season until groin injury Nov. 6 against Dallas sidelined him for five of last six games... Was second on team in passes defensed with 13... Had just one interception... Beaten by Jerry Rice for 78-yard touchdown pass in final seconds against 49ers in Week 2... Improved run support, collecting 58 tackles... Was second-round draft choice out of Cal State-Fullerton in 1986. First of four players taken by club in that round... Should push for All-Pro this year if injury bug doesn't bite... Born Jan. 16, 1964, in St. Louis... Played football, baseball and basketball in high school... Enjoys golf during offseason... 1988 salary: $175,000.

TERRY KINARD 30 6-1 200   Free Safety

Struggled during first half of season, arriving late on several of opponents' touchdown passes, but regrouped during second half and earned first trip to Pro Bowl... Was named to NFC squad by coach Mike Ditka as "need player"... Had interception in Pro Bowl... Was without an interception for first 11 weeks, then had one in three successive weeks, returning one 39 yards against Cardinals Dec. 4... Finished second on team with 85 tackles... Fully recovered from major knee surgery in December 1986 that kept him out of Super Bowl XXI ... Born Nov. 24, 1959, in Bitburg, Germany, where dad served in the Air Force... 1988 salary: $350,000... Tenth overall pick, out of Clemson, in 1983.

STEPHEN BAKER 25 5-8 165   Wide Receiver

Became starter in sixth game of the season after injuries sidelined Mark Ingram and Odessa Turner... Answered questions about his stamina and durability by posting solid performances throughout the season... Caught 40 passes for 656 yards... Seven TD catches led team... Average per catch of 16.4 yards was tops among receivers with 10 or more catches... Possesses quick feet and instant acceleration... Caught six passes for 104 yards at Atlanta Oct. 23 and three passes for 134 at New Orleans Nov. 27... Nicknamed "Touchdown Maker" after scoring 57 TDs during stellar career at Fresno State... Third-round draft pick in 1987. One of three receivers taken among top four picks... Born Aug. 30, 1964, in San Antonio and grew up in Los Angeles... 1988 salary: $132,000.

CARL BANKS 27 6-4 235   Linebacker

Missed all of training camp before signing a multi-year, $3.2-million contract days before regular-season opener against Washington... Went on to have disappointing season... Had 66 tackles to rank seventh on team after leading Giants in that category previous two years ... Had just two sacks... Missed one game with hamstring pull... Wasn't nearly as aggressive as previous seasons... Was vulnerable against the run and wasn't as intimidating on the pass rush... Also hampered by bruised knee... No. 3 draft pick out of Michigan State in 1984, where he was consensus All-America... Born Aug. 29, 1962, in Flint, Mich.... Exceptional basketball player... Was married during the offseason... 1988 salary: $750,000.

COACH BILL PARCELLS: Had Giants on verge of playoff berth despite a four-week drug suspension to Lawrence Taylor, subpar seasons by Carl Banks and Mark Bavaro and frequent personnel changes along the offensive line . . . Loss to Jets in regular-season finale knocked team out of postseason contention . . . Mended fences with players after bitter 1987 strike . . . Signed contract prior to 1988 season for $3.2 million over four years . . . Coached at Wichita State, Army, Vanderbilt, Florida State and Texas Tech before becoming head coach at Air Force . . . Was linebacker coach with Patriots in 1980 before joining Giants as defensive coordinator in 1981 . . . He became Giants' head coach when Ray Perkins left in 1983 . . . Has record of 57-44-1 in six seasons with Giants . . . Born Aug. 22, 1941, in Englewood, N.J. . . . Was a linebacker at Wichita State.

GREATEST COACH

Steve Owen coached the Giants from 1931 to 1953, compiling a record of 151-100-17 for a winning percentage of .595. He ranks eighth among all-time NFL coaches in career victories. As both a player and coach, he was a Giant institution for 28 years. He joined the club in 1926 as a 5-10, 225-pound tackle and played through 1933.

As a player, he was known as a tenacious tackler. As a coach, he gained fame for the "umbrella defense." Under Owen, the Giants won 10 division or conference titles and reached the NFL championship game eight times, winning in 1934 and 1938. He was enshrined in the Pro Football Hall of Fame in 1966.

INDIVIDUAL GIANT RECORDS
Rushing

Most Yards Game:	218	Gene Roberts, vs Chi. Cardinals, 1950
Season:	1,516	Joe Morris, 1986
Career:	5,296	Joe Morrison, 1982-88

Passing

Most TD Passes Game:	7	Y. A. Tittle, vs Washington, 1962
Season:	36	Y. A. Tittle, 1963
Career:	173	Charlie Conerly, 1948-61

Receiving

Most TD Passes Game:	4	Earnest Gray, vs St. Louis, 1980
Season:	13	Homer Jones, 1967
Career:	48	Kyle Rote, 1951-61

Scoring

Most Points Game:	24	Ron Johnson, vs Philadelphia, 1972
	24	Earnest Gray, vs St. Louis, 1980
Season:	127	Ali Haji-Sheikh, 1983
Career:	646	Pete Gogolak, 1966-74
Most TDs Game:	4	Ron Johnson, vs Philadelphia, 1972
	4	Earnest Gray, vs St. Louis, 1980
Season:	21	Joe Morris, 1985
Career:	78	Frank Gifford, 1952-60, 1962-64

PHILADELPHIA EAGLES

TEAM DIRECTORY: Owner: Norman Braman; Pres/CEO: Harry Gamble; VP-Finance: Mimi Box; VP-Marketing: Decker Uhlhorn; VP-Player Personnel: Bill Davis; Dir. Player Personnel: Joe Woolley; Dir. Pub. Rel.: Ron Howard; Head Coach: Buddy Ryan. Home field: Veterans Stadium (65,356). Colors: Kelly green, white and silver.

SCOUTING REPORT

OFFENSE: The Eagles (10-6) won their first NFC East title since 1981 partly because they beat the Giants twice and partly because Randall Cunningham is simply the most dangerous quarterback in the NFL. When you consider that a weak offensive line allowed him to be sacked 57 times and kept him under constant pressure, Cunningham's 3,808 yards passing is a true testament to his ability.

The emergence of a running game is badly needed. The Eagles averaged just 121 yards per game on the ground and someone besides Cunningham has to be the club's top groundgainer. Tight end Keith Jackson, who made the Pro Bowl as a rookie last year, and wideouts Mike Quick and Cris Carter comprise an excellent receiving corps.

The offensive line needs to be solidified and could be with a healthy Ron Solt, who had surgery on both knees.

DEFENSE: Reggie! Reggie! Reggie! Reggie White has been the heart of the Eagles' defense over the last two years, leading the NFL in sacks both seasons. But he could get more help this year from Jerome Brown, who has improved in each of his two seasons, and Mike Pitts, who is an aggressive competitor. Linebacker Seth Joyner is Philly's best-kept secret, but Todd Bell is out of position at linebacker and could be moved back to the secondary.

As for the secondary, its pass coverage was awful last year, finishing 28th (dead-last), allowing 259 yards per game. Strong safety Andre Waters is a solid player, but the other three positions could be up for grabs.

KICKING GAME: Early placekicking problems weren't solved until Luis Zendejas arrived from Dallas and took over in Week 5. He made 19 of 24 field goals with Philly and 15 of 17 from inside the 40. John Teltschik averaged a respectable 40.4 yards per punt, but the Eagles lack a threatening return specialist.

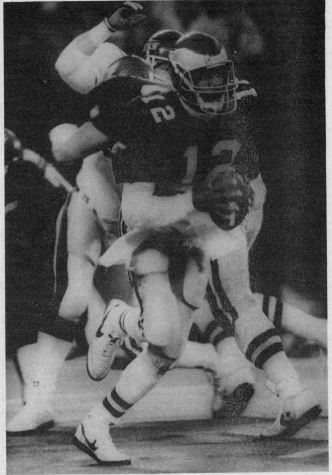

Randall Cunningham spirited Eagles to NFC East crown.

THE ROOKIES: With only four draft picks, the Eagles needed to make every selection count. Linebacker Jessie Small of Eastern Kentucky could play in pass-rush situations but needs to improve his pass coverage after being a standup defensive end in college. Syracuse running back Robert Drummond has good hands and should complement Byars.

EAGLES VETERAN ROSTER

HEAD COACH—Buddy Ryan. Assistant Coaches—Dave Atkins, Tom Bettis, Jeff Fisher, Dale Haupt, Ronnie Jones, Dan Neal, Ted Plumb, Al Roberts, Doug Scovil, Bill Walsh.

No.	Name	Pos.	Ht.	Wt.	NFL Exp.	College
32	Abercrombie, Walter	RB	6-0	210	8	Baylor
72	Alexander, David	C-G	6-3	282	3	Tulsa
21	Allen, Eric	CB	5-10	188	2	Arizona State
58	Allert, Ty	LB	6-2	238	4	Texas
87	Bailey, Eric	TE	6-5	245	2	Kansas State
63	Baker, Ron	G	6-4	275	12	Oklahoma State
49	Bell, Todd	S	6-1	212	8	Ohio State
99	Brown, Jerome	DT	6-2	292	3	Miami
51	Butcher, Paul	LB	6-0	230	4	Wayne State
4	Byars, Keith	RB	6-1	230	4	Ohio State
80	Carter, Cris	WR	6-3	194	3	Ohio State
6	Cavanaugh, Matt	QB	6-2	210	12	Pittsburgh
12	Cunningham, Randall	QB	6-4	192	5	Nevada-Las Vegas
76	Darwin, Matt	T	6-4	275	4	Texas A&M
56	Evans, Byron	LB	6-2	235	3	Arizona
77	Evans, Donald	DE	6-2	258	2	Winston-Salem State
42	Everett, Eric	CB	5-10	170	2	Texas Tech
33	Frizzell, William	S	6-3	206	6	North Carolina Central
86	Garrity, Gregg	WR	5-10	175	7	Penn State
83	Giles, Jimmie	TE	6-3	245	13	Alcorn State
90	Golic, Mike	DT	6-5	275	4	Notre Dame
95	Harris, Al	LB	6-5	265	10	Arizona State
73	Heller, Ron	T	6-6	280	6	Penn State
22	Higgs, Mark	RB	5-7	200	2	Kentucky
34	Hoage, Terry	S	6-3	201	6	Georgia
84	Holloway, Derek	WR	5-8	162	3	Arkansas
48	Hopkins, Wes	S	6-1	215	6	Southern Methodist
88	Jackson, Keith	TE	6-2	250	2	Oklahoma
46	Jenkins, Izel	CB	5-10	191	2	North Carolina State
53	Jiles, Dwayne	LB	6-4	245	5	Texas Tech
85	Johnson, Ron	WR	6-3	190	5	Long Beach State
59	Joyner, Seth	LB	6-2	241	4	Texas-El Paso
97	Klingel, John	DE	6-3	270	4	Eastern Kentucky
89	Little, David	TE	6-2	230	3	Middle Tenn. State
74	Pitts, Mike	DT	6-5	277	7	Alabama
82	Quick, Mike	WR	6-2	190	8	North Carolina State
66	Reeves, Ken	T-G	6-5	270	5	Texas A&M
55	Reichenbach, Mike	LB	6-2	235	6	East Stroudsburg
50	Rimington, Dave	C	6-3	285	7	Nebraska
79	Schad, Mike	G	6-5	290	2	Queen's (Canada)
96	Simmons, Clyde	DE	6-6	275	4	Western Carolina
68	Singletary, Reggie	G-T	6-3	285	4	North Carolina State
65	Solt, Ron	G	6-3	288	5	Maryland
61	Tamburello, Ben	G-C	6-3	278	2	Auburn
10	Telschik, John	P	6-2	210	4	Texas
25	Toney, Anthony	RB	6-0	227	4	Texas A&M
20	Waters, Andre	S	5-11	185	6	Cheyney
92	White, Reggie	DE	6-5	285	5	Tennessee
43	Young, Roynell	CB	6-1	185	10	Alcorn State
8	Zendejas, Luis	K	5-9	170	3	Arizona State

TOP DRAFT CHOICES

Rd.	Name	Sel. No.	Pos.	Ht.	Wt.	College
2	Small, Jessie	49	LB	6-4	240	Eastern Kentucky
3	Drummond, Robert	76	RB	6-1	205	Syracuse
3	Hager, Britt	81	LB	6-0	230	Texas
6	Sherman, Heath	162	RB	6-0	190	Texas A&I

OUTLOOK: Last year's division title was no fluke. With improvement in the secondary and the development of a running game, the Eagles may not get fogged out early in the playoffs this year.

EAGLE PROFILES

RANDALL CUNNINGHAM 26 6-4 192   Quarterback

One of rising stars in NFL...Was MVP of Pro Bowl...Passed for 3,808 yards and 24 touchdowns...Yardage figure was second in the NFC and third in NFL...Quarterback rating of 77.6 was seventh in the NFC...Led Eagles in rushing with 624 yards on 93 carries ...Best was Monday Night effort against Giants Oct. 10. Passed for 369 yards (31 of 41) and three TDs, including 80-yarder to Cris Carter...Was sacked the most times (57), making him leader in that category over Giants' Phil Simms (53)...Completed 53.8 percent of his passes...Brother Sam starred at USC and with Patriots... Second-round pick in 1985 out of Nevada-Las Vegas, where he became only third quarterback in NCAA history to throw for more than 2,500 yards in three consecutive seasons, joining John Elway and Doug Flutie...Born March 27, 1963, in Santa Barbara, Cal....Earned $1.35 million last season.

KEITH JACKSON 24 6-2 250   Tight End

A No. 1 draft pick who exceeded the expectations the Eagles had for him in 1988...Has the agility and speed of many wide receivers and the power of a lineman...Was voted NFC Rookie of the Year and earned spot in Pro Bowl...Caught 81 passes for 869 yards and six TDs...Reception total ranked fourth in NFC...Had at least five receptions in eight games...A consensus All-American and unanimous All-Big Eight choice as junior and senior at Oklahoma...Caught only 62 passes for 1,470 yards and 14 touchdowns out of Sooners' wishbone offense...Earned communications degree in 3½ years... Likes to play cello...Born April 19, 1965, in Little Rock, Ark....Earned $1,062,500 last year.

REGGIE WHITE 27 6-5 285   Defensive End/Tackle

Collected 18 sacks to lead NFL in that category for second consecutive season . . . Has 70 sacks in four NFL seasons . . . Agile, quick and extremely powerful player who can dominate offense rushing from an end or tackle spot . . . Had four sacks against Minnesota Sept. 25 . . . Eagles' fourth-leading tackler with 133, including 96 solo . . . Recovered two fumbles and blocked one point-after kick . . . Claimed by Eagles in first round of 1984 supplemental draft . . . Played two years with Memphis Showboats of USFL . . . Named USFL Man of the Year in 1985 . . . An ordained Baptist minister . . . Attended University of Tennessee . . . Born Dec. 19, 1961, in Chattanooga, Tenn. . . . Earned $525,000 last year.

SETH JOYNER 24 6-2 241   Linebacker

Tough, aggressive player who is one of the most underrated linebackers in the NFC . . . Finished third on the team with 136 tackles, 86 solo . . . Had four interceptions . . . Credited with 11 passes defensed . . . Forced two fumbles . . . Had at least seven tackles in 12 games . . . Had season-high 16 tackles at Phoenix Dec. 10 . . . Credited with 3½ sacks . . . Born Nov. 18, 1964, in Spring Valley, N.Y. . . . An eighth-round pick out of Texas-El Paso in 1986 . . . Was released during final preseason cut of rookie season, but re-signed within two weeks . . . Stuck with club as special-teams player . . . An avid bowler.

ANDRE WATERS 27 5-11 185   Strong Safety

Recorded 154 tackles to lead team in that category for second straight year, after sharing the honor in his first season as a starter in 1986 . . . Had 107 solo tackles . . . Has 395 tackles over last three seasons . . . Buddy Ryan's type of player, hard-nosed and well-liked around the league . . . Had three interceptions . . . Defensed nine passes . . . Forced three fumbles . . . Blocked a punt against Minnesota Sept. 25. Also had 19 tackles in that game . . . Had 10 or more tackles in 10 games . . . Plays linebacker in "46" defense . . . Signed as free agent from Cheyney State in 1984 . . . Made club with outstanding special-teams play . . . Born March 10, 1962, in Belle Glade, Fla. . . . Has degree in business administration . . . Earned $300,000 last year.

KEITH BYARS 25 6-1 230 — Running Back

Has not emerged into the consistent rushing threat the Eagles hoped he'd be when drafted No. 1 in 1986 . . . Was team's second-leading rusher with 517 yards on 152 carries, but did not have a 100-yard rushing day . . . Best outing was 86-yard effort against Phoenix Dec. 10 . . . As pass receiver, he caught 72 balls for 705 yards . . . Scored 10 touchdowns, six rushing . . . Played every game for first time in career, avoiding foot injuries that have dogged him since senior year at Ohio State . . . Second-leading rusher (3,200 yards) in OSU history behind Archie Griffin . . . Born Oct. 14, 1963, in Dayton, Ohio . . . Played on two state championship basketball teams in high school . . . Enjoys gospel music . . . Earned $375,000 last year.

JEROME BROWN 24 6-2 292 — Defensive Tackle

Showed great improvement in second season in the NFL . . . Offensive lines must start paying more attention to Brown, freeing Reggie White of double- and triple-teamed blocking . . . Ranked sixth on team with 101 tackles, starting all 16 games . . . Had 17 tackles against Giants Nov. 20 and 14 at Cleveland Oct. 16 . . . Collected five sacks . . . Intercepted one pass and forced one fumble . . . Was used as part of three-man rotation during rookie season, but held position on his own last year . . . One of few freshmen to see much action on Miami's national-championship team of 1983 . . . Born Feb. 4, 1965, in Brooksville, Fla. . . . Was ninth player chosen overall in 1987 . . . Earned $240,000 last year.

CRIS CARTER 23 6-3 194 **Wide Receiver**

Became Eagles' top wide receiver when Mike Quick went down with broken leg in fifth week of the season... Caught 39 passes for 761 yards and six touchdowns... Had memorable outing in Monday Night game against Giants Oct. 10, catching five passes for 162 yards. Had 80-yard TD that night to clinch victory... It was his only 100-yard receiving day of the season... Showed great improvement in second year ... Chosen in special supplemental draft in 1987 after losing last year of eligibility at Ohio State for accepting money from an agent... Set all-time Buckeye career record for receptions (168) and touchdown catches (27)... Born Nov. 25, 1965, in Troy, Ohio... Brother Butch played six years in the NBA... Earned $175,000 last season.

TODD BELL 30 6-1 212 **Linebacker**

Was a valuable addition to the defense after being signed as a free agent on June 14, 1988 ... Had been released by the Bears... Was undersized for position, but did adequate job, finishing seventh on the team in tackles with 92... Shared team lead with three fumble recoveries... Most productive game was against Giants Nov. 20, when he had 10 tackles... Had at least five tackles in 11 games... Originally a fourth-round draft choice of Bears in 1981... Was Pro Bowl choice at strong safety in 1984... Sat out 1985 Super Bowl season in contract dispute... Played at Ohio State... Born Nov. 28, 1958, in Middletown, Ohio... Was state long-jump champ three straight years in high school... Earned $350,000 last year.

MIKE QUICK 30 6-2 190 **Wide Receiver**

Was off to a good start in 1988 until fifth game of the season, when he broke the fibula in his left leg against Houston Oct. 2... Spent eight weeks on injured reserve... Returned against Washington Dec. 4... Finished season with 22 catches for 508 yards and four touchdowns ... Best day was third game of the season against Redskins, catching four passes for 105

yards, including a 55-yard TD... Averaged 23.1 yards per catch
... Has accounted for 5,945 receiving yards over last six seasons
... Injury snapped string of five consecutive trips to the Pro
Bowl... Was first-round round draft from North Carolina State
in 1982... Born May 14, 1959, in Hamlet, N.C.... Earned
$750,000 last year.

COACH BUDDY RYAN: Perhaps not given the credit he deserved after guiding the Eagles to their first NFC East championship since 1980... Players felt he should have been voted Coach of the Year... Never at a loss for words... Has 22-24-1 record since coming to Philadelphia... Has coached 21 years in the NFL... Innovator of the "46" defense while serving as the defensive coordinator at Chicago, where he was instrumental in helping the Bears to Super Bowl XX championship... Began coaching career at Gainesville High in Texas (1957-59)... Moved to college level as defensive coordinator for University of Buffalo (1961-65)... Was defensive-line coach under Bud Grant at Minnesota (1976-77) before going to Chicago... Born Feb. 17, 1934, in Frederick, Okla. ... Was an offensive guard at Oklahoma State and a master sergeant in the Army in Korea.

GREATEST COACH

One of the first acts of owner Alexis Thompson after acquiring the Philadelphia Eagles in 1941 was to hire Earle "Greasy" Neale as his head coach. It proved to be a move that would result in the Eagles becoming one of the NFL powers during the 1940s.

After three consecutive second-place finishes in the Eastern Conference (1944-46), the Eagles reached their first NFL championship game in 1947, losing to the Chicago Cardinals. But successive returns to the title game in 1948 and '49 resulted in two championships and a three-year mark of 28-7-1. Neale remains the Eagles' all-time winningest coach at 66-44-5.

INDIVIDUAL EAGLE RECORDS

Rushing

Most Yards Game:	205	Steve Van Buren, vs Pittsburgh, 1949
Season:	1,512	Wilbert Montgomery, 1979
Career:	6,538	Wilbert Montgomery, 1977-84

Passing

Most TD Passes Game:	7	Adrian Burk, vs Washington, 1954
Season:	32	Sonny Jurgensen, 1961
Career:	167	Ron Jaworski, 1977-85

Receiving

Most TD Passes Game:	4	Joe Carter, vs Cincinnati, 1934
	4	Ben Hawkins, vs Pittsburgh, 1969
Season:	13	Tommy McDonald, 1960 and 1961
	13	Mike Quick, 1983
Career:	79	Harold Carmichael, 1971-83

Scoring

Most Points Game:	25	Bobby Walston, vs Washington, 1954
Season:	116	Paul McFadden, 1984
Career:	881	Bobby Walston, 1951-62
Most TDs Game:	4	Joe Carter, vs Cincinnati, 1934
	4	Clarence Peaks, vs St. Louis, 1958
	4	Tommy McDonald, vs N.Y. Giants, 1959
	4	Ben Hawkins, vs Pittsburgh, 1969
	4	Wilbert Montgomery, vs Washington, 1978
	4	Wilbert Montgomery, vs Washington, 1979
Season:	18	Steve Van Buren, 1945
Career:	79	Harold Carmichael, 1971-83

PHOENIX CARDINALS

TEAM DIRECTORY: Pres.: William V. Bidwill; GM: Larry Wilson; VP-Administration: Curt Mosher; VP-Communications: Terry Bledsoe; Dir. Pro Personnel: Erik Widmark; Dir. Pub. Rel.: Paul Jensen; Head Coach: Gene Stallings. Home field: Sun Devil Stadium (72,000). Colors: Cardinal red, white and black.

SCOUTING REPORT

OFFENSE: They finished 7-9 last season, but considering they had to endure a move from the Midwest to the Southwest and an

J.T. Smith capped stellar season with Pro Bowl selection.

untimely injury to quarterback Neil Lomax, there's plenty of reason to be optimistic. Lomax is a gifted passer and leader, but needs to stay healthy. The Cards were 7-4 when he went down for two weeks with a sprained knee ligament, the first games he's missed because of injury since 1983.

Wide receivers J.T. Smith and Roy Green remain one of the league's most explosive combinations. Running back Stump Mitchell isn't the banger he used to be, so fullback Earl Ferrell should be the workhorse this year.

Offense isn't a problem. It ranked third in the NFC last year and fourth overall.

DEFENSE: The Cards were vulnerable to the run last season and tried several combinations along the defensive line to plug the holes. Freddie Joe Nunn, Rod Saddler and David Galloway should get most of the playing time this year, with Rob Clasby and Steve Alvord pushing for duty. The Cards lost E.J. Junior to free agency and will be looking for someone to fill his hole alongside steady fireplug Niko Noga.

Strong safety Tim McDonald is a promising talent and he could become a fixture in the secondary.

KICKING GAME: Placekicker Al Del Greco hopes to avoid the shaky start he had last year, when he was an erratic 12 of 21. Yet, his 78 points was the most by a Cardinal kicker since 1984. The Cards could miss punter Greg Horne, who signed as a free agent with the Redskins. Return specialist Vai Sikahema is one of the best in the game.

THE ROOKIES: Don't be surprised if linebacker Eric Hill of LSU is starting and playing effectively by midseason. Ditto for the second first-round pick Joe Wolf of Boston College, considered by many the top guard in the draft. Guard Mike Zandofsky of Washington brings added size (300 pounds) and could be a capable backup.

OUTLOOK: When Lomax is healthy, the Cardinals clearly have the talent to contend in the NFC East. But the secondary is suspect, as is the defense against the run. If those two areas can be improved, along with a more consistent kicking game, look for the Cardinals to be in the thick of it in December.

CARDINALS VETERAN ROSTER

HEAD COACH—Gene Stallings. Assistant Coaches—Marv Braden, Le-Baron Caruthers, Jim Johnson, Hank Kuhlmann, Leon McLaughlin, Mal Moore, Joe Pascale, Jim Shofner, Mike Solari, Dennis Thurman.

No.	Name	Pos.	Ht.	Wt.	NFL Exp.	College
40	Adams, Michael	CB	5-10	195	3	Arkansas State
60	Alvord, Steve	DT	6-4	272	3	Washington
80	Awalt, Robert	TE	6-5	248	3	San Diego State
55	Bell, Anthony	LB	6-3	231	4	Michigan State
82	Bellini, Mark	WR	5-11	185	3	Brigham Young
71	Bostic, Joe	G	6-3	268	11	Clemson
44	Brin, Michael	CB	6-0	186	2	Virginia Union
16	Camarillo, Rich	P	5-11	185	9	Washington
41	Carter, Carl	CB	5-11	180	4	Texas Tech
34	Clark, Jessie	RB	6-0	233	7	Arkansas
79	Clasby, Bob	DT	6-5	260	4	Notre Dame
94	Cooks, Rayford	DT	6-2	225	2	North Texas State
17	Del Greco, Al	K	5-10	191	6	Auburn
74	Dill, Scott	G	6-5	272	2	Memphis State
31	Ferrell, Earl	RB	6-0	240	8	East Tennessee State
65	Galloway, David	DE	6-3	279	8	Florida
14	Garcia, Teddy	K	5-10	190	2	Northeast Louisiana
81	Green, Roy	WR	6-0	195	11	Henderson State
73	Hadd, Gary	DT	6-4	270	2	Minnesota
56	Harvey, Ken	LB	6-2	225	2	California
13	Hogeboom, Gary	QB	6-4	208	10	Central Michigan
83	Holmes, Don	WR	5-10	180	4	Mesa, Colo.
51	Hunley, Rickey	LB	6-2	250	6	Arizona
50	Jarostchuk, Ilia	LB	6-3	231	3	New Hampshire
53	Jax, Garth	LB	6-2	222	4	Florida State
28	Jeffery, Tony	RB	5-11	208	2	Texas Christian
86	Jones, Ernie	WR	5-11	186	2	Indiana
59	Jones, Tyrone	LB	6-0	220	2	Southern University
32	Jordan, Tony	RB	6-0	220	2	Kansas State
57	Kauahi, Kani	C	6-2	273	7	Hawaii
70	Kennard, Derek	C-G	6-3	285	4	Nevada-Reno
52	Kirk, Randy	LB	6-2	235	3	San Diego State
15	Lomax, Neil	QB	6-3	215	9	Portland State
76	MacDonald, Mark	G-C	6-4	265	5	Boston College
47	Mack, Cedric	CB	6-0	194	7	Baylor
46	McDonald, Tim	CB-S	6-2	207	3	Southern California
51	McKenzie, Reggie	LB	6-1	235	5	Tennessee
95	McNanie, Sean	DE	6-5	270	7	San Diego State
25	Mitchell, Roland	CB	5-11	180	3	Texas Tech
30	Mitchell, Stump	RB	5-9	188	9	Citadel
57	Noga, Niko	DE	6-1	235	6	Hawaii
85	Novacek, Jay	TE	6-4	235	5	Wyoming
78	Nunn, Freddie Joe	DE	6-4	255	5	Mississippi
64	Peat, Todd	G	6-2	294	3	Northern Illinois
48	Phillips, Reggie	CB	5-10	175	5	Southern Methodist
12	Prindle, Michael	K	5-9	163	2	Western Michigan
63	Robbins, Tootie	T	6-5	302	8	East Carolina
72	Saddler, Rod	DE	6-5	276	3	Texas A&M
87	Schillinger, Andy	WR	5-11	179	2	Miami, Ohio
67	Sharpe, Luis	T	6-4	260	8	UCLA
36	Sikahema, Vai	RB-KR	5-9	191	4	Brigham Young
84	Smith, J.T.	WR	6-2	185	2	North Texas State
61	Smith, Lance	T-G	6-2	262	5	Louisiana State
19	Tupa, Tom	QB-P	6-4	220	2	Ohio State
89	Walczak, Mark	TE	6-6	246	3	Arizona
24	Wolfley, Ron	RB	6-0	222	5	West Virginia
43	Young, Lonnie	S	6-1	182	5	Michigan State
38	Zordich, Mike	S	5-11	207	3	Penn State

TOP DRAFT CHOICES

Rd.	Name	Sel. No.	Pos.	Ht.	Wt.	College
1	Hill, Eric	10	LB	6-1	250	LSU
1	Wolf, Joe	17	G	6-6	284	Boston College
2	Reeves, Walter	40	TE	6-3	250	Auburn
3	Zandofsky, Mike	67	G	6-2	300	Washington
4	Wahler, Jim	94	DT	6-4	265	UCLA

CARDINAL PROFILES

NEIL LOMAX 30 6-3 215   Quarterback

It isn't difficult to find the main reason for the Cardinals' collapse in 1988. Look no further than Nov. 13, when Lomax sprained a ligament in his left knee and was sidelined for two weeks...That injury, coupled with arthritic hip problems, left the quarterback less than 100 percent for the remainder of the season ...Finished the year completing 255 of 443 for 3,395 yards for 20 TDs with 11 interceptions...Was NFC Offensive Player of the Month for October and NFC Offensive Player of the Week after completing 28 of 43 passes for 342 yards and two TDs in Cards' 41-27 win over Rams Oct. 2...Was fourth-rated quarterback in NFC with 86.7 rating...Passing yardage was third-highest in NFC...Second-round draft pick in 1981 out of Portland State...Born Feb. 17, 1959, in Lake Oswego, Ore....Earned $1.5 million last year.

STUMP MICHELL 30 5-9 188   Running Back

Racked up his fourth straight season rushing for 700-plus yards, carrying 164 times for 726 yards and four TDs...Rushed for 110 yards against Cincinnati Sept. 4 and Tampa Bay Sept. 18...Owns the club's second-best career yards-per-carry average at 4.76...Is Cards' all-time leader in combined yardage with a total of 11,807 (4,484 rushing, 1,945 receiving, 1,377 punt returns, 4,001 kickoff returns)... Sidelined by ankle injury against Cleveland Oct. 23 and Dallas Oct. 31...Real name is Lyvonia Albert...Ninth-round draft choice out of the Citadel in 1981...Born March 15, 1959, in Kingsland, Ga....Earned $400,000 last year.

ROY GREEN 32 6-0 195   Wide Receiver

Playing and practicing on grass must have done wonders for Green, who took a big step in re-establishing his nickname "Jet Stream" ...Enjoyed his first injury-free season since Pro Bowl campaign of 1984...Caught 68 passes for 1,097 yards and seven TDs, his best numbers in four years...Had nine catches for 176 yards in 24-17 victory over the Giants Nov. 13. It was his best production in 46 games...Also had 119 yards receiving against Pittsburgh Oct. 9...Longest catch was

52-yarder against Washington Sept. 25 . . . In 1981, he was first player since 1957 to catch a TD pass and intercept a pass in the same game . . . Fourth-round draft choice out of Henderson State in 1979 . . . Born June 30, 1957, in Magnolia, Ark. . . . Earned $675,000 last year.

LUIS SHARPE 29 6-4 260   Tackle

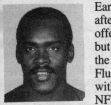

Earned second consecutive trip to Pro Bowl after helping Cardinals become fourth-rated offense in the NFL . . . Forte is pass protection, but is also a bulldozer on the run . . . One of the most quoted linemen in the league . . . Fluent in two languages, he does interviews with Spanish radio stations in a number of NFL cities . . . Moved with family from Havana, Cuba, to Detroit when he was six . . . First-round draft choice out of UCLA in 1982 . . . Went from St. Louis to Memphis Showboats of USFL in spring of 1985. Went back to Cardinals that fall . . . Born June 16, 1960, in Havana . . . Has a degree in political science . . . Earned $415,000 last year.

ROBERT AWALT 25 6-5 248   Tight End

No sophomore jinx here . . . Followed *Sporting News* NFL Rookie of the Year selection in 1987 with solid performance in 1988 . . . Was Cards' third-leading receiver, catching 39 passes for 454 yards and four TDs while splitting time with Jay Novacek (39, 569 yards, 4 TDs) . . . Had 52-yard touchdown reception at Houston Nov. 20 . . . Was a high-school quarterback in Sacramento and freshman quarterback at Nevada-Reno before transferring to San Diego State, where he was moved to tight end . . . Was a third-round draft choice . . . Born April 9, 1964, in Landsthul, West Germany . . . Earned $125,000 last year.

J.T. SMITH 33 6-2 185   Wide Receiver

Earned trip to Pro Bowl after 49ers' Jerry Rice bowed out with injury . . . Enjoyed banner season in 1988 . . . His 83 receptions were second only to his own club record of 91, set in 1987 . . . Has caught more passes (254) over the last three seasons than any other NFL player . . . Fell 14 yards short of third consecutive 1,000-yard season . . . Had 10 receptions for 114 yards against Houston Nov. 20...Caught nine passes for 90 yards at Philadelphia Nov. 27...Signed with Cards as free agent in 1985...Originally signed with Redskins as free agent in 1978. Was released after six games and signed with Chiefs... Played at North Texas State as wide receiver and kick-returner ...Born Oct. 29, 1955, in Leonard, Tex....Earned $450,000 last year.

TIM McDONALD 24 6-2 207   Strong Safety

A promising defensive back who showed glimpses of greatness in 1988...Spent all but the final four games of 1987 rookie season on injured reserve with a broken ankle, then stepped into starting lineup last year when Leonard Smith was traded to Buffalo...Went on to lead the team in tackles with 115 and forced fumbles (four)...His 101 solo tackles was 46 more than nearest teammate...Had seven or more tackles in nine games...Collected two interceptions and two sacks...A second-round pick from USC...Born Jan. 6, 1965, in Fresno, Cal....Earned $165,000 last year.

CARL CARTER 25 5-11 180   Cornerback

A young cornerback who struggled early in the year but stepped up intensity as season progressed...Starter for second straight year on left side...Had a team-high 15 passes defensed...Started all 16 games and was third on team with 60 tackles...Had three interceptions and two fumble recoveries...Has 150 tackles in three seasons...Fourth-round draft choice in 1986 out of Texas Tech...Set Texas Tech 100-meter track record with 10.12 timing, competing against such speedsters as Carl Lewis, Harvey Glance and Calvin Smith... Born March 7, 1964, in Fort Worth, Tex....Earned $105,000 last year.

NIKO NOGA 27 6-1 235   Middle Linebacker

Continues to be prolific tackler for Cardinals, despite his relative lack of size...Was second on the team with 62 tackles...Had one sack and forced one fumble...Has 314 stops in five-year NFL career...Eighth-round draft choice out of Hawaii in 1984...Paid dues on special teams as rookie before getting starting job midway through 1985 season...Had career-high 90 tackles in 1986...A four-year starter at Hawaii ...Born March 2, 1962, in American Samoa...Real name is Falaniko...Wife Poufa is professional singer who has recorded native island songs...Earned $275,000 last year...One of nine children.

VAI SIKAHEMA 27 5-9 191   Kick Returner

Could have become the first player ever to lead the NFL in punt-return yardage three consecutive seasons, but knee injury forced him to spend four weeks on the injured-reserve list ...Returned 33 punts for 341 yards, a 10.3 average that ranked him fourth in the NFC... Returned 23 kickoffs for 475 yards and 20.7 average...Voted to Pro Bowl in 1986 and 1987 after leading league in punt-return yardage...Is Cardinals' leader in career punt-return yardage with 1,413...A longshot to make the team after being a 10th-round draft choice out of Brigham Young in 1986...Served on Mormon mission in South Dakota in 1982-83 before returning to school in 1984...Born Aug. 29, 1962, in Nyku' Alofa, Tonga...Earned $175,000 last year.

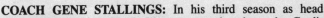

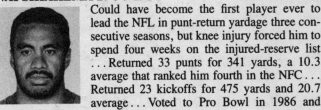

COACH GENE STALLINGS: In his third season as head coach, Stallings appeared to have the Cardinals in contention for a NFC East title after a 24-17 victory over the Giants on Nov. 13. That gave Cards a 7-4 record and share of division lead, but injuries to key players, including quarterback Neil Lomax, contributed to five straight losses to dissolve what had been a promising season...Is 18-28-1 in three seasons as head coach...A defensive-minded disciple of Tom Landry...An All-Southwest Conference receiver at Texas A&M...Began coaching as assistant at Alabama...Later became head coach at Texas A&M...Fired after 1971 season, then joined Cowboys as secondary coach...Replaced Jim Hanifan in 1986...Born March 2, 1935, in Paris, Tex.

GREATEST COACH

There have been many highs and lows during the Cardinals' 69-year history in the NFL. But certainly one of the bright spots came in the mid-70s when Don Coryell turned the Cardinals into one of the league's most exciting teams.

"Cardiac Cards" is the nickname the club carried during the 1974, '75, and '76 seasons, a period when heart-stopping finishes helped St. Louis win two NFC Eastern Division championships and compile a three-year regular-season record of 31-11.

It was in St. Louis where Air Coryell first took off as the pass-happy Cardinals captured the imagination of the NFL as they terrorized secondaries. After five years and a 42-27-1 record, Coryell left St. Louis in 1978 for San Diego.

INDIVIDUAL CARDINAL RECORDS

Rushing

Most Yards Game:	203	John David Crow, vs Pittsburgh, 1960	
Season:	1,605	Ottis Anderson, 1979	
Career:	7,999	Ottis Anderson, 1979-86	

Passing

Most TD Passes Game:	6	Jim Hardy, vs Baltimore, 1950
	6	Charley Johnson, vs Cleveland, 1965
	6	Charley Johnson, vs New Orleans, 1969
Season:	28	Charley Johnson, 1963
	28	Neil Lomax, 1984
Career:	205	Jim Hart, 1966-82

Receiving

Most TD Passes Game:	5	Bob Shaw, vs Baltimore, 1950
Season:	15	Sonny Randle, 1960
Career:	60	Sonny Randle, 1959-66

Scoring

Most Points Game:	40	Ernie Nevers, vs Chicago, 1929
Season:	117	Jim Bakken, 1967
	117	Neil O'Donoghue, 1984
Career:	1,380	Jim Bakken, 1962-78
Most TDs Game:	6	Ernie Nevers, vs Chicago, 1929
Season:	17	John David Crow, 1962
Career:	60	Sonny Randle, 1959-66

SAN FRANCISCO 49ERS

TEAM DIRECTORY: Owner/Pres.: Edward J. DeBartolo Jr.: Exec. VP Front Office/League Relations: Carmen Policy; Exec. VP Football Oper.: Bill Walsh; Dir. Publicity: Jerry Walker. Head Coach: George Seifert. Home field: Candlestick Park (61,499). Colors: 49er gold and scarlet.

SCOUTING REPORT

OFFENSE: Want to unnerve a defensive back? Then whisper the phrase "Montana to Rice." Montana as in Joe; Rice as in Jerry. Together they form the NFL's most exciting passing combination. Between them, they've shared the MVP award in three Super Bowls and numerous other awards that would satisfy most careers. But don't expect Rice or Montana to let up in 1989. Both are extremely competitive and will be looking to pad their Hall of Fame credentials.

Roger Craig's total yardage made him No. 1 in the NFL.

The remainder of the 49ers' offense should be as solid for new head coach George Seifert as it was last year for Bill Walsh. Roger Craig led the NFC in total yards with 2,036, and blocking fullback Tom Rathman handles his role well. John Taylor, recipient of the winning TD pass in Super Bowl XXIII, is a budding star for a team that went 10-6 in the regular season.

The lone question mark is at center, where Jesse Sapolu is the top candidate to replace Randy Cross, who retired after 13 seasons and three Super Bowl rings.

DEFENSE: The frightening thought for the rest of the NFL is the relative youth of the 49er defense. Rookie linemen Danny Stubbs and Pierce Holt had 14 sacks between them, including the playoffs. Bill Romanowski, another rookie, was the team's seventh-leading tackler and often started in place of the injured Keena Turner. Third-year linebacker Charles Haley led the club with 15 sacks and made the Pro Bowl. And the 49ers chose linebacker Keith DeLong as their No. 1 in the draft.

Cornerbacks Tim McKyer and Don Griffin also have just three years of experience, meaning the 49ers should field a tough defense for many years. The anchor of the unit is veteran nose tackle Michael Carter, the immovable force. Overshadowed by their offense, the 49er defense was the league's third-best last year and should be just as good this season.

KICKING GAME: Former free-agent Mike Cofer has found a home in the Bay Area after setting club records last year for field-goal attempts (38) and field-goals made (27). Punter Barry Helton probably won't be cut, as he was during training camp last year. He averaged 39.3 yards per punt, landing 22 inside the 20. Taylor, who made the Pro Bowl as a special-teams player, can break a game open with kick-return ability.

THE ROOKIES: Tennessee's DeLong is light (230 pounds) for an inside linebacker, but he's tough, smart and loaded with athletic skill. Tight end Wesley Walls, primarily an outside linebacker at Mississippi, needs to work on sharper pass routes, but has the size and stamina.

OUTLOOK: No team has won back-to-back Super Bowls since the 1979 Steelers, but who's to say the 49ers can't do it again? They've got the personnel, but they've also got to adjust to a new coach in his first NFL head-coaching assignment.

49ERS VETERAN ROSTER

HEAD COACH—George Seifert. Assistant Coaches—Jerry Attaway, Dennis Green, Mike Holmgren, Al Lavan, Sherman Lewis, John Marshall, Bobb McKittrick, Bill McPherson, Ray Rhodes, Lynn Stiles.

No.	Name	Pos.	Ht.	Wt.	NFL Exp.	College
79	Barton, Harris	T	6-4	280	3	North Carolina
65	Bregel, Jeff	G	6-4	280	3	Southern California
31	Brooks, Chet	CB	5-11	191	2	Texas A&M
95	Carter, Michael	NT	6-2	285	6	Southern Methodist
66	Cochran, Mark	T	6-5	285	2	Baylor
6	Cofer, Mike	K	6-1	190	2	North Carolina State
69	Collie, Bruce	G-T	6-6	275	5	Texas-Arlington
33	Craig, Roger	RB	6-0	224	7	Nebraska
25	Dubose, Doug	RB	5-11	190	2	Nebraska
50	Ellison, Riki	LB	6-2	225	7	Southern California
75	Fagan, Kevin	DE	6-3	260	3	Miami
55	Fahnhorst, Jim	LB	6-4	230	6	Minnesota
32	Flagler, Terrance	RB	6-0	200	3	Clemson
49	Fuller, Jeff	S	6-2	216	6	Texas A&M
83	Greer, Terry	WR	6-1	192	4	Alabama State
29	Griffin, Don	CB	6-0	176	4	Tenn. State
54	Hadley, Ron	LB	6-2	240	3	Washington
94	Haley, Charles	LB-DE	6-5	230	4	James Madison
9	Helton, Barry	P	6-3	205	2	Colorado
46	Holmoe, Tom	S	6-2	195	6	Brigham Young
78	Holt, Pierce	NT	6-4	280	2	Angelo State
84	Jones, Brent	TE	6-4	230	3	Santa Clara
57	Kennedy, Sam	LB	6-2	235	2	San Jose State
67	Kugler, Pete	DE	6-4	255	7	Penn State
42	Lott, Ronnie	S	6-0	200	9	Southern California
62	McIntyre, Guy	G	6-3	265	6	Georgia
22	McKyer, Tim	CB	6-0	174	3	Texas-Arlington
16	Montana, Joe	QB	6-2	195	11	Notre Dame
20	Nixon, Tory	CB	5-11	186	5	San Diego State
64	O'Connor, Paul	G	6-3	258	2	Miami
77	Paris, Bubba	T	6-6	306	6	Michigan
15	Paye, John	QB	6-3	205	2	Stanford
26	Pollard, Darryl	CB	5-11	187	3	Weber State
44	Rathman, Tom	RB	6-1	232	4	Nebraska
80	Rice, Jerry	WR	6-2	200	5	Miss. Valley State
91	Roberts, Larry	DE	6-3	275	4	Alabama
35	Rogers, Del	RB	5-10	203	5	Utah
53	Romonowski, Bill	LB	6-4	231	2	Boston College
61	Sapolu, Jessie	G-C	6-4	260	4	Hawaii
88	Sherrard, Mike	WR	6-2	187	2	UCLA
72	Stover, Jeff	DE	6-5	275	8	Oregon
96	Stubbs, Daniel	DE	6-4	260	2	Miami
24	Sydney, Harry	RB	6-0	217	3	Kansas
10	Sweeney, Kevin	QB	6-0	193	3	Fresno State
66	Tausch, Terry	G	6-4	278	8	Texas
82	Taylor, John	WR	6-1	185	3	Delaware State
60	Thomas, Chuck	C	6-3	280	4	Oklahoma
23	Tillman, Spencer	RB	5-11	206	3	Oklahoma
58	Turner, Keena	LB	6-2	222	10	Purdue
74	Wallace, Steve	T	6-5	276	4	Auburn
99	Walter, Michael	LB	6-3	238	7	Oregon
51	Washington, Chris	LB	6-4	240	7	Iowa State
81	Williams, Jamie	TE	6-4	245	7	Nebraska
85	Wilson, Mike	WR	6-3	215	9	Washington State
21	Wright, Eric	CB	6-1	185	8	Missouri
8	Young, Steve	QB	6-2	200	5	Brigham Young

TOP DRAFT CHOICES

Rd.	Name	Sel. No.	Pos.	Ht.	Wt.	College
1	DeLong, Keith	28	DE	6-4	230	Tennessee
2	Walls, Wesley	56	TE	6-5	245	Mississippi
3	Henderson, Keith	84	RB	6-2	202	Georgia
4	Barber, Mike	112	WR	5-10	170	Marshall
5	Jackson, Johnny	122	DB	6-1	200	Houston

49ER PROFILES

JERRY RICE 26 6-2 200   Wide Receiver

Played key role in 49ers' climb to Super Bowl with splendid postseason... Caught 21 passes for 409 yards and six TDs in three playoff games... Was MVP of Super Bowl XXIII, in which he caught 11 passes for record 215 yards and one TD... Was league MVP in 1987... Was second in NFL receiving yards in 1988 with 1,306... Average-per-catch of 20.4 yards was tops among NFC receivers... Voted to third consecutive Pro Bowl, but did not play because of injury... Had nine TDs during regular season after posting 22 in 1987... First-round draft choice (16th overall) in 1985... Totaled 4,693 yards and set 18 NCAA Division 1-AA records during four years at Mississippi Valley State... 1988 salary: $950,000... Born Oct. 13, 1962, in Starkville, Miss.

JOE MONTANA 33 6-1 195   Quarterback

Enhanced his legendary status by leading 49ers to winning touchdown drive in closing seconds of Super Bowl XXIII... Ten-yard touchdown pass to John Taylor with 34 seconds left sealed 20-16 win... Survived mid-season quarterback controversy with Steve Young... MVP of Super Bowls XVI and XIX... Passed for 2,981 yards and 18 touchdowns during 1988 regular season... QB rating of 87.9 was third highest in NFC... Had rating of 117.0 during playoffs, throwing for 823 yards and eight touchdowns... Completed longest play from scrimmage in team history, connecting with Jerry Rice on 96-yard touchdown pass at San Diego Nov. 27... 1988 salary: $1,100,000... Born June 11, 1956, in New Eagle, Pa.

ROGER CRAIG 29 6-0 224   Running Back

Earned NFC Offensive Player of the Year honors after rushing for 1,502 yards during regular season... Caught a team-high 76 passes for 534 yards... Is 49ers' all-time leader in total yards (rushing, receiving) with 9,339 over six seasons... Voted to second straight Pro Bowl and third overall... Made postseason NFL-record 80-yard run against

Vikings Jan. 1, highlighting 135-yard rushing day . . . Gained 430 (260 rushing) all-purpose yards during playoffs, with two TDs . . . Only player in NFL history to surpass 1,000 yards rushing and 1,000 receiving in a single season (1985) . . . Second-round draft choice out of Nebraska in 1983 . . . 1988 salary: $600,000 . . . Born July 10, 1960, in Preston, Miss.

MICHAEL CARTER 28 6-2 285   Nose Tackle

Strong, aggressive and agile . . . Not many centers can contain him . . . Had career-high 71 tackles and 6½ sacks in regular season . . . Also credited with nine passes defensed, including one interception . . . Voted to second consecutive Pro Bowl and third overall . . . Silver medalist in shot-put in 1984 Olympics . . . Holds Texas high-school record for discus throw (204 feet, 8 inches) . . . Born Oct. 29, 1960, in Dallas . . . Roomed with Indianapolis Colts running back Eric Dickerson during collegiate days at Southern Methodist . . . Received degree in sociology . . . 1988 salary: $450,000.

RONNIE LOTT 30 6-0 200   Free Safety

Acknowledged as one of the hardest hitters ever to play defensive back in the NFL . . . Sets standard for intensity and desire . . . Earned third straight trip to Pro Bowl and seventh overall . . . Posted 74 tackles and five interceptions during regular season . . . Ranks second on club's all-time list with 43 interceptions . . . Had two interceptions in playoff win over Vikings . . . Selected out of USC in first round (8th overall) of 1981 draft . . . Born May 8, 1959, in Albuquerque, N.M. . . . Earned degree in public administration . . . Co-owner of restaurant in Cupertino, Cal. . . . 1988 salary: $842,500.

CHARLES HALEY 25 6-5 230   Linebacker

Budding superstar . . . Moved from left defensive end to linebacker and earned first trip to Pro Bowl after posting 11½ sacks to lead 49ers and tie for seventh in the NFC . . . Skilled at applying pressure on quarterbacks . . . Has 29½ sacks in three pro seasons . . . Was NFC Defensive Player of the Month for October . . . Was surprise of 1986 draft as fourth-round selection... Had 12 sacks as a rookie... Posted 506 tackles during four-year career at James Madison, where he played inside and outside linebacker... Never missed a collegiate game... Was football, basketball and track star in high school... Born Jan. 6, 1964, in Gladys, Va.... 1988 salary: $100,000.

TOM RATHMAN 26 6-1 232   Fullback

Like Roger Craig, a Nebraska product... Good blocker with bruising style... Opens holes for Craig, but also can grind out tough yardage on his own... Rushed for 427 yards and two touchdowns during regular season... Had 382 receiving yards... Established career high with 79 yards rushing on 15 attempts at Seattle Sept. 25... Gained 88 yards and scored one TD during playoffs... First of three 49er third-round draft picks in 1986... Born Oct. 7, 1962, in Grand Island, Neb.... Was backup to Craig during first season at Nebraska... 1988 salary: $175,000.

MICHAEL WALTER 28 6-3 238   Linebacker

An underrated player who just keeps getting better... Claimed off waivers from Dallas in 1984, he has developed into one of the NFC's top inside backers... Led team in tackles for second straight season... Had 97 stops, 60 solo... Had good postseason with 10 tackles against Vikings and 11 against Bears... Was selected in second round of 1983 draft by Cowboys, but released a year later... Earned telecommunications degree at Oregon... Born Nov. 3, 1960, in Eugene, Ore.... Went to same high school as Raiders' Todd Christensen and Falcons' Chris Miller... 1988 salary: $275,000.

TIM McKYER 25 6-0 174   Cornerback

Most vocal member of squad... Will often speak his mind even if it belittles opponents... Guaranteed 49ers' victory in Super Bowl XXIII... Backed up prediction by sharing team lead in tackles with six... Has been a starter for all three years of his pro career... Led team with seven interceptions and 19 passes defensed... Collected 39 tackles...

Was angry at not being voted to Pro Bowl . . . Second of three third-round 49er selections in 1986 draft . . . Extremely quick . . . Last player drafted out of Texas-Arlington before school closed football program . . . Born Sept. 5, 1963, in Orlando, Fla. . . . 1988 salary: $363,000.

JOHN TAYLOR 27 6-1 185   Wide Receiver

Caught winning 10-yard TD pass from Joe Montana with 34 seconds left in Super Bowl XXIII . . . It was his only reception of the day . . . Rebounded from four-week drug suspension at beginning of the season to earn first trip to the Pro Bowl as kick-return specialist . . . Led 49ers with 23.2 average-per-catch . . . Led NFL in punt-return yardage (556) and average yards-per-return (12.6) . . . Had team-record 95-yard punt return for touchdown against Redskins Nov. 21 . . . Born March 31, 1962, in Pennsauken, N.J. . . . Was third of three 49er third-round draft choices in 1986 out of Delaware State . . . An avid bowler . . . 1988 salary: $155,000.

COACH GEORGE SEIFERT: Named 49ers' head coach when

Bill Walsh announced his retirement four days after Super Bowl XXIII . . . He got the word when he was on a flight to Cleveland to be interviewed for the Browns' head coaching vacancy . . . A highly respected defensive specialist, he was an assistant 49er coach under Walsh for nine seasons, coach of the secondary for the first three before becoming defensive coordinator . . . His 1987 defensive unit led the league in fewest total yards allowed . . . Coached for 15 years in collegiate ranks . . . Only previous head coaching posts were at Westminster College in Salt Lake City and at Cornell, where he was 1-8 in 1975 and 2-7 in 1976 . . . Had two stints under Walsh at Stanford . . . Born Jan. 22, 1940, in San Francisco . . . Played end and guard at Utah, and graduated in 1963 with a degree in zoology.

Tennessee LB Keith DeLong was 49ers' first-rounder.

GREATEST COACH

If the 49ers are the team of the 80s, then certainly Bill Walsh is the coach of the 80s. In his 10 years as head coach, Walsh used his offensive creativity and philosophical powers of motivation to lead a once-struggling franchise to victories in Super Bowls XVI, XIX and XXIII.

Also included were six NFC Western Division titles and an overall won-lost record of 102-63-1, including a 10-4 playoff mark. Last January, four days after the 49ers beat the Bengals in Super Bowl XXIII, the 57-year-old Walsh announced his retirement from coaching.

INDIVIDUAL 49ER RECORDS
Rushing

Most Yards Game:	194	Delvin Williams, vs St. Louis, 1976
Season:	1,502	Roger Craig, 1988
Career:	7,344	Joe Perry, 1948-60, 1963

Passing

Most TD Passes Game:	5	Frank Albert, vs Cleveland (AAC), 1949
	5	John Brodie, vs Minnesota, 1965
	5	Steve Spurrier, vs Chicago, 1972
	5	Joe Montana, vs Atlanta, 1985
Season:	31	Joe Montana, 1987
Career:	214	John Brodie, 1957-73

Receiving

Most TD Passes Game:	3	Alyn Beals, vs Brooklyn (AAC), 1948
	3	Alyn Beals, vs Chicago (AAC), 1949
	3	Gordy Soltau, vs Los Angeles, 1951
	3	Bernie Casey, vs Minnesota, 1962
	3	Dave Parks, vs Baltimore, 1965
	3	Gene Washington, vs San Diego, 1972
	3	Jerry Rice, vs Indianapolis, 1986
	3	Jerry Rice, vs St. Louis, 1986
	3	Jerry Rice, vs Tampa Bay, 1987
	3	Jerry Rice, vs Cleveland, 1987
	3	Jerry Rice, vs Chicago, 1987
	3	Jerry Rice, vs Tampa, 1988
	3	Jerry Rice, vs Minnesota, 1988
Season:	22	Jerry Rice, 1987
Career:	59	Gene Washington, 1969-76

Scoring

Most Points Game:	26	Gordy Soltau, vs Los Angeles, 1951
Season:	138	Jerry Rice, 1987
Career:	896	Ray Wersching, 1977-86
Most TDs Game:	4	Bill Kilmer, vs Minnesota, 1961
Season:	23	Jerry Rice, 1987
Career:	61	Ken Willard, 1965-73

TAMPA BAY BUCCANEERS

TEAM DIRECTORY: Owner-Pres.: Hugh Culverhouse; VP: Joy Culverhouse; VP-Head Coach: Ray Perkins; VP-Community Rel.: Dr. Gay Culverhouse; VP-Adm.: William Klein; Asst. to Pres.: Phil Krueger; Dir. Player Personnel: Jerry Angelo; Dir. Pub. Rel.: Rick Odioso; Home field: Tampa Stadium (74,317). Colors: Florida orange, white and red.

SCOUTING REPORT

OFFENSE: Vinny Testaverde hasn't set the world on fire in his first two years in the NFL, but few young quarterbacks have. He still possesses the necessary skills to be a top quarterback.

A great help would be the emergence of a running game. The Bucs averaged just 110 yards rushing per game last year, but are hoping for better things from second-year men William Howard and Lars Tate and veteran back James Wilder.

When the passing game is effective, wideouts Bruce Hill and Mike Carrier can produce. They combined for 2,000 yards last year, but neither will dominate a game. The offensive line should start to solidify now that all the pieces are in place, especially at left tackle, where Paul Gruber had a fine rookie year.

DEFENSE: The Bucs were outstanding against the run, leading the NFL in fewest yards allowed per rush at 3.2 and finishing second in total yards allowed. A key newcomer was ninth-round draft choice Reuben Davis, who became a force at left defensive end.

The pass rush is a major weakness; the Bucs produced an NFC-low 20 sacks. Starting outside linebackers Kevin Murphy and Winston Moss combined for just one sack. Seven of the eight linebackers on the final 1988 roster had been in the league less than five years. They'll welcome instant input from linebacker Broderick Thomas, No. 6 overall in the '89 draft.

Safeties Mark Robinson and Harry Hamilton provide good leadership in the secondary, although both will be pushed by Odie Harris. Ricky Reynolds is solid at left cornerback, while Rod Jones and Bobby Futrell will battle for the starting job on the right side.

KICKING GAME: Reserve cornerback Donnie Elder averaged 23.0 yards as the primary kickoff-return man. Placekicker Donald Igwebuike can convert from 50 yards and out, but punter Ray

Donnie Elder's kickoff returns justified free-agent signing.

Criswell averaged just 36.1 yards and will have to battle to keep his job.

THE ROOKIES: Nebraska's Thomas could be the answer to the Bucs' pass-rush problems. He'll be tried at right outside linebacker, where he'll rush from the quarterback's blind side. North

BUCCANEERS VETERAN ROSTER

HEAD COACH—Ray Perkins. Assistant Coaches—John Bobo, Louis Campbell, Sylvester Croom, Mike DuBose, Doug Graber, Kent Johnston, Joe Kines, Mike Shula, Rodney Stokes, Richard Williamson.

No.	Name	Pos.	Ht.	Wt.	NFL Exp.	College
45	Anno, Sam	LB	6-2	230	3	Southern California
11	Bell, Kerwin	QB	6-3	205	2	Florida
69	Bruhin, John	G	6-3	280	2	Tennessee
78	Cannon, John	DE	6-5	260	8	William & Mary
4	Carney, John	K	5-11	160	2	Notre Dame
88	Carrier, Mark	WR	6-0	182	3	Nicholls State
21	Cocroft, Sherman	CB-S	6-1	190	5	San Jose State
53	Coleman, Sidney	LB	6-2	250	2	Southern Mississippi
71	Cooper, Mark	T	6-5	280	7	Miami
13	Criswell, Ray	P	6-0	195	3	Florida
79	Davis, Reuben	DE	6-4	290	2	North Carolina
87	Drewrey, Willie	WR	5-7	165	5	West Virginia
40	Elder, Donnie	CB-S	5-9	175	5	Memphis State
12	Ferguson, Joe	QB	6-1	190	17	Arkansas
36	Futrell, Bobby	CB-S	5-11	190	4	Elizabeth City State
44	Gladman, Charles	RB	5-11	205	2	Pittsburgh
94	Goff, Robert	DE	6-3	270	2	Auburn
60	Grimes, Randy	C	6-4	275	7	Baylor
74	Gruber, Paul	T	6-5	290	2	Wisconsin
82	Hall, Ron	TE	6-4	245	3	Hawaii
39	Hamilton, Harry	CB-S	6-0	195	6	Penn State
20	Harris, Odie	CB-S	6-0	190	2	Sam Houston State
84	Hill, Bruce	WR	6-0	180	3	Arizona State
90	Holmes, Ron	DE	6-4	265	5	Washington
43	Howard, William	RB	6-0	240	2	Tennessee
1	Igwebuike, Donald	K	5-9	185	5	Clemson
95	Jarvis, Curt	NT	6-2	265	2	Alabama
45	Johnson, Sidney	CB-S	5-9	175	2	California
22	Jones, Rod	CB-S	6-0	185	4	Southern Methodist
75	Kellin, Kevin	DE	6-5	270	4	Minnesota
97	Lee, Shawn	NT	6-2	290	2	North Alabama
68	Mallory, Rick	G	6-2	265	5	Washington
99	Marve, Eugene	LB	6-2	240	8	Saginaw Valley State
73	McHale, Tom	G	6-4	275	3	Cornell
58	Moss, Winston	LB	6-3	235	3	Miami
59	Murphy, Kevin	LB	6-2	235	4	Oklahoma
57	Najarian, Pete	LB	6-2	230	2	Minnesota
85	Parks, Jeff	TE	6-4	240	4	Auburn
80	Pillow, Frank	WR	5-10	170	2	Tennessee State
54	Randle, Ervin	LB	6-1	250	5	Baylor
29	Reynolds, Ricky	CB-S	5-11	190	3	Washington State
30	Robinson, Mark	CB-S	5-11	200	6	Penn State
55	Rolling, Henry	LB	6-2	225	2	Nevada-Reno
47	Smith, Don	RB-WR	5-11	195	2	Mississippi State
35	Smith, Jeff	FB	5-9	205	5	Nebraska
93	Smith, Robert	DE	6-7	270	2	Grambling
24	Stamps, Sylvester	RB	5-7	185	5	Jackson State
70	Swayne, Harry	DE	6-5	270	3	Rutgers
34	Tate, Lars	RB	6-2	215	2	Georgia
72	Taylor, Rob	T	6-6	295	4	Northwestern
14	Testaverde, Vinny	QB	6-5	218	3	Miami
64	Thomas, Kevin	C	6-2	265	2	Arizona State
50	Turk, Dan	G	6-4	260	4	Wisconsin
33	Valentine, Ira	RB	6-1	220	2	Texas A&M
32	Wilder, James	FB	6-3	225	9	Missouri
46	Wonsley, Nathan	FB	5-9	185	2	Mississippi

TOP DRAFT CHOICES

Rd.	Name	Sel. No.	Pos.	Ht.	Wt.	College
1	Thomas, Broderick	6	LB	6-2	250	Nebraska
2	Peebles, Danny	33	WR	5-11	170	N.C. State
4	Florence, Anthony	90	DB	5-11	185	Bethune-Cookman
5	Lawson, Jamie	117	RB	5-10	250	Nicholls State
6	Mohr, Chris	146	P	6-4	215	Alabama

Carolina State wide receiver Danny Peebles is a sprinter and long-jumper who can get deep in a hurry.

OUTLOOK: The Bucs, thanks to excellent drafts in 1987 and 1988, are moving closer to respectability. If Testaverde matures and the running game produces more than token yardage, Tampa Bay could push for a .500 season, although their non-division foes include San Francisco, New Orleans, Washington, Cincinnati, Houston and Cleveland.

BUCCANEER PROFILES

VINNY TESTAVERDE 25 6-5 218   Quarterback

His second year in the NFL proved to be a difficult learning experience... Threw an NFL-high 35 interceptions; Dan Marino was second with 23... Quarterback rating of 48.8 was lowest among those with 200-or-more pass attempts... Was sacked 33 times... Became undisputed starter when Steve DeBerg was traded to Kansas City during offseason ...Completed just 47.6 percent of his passes (222 of 466) for 3,240 yards and 13 TDs... Had NFC's high passing-yardage game, completing 25 of 42 for 469 yards against Colts Oct. 16 ... Gained 138 yards on 28 carries and scored one TD... Heisman Trophy winner in 1986 out of Miami and first player selected in 1987 draft... Led Hurricanes to 11-0 regular-season mark in 1986... Born Nov. 13, 1963, in Brooklyn, N.Y.... Although a right-hander, he writes lefty... Earned $966,000 last year.

BRUCE HILL 25 6-0 180   Wide Receiver

Established himself as a capable receiver in his second season... Led the team in receptions (58), receiving yardage (1,040), average per catch (17.9) and TD receptions (nine)... Was NFC's seventh-leading receiver... Had one TD catch of 42 yards... Was a fourth-round draft choice in 1987... Spent first seven weeks of rookie season on injured reserve with strained knee ligaments... Showed promise by totaling 329 reception yards during a four-game stretch... A product of

Arizona State, where he spent first two seasons at cornerback ... Born Feb. 29, 1964, in Fort Dix, N.J. ... Worked in law firm during offseason ... Earned $110,000 last year.

MARK CARRIER 23 6-0 182   Wide Receiver

Another cog in Bucs' potent, young passing attack ... Like Bruce Hill, Carrier displayed big-play qualities, catching 57 passes for 970 yards and five TDs ... Averaged 17 yards per catch and had a 59-yard TD catch ... Has speed and the ability to catch the ball over the middle ... Caught 26 passes for 423 yards in rookie season, including 212 yards against Saints ... A third-round draft pick in 1987 out of Nicholls State ... Was school's all-time leading receiver with 132 catches for 2,407 yards. Was also punt- and kickoff-return specialist ... Born Oct. 28, 1965, in Lafayette, La. ... Earned $155,000 last year.

PAUL GRUBER 24 6-5 290   Tackle

Bucs showed faith and wallet by awarding him a five-year contract worth $3.8 million, an unprecedented amount for a rookie lineman ... He responded with a sensational season ... A starter in all 16 games at tackle ... Consensus All-Rookie selection ... A key reason Bucs went from the league's 21st-best rushing team in 1987 to second-best last season ... Was the first offensive lineman chosen in 1988 draft, fourth pick overall ... Was a first-team All-American as a senior at Wisconsin ... Started 32 of 33 games during his collegiate career ... Born Feb. 24, 1965, in Madison, Wis. ... Hobbies include deer- and bird-hunting ... Earned $1,550,000 last year.

LARS TATE 23 6-2 215   Running Back

A talented back with good size and speed ... Should develop into the type of rushing threat Bucs need to take pressure off Testaverde ... As a rookie last season, he led team with 467 yards on 122 carries ... Scored seven rushing TDs ... Had average-per-carry of 3.8 yards ... Caught five passes for 23 yards and one TD ... Second-round draft pick. Bucs got him after draft-day trades with Philadelphia and San Francisco... Was second-leading rusher in University of Georgia history (3,017 yards, behind only Herschel Walker)... In 1986, he became the first player in Bulldog history to lead team in rushing (954 yards), receiving (22 catches) and scoring (102 points) in a single season... Born Feb. 2, 1966, in Indianapolis... Earned $360,000 last year.

HARRY HAMILTON 26 6-0 195   Safety

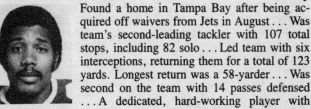

Found a home in Tampa Bay after being acquired off waivers from Jets in August... Was team's second-leading tackler with 107 total stops, including 82 solo... Led team with six interceptions, returning them for a total of 123 yards. Longest return was a 58-yarder... Was second on the team with 14 passes defensed ... A dedicated, hard-working player with good leadership qualities... An excellent tackler... Originally a seventh-round draft choice of Jets in 1984... Started 34 of 46 games with Jets... Has pre-law degree from Penn State... Father Stan was writer for "Sesame Street"... Born Nov. 29, 1962, in Jamaica, N.Y.... Earned $250,000 last year.

DONALD IGWEBUIKE 28 5-9 185   Kicker

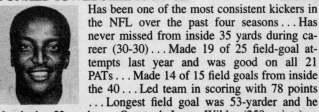

Has been one of the most consistent kickers in the NFL over the past four seasons... Has never missed from inside 35 yards during career (30-30)... Made 19 of 25 field-goal attempts last year and was good on all 21 PATs... Made 14 of 15 field goals from inside the 40... Led team in scoring with 78 points ... Longest field goal was 53-yarder and he also had a 52-yarder... Overtook James Wilder (258 points) as Bucs' all-time career scoring with 317 points... Has made 72 of 99 career field goals and 101 of 119 PATs... Taken in 10th round of 1985 draft out of Clemson... Holds school record of five field goals over 50 yards... Only Tiger to play on two nationally-ranked teams (football and soccer) in same year (1981) ... Has degree in economics... Born Dec. 27, 1960, in Anambra, Nigeria... Name is pronounced Ig-way-BWEE-kay ... Teammates call him Iggy... Earned $176,000 last season.

EUGENE MARVE 29 6-2 240   Linebacker

Acquired June 13, 1988, from Buffalo for bargain price of an eighth-round draft choice in 1989 . . . Made immediate impact in first season with Bucs . . . Led team in tackles with 121, a team-high 88 of which were solo . . . Had 1½ sacks and 10 tackles for losses . . . Intercepted one pass and recovered one fumble . . . Blocked a field goal against Green Bay Sept. 18 . . . Started 74 of 76 appearances at inside linebacker during six-year career with Buffalo . . . Led Bills in tackles three times (1983, '84, and '86) . . . A third-round draft choice by Bills in 1982 out of Saginaw (Mich.) Valley State . . . First player in school's history to be named All-America . . . Has degree in criminal justice . . . Born Aug. 14, 1960, in Flint, Mich. . . . Earned $340,000 last year.

DONNIE ELDER 25 5-9 175   Cornerback

One of the pleasant success stories of the Bucs' 1988 season . . . Made team as free agent and became NFL's top kickoff-return man . . . Handled 34 kickoffs for 772 yards, including a 51-yarder . . . Average of 22.7 yards-per-return was highest in the NFL . . . Was third on the team with three interceptions . . . Defensed six passes . . . Totaled 26 tackles, 25 solo . . . Originally a third-round draft choice of Jets in 1985 . . . Played one season in New York before being waived . . . Signed and waived by Pittsburgh in 1986 . . . Spent 1987 with Detroit . . . Teamed with Buffalo's Derrick Burroughs at Memphis State, giving Tigers top cornerback duo . . . Born Dec. 13, 1963, in Chattanooga, Tenn. . . . Earned $75,000 last year.

RAY CRISWELL 26 6-0 195   Punter

Spent his first full season in the NFL after bouncing around for two years . . . Won job in training camp and was the Bucs' punter . . . Averaged 36.4 yards on 68 punts . . . Landed 20 kicks inside the 20 . . . Longest punt was 62-yarder . . . Drafted by Philadelphia in fifth round in 1986 and later waived by the Eagles during the preseason . . . Signed as a free agent with the Raiders in 1987 and subsequently was waived during preseason . . . Signed with Tampa Bay and punted during the replacement games, but was waived when strike ended . . . Resigned during offseason . . . Originally a fifth-round draft choice of the Eagles in 1986 out of University of Florida . . . Only punter in Florida history to lead Gators in punting four straight seasons (1982-85) . . . Coached in high school by his father Wink . . . Born Aug. 16, 1963, in Lake City, Fla.

COACH RAY PERKINS: This could be the year that the Perkins touch pushes the Bucs toward a winning season . . . With young players like Testaverde maturing at key positions, the Bucs could become a respectable contender in 1989. "We have the nucleus in place," Perkins said. "We have some work to do, but I feel we are on the verge of being able to win on a consistent basis." . . . So far, it's been two tough seasons, 4-11 in 1987 and 5-11 last year . . . Was All-American receiver at Alabama . . . Played five seasons with Colts . . . Started coaching in 1973 as an assistant at Mississippi State before moving to Patriots in 1974 . . . Joined Chargers in 1978 before being named the Giants' head coach in 1979, taking team to playoffs in 1981 . . . Left two years later to succeed Bear Bryant at Alabama . . . Named Bucs' head coach on Dec. 31, 1986 . . . Born Nov. 6, 1941, in Mount Olive, Miss.

GREATEST COACH

When you contrast John McKay's NFL coaching career with that of his collegiate reign, it's a story of extremes. McKay won four national championships while at the University of Southern California, where he had a 127-40-8 record. He was 44-88-1 in nine seasons at Tampa Bay.

The Bucs won just seven of their first 44 games during their first three seasons, including an 0-14 mark in 1976, the inaugural campaign. But in 1979, McKay achieved the coaching feat of the decade when he guided the Bucs to the NFC Central Division title and a berth in the NFC championship game. And they were first again in their division in 1981. These were the high points of McKay's tenure.

His successor in 1985, Leeman Bennett, lasted through two sad seasons and, since 1987, it has been the goal of Ray Perkins, the third coach in Buc history, to give the franchise a rare touch of glory.

INDIVIDUAL BUCCANEER RECORDS

Rushing

Most Yards Game:	219	James Wilder, vs Minnesota, 1983	
Season:	1,544	James Wilder, 1984	
Career:	5,713	James Wilder, 1981-88	

Passing

Most TD Passes Game:	5	Steve DeBerg, vs Atlanta, 1987
Season:	20	Doug Williams, 1980
Career:	73	Doug Williams, 1978-82

Receiving

Most TD Passes Game:	4	Jimmie Giles, vs Miami, 1985
Season:	9	Kevin House, 1981
	9	Bruce Hill, 1988
Career:	34	Jimmie Giles, 1978-86

Scoring

Most Points Game:	24	Jimmie Giles, vs Miami, 1985
Season:	96	Donald Igwebuike, 1985
Career:	317	Donald Igwebuike, 1985-88
Most TDs Game:	4	Jimmie Giles, vs Miami, 1985
Season:	13	James Wilder, 1984
Career:	43	James Wilder, 1981-88

WASHINGTON REDSKINS

TEAM DIRECTORY: Chairman: Jack Kent Cooke; Exec. VP: John Kent Cooke; GM: Charlie Casserly; Dir. Player Personnel: Dick Daniels; VP-Communications: Charlie Dayton; Dir. Information: John Konoza; Dir. Pub. Rel.: Marty Hurney; Head Coach: Joe Gibbs. Home field: Robert F. Kennedy Stadium (55,750). Colors: Burgundy and gold.

SCOUTING REPORT

OFFENSE: The Redskins' rushing game, the backbone to three Super Bowl appearances in the 1980s, never got on track last year. The Skins (7-9) finished the year ranked 25th, producing just 96.4 rushing yards per game.

Super Bowl XXII star Timmy Smith was a bust and has moved on to San Diego. Kelvin Bryant is capable, but can't

Wilber Marshall looks forward to second year as a Redskin.

avoid injury. Jamie Morris provided some productive moments, but his lack of size hurts his chances of holding up through a 16-game schedule in a one-back offense. Offseason additions Earnest Byner and Gerald Riggs can only help.

With the ground game stalled, the Redskins' passing game emerged into one of the league's best. Doug Williams and Mark Rypien will likely split time at quarterback. Both don't mind going deep to Art Monk, Ricky Sanders or Gary Clark. The offensive line was in constant transition last year and should stabilize.

DEFENSE: Charles Mann and Dexter Manley are the best pair of pass-rushing defensive ends in football, but both had their problems. Mann was hindered by leg injuries and Manley was suspended during training camp for violating the league's substance-abuse policy. With Dave Butz retired, nine-year veteran Darryl Grant remains to plug the middle.

The secondary was plagued by injuries to Brian Davis, Darrell Green, Barry Wilburn and Johnny Thomas. Green wanted to be traded during the offseason.

Wilber Marshall was less than spectacular in his first season in D.C. and will likely blitz more this year to make his presence felt. The rest of the linebacking corps will be revamped.

KICKING GAME: Placekicker Chip Lohmiller missed an extra-point and late field goal in a one-point loss to the Giants early in the year, but he rallied later in the season and converted 10 straight field goals up to the final week. Punter Greg Horne, a free agent acquired from the Cardinals, will compete with Tom Barnhardt and Greg Coleman.

THE ROOKIES: Tracy Rocker, a defensive tackle from Auburn, could be the successor to Butz. Rocker's work habits have been questioned, but Skins couldn't overlook his production during stellar collegiate career. Fourth-round quarterback Jeff Graham from Long Beach State is a pocket passer with a strong arm. He could be a long-range project.

OUTLOOK: The Redskins lost their season-opener to the Giants and never came close to defending their Super Bowl XXII title. But there's plenty of talent on this team and with the genius of coach Joe Gibbs (and despite the departure of esteemed GM Bobby Beathard), the Redskins should bounce back and contend for a playoff berth.

REDSKINS VETERAN ROSTER

HEAD COACH—Joe Gibbs. Assistant Coaches—Don Breaux, Joe Bugel, Jack Burns, Bobby De Paul, Larry Peccatiello, Richie Petitbon, Frank Raines, Dan Riley, Wayne Sevier, Warren Simmons, Charley Taylor, Emmitt Thomas, LaVern Torgeson.

No.	Name	Pos.	Ht.	Wt.	NFL Exp.	College
14	Barnhardt, Tom	P	6-3	205	3	North Carolina
80	Beals, Shawn	WR-KR	5-10	178	2	Idaho State
69	Benish, Dan	DT	6-5	275	6	Clemson
53	Bostic, Jeff	C	6-2	260	10	Clemson
23	Bowles, Todd	S	6-2	203	4	Temple
29	Branch, Reggie	RB	5-11	235	4	East Carolina
67	Brown, Ray	G-T	6-5	280	4	Arkansas State
24	Bryant, Kelvin	RB	6-2	195	4	North Carolina
21	Byner, Earnest	RB	5-10	215	6	East Carolina
50	Caldwell, Ravin	LB	6-3	229	3	Arkansas
84	Clark, Gary	WR	5-9	173	5	James Madison
51	Coleman, Monte	LB	6-2	230	11	Central Arkansas
34	Davis, Brian	CB	6-2	190	3	Nebraska
36	Dillahunt, Ellis	S	5-11	190	2	East Carolina
92	Elam, Onzy	LB	6-2	225	3	Tennessee State
54	Gouveia, Kurt	LB	6-1	227	3	Brigham Young
57	Graham, Don	LB	6-2	244	2	Penn State
77	Grant, Darryl	DT	6-1	275	9	Rice
28	Green, Darrell	CB	5-8	170	7	Texas A&I
68	Grimm, Russ	G	6-3	275	9	Pittsburgh
78	Hamel, Dean	DT	6-3	280	5	Tulsa
59	Harbour, Dave	C	6-4	265	2	Illinois
62	Hitchcock, Ray	C	6-3	289	2	Minnesota
4	Horne, Greg	P	6-0	188	3	Arkansas
66	Jacoby, Joe	T	6-7	305	9	Louisville
55	Kaufman, Mel	LB	6-2	230	8	Cal Poly-SLO
74	Koch, Markus	DE	6-5	275	4	Boise State
79	Lachey, Jim	T	6-6	290	5	Ohio State
8	Lohmiller, Chip	K	6-3	213	2	Minnesota
41	Mandeville, Chris	S	6-1	213	3	Calif.-Davis
72	Manley, Dexter	DE	6-3	257	9	Oklahoma State
71	Mann, Charles	DE	6-6	270	7	Nevada-Reno
91	Manusky, Greg	LB	6-1	242	2	Colgate
58	Marshall, Wilbur	LB	6-1	225	6	Florida
96	Maxey, Curtis	DT	6-3	298	2	Grambling
73	May, Mark	G-T	6-6	295	9	Pittsburgh
32	McEwen, Craig	RB	6-1	220	3	Utah
63	McKenzie, Raleigh	C-G	6-2	270	5	Tennessee
86	Middleton, Ron	TE	6-2	252	4	Auburn
81	Monk, Art	WR	6-3	209	10	Syracuse
22	Morris, Jamie	RB	5-7	185	2	Michigan
61	Morris, Mike	C-G	6-5	275	2	NE Missouri State
52	Olkewicz, Neal	LB	6-0	230	11	Maryland
87	Orr, Terry	TE	6-3	227	4	Texas
59	Price, Stacy	LB	6-3	220	2	Arkansas State
48	Profit, Eugene	CB	5-10	175	2	Yale
39	Riggs, Gerald	RB	6-1	232	8	Arizona State
11	Rypien, Mark	QB	6-4	234	2	Washington State
83	Sanders, Ricky	WR	5-11	180	4	Southwest Texas State
76	Simmons, Ed	T	6-5	280	3	Eastern Washington
60	Stokes, Fred	DE	6-3	262	3	Georgia Southern
86	Tice, Mike	TE	6-7	244	9	Maryland
31	Vaughn, Clarence	S	6-0	202	3	Northern Illinois
40	Walton, Alvin	S	6-0	180	4	Kansas
85	Warren, Don	TE	6-4	242	11	San Diego State
82	Whisenhunt, Ken	RB	6-3	240	5	Georgia Tech
45	Wilburn, Barry	CB	6-3	186	5	Mississippi
17	Williams, Doug	QB	6-4	220	9	Grambling

TOP FIVE DRAFT CHOICES

Rd.	Name	Sel. No.	Pos.	Ht.	Wt.	College
3	Rocker, Tracy	66	DT	6-2	280	Auburn
4	Graham, Jeff	87	QB	6-4	200	Long Beach State
5	Smiley, Tim	129	DB	6-0	190	Arkansas State
5	Robinson, Lybrant	140	DE	6-4	225	Delaware State
6	Johnson, A.J.	149	DB	5-8	176	SW Texas State

REDSKIN PROFILES

DOUG WILLIAMS 34 6-4 220   Quarterback

He proved to be mortal after all . . . Following a fairy-tale 1987 season in which he led the Redskins to the Super Bowl XXII title, he struggled through a disappointing 1988 . . . Missed five weeks after undergoing emergency appendectomy . . . Started 10 games, splitting time with Mark Rypien . . . Completed 213 of 380 passes for 2,609 yards and 15 TDs, with 12 INTs . . . Passed for season-high 430 yards (2 TDs) against Steelers in Week 2 . . . Was named MVP of Super Bowl XXII, setting records for most passing yards (340) and most yards passing in a quarter (228), most TD passes (4) and longest completion (80 yards) . . . Tampa Bay's first-round draft pick out of Grambling in 1978 . . . Spent five years with Bucs and two in USFL before signing with Redskins in 1986 . . . Born Aug. 9, 1955, in Baton Rouge, La. . . . Earned $1 million in 1988.

ALVIN WALTON 25 6-0 180   Safety

One of the hardest-hitting defensive backs in the NFL . . . Excellent defender against the run . . . Averaged nearly 12 tackles a game, totaling 189 (113 solo) for the season . . . Has 337 total tackles in last two seasons . . . Had eight tackles behind the line of scrimmage . . . Also intercepted three passes, collected one sack and forced three fumbles . . . Passed over until Redskins selected him in third round of 1986 draft . . . Probably went unnoticed because he did not play senior year at Kansas due to academic mix-up . . . Attended Mt. Jacinto Junior College . . . Born March 14, 1964, in Riverside, Cal. . . . Earned $170,000 last year.

MARK RYPIEN 26 6-4 234   Quarterback

Proved himself to be a capable quarterback after Doug Williams went out with appendectomy . . . Started six games and played in nine . . . Completed 114 of 208 passes for 1,730 yards and 18 TDs, 13 INTs . . . Passed for 303 yards and four TDs against Phoenix Oct. 16 . . . Was virtual unknown before season but earned backup job after Jay

Schroeder was traded to Raiders . . . He did little to distinguish his first two NFL seasons . . . Was a sixth-round draft pick in 1986 out of Washington State . . . But injuries—knee in his first season and back in '87—put him on injured reserve, so he never got to play . . . Has good mobility and instincts . . . Could be a comer . . . Born Oct. 2, 1962, in Calgary, Canada . . . Earned $210,000 last year.

CHARLES MANN 28 6-6 270   Defensive End

Though bothered by injuries for most of the season, he still turned in good enough year to earn second straight trip to Pro Bowl . . . Was sixth on team with 68 tackles and second in sacks with 5½ . . . Forced one fumble and credited with 17 quarterback pressures . . . Has 40 sacks over the last four seasons . . . Earned first trip to Pro Bowl after 1987 Super Bowl season in which he led club with 10 sacks and 21 quarterback hurries . . . Passed over for postseason honors despite collecting 14½ sacks in 1985 . . . A third-round pick out of Nevada-Reno in 1983. Became a starter in 1984 . . . Born April 12, 1961, in Sacramento, Cal. . . . Dabbles in real estate, acting and modeling during the offseason . . . Earned $450,000 last year.

WILBER MARSHALL 27 6-1 225   Linebacker

Became the first NFL player since Norm Thompson in 1977 to take free agency and switch teams when Redskins signed him to a five-year deal worth $6 million after 1987 season . . . Did his best to be worthy of that heavy price tag . . . Was fourth on the team in tackles with 133, including 78 solo . . . Had four sacks and three interceptions . . . Also forced three fumbles and totaled 10 quarterback pressures . . . Earned Pro Bowl trips in 1986 and 1987 while with the Bears . . . Recorded a fumble recovery and sack in Super Bowl XX . . . Was Bears' No. 1 draft choice out of Florida in 1984 . . . Comes from a family of 13 children . . . Born April 18, 1962, in Titusville, Fla. . . . A high-school teammate of Bengal receiver Cris Collinsworth . . . Earned $1.4 million last year.

RICKY SANDERS 27 5-11 180   Wide Receiver

One of the few Redskins who had a better season in 1988 than in 1987... Totaled a NFL career-high 73 receptions (sixth in NFC)... Had 1,148 receiving yards to rank fifth in the NFL and fourth in the NFC... Led the NFC with 12 TD receptions... Set foundation for good season with spectacular performance in Super Bowl XXII, where he caught nine passes for a then-record 193 yards and TDs of 80 and 50 yards ... Started pro career playing two seasons with Houston Gamblers of USFL, totaling 1,916 receiving yards and 18 TDs... Signed by Redskins on Aug. 11, 1986... Was a running back at Southwest Texas State... Born Aug. 30, 1962, in Temple, Tex.... Earned $560,000 last year.

DEXTER MANLEY 30 6-3 257   Defensive End

Missed four weeks during training camp after failing a preseason drug test... Returned for season opener against Giants and went on to lead team in sacks with 10... Had three against Giants Oct. 2... Was 11th on team in tackles with 54... Had 16 stops behind line of scrimmage... Credited with 10 quarterback pressures... Brash and outspoken, he remains one of the league's most loved and hated personalities... Is Redskins' career leader in sacks with 88... His speed (4.6 in the 40-yard dash) makes him tough for most offensive tackles to handle... A fifth-round draft choice in 1981 out of Oklahoma State... Born Feb. 2, 1959, in Houston... Has his own radio show during the season... Earned $405,000 last year.

ART MONK 31 6-3 209   Wide Receiver

When it comes to consistency, durability and reliability, Monk's name is at the top of each list... Entering his 10th year as one of the league's most respected receivers... Caught 72 passes last year for 946 yards and five TDs ... Reception total tied for seventh (with Anthony Carter) in NFC... Remains second behind Charley Taylor on the club's all-time list of receptions (576) and receiving yardage (7,979)... Missed last three games of 1987 regular season and first two playoff games after tearing knee ligaments. Caught one pass for 40 yards in Super Bowl XXII... Was Redskins' first pick in 1980, out of Syracuse... Nicknamed "Money" for his clutch play... Born Dec. 5, 1957, in White Plains, N.Y.... Earned $700,000 last year.

JAMIE MORRIS 24 5-7 185   Running Back

Should see more playing time now that Timmy Smith has moved on to San Diego... May push injury-prone Kelvin Bryant for starting role... Finished rookie season by setting NFL record with 45 carries (152 yards) against Cincinnati Dec. 17... Totaled 437 yards (2 TDs) on 126 carries for the season... Handled kickoff-return duties, averaging 19.7 yards on 21 returns... Was a fourth-round pick out of Michigan, where he became the Wolverines' all-time leading rusher with 4,393 yards... Was the first player in Michigan history to gain 1,000 yards three years running... Younger brother of Giants' running back Joe Morris... Born June 6, 1965, in Ayer, Mass.... Earned $175,000 last year.

GERALD RIGGS 28 6-1 232   Running Back

Joins Redskins following draft-pick exchange with Falcons... Missed almost half of 1988 (7½ games) with sprained knee... Still finished as Falcons' second-leading rusher with 488 yards on 113 carries... Scored one touchdown... Caught 22 passes for 171 yards... Was NFC Player of the Week after gaining 115 yards rushing and 64 yards receiving in 34-17 win at San Francisco Sept. 18... Now has 8,015 career yards rushing and receiving, just 687 behind Atlanta record-holder William Andrews... Added to 17 club records that include 6,631 yards rushing, 48 TDs and 25 100-yard games... Continues streak of 186 pass receptions without scoring a TD... Second only to Eric Dickerson in yards gained over the last five years... First-round draft choice out of Arizona State in 1982... Born Nov. 6, 1960, in Tullos, Cal.... Earned $530,000 last year.

EARNEST BYNER 26 5-10 215   **Running Back**

Came to Redskins from Browns in April trade for Mike Oliphant . . . Led Browns last year in rushing and receiving, gaining 576 yards in each category . . . His 59 receptions ranked ninth in AFC . . . His dedication gained respect of teammates . . . Owns Browns' top two postseason rushing games, 161 vs. Miami in 1986 and 122 vs. Colts in '88 . . . Caught more passes (193) than any other Brown in last four years . . . Wasn't drafted until 10th round in 1984, the 280th pick overall . . . Started three years at fullback at East Carolina . . . One of eight ECU players drafted in 1984 . . . 1988 salary: $350,000 . . . Born Sept. 15, 1962, in Milledgeville, Ga.

GARY CLARK 27 5-9 173   **Wide Receiver**

Analyst John Madden likes Clark because, "He's the guy who keeps first downs coming, then he'll lull you to sleep and slip behind you for a deep one." . . . Clark slipped behind many defensive backs in 1988, catching 59 balls for 892 yards and seven TDs . . . Was more of a possession receiver than in previous years . . . One of the more emotional players on the team . . . Has amassed 3,223 receiving yards and 21 TDs over last three seasons . . . An intelligent player who is all business on the field . . . Signed with Redskins as a free agent in 1985 after playing two seasons in the USFL . . . Became all-time leading receiver with 155 catches at James Madison University . . . Born May 1, 1962, in Dublin, Va. . . . Earned $247,000 last year.

COACH JOE GIBBS:

He'll be working harder than ever to help the Redskins rebound from last year's 7-9 record, the first losing season in his eight years as head coach . . . Despite trading Jay Schroeder, he still had to deal with a quarterback controversy when Mark Rypien played so well in place of Doug Williams . . . Learned offensive philosophy from Don Coryell . . . Played tight end for Coryell at San Diego

State, later worked for him there as a graduate assistant and at St. Louis and San Diego as offensive backfield coach . . . Assisted John McKay at USC and Tampa Bay . . . Born Nov. 25, 1940, in Mocksville, N.C. . . . Is outstanding racquetball player.

Appendix out, Doug Williams will go all out.

GREATEST COACH

Old-timers will vote for Ray Flaherty, whose Redskins won the NFL title in their first year in Washington, 1937, and won it again in 1942, his sixth and final season. Flaherty's regular-season record of 47-16-3 (.735) tops all of the 17 coaches in club history.

George Allen's 67-30-1 (.689) from 1971-77 marked a successful tenure, but there were no NFL championships—despite some play suggestions from Richard M. Nixon, the other Washington quarterback. The closest Allen came was a loss to Miami in Super Bowl VII.

Joe Gibbs, the Redskin coach longer than anyone else (entering his ninth season), has brought Washington two Super Bowl victories, three NFC championships and four NFC Eastern Division titles. Gibbs' regular-season record is 81-39 (.457), but significantly he is 11-3 where it pays off—in the playoffs. And to think that he had an 0-5 start in his rookie season in 1981!

How to compare Flaherty's two titles in the pre-Super Bowl era with Gibbs' two Super Bowl rings? And no question Flaherty has the better won-lost percentage. Okay, Flaherty has a blot on the escutcheon—his Redskins were also notable for having been whipped, 73-0, by Chicago's Monsters of the Midway in 1940.

Flaherty? Gibbs? The late Vince Lombardi, 7-5-2 in 1969, his one year as Redskin coach before cancer felled him, would have an opinion. So can the reader.

INDIVIDUAL REDSKIN RECORDS

Rushing

Most Yards Game:	206	George Rogers, vs St. Louis, 1985
Season:	1,347	John Riggins, 1983
Career:	7,472	John Riggins, 1976-79, 1981-85

Passing

Most TD Passes Game:	6	Sam Baugh, vs Brooklyn, 1943
	6	Sam Baugh, vs St. Louis, 1947
Season:	31	Sonny Jurgensen, 1967
Career:	187	Sammy Baugh, 1937-52

Receiving

Most TD Passes Game:	3	Hugh Taylor (5 times)
	3	Jerry Smith, vs Los Angeles, 1967
	3	Jerry Smith, vs Dallas, 1969
	3	Hal Crisler
	3	Joe Walton
	3	Pat Richter, vs Chicago, 1968
	3	Larry Brown, vs Philadelphia, 1973
	3	Jean Fugett, vs San Francisco, 1976
	3	Alvin Garrett, vs Lions, 1982
	3	Art Monk, vs Indianapolis, 1984
Season:	12	Hugh Taylor, 1952
	12	Charley Taylor, 1966
	12	Jerry Smith, 1967
	12	Ricky Sanders, 1988
Career:	79	Charley Taylor, 1964-77

Scoring

Most Points Game:	24	Dick James, vs Dallas, 1961
	24	Larry Brown, vs Philadelphia, 1973
Season:	161	Mark Moseley, 1983
Career:	1,176	Mark Moseley, 1974-85
Most TDs Game:	4	Dick James, vs Dallas, 1961
	4	Larry Brown, vs Philadelphia, 1973
Season:	24	John Riggins, 1983
Career:	90	Charley Taylor, 1964-77

INSIDE THE AFC

By BRIAN WHITE

PREDICTED ORDER OF FINISH

EAST	CENTRAL	WEST
Buffalo	Cincinnati	Denver
New England	Houston	Seattle
Indianapolis	Cleveland	L. A. Raiders
Miami	Pittsburgh	Kansas City
New York Jets		San Diego

AFC Champion: Buffalo

The 1988 season proved, among other things, that the AFC has the ability to compete in the Super Bowl, after all. It also gave hope and inspiration to teams such as Kansas City, Miami and Pittsburgh, who are coming off disastrous seasons.

Both of those lessons came courtesy of the Cincinnati Bengals, who went from 4-11 bumblers to 12-4 giants and fell seconds short of a Super Bowl title. Now, in a drastic role reversal, the Bengals are the team to beat.

The primary challenge to Cincinnati comes from the AFC East, where Marv Levy's Buffalo Bills ran away from the pack in '88 and should do so again this year. Bruce Smith and Cornelius Bennett lead an imposing defensive unit that would love for quarterback Jim Kelly and the offense to catch fire. The combination could be deadly.

The rest of the East will be tight. The Patriots want running back John Stephens, last year's top rookie, to combine with the arm of Tony Eason to bring much-needed offensive balance to

---

Brian White of the Ft. Myers News Press *regularly covers the Miami Dolphins and follows all else in the NFL.*

New England. With Eric Dickerson, the Colts have the potential to beat anybody. Miami drafted Sammie Smith to give a lift to the league's worst rushing atttack, but the Dolphins still have major questions on defense. The Jets continue to try to shore up glaring weak spots.

The Central should provide the best race, with Houston and Cleveland pushing Cincinnati from start to finish. The Bengals are a strange team. In '88, they added an unheralded, pony-tailed running back named Ickey Woods and moved from among the worst teams to the best. Now coach Sam Wyche has a new five-year contract. Are the Bengals satisfied? Will they do another about-face?

If so, the big, bad Oilers are aching to take over. Houston lost a league-high 15 players to free agency, but the personnel and the desire appear to still be there. Cleveland, under new coach Bud Carson, is anxious to show once again what it can do with a healthy Bernie Kosar. The Browns dumped Earnest Byner and added speed to their offense, but several veterans must perform well if the Central is to send three teams to the playoffs again. Pittsburgh continues to improve with a no-name lineup.

The West is weak once again. Denver is expected to return to the high-flying offensive style that brought it to consecutive Super Bowls a few years ago. Seattle has a new star in fullback John L. Williams, and Curt Warner is still effective. Those two teams will fight it out.

The Raiders have the talent to contend, but are unpredictable. If quarterback Jay Schroeder relaxes and masters the playbook, the men in black and silver will be exciting. Kansas City, with Marty Schottenheimer calling the shots, could be the turnaround team of '89. The Chiefs were 4-11-1 last year but weren't blown out very often. San Diego has speed and a new coach, Dan Henning, but must find consistency at quarterback.

The division winners will be Buffalo, Cincinnati and Denver, with Houston and New England claiming wild-card berths. Look for the Bills to cap Kelly's best NFL season with a vengeful AFC championship victory over Cincinnati and a trip to the Super Bowl.

BUFFALO BILLS

TEAM DIRECTORY: Pres.: Ralph Wilson; GM/VP-Administration: Bill Polian; Dir. Pro Personnel: Bob Ferguson; Mgr. Media Rel.: Scott Berchtold; Dir. Pub. and Community Rel.: Denny Lynch; Head Coach: Marv Levy. Home field: Rich Stadium (80,290). Colors: Scarlet red, royal blue and white.

SCOUTING REPORT

OFFENSE: There were times last year when Buffalo won despite its lackluster offense. The Bills (12-4) scored fewer than 10 points four times, winning two of those battles.

Quarterback Jim Kelly is a good leader, but his statistics were unspectacular in 1988 (15 TDs, 17 interceptions). Coach Marv Levy feels the Bills must develop a respectable running game to take pressure off Kelly.

"Jim Kelly threw into coverage all season because teams weren't concerned about our running game," Levy said.

Rookie running back Thurman Thomas gained 881 yards with a 4.3 average, and Robb Riddick was successful in short-yardage situations. But the Bills' line is aging and needs new blood. Levy also went shopping for new ball-carriers in the offseason, signing Kenneth Davis (Packers), Larry Kinnebrew (Bengals) and Tim Tyrell (Rams).

Kelly also needs more speed on the outside to go along with Andre Reed, who caught a team-record 71 passes last year for 968 yards and six TDs.

DEFENSE: The Bills' all-star cast on defense carried the team while the offense struggled. There's no sign of letting up, either. In the group that allowed the fewest points (237) in the AFC, only two defenders, Art Still and Fred Smerlas, are in their 30s.

Where do you start in describing this unit? End Bruce Smith, nose tackle Smerlas and linebackers Cornelius Bennett and Shane Conlan are among the best in the business, and Still, an end, gained new life under his old coach.

Safety Leonard Smith brought toughness to the secondary, but that aggressiveness sometimes resulted in unnecessary cheap shots that cost the team in big games.

The Bills' defense ranked fourth overall in the NFL, but only 12th against the run. Opponents gained 3.9 yards per carry. Levy would like to see his defense cause more turnovers.

Sacks propelled Bruce Smith to second Pro Bowl.

KICKING GAME: Scott Norwood was the best kicker in the NFL last year, making 32 of 37 field-goal attempts, including 26 of 27 inside 40 yards. John Kidd was in the middle of the pack of AFC punters with a 39.5 average. Several Bills returned kicks, and the team's most active punt-returner, Flip Johnson, averaged just 4.5 yards. Kick coverage was good once again.

THE ROOKIES: The Bills, without a draft choice until late in the third round, sought help for their receiving corps. They got a burner in 24-year-old Don Beebe of Chadron (Neb.) State, then went for a possession receiver in Michigan's John Kolesar in the fourth. Beebe has run a 4.38 40-yard dash and can be the deep threat Kelly needs. Kolesar is a clutch player who had an injury-hampered college career.

BILLS VETERAN ROSTER

HEAD COACH—Marv Levy. Assistant Coaches—Tom Bresnahan, Walt Corey, Ted Cottrell, Bruce DeHaven, Chuck Dickerson, Rusty Jones, Chuck Lester, Ted Marchibroda, Nick Nicolau, Elijah Pitts, Dick Roach.

No.	Name	Pos.	Ht.	Wt.	NFL Exp.	College
54	Bailey, Carlton	LB	6-2	240	2	North Carolina
75	Ballard, Howard	T	6-6	300	2	Alabama A&M
1	Bell, Albert	WR	6-0	170	2	Alabama
55	Bennett, Cornelius	LB	6-2	235	3	Alabama
50	Bentley, Ray	LB	6-2	235	4	Central Michigan
71	Broughton, Walter	WR	5-10	180	3	Jacksonville State
85	Burkett, Chris	WR	6-4	210	5	Jackson State
29	Burroughs, Derrick	CB	6-1	180	5	Memphis State
61	Burton, Leonard	T	6-3	275	4	South Carolina
58	Conlan, Shane	LB	6-3	235	3	Penn State
71	Davis, John	C-T	6-4	304	3	Georgia Tech
23	Davis, Kenneth	RB	5-10	209	4	Texas Christian
21	Davis, Wayne	CB	5-11	180	5	Indiana State
70	Devlin, Joe	T	6-5	280	13	Iowa
45	Drane, Dwight	S	6-2	205	4	Oklahoma
53	Erlandson, Tom	LB	6-1	220	2	Washington
59	Frerotte, Mitch	T-G	6-3	275	1	Penn State
99	Garner, Hal	LB	6-4	235	4	Utah State
8	Gelbaugh, Stan	QB	6-3	207	3	Maryland
41	Guggemos, Neal	S	6-1	190	4	St. Thomas (Minn.)
49	Hagy, John	S	5-11	190	2	Texas
33	Harmon, Ronnie	RB	5-11	200	4	Iowa
67	Hull, Kent	C	6-4	275	4	Mississippi State
47	Jackson, Kirby	CB	5-10	180	3	Mississippi State
80	Johnson, Flip	WR	5-10	185	2	McNeese State
86	Johnson, Trumaine	WR	6-1	196	5	Grambling
12	Kelly, Jim	QB	6-3	218	4	Miami
38	Kelso, Mark	S	5-11	185	4	William & Mary
4	Kidd, John	P	6-3	208	6	Northwestern
28	Kinnebrew, Larry	RB	6-2	258	6	Tennessee State
63	Lingner, Adam	C	6-4	265	7	Illinois
84	McKeller, Keith	TE	6-6	245	2	Jacksonville State
74	Mesner, Bruce	NT	6-5	280	2	Maryland
88	Metzelaars, Pete	TE	6-7	250	8	Wabash
39	Mueller, Jamie	RB	6-1	225	3	Benedictine
11	Norwood, Scott	K	6-0	207	5	James Madison
37	Odomes, Nate	CB	5-10	188	3	Wisconsin
94	Pike, Mark	DE	6-4	272	3	Georgia Tech
97	Radecic, Scott	LB	6-3	242	6	Penn State
83	Reed, Andre	WR	6-0	190	5	Kutztown State
14	Reich, Frank	QB	6-4	210	5	Maryland
62	Rentie, Caesar	T	6-3	291	2	Oklahoma
40	Riddick, Robb	RB	6-0	195	8	Millersville State
98	Ridgle, Elston	DE	6-6	270	2	Nevada-Reno
51	Ritcher, Jim	G	6-3	265	10	North Carolina State
87	Rolle, Butch	TE	6-3	242	4	Michigan State
96	Seals, Leon	DE	6-4	265	3	Jackson State
76	Smerlas, Fred	NT	6-3	280	11	Boston College
78	Smith, Bruce	DE	6-4	285	5	Virginia Tech
46	Smith, Leonard	S	5-11	202	7	McNeese State
72	Still, Art	DE	6-7	255	12	Kentucky
64	Strenger, Rich	T	6-7	285	4	Michigan
56	Talley, Darryl	LB	6-4	235	7	West Virginia
89	Tasker, Steve	WR-KR	5-9	185	5	Northwestern
34	Thomas, Thurman	RB	5-10	198	2	Oklahoma State
22	Tucker, Erroll	KR-DB	5-8	170	2	Utah
25	Tyrell, Tim	RB	6-2	215	6	Northern Illinois
65	Vogler, Tim	C	6-3	285	11	Ohio State
73	Wolford, Will	T	6-5	280	4	Vanderbilt
91	Wright, Jeff	NT	6-2	270	2	Central Missouri State
90	Young, Theo	TE	6-2	233	2	Arkansas

TOP DRAFT CHOICES

Rd.	Name	Sel. No.	Pos.	Ht.	Wt.	College
3	Beebe, Don		82	WR	5-10	175	Clarion State
4	Kolesar, John		109	WR	5-11	185	Michigan
5	Andrews, Michael		138	DB	5-11	180	Alcorn State
6	Doctor, Sean		164	RB	6-2	237	Marshall
7	Jordan, Brian		173	DB	6-1	205	Richmond

OUTLOOK: There's nothing wrong with the defense. If the Bills establish a running game to free Kelly up a bit, Buffalo could reach the Super Bowl.

BILL PROFILES

BRUCE SMITH 26 6-4 285 Defensive End

Created confusion and panic on opposing offensive lines once again, leading Bills with 11 sacks in just 12 games... Underwent 30-day suspension for violation of NFL substance-abuse policy... Accused Bills' management of having off-duty police follow him after suspension... Still finished second in AFC sacks for third consecutive year... Has 44½ sacks in four years... Was off to great start against Bengals' Anthony Munoz in AFC championship game before leg injury slowed him down... Went to Pro Bowl for second time... Forced three fumbles... 1985 Outland Trophy winner from Virginia Tech was first player taken in draft... Had 22 sacks as a junior and 16 as a senior... Signed five-year, $7.5 million offer sheet with Broncos but Bills matched it in March... "Buffalo, I think, made a very wise decision to keep him," said Denver coach Dan Reeves... Born June 18, 1963, in Norfolk, Va.

JIM KELLY 29 6-3 218 Quarterback

Led unappreciated offense with 3,380 yards passing... His completion percentage of 59.5 was second in AFC and fell just short of club record of 59.7 he set in 1987... Quarterback rating of 78.2, a career low, was seventh in AFC... Threw more interceptions (17) than touchdowns (15)... Shrugged off late-season public criticism by teammate Robb Riddick, who claimed Kelly makes bad decisions... Starred in 1984-85 in USFL... Former University of Miami star originally was first-round pick by Bills in '83... Went to Buffalo in '86... 1988 salary: $1.2 million. 1989 salary: $1.3 million. 1990 salary: $1.4 million... Born Feb. 14, 1960, in East Brady, Pa.

CORNELIUS BENNETT 23 6-2 235   Linebacker

Pro Bowl performer in his first full NFL season... Second on team with 103 tackles and 9½ sacks but was first with 85 initial hits... Made two interceptions... Lean and mean... Acquired in midseason of 1987 in blockbuster Eric Dickerson trade... Played in final eight games. Bills recorded 22 sacks in those eight after compiling eight in first four games... Had 17 tackles, four sacks and three forced fumbles in '87 season finale vs. Philadelphia... Second player picked (by Colts) in '87 draft... Made 287 tackles in career at Alabama... 1988 salary: $375,000. 1989 salary: $475,000. 1990 salary: $575,000. 1991 salary: $675,000... Born Aug. 25, 1966, in Birmingham, Ala.

THURMAN THOMAS 23 5-10 198   Running Back

Bills gambled by drafting Thomas, who had past knee problems, but are happy they took risk... Led team in rushing with 881 yards, the first rookie to do so since Greg Bell in 1984... Had two 100-yard games—116 vs. Green Bay and 106 vs. Raiders... Leg injury prevented him from gaining 1,000 yards. Limited to six carries Nov. 6 vs. Seattle and none Nov. 14 vs. Miami... Ninth in AFC rushing... Despite 207 carries, he scored just two TDs... Second-round pick out of Oklahoma State who ran for 4,595 yards and 43 TDs in four years... Racked up 1,613 yards and 18 TDs as a senior... Slowed as junior after knee surgery. Injury was suffered in pickup basketball game... Born July 16, 1966, in Missouri City, Tex.

SHANE CONLAN 25 6-3 235   Linebacker

Led Bills in tackles for most of season, but foot injury caused him to miss three games and part of another late in year... Finished with 84 stops, third-best on team... He, Smith and Bennett are nucleus of strong defense for years to come... Tireless worker who is tough to block... Led club in tackles in 1987 as a rookie with 114... Was NFL Rookie of the Year... Moved from outside to inside upon Bennett's arrival in 1987... First-round draft pick out of Penn State... Nittany

Lions coach Joe Paterno called him the best linebacker ever to play at Linebacker U.... Grew up in Fewsburg, N.Y., about 70 miles from Rich Stadium... 1988 salary: $955,000... Born April 3, 1964, in Olean, N.Y.

FRED SMERLAS 32 6-3 280   Nose Tackle

Age hasn't slowed this hard-nosed veteran... Has started every non-strike game since 1980 ... Returned to Pro Bowl for first time since 1983, when he went for the fourth straight year... Finished 10th on team in tackles with 54 and had four sacks... Made career-high 87 tackles (55 solo) in 1983... Second-round pick in 1979 out of Boston College, where he played on winless team his senior year... Has considered a career in professional wrestling following football... Was a two-time New England prep wrestling champion... 1988 salary: $625,000... Born April 8, 1957, in Waltham, Mass.

ANDRE REED 25 6-0 190   Wide Receiver

Received overdue recognition in Pro Bowl year... Set club record with 71 receptions, fourth-best in the AFC... Led Bills in receptions for third straight year... Gained 968 yards and scored six TDs... Voted as Pro Bowl alternate, but played after Houston's Drew Hill withdrew because of neck injury ... Broke 100-yard mark three times and had games of 99 and 98 yards... Missed one game with knee injury ... Best day was 132-yard game Oct. 17 vs. Jets... Fourth-round draft choice out of Kutztown (Pa.) University, then won starting job in training camp... Was high-school quarterback... 1988 salary: $295,000... Born Jan. 29, 1964, in Philadelphia.

SCOTT NORWOOD 29 6-0 207   Kicker

Quite simply, the best kicker in football in 1988... Led NFL in scoring with 129 points ... Named to Pro Bowl and All-Pro teams... Hit 32 of 37 field goals and was only NFL kicker to make 30 or more... Booted 30-yarder in overtime Nov. 20 vs. Jets to give Bills AFC East title... Kicked last-minute field goals in both victories over Patriots...

Has made 75 straight extra-point kicks and 10 consecutive field goals ... Highest previous point total was 83 in 1986 ... Signed as free agent in 1985 after playing in USFL ... Failed in 1982 tryout with Atlanta ... Made 32 of 57 field goals at James Madison University in Harrisonburg, Va. ... Once kicked winning field goal and scored winning goal for JMU soccer team in same day ... 1988 salary: $125,000 ... Born July 17, 1960, in Alexandria, Va.

KENT HULL 28 6-4 275   Center

Former USFL standout made Pro Bowl in third season with Bills ... Part of reason Bills rushed for 2,133 yards, best since 1980 ... Durable player who put on 20 pounds since coming to NFL in 1986 ... Signed with Buffalo in middle of '86 training camp and became starter five days after arrival ... Blocked for Herschel Walker with New Jersey Generals, who made him a seventh-round draft pick ... Started four years at Mississippi State ... Father Charles is Mississippi director of agriculture ... 1988 salary: $275,000 ... Born Jan. 13, 1961, in Ponotoc, Miss.

ART STILL 33 6-7 255   Defensive End

Outstanding career was given new life with trade from Chiefs in June, 1988 ... Finished as Bills' fourth-leading tackler with 79 and had six sacks ... Holds Kansas City's sack record with $72\frac{1}{2}$ in 10 seasons ... Four-time Pro Bowler was named to Chiefs' all-time team in '87 ... Best year of career was 1980, when he made 140 tackles and was KC's MVP ... Second player picked in 1978 draft, behind Earl Campbell ... Four-year starter at Kentucky ... 1988 salary: $650,000. 1989 salary: $715,000 ... Born Dec. 5, 1955, in Camden, N.J.

RAY BENTLEY 28 6-2 235   Linebacker

Bentley's name isn't first to come to mind upon mention of Bills' defense, but former Central Michigan star led AFC's top defense in tackles ... Made 122 tackles, 19 more than runnerup Cornelius Bennett ... Full-time starter for first time in three years with Bills ... Had club-high 15 tackles Nov. 27 vs. Cincinnati and added 14 Dec. 18 at

Indianapolis ... Signed with Buffalo as free agent in 1986 after three years in USFL ... Cut by Tampa Bay, was waived and re-signed by Bills during '86 season ... Mid-American Conference Defensive Player of the Year in 1982 ... Writes childrens' books in spare time ... 1988 salary: $205,000 ... Born Nov. 25, 1960, in Grand Rapids, Mich.

COACH MARV LEVY: Brainy Harvard man has put together a young, powerful team in just over two seasons ... Overhauled roster and pieced together defense full of superstars ... Is 22-18 with Bills ... Took over after Hank Bullough was fired with seven games left in 1986 season. Went 2-5, then 7-8 and 12-4 ... Organization is a big key to his preparation ... "Our goal is to win the Super Bowl and win it again and again," he says ... Graduate of Coe College, where he was a standout running back, and has master's degree in English history from Harvard ... Coached USFL's Chicago Blitz in 1984, NFL's Kansas City Chiefs from 1978-82 and CFL's Montreal Alouettes from 1973-77 ... Was 31-41 with Chiefs ... Won two CFL titles with the Alouettes ... Was an assistant under Jerry Williams with the Eagles and George Allen with the Rams and Redskins ... Present emphasis on special teams stems from his work as an assistant overseeing that area ... Was head coach at New Mexico, California and William & Mary ... Born Aug. 3, 1928, in Chicago.

GREATEST COACH

The much-traveled Lou Saban made two stops in Buffalo, winning two AFL championships the first time around and returning the Bills to respectability the next.

An AFL pioneer while coaching the Boston Patriots from 1960-61, Saban took over the Bills in '62. After two 7-6-1 years, the Bills won league titles in 1964 and '65. Saban left to coach the University of Maryland and later the Denver Broncos. In the meantime, the Bills stumbled.

Buffalo went 1-13 in 1971, paving the way for Saban's return.

With an offense that featured O.J. Simpson, the Bills climbed back into contention. In 1973, they became the first team in NFL history to rush for more than 3,000 yards. In '74, they made the playoffs, losing to eventual Super Bowl winner Pittsburgh.

Saban was replaced by Jim Ringo four games into the 1976 season. He left with a 68-44-4 mark, the best in team history.

INDIVIDUAL BILL RECORDS

Rushing

Most Yards Game:	273	O. J. Simpson, vs Detroit, 1976
Season:	2,003	O. J. Simpson, 1973
Career:	10,183	O. J. Simpson, 1969-77

Passing

Most TD Passes Game:	5	Joe Ferguson, vs N.Y. Jets, 1979
Season:	26	Joe Ferguson, 1983
Career:	181	Joe Ferguson, 1973-84

Receiving

Most TD Passes Game:	4	Jerry Butler, vs N.Y. Jets, 1979
Season:	10	Elbert Dubenion, 1964
Career:	35	Elbert Dubenion, 1960-67

Scoring

Most Points Game:	30	Cookie Gilchrist, vs N.Y. Jets, 1963
Season:	138	O. J. Simpson, 1975
Career:	420	O. J. Simpson, 1969-77
Most TDs Game:	5	Cookie Gilchrist, vs N.Y. Jets, 1963
Season:	23	O. J. Simpson, 1975
Career:	70	O. J. Simpson, 1969-1977

CINCINNATI BENGALS

TEAM DIRECTORY: Chairman: Austin E. Knowlton; Pres.: John Sawyer; VP/GM: Paul Brown; Asst. GM: Michael Brown; Dir. Player Personnel: Pete Brown; Dir. Pub. Rel.: Allan Heim; Bus Mgr.: Bill Connelly; Head Coach: Sam Wyche. Home field: Riverfront Stadium (59,754). Colors: Orange, black and white.

SCOUTING REPORT

OFFENSE: The Cincinnati offensive attack is so well-rounded, it's scary. The unit that ranked No. 1 in the NFL last year heads into 1989 having finally put together all its talented parts.

Quarterback Boomer Esiason, the league MVP, was awesome early in the year before handing things over to the running game. However, late-season injuries that were slow to heal during the offseason have Bengal followers concerned about Esiason. The arrival of rookie fullback Ickey Woods brought new life to James Brooks, who just missed out matching Woods' 1,000-yard sea-

Ickey Woods leads "Ickey Shuffle" during Super Bowl Week.

son. It also added an unstoppable diversity to the Bengals (12-4), who led the NFL in scoring, total offense and rushing.

Receiver Eddie Brown and tight end Rodney Holman had Pro Bowl years, and speedster Tim McGee also had a big season with 36 receptions and six TDs. Veteran Cris Collinsworth is slowing down and fading from the team's plans.

The offense's major question mark is right tackle Joe Walter, who proved to be one of the league's best pass-blockers until a severe knee injury kept him out of the playoffs.

DEFENSE: If not for the question hanging over Tim Krumrie, all would be well for years to come for the Bengal defense. Krumrie, the team's leading tackler the past four years, broke a leg in the Super Bowl and will be watched carefully in his comeback.

The Bengal defense is young. Linebacker Reggie Williams was the oldest regular at 34, and many consider him relatively easy to replace.

The secondary played well enough to keep No. 1 draft choice Rickey Dixon at a backup position. Pro Bowl starter David Fulcher made things happen, while cornerbacks Eric Thomas and Lewis Billups were steady.

Cincy doesn't have a feared pass-rusher, but Jim Skow and Jason Buck are improving.

KICKING GAME: The Bengals won in 1988 despite their special teams. The kicking squad cost Cincinnati games against Cleveland and Kansas City. The Bengals had five kicks blocked —two punts, two extra points and one field goal—giving them 18 in the last three years.

Kicker Jim Breech is accurate but doesn't have great range. Lee Johnson has good range on field goals and can handle kickoff and punting duties.

The Bengals ranked near the bottom of the AFC in both punt returns (7.6) and kickoff returns (18.5).

THE ROOKIES: The Bengals hope UCLA running back Eric Ball can provide immediate backup help for Brooks and Woods. Ball showed flashes of greatness in his injury-filled career, especially with 227 yards and four TDs in the Rose Bowl as a freshman. Arkansas guard Freddie Childress, primarily a run-blocker, is a load at 322 pounds. Erik Wilhelm, from Oregon State, gives the Bengals two left-handed quarterbacks.

OUTLOOK: The Bengals showed how good they can be in 1988. Now it's up to coach Sam Wyche to keep his team level-

BENGALS VETERAN ROSTER

HEAD COACH—Sam Wyche. Assistant Coaches—Jim Anderson, Bruce Coslet, Bill Johnson, Dick LeBeau, Jim McNally, Dick Selcer, Mike Stock, Chuck Studley, Kim Wood.

No.	Name	Pos.	Ht.	Wt.	NFL Exp.	College
35	Barber, Chris	S	6-0	187	2	North Carolina A&T
53	Barker, Leo	LB	6-2	227	6	New Mexico State
24	Billups, Lewis	CB	5-11	190	4	North Alabama
74	Blados, Brian	G	6-5	295	6	North Carolina
55	Brady, Ed	LB	6-2	235	6	Illinois
3	Breech, Jim	K	5-6	161	11	California
21	Brooks, James	RB	5-10	182	9	Auburn
81	Brown, Eddie	WR	6-0	185	5	Miami
99	Buck, Jason	DE	6-5	264	3	Brigham Young
27	Bussey, Barney	S	6-0	195	4	South Carolina
80	Collinsworth, Cris	WR	6-5	192	9	Florida
29	Dixon, Rickey	CB	5-11	177	2	Oklahoma
7	Esiason, Boomer	QB	6-5	225	6	Maryland
33	Fulcher, David	S	6-3	228	4	Arizona State
17	Fulhage, Scott	P	5-11	191	3	Kansas State
98	Grant, David	NT	6-4	277	2	West Virginia
71	Hammerstein, Mike	DE	6-4	270	3	Michigan
89	Hillary, Ira	WR	5-11	190	3	South Carolina
82	Holman, Rodney	TE	6-3	238	8	Tulane
37	Jackson, Robert	S	5-10	186	7	Central Michigan
36	Jennings, Stanford	RB	6-1	205	6	Furman
11	Johnson, Lee	P	6-2	198	5	Brigham Young
34	Kattus, Eric	TE	6-5	235	5	Michigan
58	Kelly, Joe	LB	6-2	231	4	Washington
42	Knapczyk, Ken	WR	6-0	185	2	Northern Iowa
64	Kozerski, Bruce	C-G	6-4	275	6	Holy Cross
69	Krumrie, Tim	NT	6-2	268	7	Wisconsin
38	Martin, Mike	WR	5-10	186	7	Illinois
72	McClendon, Skip	DE	6-7	275	3	Arizona State
85	McGee, Tim	WR	5-10	175	4	Tennessee
65	Montoya, Max	G	6-5	275	11	UCLA
78	Munoz, Anthony	T	6-6	278	10	Southern California
86	Parker, Carl	WR	6-2	201	2	Vanderbilt
75	Reimers, Bruce	T	6-7	280	6	Iowa State
87	Riggs, Jim	TE	6-5	245	3	Clemson
94	Romer, Rich	LB	6-3	214	2	Union College
15	Schonert, Turk	QB	6-1	196	10	Stanford
70	Skow, Jim	DE	6-3	255	4	Nebraska
22	Thomas, Eric	CB	5-11	181	3	Tulane
59	Walker, Kevin	LB	6-2	238	2	Maryland
63	Walter, Joe	T	6-6	290	5	Texas Tech
51	White, Leon	LB	6-3	245	4	Brigham Young
41	Wilcots, Solomon	CB	5-11	185	3	Colorado
57	Williams, Reggie	LB	6-1	232	14	Dartmouth
30	Woods, Ickey	RB	6-2	232	2	Nevada-Las Vegas
91	Zander, Carl	LB	6-2	235	5	Tennessee

TOP DRAFT CHOICES

Rd.	Name	Sel. No.	Pos.	Ht.	Wt.	College
2	Ball, Eric	35	RB	6-1	215	UCLA
2	Childress, Freddie	55	G	6-4	322	Arkansas
3	Wilhelm, Erik	83	QB	6-2	215	Oregon State
4	Owens, Kerry	89	LB	6-2	235	Arkansas
4	Woods, Rob	111	OT	6-5	275	Arizona

headed after a most startling turnaround. The talent is there to repeat as AFC champs, but the Browns and Oilers will provide strong challenges in the Central Division.

BENGAL PROFILES

BOOMER ESIASON 28 6-5 225　　　　　**Quarterback**

Was named NFL MVP after guiding explosive Bengal offense to Super Bowl, but had disappointing Super Sunday... His 97.4 QB rating was league's best... Completed 223 of 388 passes for 3,572 yards and 28 TDs... Only Dan Marino, Jim Everett and Randall Cunningham threw for more yardage... Stats were even more impressive in light of Bengals' success running the ball late in season... Was banged up late in year... Sore arm was slow healing in offseason... Threw twice as many TDs as interceptions after tossing 19 interceptions and 16 TDs in '87... Went from Cincy's villain during players' strike and losing season in '87 to city's hero in '88... Became full-time starter in third game of 1985 season... Second-round pick out of Maryland in 1984. Holds all Terp passing records, including 42 TD passes... 1989 salary: $1.2 million... Born April 17, 1961, in East Islip, N.Y.

ANTHONY MUNOZ 31 6-6 278　　　　　**Tackle**

Continues to have Hall of Fame career... Some consider him the best tackle ever... Has been selected to play in eight straight Pro Bowls... His strength is his athletic ability. He has depended more on technique than muscle as he has gotten older... Has caught four touchdown passes in career as a tackle-eligible receiver... First-round pick out of Southern California in 1980... Was a standout baseball player as a schoolboy... Has appeared in two movies, including *The Right Stuff*... Is a licensed realtor... A bargain at $540,000... Born Aug. 19, 1958, in Ontario, Cal.

EDDIE BROWN 26 6-0 185   Wide Receiver

Boomer Esiason's deep threat . . . Led AFC in receiving yards with 1,273 . . . Yardage was club record . . . Caught 53 passes for 24-yard average. Among NFL's top receivers, only 49ers' Jerry Rice, with 20.4, bettered 20-yard average . . . Pro Bowl starter . . . Scored career-high nine TDs . . . Only fifth Bengal to catch 50 or more passes in a season. Has done it in three of his four seasons, including 58 in 1986 . . . Former Miami U. star was 13th player selected in 1985 draft . . . Was first Miami player to gain 1,000 yards in a season . . . Got to go home for Super Bowl . . . 1988 salary: $350,000 . . . Born Dec. 18, 1962, in Miami.

ICKEY WOODS 23 6-2 232   Running Back

Pony-tailed rookie shuffled way into hearts of nation with trademark scoring dance . . . Used the dance frequently as he led AFC with 15 rushing touchdowns . . . No. 4 rusher in AFC with 1,066 yards, an impressive average of 5.3 yards per carry . . . Caught 21 passes for 199 yards . . . Punishing straight-ahead runner who showed great instinct with cutback ability . . . Second-round draft pick out of UNLV . . . Considered risky draft pick despite leading nation in rushing with 1,658 yards in 1987 . . . Gained just 267 yards and scored five TDs in first three years of college . . . First name is Elbert . . . 1988 salary: $438,000 . . . Born Feb. 28, 1966, in Fresno, Cal.

JAMES BROOKS 30 5-10 182   Running Back

Bounced back from worst year of career to give Bengals a powerful backfield combination . . . Rushed 182 times for 931 yards for 5.1 average after '87 career lows of 290 yards, one TD and a 3.1 average . . . His career-high 14 TDs (eight rushing, six receiving) put him one off AFC lead, shared by teammate Ickey Woods and Colts' Eric Dickerson . . . Caught 29 passes for 287 yards . . . Pro Bowl backup . . . Started in '86 Pro Bowl after rushing for 1,087 yards and amassing 1,773 total yards . . . Bengals robbed San Diego to get Brooks in '84, trading Pete Johnson straight up . . . Led NFL in total yards while with Chargers in 1981 and '82 . . . First-round draft choice out of Auburn in '81 . . . 1989 salary: $550,000 . . . Born Dec. 28, 1958, in Warner Robbins, Ga.

MAX MONTOYA 33 6-5 275   Guard

Along with Anthony Munoz, provides veteran leadership on huge offensive line . . . Ten-year veteran started in Pro Bowl for second time. Also made it in 1986 . . . His '87 season was hampered by back injury that forced him to miss five games . . . Superb pass-blocker . . . Seventh-round draft choice out of UCLA in 1979 . . . Present weight is close to college weight . . . Avid cook who owns "Montoya's Homemade Mexican Food" restaurant in northern Kentucky . . . 1988 salary: $390,000 . . . Born May 12, 1956, in Montebello, Cal.

RODNEY HOLMAN 29 6-3 238   Tight End

Finally made it to spotlight after years of quiet success . . . Was second on Bengals with 39 receptions, good for 527 yards and three TDs . . . Went to Pro Bowl for first time . . . A good blocker, his size and speed help open things up for Cincy's outside receivers . . . Caught 28 passes for 15.9 average in '87 despite leg injuries . . . Had sensational 1986, catching 40 passes for 570 yards . . . Dedicated practice player who helped coach Tulane, his alma mater, during spring practice . . . Third-round pick in 1982 . . . Is Green Wave's all-time leading receiver with 135 . . . Cousin of former NFL running back Preston Pearson . . . 1988 salary: $217,000 . . . Born April 20, 1960, in Ypsilanti, Mich.

TIM KRUMRIE 29 6-2 268   Nose Tackle

The heart of the Bengals' defense . . . Tough, blue-collar player who seemed invincible until leaving Super Bowl with broken leg . . . Going through extensive rehabilitation but could be ready for start of season . . . Led team in tackles fourth straight year, rare for a nose tackle . . . His 152 total stops were 43 more than any teammate . . . Had three sacks and a fumble recovery . . . Despite second straight Pro Bowl selection, he still thinks he has to prove every day that he is not a 10th-round draft choice. "That still haunts me," he said. "The computer said I was too short, too slow and too light. But a computer can't measure your heart or your desire." . . . Revved-up practice player who is frequently involved in fights, even during Super Bowl week . . . Was All-American at Wisconsin . . . Also wrestled for Badgers . . . 1988 salary: $275,000 . . . Born May 20, 1960, in Eau Claire, Wis.

DAVID FULCHER 24 6-3 228   Safety

Size, speed and toughness makes him half-safety and half-linebacker . . . Can take on linemen or sprint to outside to catch halfbacks . . . Second on team in tackles (109 total, 73 solo) and interceptions (five) . . . Added 1½ sacks . . . A third-round pick in 1986 who has started all three years . . . Nicknamed "Rock" for his punishing hits . . . All-American at Arizona State who left school a year early . . . Unsettled college career left doubts about his stability, but Bengals are thrilled . . . 1988 salary: $350,000 . . . Born Sept. 28, 1964, in Los Angeles.

JASON BUCK 26 6-5 264   Defensive End

Former No. 1 pick came on strong after terrible rookie year . . . Made 35 tackles and finished second on team with six sacks . . . After All-American career at Brigham Young, he missed training camp because of a holdout and never was a force . . . He and Jim Skow (9½ sacks) give Bengals bright future at defensive-end position . . . Used as pass-rusher as a rookie . . . Was Western Athletic Conference Player of the Year in 1985 and '86 . . . Went to junior college as a quarterback, put on weight and now bench-presses 490 pounds . . . 1989 salary: $260,000 . . . Born July 27, 1963, in St. Anthony, Idaho.

COACH SAM WYCHE: In eyes of public, he went from buffoon to genius in one short year . . . Fans were clamoring for his firing after 4-11 season in 1987. Now has new contract as Bengal boss . . . Agreed to stipulations set by Paul Brown before '88 season that cut down, among other things, his hours on the job. Brown felt stress played a part in Wyche's late-game blunders in '87 . . . Known as one of football's most inno-

vative offensive minds, his no-huddle offense has caused fits around the league . . . Was tickled to be matched up against mentor Bill Walsh in Super Bowl . . . Has 41-38 regular-season record since replacing Forrest Gregg in 1984 . . . Was an assistant with 49ers from 1979-82, monitoring development of Joe Montana . . . Was Indiana University's head coach in 1983, when he went 3-8 . . . Was a Bengal quarterback whom Brown remembered for his intellect and enthusiasm . . . Was walk-on at Furman who played with Wheeling Ironmen of Continental Football League before landing on expansion Cincinnati team. Later played for Redskins, Lions, Cardinals and Bills . . . Ran Sam Wyche Sports World sporting goods for three years before getting into coaching . . . Born Jan. 5, 1945, in Atlanta.

GREATEST COACH

When the Bengals' franchise began in the AFL in 1968, a figure familiar to Ohioans as well as all football fans was the driving force. Paul Brown, who had achieved legendary success at Massilon High, Ohio State and with the Cleveland Browns in the All-America Football Conference and the NFL, became the Bengals' general manager and coach.

It took Brown only three years to win the AFC Central Division title (1970), quickest ever for an expansion team in the NFL. In his eight years as coach, before he became fulltime general manager, Brown led the Bengals to two AFC Central Division championships.

His Bengal mark was 55-59-1 and even though he was no longer the coach, the Brown touch was evident as Cincinnati reached two Super Bowls—XVI under Forrest Gregg and XXIII under Sam Wyche.

INDIVIDUAL BENGAL RECORDS
Rushing

Most Yards Game:	163	James Brooks, vs New England, 1986	
Season:	1,087	James Brooks, 1986	
Career:	5,421	Pete Johnson, 1977-83	

Passing

Most TD Passes Game:	5	Boomer Esiason, vs N.Y. Jets, 1986
Season:	29	Ken Anderson, 1981
Career:	196	Ken Anderson, 1971-85

Receiving

Most TD Passes Game:	3	Bob Trumpy, vs Houston, 1969
	3	Isaac Curtis, vs Cleveland, 1973
	3	Isaac Curtis, vs Baltimore, 1979
Season:	10	Isaac Curtis, 1974
Career:	53	Isaac Curtis, 1973-83

Scoring

Most Points Game:	24	Larry Kinnebrew, vs Houston, 1984
Season:	115	Jim Breech, 1981
Career:	802	Jim Breech, 1981-88
Most TDs Game:	4	Larry Kinnebrew, vs Houston, 1984
Season:	16	Pete Johnson, 1981
Career:	70	Pete Johnson, 1977-83

CLEVELAND BROWNS

TEAM DIRECTORY: Owner/Pres.: Art Modell; Exec. VP-Legal Administration: James Bailey; VP-Football Operations: Ernie Accorsi; Dir. Player Relations: Ricky Feacher; VP-Pub. Rel.: Kevin Byrne; Head Coach: Bud Carson. Home field: Cleveland Stadium (80,098). Colors: Seal brown, orange and white.

SCOUTING REPORT

OFFENSE: The experiment of Marty Schottenheimer as offensive coordinator is over, and Cleveland fans hope the quarterback shuttle to the hospital is, too. With Bernie Kosar healthy and Marc Trestman moving from QB coach to offensive coordinator, the Browns (10-6) will try to be a more attack-oriented offense with more deep passes. Mistake-free Kosar also is deadly on short possession routes.

Something, however, must be done up front. After center

Bernie Kosar had highest AFC completion percentage.

Mike Baab was traded to the Patriots in the 1988 preseason, replacement Gregg Rakoczy struggled. The Browns probably will reconstruct the left side of their line, with free-agent guard Ted Banker (Jets) getting a shot.

The Browns sought greater speed at running back and they have it now in Eric Metcalf, 13th pick in the draft. They gave up Ernest Byner (576 yards rushing, 576 receiving) in a trade to Washington for running back Mike Oliphant (30 yards on eight carries). But they still have tough Kevin Mack (485 yards on 123 attempts for a 3.9-yard average). Cleveland averaged just 3.6 yards per carry last year and ranked 24th in the league. What's worse, the highest-scoring team in the AFC in 1987 dropped to 11th in 1988.

DEFENSE: Owner Art Modell, tired of seeing his defense blow late leads in big games the past four years, was determined to hire a defensive-minded man as his head coach, and he got him from the Jets. Bud Carson makes his debut with a promising squad.

Cleveland had the NFL's No. 6 defense a year ago, but still will make some changes. Nose tackle Bob Golic and end Sam Clancy are gone, so the Browns acquired linebacker Barry Krauss from Indy and end Robert Banks from Houston. Clay Matthews made the Pro Bowl last year, but the other linebackers aren't spectacular.

The secondary, led by Frank Minnifield and Hanford Dixon, is intimidating and outstanding. Strong safety Brian Washington beefed up in the offseason.

KICKING GAME: The Browns feel they have upgraded their punting game with the acquisition of Bryan Wagner, who ranked second (41.5 avg.) in the NFC with the Bears in 1988. Last year's punter, Max Runager, signed with the Chiefs. Matt Bahr made 24 of 29 field goals, including five of six from 40-49 yards. The Browns had five kicks blocked.

Gerald McNeil had a career-low 8.3 average on punt returns and kick returner Glen Young slipped slightly from 23 to 21.9 on kickoffs.

THE ROOKIES: The Browns traded up twice in order to add speed and excitement to their offense. Metcalf, the University of Texas open-field runner who is the son of former Cardinal running back Terry Metcalf, has superb quickness and can return kicks. Despite his size (5-9½, 177), Metcalf is durable. Auburn wide receiver Lawyer Tillman is big (6-4, 222) and might have a future at tight end.

BROWNS VETERAN ROSTER

HEAD COACH—Bud Carson. Assistant Coaches—Jed Hughes, Hal Hunter, Stan Jones, Paul Lanham, Richard Mann, Joe Popp, Dan Radakovich, George Sefcik, Lionel Taylor, John Teerlinck, Marc Trestman, Gary Wroblewski.

No.	Name	Pos.	Ht.	Wt.	NFL Exp.	College
70	Aronson, Doug	G	6-3	209	2	San Diego State
9	Bahr, Matt	K	5-10	175	11	Penn State
60	Baker, Al	DE	6-6	280	12	Colorado State
43	Baker, Tony	RB	5-10	180	3	East Carolina
68	Banker, Ted	G	6-2	275	6	SE Missouri
97	Banks, Robert	DE	6-5	254	3	Notre Dame
64	Baugh, Tom	C	6-3	290	4	Southern Illinois
93	Bennett, Charles	DE	6-6	280	2	SW Louisiana
24	Blaylock, Anthony	CB	5-11	190	2	Winston-Salem
77	Bolden, Rickey	T	6-4	280	6	Southern Methodist
36	Braggs, Stephen	CB	5-10	180	3	Texas
86	Brennan, Brian	WR	5-9	178	6	Boston College
72	Buchanan, Charles	DE	6-3	245	2	Tennessee State
83	Butler, Ray	WR	6-3	203	10	Southern California
58	Charlton, Clifford	LB	6-3	240	2	Florida
25	Collins, Patrick	RB	5-9	188	2	Oklahoma
17	Crawford, Derrick	WR	5-10	185	2	Memphis State
52	Dean, Kevin	LB	6-2	226	2	Texas Christian
29	Dixon, Hanford	CB	5-11	195	9	Southern Mississippi
74	Farren, Paul	T-G	6-6	280	7	Boston University
69	Fike, Dan	G	6-7	280	5	Florida
30	Gash, Thane	S	6-0	200	2	East Tennessee State
39	Glenn, Kerry	CB	5-9	175	3	Minnesota
56	Grayson, David	LB	6-2	230	3	Fresno State
78	Hairston, Carl	DE	6-2	280	14	Maryland-E.S.
23	Harper, Mark	CB	5-9	185	4	Alcorn State
35	Hill, Will	S	6-0	200	2	Bishop College
51	Johnson, Eddie	LB	6-1	225	9	Louisville
59	Johnson, Mike	LB	6-1	225	4	Virginia Tech
95	Jones, Marlon	DE	6-4	260	2	Central State (Ohio)
66	Jones, Tony	T	6-5	280	2	Western Carolina
19	Kosar, Bernie	QB	6-5	210	5	Miami
55	Krauss, Barry	LB	6-3	255	11	Alabama
88	Langhorne, Reggie	WR	6-2	200	5	Elizabeth City State
34	Mack, Kevin	RB	6-0	235	5	Clemson
42	Manoa, Tim	RB	6-1	227	3	Penn State
57	Matthews, Clay	LB	6-2	245	12	Southern California
89	McNeil, Gerald	WR-KR	5-7	147	4	Baylor
31	Minnifield, Frank	CB	5-9	185	6	Louisville
82	Newsome, Ozzie	TE	6-2	232	12	Alabama
7	Norseth, Mike	QB	6-2	200	3	Kansas
28	Oliphant, Mike	RB	5-10	183	2	Puget Sound
10	Pagel, Mike	QB	6-2	211	8	Arizona State
71	Perkins, Ray	DE	6-6	255	2	Virginia
92	Perry, Michael Dean	DE	6-0	285	2	Clemson
73	Rakoczy, Gregg	C	6-6	290	3	Miami
63	Risien, Cody	T	6-7	280	10	Texas A&M
99	Sims, Darryl	DE	6-3	290	5	Wisconsin
84	Slaughter, Webster	WR	6-1	170	4	San Diego State
12	Strock, Don	QB	6-5	220	16	Virginia Tech
97	Strozier, Wilbur	TE	6-4	255	3	Georgia
81	Tennell, Derek	TE	6-5	245	3	UCLA
15	Wagner, Bryan	P	6-2	200	3	Cal State-Northridge
50	Waiters, Van	LB	6-4	240	2	Indiana
48	Washington, Brian	S	6-0	210	2	Nebraska
1	Woods, Chris	WR	5-11	190	2	Auburn
22	Wright, Felix	S	6-2	190	5	Drake

TOP DRAFT CHOICES

Rd.	Name	Sel. No.	Pos.	Ht.	Wt.	College
1	Metcalf, Eric	13	RB	5-9	177	Texas
2	Tillman, Lawyer	31	WR	6-4	222	Auburn
4	Stewart, Andrew	107	DE	6-4	260	Cincinnati
5	Kramer, Kyle	114	S	6-2	175	Bowling Green
5	Jones, Vernon	116	WR	6-1	195	Maryland

OUTLOOK: Modell is tired of coming close. Shortly after the 1988 season ended, he said, "What I see out there is the Oilers' and Bengals' franchises surging ahead, and I see us treading water. Frankly, if I were to handicap next year ['89], we would be the third-favorite in the division." He may be right.

The Browns, so close to being the best just a few years ago, have too many holes.

BROWN PROFILES

BERNIE KOSAR 25 6-5 210   Quarterback

Injury-filled season for Kosar and rest of Cleveland quarterbacks . . . Hurt arm in season opener, missed next six games and never regained complete strength . . . Returned to lead Browns to wins over Cardinals and Bengals . . . Knocked out of Week 15 game at Miami with knee injury . . . Returned the next week and suffered sprained wrist . . . Somehow managed to squeeze in 1,890 yards and 10 touchdowns in the season . . . Rating of 84.3 ranked fourth in AFC . . . Intelligent player who rarely gets sacked despite lack of foot speed . . . Led Browns to three straight division titles after coming to NFL as 22-year-old . . . Won AFC passing title in 1987 with 95.4 rating . . . Is 12 days younger than Vinny Testaverde of Tampa Bay, who succeeded him at the University of Miami . . . Picked in special supplemental draft after playing just two seasons for Hurricanes and graduating . . . 1989 salary: $1 million . . . Born Nov. 25, 1963, in Boardman, Ohio.

FRANK MINNIFIELD 29 5-9 185   Cornerback

Aggressive, integral part of Browns' cocky secondary . . . Has been to Pro Bowl three straight years, the last two as starter . . . Second on Browns with four interceptions, tying a career high . . . Led team with 14 passes defensed . . . Missed one game with calf and groin injuries . . . Has been mainstay at left cornerback since coming from the USFL in 1984 . . . Wasn't drafted by NFL because of early signing with Chicago Blitz . . . Walk-on at Louisville who ended up starting three years and leading nation in kickoff returns . . . Vertical leap

was measured at 44 inches in college...Cousin of NBA's Dirk Minniefield...1989 salary: $600,000...Born Jan. 1, 1960, in Lexington, Ky.

HANFORD DIXON 30 5-11 195   Cornerback

Performance of "Dawgs" defense founder slipped in 1988 after two stellar seasons... Made career-low two interceptions... Considered by some as NFL's top man-to-man defender...Aggressive player who's not afraid to hit...Missed last game of regular season with hamstring and quadriceps injuries —first game he missed because of injury in seven-year career...Was hurt in Week 15 against Miami but continued to play and was beaten deep by former Brown Fred Banks to set up Dolphins' winning TD...Was 22nd player picked in 1981 draft...Four-year letterman at Southern Mississippi...1988 salary: $550,000...Born Dec. 25, 1958, in Mobile, Ala.

REGGIE LANGHORNE 26 6-2 200   Wide Receiver

Emerged as big-play threat in absence of Webster Slaughter, who missed seven games with a broken arm...Led Browns with 780 receiving yards and seven TDs...Ranked 12th in AFC receptions...Ran the ball two times, once for a 20-yard TD...His 57 receptions were two behind team leader Earnest Byner...Previous highs were 39 receptions, 678 yards, one TD in 1986...Runs 40-yard dash in under 4.4 seconds...Seventh-round pick out of little Elizabeth City State, where he started for three-plus years...1988 salary: $210,000...Born April 7, 1963, in Suffolk, Va.

FELIX WRIGHT 30 6-2 190   Safety

Stayed healthy and dependable while Browns' high-profile cornerbacks battled injuries... Browns' defensive MVP...Led team in interceptions (five), was second in tackles (120) and third in passes defensed (10)...Was quiet contributor until cracking the starting lineup midway through 1987 season...Started just seven games but shared team lead in pickoffs with four... Signed as a free agent in 1985 after three years in Canadian Football League... Stuck with Browns partly because of special-teams effort and play as nickel back... Oilers had their chance, but cut him in 1982... Never missed a game in four-year career at Drake... 1988 salary: $295,000... Born June 22, 1959, in Carthage, Mo.

KEVIN MACK 27 6-0 235   Fullback

Had frustrating year in which he missed all or part of 10 games with neck, shoulder, calf and knee injuries... Managed just 485 yards and three TDs on 123 carries, all career lows... Hopes to bounce back and resume climb up Browns' rushing charts... Ranks sixth on team's all-time rushing list in just three full seasons... Two-time Pro Bowl player... Broke Jim Brown's team rookie rushing mark with 1,104 yards in 1985... First-round pick in 1984 supplemental draft after being waived by USFL Los Angeles Express... In 1986, finished second in AFC with 10 rushing TDs despite missing four games with shoulder injury... In 1985, he and Earnest Byner formed third NFL backfield with two 1,000-yard runners... Helped Clemson go 9-1-1 in 1984... Ran 9.5-second 100-yard dash in high school... 1988 salary: $400,000... Born Aug. 9, 1962, in Kings Mountain, N.C.

CLAY MATTHEWS 33 6-2 245   Linebacker

A fixture at right outside linebacker who made it to his fourth Pro Bowl... Browns' third-leading tackler with 101... Tied Michael Dean Perry for team lead in sacks with six. Also had 39 quarterback pressures... Has averaged 100 tackles over last eight years... Failed to make interception for first time in career... Was 12th player picked in 1978 draft... Played middle linebacker at Southern California but made immediate switch outside in NFL... Brother Bruce is starting offenisve lineman for Oilers... Father Clay played end for 49ers in the '50s... 1988 salary: $685,000... Born March 15, 1956, in Palo Alto, Cal.

BRIAN BRENNAN 27 5-9 178   Wide Receiver

Diminutive five-year veteran was third on team in receiving with 46 catches for 579 yards... TD production fell off from six each of the past two years to one... Led Browns in receptions first three years and was second in 1987... Best year was 1986, when he caught 55 passes for 838 yards and six TDs. It was first year since 1980 that tight end Ozzie Newsome didn't lead the club in receptions... Fourth-round pick in 1984... All-time leading receiver in Boston College history... Was favorite target of Heisman Trophy winner Doug Flutie in college... 1988 salary: $255,000... Born Feb. 15, 1962, in Bloomfield, Mich.

MIKE JOHNSON 26 6-1 225   Linebacker

Relatively unknown for a player who has led defense-minded team in tackles last two years ... Had 132 tackles in 1988, 12 more than runnerup Felix Wright... Added two interceptions... In 1987, made 48 tackles in last four games to finish with 98... First-round pick in 1984 NFL supplemental draft after two years in USFL, including two title games... Two-time All-American at Virginia Tech... Played on same college team as Bruce Smith (Bills), Jesse Penn (Cowboys) and Tony Paige (Jets)... Also was Academic All-America while studying architecture... Played basketball for powerhouse DeMatha High (Md.)... 1988 salary: $395,000... Born Nov. 26, 1962, in Southport, N.C.

COACH BUD CARSON:

Former Jets' defensive coordinator took over after messy departure by Marty Schottenheimer... Inherits strong, talented team... Becomes head coach for first time since directing Georgia Tech from 1967-71 ... Spent past few years patching up injury-plagued New York defense. That should be good practice for handling hobbling Browns ... Also has been defensive coordinator for Browns, Chiefs, Colts, Rams and Steelers... Oversaw domination of Steelers' "Steel Curtain" from 1972-77... Has been defensive coordinator in three Super Bowls, two with Steelers and one with Rams... Spent 30 years in the Marines after playing defensive back at North Carolina... Born April 28, 1931, in Freeport, Pa.

GREATEST COACH

A master innovator and teacher, Paul Brown changed the face of pro football when he helped found the Cleveland Browns in 1946.

Brown's success came early and often. After winning the All-America Conference four years in a row (1946-49) with a 52-4-3 record, the Browns joined the NFL in 1950. Cleveland reached the championship game in seven of its first eight NFL seasons, winning in 1950, '54 and '55. Brown's only losing season in 17 years in Cleveland came in 1956.

Brown won with ingenuity. Among his contributions to football are use of notebooks and classroom techniques; grading players on film; intelligence tests for players; and shuttling in plays from the sideline.

Brown was inducted into the Pro Football Hall of Fame in 1967. The next year, he became coach of the Cincinnati Bengals.

Browns hope Kevin Mack rebounds from assorted injuries.

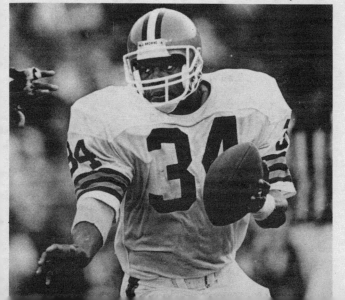

INDIVIDUAL BROWN RECORDS

Rushing

Most Yards Game:	237	Jim Brown, vs Los Angeles, 1957
	237	Jim Brown, vs Philadelphia, 1961
Season:	1,863	Jim Brown, 1963
Career:	12,312	Jim Brown, 1957-65

Passing

Most TD Passes Game:	5	Frank Ryan, vs N.Y. Giants, 1964
	5	Bill Nelsen, vs Dallas, 1969
	5	Brian Sipe, vs Pittsburgh, 1979
Season:	30	Brian Sipe, 1980
Career:	154	Brian Sipe, 1974-83

Receiving

Most TD Passes Game:	3	Mac Speedie, vs Chicago, 1951
	3	Darrell Brewster, vs N.Y. Giants, 1953
	3	Ray Renfro, vs Pittsburgh, 1959
	3	Gary Collins, vs Philadelphia, 1963
	3	Reggie Rucker, vs N.Y. Jets, 1976
	3	Larry Poole, vs Pittsburgh, 1977
	3	Calvin Hill, vs Baltimore, 1978
Season:	13	Gary Collins, 1963
Career:	70	Gary Collins, 1962-71

Scoring

Most Points Game:	36	Dub Jones, vs Chicago Bears, 1951
Season:	126	Jim Brown, 1965
Career:	1,349	Lou Groza, 1950-59, 1961-67
Most TDs Game:	6	Dub Jones, vs Chicago Bears, 1951
Season:	21	Jim Brown, 1965
Career:	126	Jim Brown, 1957-65

DENVER BRONCOS

TEAM DIRECTORY: Owner: Patrick D. Bowlen; GM: John Beake; Dir. Media Rel.: Jim Saccomano; Head Coach: Dan Reeves. Home field: Mile High Stadium (76,273). Colors: Orange, blue and white.

SCOUTING REPORT

OFFENSE: The Broncos were faced once again last year with a weak running game, then compounded it by trying to force things with Tony Dorsett. The club eventually abandoned the wide-open shotgun offense that got it to consecutive Super Bowls and never got untracked.

The Broncos (8-8) probably will go back to the exciting style of '87, with John Elway throwing the ball all over the place. With Mark Jackson, Vance Johnson and Ricky Nattiel on board, that makes sense. Dorsett will be a factor only if he improves his receiving skills.

Perhaps this is the pause that refreshes John Elway in '89.

Elway was bothered by ankle and elbow problems, throwing 17 touchdown passes and 19 interceptions. The Broncos were just eighth in AFC scoring. The concern is minimal, however, because when they're hot, Elway and the Broncos can score almost at will.

DEFENSE: Problems, problems. After his defense ranked 22nd overall and 27th against the run, coach Dan Reeves cleaned house. Former Eagles' defensive coordinator Wade Phillips replaces veteran Joe Collier, who was fired along with four other defensive assistants.

Phillips promises to bring an aggressive brand of play much unlike the Denver style that gave up 400 yards four times in '88. That will please Reeves, who would like to see his team force more turnovers.

"I want to attack, try to make things happen," said Phillips, son of former NFL coach Bum Phillips. "I think the players like it better. It's an aggressive, stunting type designed to make big plays."

The Broncos are strong at linebacker with Karl Mecklenburg and Simon Fletcher. And they made Steve Atwater their first choice in the draft to augment safeties Dennis Smith and Mike Harden. But they need improvement at other spots. They still are trying to shore up their line, something they incorrectly thought they accomplished by drafting Ted Gregory last year.

KICKING GAME: Punter Mike Horan went to the Pro Bowl after leading the NFL with a net average of 37.8. Rich Karlis missed seven tries from 30-39 yards and was left unprotected in the free-agent pool. Nattiel is an exciting punt-returner (9.9 average), but the Broncos allowed opponents a return average of 11.0.

THE ROOKIES: Reeves passed up Florida's Louis Oliver for Arkansas safety Atwater, who made 15 interceptions in college and figures to battle Harden for a starting job. Offensive lineman Doug Widell, taken in the second round out of Boston College, is a good pass-blocker and could start at right guard or right tackle. Defensive end Warren Powers, another second-round pick, is 6-6, 277, but was inconsistent at Maryland.

OUTLOOK: The Broncos have the offense to win the weak AFC West, but the defense is going to need more than a new attitude to get back to the Super Bowl. But then again, when Elway's hot, strange things can happen.

BRONCOS VETERAN ROSTER

HEAD COACH—Dan Reeves. Assistant Coaches—Marvin Bass, Barney Chavous, Mo Forte, Chan Gailey, George Henshaw, Earl Leggett, Pete Mangurian, Al Miller, Mike Nolan, Wade Phillips, Harold Richardson, Charlie Waters.

No.	Name	Pos.	Ht.	Wt.	NFL Exp.	College
35	Bell, Ken	RB	5-10	190	4	Boston College
54	Bishop, Keith	C-G	6-3	265	9	Baylor
68	Blair, Paul	T	6-4	280	3	Oklahoma State
34	Braxton, Tyrone	S	5-11	174	3	North Dakota State
56	Brooks, Michael	LB	6-1	235	3	Louisiana State
64	Bryan, Billy	C	6-2	255	13	Duke
95	Bryan, Steve	NT	6-2	256	3	Oklahoma
92	Carreker, Alphonso	DE	6-5	252	6	Florida State
28	Castille, Jeremiah	CB	5-10	175	7	Alabama
63	Contz, Bill	T	6-5	270	7	Penn State
86	Cosbie, Doug	TE	6-6	238	11	Santa Clara
58	Curtis, Scott	LB	6-1	227	2	New Hampshire
55	Dennison, Rick	LB	6-3	220	8	Colorado State
33	Dorsett, Tony	RB	5-11	189	13	Pittsburgh
7	Elway, John	QB	6-3	210	7	Stanford
73	Fletcher, Simon	LB	6-5	240	5	Houston
90	Gilbert, Freddie	DE	6-4	275	4	Georgia
22	Goode, Kerry	RB	5-11	203	2	Alabama
37	Guidry, Kevin	CB	6-0	176	2	Louisiana State
31	Harden, Mike	S	6-1	192	10	Michigan
36	Haynes, Mark	CB	5-11	195	10	Colorado
24	Henderson, Wymon	CB	5-9	181	3	Nevada-Las Vegas
78	Hood, Winford	G	6-3	262	6	Georgia
2	Horan, Mike	P	5-11	190	6	Long Beach State
79	Humphries, Stefan	G	6-3	268	5	Michigan
80	Jackson, Mark	WR	5-9	180	4	Purdue
82	Johnson, Vance	WR	5-11	185	5	Arizona
75	Jones, Rulon	DE	6-6	260	10	Utah State
66	Juriga, Jim	G-T	6-6	269	2	Illinois
12	Karcher, Ken	QB	6-3	205	3	Tulane
3	Karlis, Rich	K	6-0	180	8	Cincinnati
72	Kartz, Keith	G-T	6-4	270	3	California
88	Kay, Clarence	TE	6-2	237	6	Georgia
87	Kelly, Pat	TE	6-6	252	2	Syracuse
97	Klostermann, Bruce	LB	6-4	232	3	South Dakota State
99	Knight, Shawn	NT-DE	6-6	288	3	Brigham Young
71	Kragen, Greg	NT	6-3	265	5	Utah State
8	Kubiak, Gary	QB	6-0	192	7	Texas A&M
76	Lanier, Ken	T	6-3	269	9	Florida State
59	Lucas, Tim	LB	6-3	230	3	California
85	Massie, Rick	WR	6-1	190	3	Kentucky
77	Mecklenburg, Karl	LB	6-3	230	7	Minnesota
89	Mobley, Orson	TE	6-5	256	4	Salem College
51	Munford, Marc	LB	6-2	231	3	Nebraska
84	Nattiel, Ricky	WR	5-9	180	3	Florida
60	Perry, Gerald	T	6-6	305	2	Southern University
74	Provence, Andrew	NT	6-3	270	6	South Carolina
48	Robbins, Randy	S	6-2	189	6	Arizona
57	Ruether, Mike	C	6-4	275	4	Texas
50	Ryan, Jim	LB	6-1	225	11	William and Mary
30	Sewell, Steve	RB	6-3	210	5	Oklahoma
49	Smith, Dennis	S	6-3	200	9	Southern California
70	Studdard, Dave	T	6-4	260	11	Texas
61	Townsend, Andre	DE-NT	6-3	265	6	Mississippi
81	Watson, Steve	WR	6-4	195	10	Temple
47	Willhite, Gerald	RB	5-10	200	8	San Jose State
23	Winder, Sammy	RB	5-11	203	8	Southern Mississippi
21	Woodberry, Dennis	CB	5-10	180	4	Southern Arkansas
83	Young, Mike	WR	6-1	183	5	UCLA

TOP DRAFT CHOICES

Rd.	Name	Sel. No.	Pos.	Ht.	Wt.	College
1	Atwater, Steve	20	S	6-3	215	Arkansas
2	Widell, Doug	41	T	6-4	285	Boston College
2	Powers, Warren	47	DT	6-6	277	Maryland
3	Hamilton, Darrell	69	T	6-6	290	North Carolina
4	McCollough, Richard	97	DE	6-5	265	Clemson

BRONCO PROFILES

JOHN ELWAY 29 6-3 210   Quarterback

Performance dropped off after MVP year... Quarterback rating of 71.4 ranked ninth in AFC... Left off all postseason all-star teams ... Completed 274 of 496 passes for 3,309 yards and 17 TDs... Became first player in NFL history with 3,000 yards passing and 200 yards rushing four straight years... Threw 19 interceptions, most since he tossed 23 in 1985 ... Suffered when Broncos, seeking to best utilize Tony Dorsett, abandoned shotgun offense that got them to two straight Super Bowls... All-American at Stanford, he was first player picked in '83 draft, by Colts, before being traded to Denver shortly after ... 1989 salary: $1.425 million... Earnings will rise to $2 million by 1993... Born June 28, 1960, in Port Angeles, Wash.

RICKY NATTIEL 23 5-9 180   Wide Receiver

Speedster from Florida improved on outstanding rookie year... Caught 46 passes for 574 yards... Still is not a TD scorer, though. Had just one in '88 and two in '87... Caught 15 more passes, but average-per-reception dropped from 20.3 to 12.5... Had 74-yard TD vs. Steelers... Fifth among AFC punt-returners with 9.7 average on 22 tries... First-round draft pick in '87... Sixth-leading receiver in Florida history with 117... High-school option quarterback in Newberry, Fla., who ran for 15 TDs as a senior... 1989 salary: $200,000 ... Born Jan. 25, 1966, in Gainesville, Fla.

SAMMY WINDER 30 5-11 203   Running Back

Suffered along with rest of Bronco offense... Failed to win team rushing title for first time in six years, losing out to Tony Dorsett... Rushed 149 times for 543 yards, his lowest numbers since he was a rookie in 1982... Scored four touchdowns... Along with John Elway, was voted Denver offensive MVP by teammates... Second-leading rusher in Bronco history with 4,957 yards. Floyd Little leads with 6,323 ... Is two TDs behind Little's career club-record of 54... Hard worker who fights hard for each yard... Best season was 1984, when he rushed for 1,153 yards... Fifth-round pick out of Southern Mississippi in 1982... Played on same college team as

Hanford Dixon and Louis Lipps... 1988 salary: $380,000...
Born July 15, 1959, in Madison, Miss.

TONY DORSETT 35 5-11 189   Running Back

Superb career is nearing an end... Presence of Herschel Walker in Dallas made Dorsett expendable, so Cowboys sent him to Denver for a conditional fifth-round draft choice in 1988 ... Twelve-year veteran led Broncos in rushing with 703 yards and ran for five touchdowns... Playing time decreased as season went on... Became NFL's No. 2 all-time rusher with 12,739 yards... Gained more than 1,000 yards eight times in career, including career-high 1,646 in 1981... Hit 1,000 mark eight of first nine seasons. Failed only in strike-shortened 1982 (745 yards)... Was 1976 Heisman Trophy winner at Pitt ... 1988 salary: $560,000... Born April 7, 1954, in Rochester, Pa.

VANCE JOHNSON 26 5-11 185   Wide Receiver

Most active member of Broncos' talented receiver corps, catching 68 passes for 896 yards, both career highs... Sixth among AFC receivers... Gained 134 yards vs. Raiders... Scored five TDs... Led all receivers in 1987 Super Bowl with five catches for 121 yards, including 47-yard TD... Ran a Bronco record 4.36 in the 40-yard dash as a rookie... Second-round draft pick (1985) out of Arizona State, where he played tailback and led Pac-10 with 13 TDs as a senior... Won 1982 NCAA long-jump title with 26-11½ leap... Was alternate on '84 Olympic team... 1988 salary: $285,000... Born March 13, 1963, in Trenton, N.J.

MIKE HORAN 30 5-11 190   Punter

On everybody's All-Pro team after leading NFL with 37.9 net average and ranking third with 44.0 overall average... Landed 19 punts inside the 20 after doing so just 11 times in '87... Had 70-yard punt vs. Raiders... Signed as a free agent in 1986 after playing for Eagles for two years... Was first team All-NFC and named All-Rookie by *Pro Football Weekly* in '84, when he had an average of 42.2 and put 21 inside 20... Was ninth-round draft pick of Falcons in 1982... Didn't hook on until Philadelphia in 1984... Two-year letterman at

Long Beach State . . . Has a degree in mechanical engineering and has worked in offseason for Hughes Aircraft Corp., helping design radar and sonar equipment . . . 1988 salary: $158,000 . . . Born Feb. 1, 1959, in Orange, Calif.

SIMON FLETCHER 27 6-5 240   Linebacker

Blossomed in second season as linebacker after two as a defensive end . . . Named defensive MVP by teammates . . . Led Broncos with nine sacks, four more than any teammate . . . Made 115 tackles and had an interception . . . Coaches moved him to strong outside linebacker to take advantage of his size and ability to drop into pass coverage . . . Broncos' fastest linebacker . . . Had six passes defensed . . . Second-round draft choice out of Houston in 1985 . . . Played tackle for two years in college . . . 1988 salary: $220,000 . . . Born Feb. 18, 1962, in Bay City, Tex.

KARL MECKLENBURG 29 6-3 230   Linebacker

Injuries helped end this 12th-round draft pick's Pro Bowl string at three . . . Made 102 tackles, but sacks dropped from six to 1½ and interceptions from three to none . . . Has 40 sacks in six seasons, including 13 in 1985, his first year as a starter . . . Versatility has been key to success . . . Holds degree in biology from Minnesota . . . Mother is former deputy secretary of Department of Health, Education and Welfare . . . 1988 salary: $400,000 . . . Born Sept. 1, 1960, in Edina, Minn.

MARK JACKSON 26 5-10 180   Wide Receiver

This Amigo continues to prove he is better than a sixth-round draft pick . . . Set career-highs in receptions (46), yards (852) and TDs (six) . . . Had 18.5-yard-per-catch average, easily outdistancing other Denver receivers . . . Had 145 receiving yards vs. Raiders . . . Sped into spotlight in 1987 AFC championship game with 80-yard TD . . . Pulled another stunner in 1986 championship, catching a five-yard TD pass to bring Denver to within an extra point with 37 seconds left in regulation . . . In 1986, broke Vance Johnson's record for reception yardage by a Denver rookie with a team-high 738 yards on 38 catches . . . Caught 47 passes for 732 yards and five TDs as senior at Purdue...1988 salary: $100,000...Born May 23, 1963, in Chicago, but grew up in Terre Haute, Ind.

MIKE HARDEN 30 6-1 192   Safety

Dependable veteran led Broncos in interceptions for fifth straight year...Had four pickoffs and 10 passes defensed...Has been starter since 1982...Was team's defensive MVP in 1986 after making six interceptions, running two back for TDs...Has played cornerback, strong safety and free safety... Fifth-round pick out of Michigan in 1980...Was All-Big Ten twice...Has degree in political science and is working toward law degree...1988 salary: $450,000...Born Feb. 16, 1959, in Memphis, Tenn.

STEVE SEWELL 26 6-3 210   Running Back

Perfect match for wide-open Bronco offense ...Runs the ball, catches it and occasionally throws it...Set career highs for receptions (38), receiving yards (507) and TDs (six)... Rushed for 135 yards on 32 carries...His 1987 season was cut short by a broken jaw... Missed final five regular-season games... Had career-high 275 rushing yards in 1985 despite not having an attempt until seventh game of year... Versatility is complemented with dedication...Former Oklahoma Sooner was first-round draft choice in 1985...Ran track as a sophomore and was Academic All-Big Eight...Has degree from OU in communication...1988 salary: $255,000...Born April 2, 1963, in San Francisco.

COACH DAN REEVES: Had toughest season after reaching

Super Bowl two years in a row...Aside from injuries and losses, he lost his offensive coordinator, Mike Shanahan, to the Raiders, his father had a stroke and he fired popular assistant head coach Joe Collier and Collier's defensive staff...Still boasts lofty 74-51-1 (.621) regular-season record, fifth-best among active coaches...His 48-13 (.787) record at home is NFL's best from 1981-88 . . . Was youngest coach in NFL (37) in 1981 when he took over Broncos . . . Played quarterback at South Carolina . . . Joined Cowboys as free-agent running back in 1965 . . . Finished career as Dallas' fifth-leading rusher with 1,990 yards and 25 TDs . . . Also caught 129 passes for 1,693 yards and 17 TDs . . . Played in 1966, '67 and '70 NFL championship games . . . Has played or coached in seven Super Bowls . . . Started in coaching when he was a player-assistant coach for the Cowboys from 1970-72 . . . Spent 1973 in private business and returned as a Cowboy assistant from 1974-81 . . . Born Jan. 19, 1944, in Americus, Ga.

GREATEST COACH

In his four years as coach at Denver, Red Miller brought the Broncos to new heights. Since replacing Miller in 1981, however, Dan Reeves has taken them further.

Reeves, a former Dallas Cowboys' halfback and offensive co-ordinator, has led Denver to two Super Bowls. His teams have been in the playoffs in four of the last six years, and his career record is 78-49-1.

After getting out of the gate quickly with a 10-6 record in '81, Reeves stumbled to 2-7 in '82. With the coming of John Elway in 1983, success began to be commonplace in Denver. The Broncos set a club record with 13 wins in 1984, but fell in the playoffs. Denver won consecutive AFC titles in 1986 and '87, making Reeves the first coach to do so since Pittsburgh's Chuck Noll in 1978 and '79. However, the Broncos were blown out in Super Bowls by the Giants (XXI) and Redskins (XXII).

Reeves' regular-season record of 74-45-1 is fifth-best among active NFL coaches.

INDIVIDUAL BRONCO RECORDS
Rushing

Most Yards Game:	183	Otis Armstrong, vs Houston, 1974	
Season:	1,407	Otis Armstrong, 1974	
Career:	6,323	Floyd Little, 1967-75	

Passing

Most TD Passes Game:	5	Frank Tripucka, vs Buffalo, 1962
	5	John Elway, vs Minnesota, 1984
Season:	24	Frank Tripucka, 1960
Career:	102	John Elway, 1983-88

Receiving

Most TD Passes Game:	3	Lionel Taylor, vs Buffalo, 1960
	3	Bob Scarpitto, vs Buffalo, 1966
	3	Haven Moses, vs Houston, 1973
	3	Steve Watson, vs Baltimore, 1981
Season:	13	Steve Watson, 1981
Career:	44	Lionel Taylor, 1960-66
	44	Haven Moses, 1972-81

Scoring

Most Points Game:	21	Gene Mingo, vs Los Angeles, 1960
Season:	137	Gene Mingo, 1962
Career:	736	Jim Turner, 1971-79
Most TDs Game:	3	Lionel Taylor, vs Buffalo, 1960
	3	Don Stone, vs San Diego, 1962
	3	Bob Scarpitto, vs Buffalo, 1966
	3	Floyd Little, vs Minnesota, 1972
	3	Floyd Little, vs Cincinnati, 1973
	3	Haven Moses, vs Houston, 1973
	3	Otis Armstrong, vs Houston, 1974
	3	Jon Keyworth, vs Kansas City, 1974
	3	Steve Watson, vs Baltimore, 1981
	3	Gerald Willhite, vs Dallas, 1986
	3	Gerald Willhite, vs Kansas City, 1986
Season:	13	Floyd Little, 1972
	13	Floyd Little, 1973
	13	Steve Watson, 1981
Career:	54	Floyd Little, 1967-75

HOUSTON OILERS

TEAM DIRECTORY: Pres./Owner K.S. (Bud) Adams; GM: Mike Holovak; Dir. College Scouting: Dick Corrick; Exec. Adm.: Lewis Mangum; Dir. Media Rel.: Chip Namias; Dir. Marketing: Gregg Stengel; Head Coach: Jerry Glanville. Home field: Astrodome (61,000). Colors: Scarlet, Columbia blue and white.

SCOUTING REPORT

OFFENSE: When the Oilers have the ball, the end zone is never far away. Even with Pro Bowl quarterback Warren Moon missing almost six games last year because of a broken shoulder blade, the Oilers (10-6) finished second in AFC scoring (424 points) behind division-rival Cincinnati. Moon was remarkable, throwing for 17 TDs and just eight interceptions.

Lose a former All-American running back? He's probably in Houston, mired somewhere down the depth chart behind Mike Rozier. While Allen Pinkett, Lorenzo White and fullback Alonzo Highsmith carried the ball infrequently, Rozier ran for 1,002 yards and 10 TDs. Highsmith was an awesome blocker and rambled for 466 yards and a 5.2 average. But unfortunately for the Oilers, only one man can carry the ball at a time.

The offensive line is still dominating. Guards Bruce Matthews and Mike Munchak went to the Pro Bowl and the unit that allowed just 24 sacks last year is intact.

Ernest Givins and Drew Hall give the Oilers one of the top receiving tandems in the NFL.

DEFENSE: The Oilers' problem is that the offense can't stay on the field all the time. Houston allowed 27 or more points seven times in 1988, and only three AFC teams gave up more points. Still, the Oiler defense somehow ranked eighth in the league.

Pass-rushing is no longer the Oilers' weakness. Emerging star Ray Childress had 8½ sacks, as did William Fuller. Linebacker Johnny Meads added eight. The addition of Sean Jones, who had 7½ sacks, helped elevate the rest of the defense.

Safety Jeff Donaldson probably was the best player in Houston's secondary in 1988. Cornerbacks Patrick Allen and Steve Brown had off-years. So did safety Keith Bostic, who was let go as a free agent. The Oiler defense let too many big plays go by.

KICKING GAME: The Oilers tied an NFL record with five blocked punts, including two by Eugene Seale, and allowed just

Warren Moon hit jackpot with 5-year, $10-million pact.

5.9 yards per punt return. Unfortunately, they weren't much better on their own returns. Only Buffalo and Green Bay were worse than Houston's 6.3 yards per return.

After a poor start, kicker Tony Zendejas wound up with 22 of 34 field-goal attempts. Rookie Greg Montgomery averaged 38.8 yards on 65 punts.

THE ROOKIES: Florida tackle David Williams was drafted in the first round to provide much-needed backup help on the line.

OILERS VETERAN ROSTER

HEAD COACH—Jerry Glanville. Assistant Coaches—Kevin Gilbride, Kim Helton, Frank Novak, Floyd Reese, Nick Saban, Ray Sherman, Doug Shively, Richard Smith, Steve Watterson.

No.	Name	Pos.	Ht.	Wt.	NFL Exp.	College
29	Allen, Patrick	CB	5-10	182	6	Utah State
24	Brown, Steve	CB	5-11	192	7	Oregon
38	Bryant, Domingo	S	6-4	178	3	Texas A&M
71	Byrd, Richard	NT	6-4	267	5	Southern Mississippi
35	Byrum, Carl	RB	6-1	237	4	Mississippi Valley
14	Carlson, Cody	QB	6-3	199	3	Baylor
79	Childress, Ray	DE	6-6	270	5	Texas A&M
77	Davis, Bruce	T	6-6	315	11	UCLA
28	Dishman, Cris	CB	6-0	180	2	Purdue
31	Donaldson, Jeff	S	6-0	190	6	Colorado
80	Duncan, Curtis	WR	5-11	185	3	Northwestern
51	Fairs, Eric	LB	6-3	240	4	Memphis State
95	Fuller, William	DE	6-3	269	4	North Carolina
97	Garalczyk, Mark	DT-DE	6-6	275	3	Western Michigan
81	Givins, Ernest	WR	5-9	172	4	Louisville
59	Grimsley, John	LB	6-2	238	6	Kentucky
83	Harris, Leonard	WR-KR	5-8	162	4	Texas Tech
32	Highsmith, Alonzo	RB	6-1	234	3	Miami
85	Hill, Drew	WR	5-9	175	10	Georgia Tech
86	Jackson, Kenny	WR	5-11	180	6	Penn State
84	Jeffries, Hawood	WR	6-2	198	2	North Carolina State
22	Johnson, Kenny	S	5-10	175	10	Mississippi State
23	Johnson, Richard	CB	6-1	190	5	Wisconsin
27	Jones, Quintin	CB	5-11	193	2	Pittsburgh
96	Jones, Sean	DE	6-7	273	6	Northeastern
93	Lyles, Robert	LB	6-1	230	6	Texas Christian
73	Maarleveld, J.D.	T	6-6	280	3	Maryland
89	Magee, Calvin	TE	6-3	255	5	Southern University
78	Maggs, Don	T-G	6-5	285	3	Tulane
74	Matthews, Bruce	G	6-5	293	7	Southern California
91	Meads, Johnny	LB	6-2	235	6	Nichols State
9	Montgomery, Greg	P	6-3	213	2	Michigan State
50	Monger, Matt	LB	6-1	238	4	Oklahoma State
1	Moon, Warren	QB	6-3	210	6	Washington
63	Munchak, Mike	G	6-3	284	8	Penn State
52	Pennison, Jay	C	6-1	282	4	Nicholls State
20	Pinkett, Allen	RB	5-9	192	4	Notre Dame
30	Rozier, Mike	RB	5-10	213	5	Nebraska
98	Ruth, Mike	NT	6-2	275	3	Boston College
69	Scotts, Colin	NT	6-6	285	2	Hawaii
53	Seale, Eugene	LB	5-10	240	3	Lamar
54	Smith, Al	LB	6-1	236	3	Utah State
99	Smith, Doug	NT	6-5	282	5	Auburn
70	Steinkuhler, Dean	T	6-3	291	6	Nebraska
75	Stroth, Vince	T	6-4	275	3	Brigham Young
88	Verhulst, Chris	TE	6-2	249	2	Chico State
44	White, Lorenzo	RB	5-11	209	2	Michigan State
66	Yarno, George	C-G	6-2	270	9	Washington State
68	Young, Almon	G	6-3	285	2	Bethune-Cookman
7	Zendejas, Tony	K	5-8	165	5	Nevada-Reno

TOP DRAFT CHOICES

Rd.	Name	Sel. No.	Pos.	Ht.	Wt.	College
1	Williams, David	23	OT	6-4	295	Florida
2	Kozak, Scott	50	LB	6-2	225	Oregon
3	McDowell, Bubba	77	DB	6-0	195	Miami
4	Harris, Rod	104	WR	5-10	180	Texas A&M
5	Montgomery, Glenn	131	DT	6-0	270	Houston

Linebacker Scott Kozak has excellent pass-coverage skills but had shoulder, neck and back problems at Oregon. Third-round pick Bubba McDowell of Miami could provide immediate help at the safety position vacated by Bostic.

OUTLOOK: The Oilers are young, mean and extremely talented, but they let a division title slip away last year. If they can raise the level of their defense a bit and play half as well on the road as they do at home, they can win the AFC Central.

OILER PROFILES

WARREN MOON 32 6-3 210   Quarterback

Missed five games after suffering fractured scapula in opener but returned to have his best NFL season . . . Was selected to Pro Bowl for first time . . . Didn't throw an interception in six of his 11 regular-season games . . . Threw 17 TDs and only eight interceptions . . . Completed 160 of 294 passes for 2,327 yards and had third-best AFC rating (88.4) . . . Showed gratitude for the help he got by buying watches and trips for two to Puerto Vallarta, Mexico, for Oilers' starting offensive linemen . . . Played playoff loss to Buffalo with torn bursa sac in right elbow . . . When healthy, his strong arm and ability to run keeps defenses on edge . . . Most yardage in a season was 3,489 in 1986, but he threw 26 interceptions and just 13 TDs that year . . . Came to Houston in 1984 after six years in Canadian Football League . . . Played college ball at Washington and was MVP of 1978 Rose Bowl win over Michigan . . . Born Nov. 18, 1956, in Los Angeles . . . Signed five-year, $10-million contract last spring.

MIKE ROZIER 28 5-10 213   Running Back

First Oiler since Earl Campbell in 1983 to rush for over 1,000 yards . . . Finished with 1,002, sixth-best in AFC . . . Named Pro Bowl backup . . . Scored NFL career high of 11 TDs, the most by an Oiler since Campbell scored 12 in '83 . . . Had three 100-yard games . . . Rushed for 126 yards and three TDs in win over Bengals . . . Production has gone up every year since going to Houston from USFL in '85 . . . Gained 2,153 yards in two seasons in USFL . . . Played two seasons in 1985, rushing for 1,361 yards for Jacksonville Bulls and 462 for Oilers . . . Heisman Trophy winner at Nebraska, he was first player picked in '84 USFL draft . . . Rushed for 4,780 yards and 49 TDs in three years as a Cornhusker . . . 1988 salary: $300,000 . . . Born March 1, 1961, in Camden, N.J.

DREW HILL 32 5-9 175   Wide Receiver

Steady player who can be spectacular, he has led Oilers in receiving yards each of his four years with the team . . . Caught 72 passes for 1,141 yards, second-best in AFC . . . Has 4,411 yards over last four years, more than any other NFL player except Jerry Rice . . . Has 10 100-yard games in past two years . . . Had 148-yard, three-TD day against Redskins . . . Has started 62 straight non-strike games . . . Has scored 40 TDs in nine NFL seasons . . . Oilers gave up fourth-and seventh-round picks for him in 1985 . . . A 12th-round pick out of Georgia Tech by Rams in 1979 . . . Caught TD pass in Super Bowl as a rookie . . . 1988 salary: $400,000 . . . Born Oct. 5, 1956, in Newnan, Ga.

RAY CHILDRESS 26 6-6 270   Defensive End

Outstanding player, but Oilers always will be reminded of how they passed up Bruce Smith to make him third player picked in 1985 draft . . . Gets better each year, especially as pass-rusher . . . Made Pro Bowl last year after recording $8\frac{1}{2}$ sacks . . . Has led Oiler linemen in tackles each of his four seasons . . . Had team-high seven fumble recoveries last year, two shy of NFL record . . . Has started 62 straight games . . . Made incredible 172 tackles in 1986 . . . Made 135 as rookie starter in '85 . . . All-American at Texas A&M who started $3\frac{1}{2}$ years . . . Owns a construction business in Dallas . . . 1988 salary: $325,000 . . . Born Oct. 20, 1962, in Memphis, Tenn.

BRUCE MATTHEWS 28 6-5 293   **Guard**

Found home at guard after bouncing around line for years . . . Only Oiler Pro Bowl starter of six selected for game . . . Associated Press and *Sporting News* first-team All-Pro . . . Big reason Oilers gave up just 24 sacks, fourth-fewest in NFL . . . Started every game after starting just five in 1987 after contract holdout . . . Played left tackle in '86, after which he had back surgery . . . Ninth pick overall in 1983 after outstanding career at Southern California . . . Has degree in industrial engineering . . . 1989 salary: $400,000. . . . Born Aug. 8, 1961, in Raleigh, N.C.

MIKE MUNCHAK 29 6-3 284   **Guard**

Becoming a regular in the Pro Bowl . . . Went for fourth time . . . *Pro Football Weekly* named him best guard in NFL in 1987 after he came back from severe knee injury . . . Injury ended streak of 53 consecutive starts . . . First offensive lineman taken in 1982 draft, eighth overall . . . Won starting job as rookie but missed most of year with broken ankle . . . Teamed with Sean Farrell (Patriots) to give Penn State a dominating line . . . Has B.S. in business logistics and owns four Gold's Gyms in Houston . . . 1988 salary: $400,000 . . . Born March 5, 1960, in Scranton, Pa.

ERNEST GIVINS 24 5-9 172   **Wide Receiver**

This miniature speedster teamed with Drew Hill for NFL's most combined receiving yards (2,117) for second straight year . . . Second behind Hill among Oilers in receptions (60) and yards (976) . . . His 16.3 yards-per-catch was team high . . . Had four 100-yard games . . . Led Oilers in 1987 with 53 receptions . . . Second-round draft pick in 1986 . . . Was only ninth rookie receiver in NFL history to have 1,000-yard season . . . All-purpose player at Louisville who accounted for 34 percent of Cardinals' offense as a senior . . . MVP of '86 Senior Bowl . . . Runs 4.36-second 40-yard dash . . . 1989 salary: $220,000 . . . Born Sept. 3, 1964, in St. Petersburg, Fla.

PATRICK ALLEN 28 5-10 182   Cornerback

Consistent performer who is starting to get noticed... Was honorable mention All-Pro after leading team in passes defensed (17) for third straight season... Strength is man-to-man coverage...... Has run 4.28-second 40-yard dash... Allowed just one reception in man-to-man coverage in six different games ... Had one interception... Did not allow a TD pass in 1986... Starter since 1985... Drafted in fourth round in 1984 after starting four years at Utah State... Holds B.A. in broadcast journalism... 1988 salary: $325,000... Born Aug. 26, 1961, in McComb, Miss.

SEAN JONES 26 6-7 273   Defensive End

Oilers got this imposing physical specimen from Raiders last year along with second- and third-round picks in exchange for first-, third- and fourth-round selections... Continued to be prolific sack artist, turning in 7½ to give him 37½ in the last four years... Played behind William Fuller all year... Drafted in second round of 1984 draft... Full-time starter in 1986-87... Had 15½ sacks in 1986... Played football and lacrosse at Northeastern... Has B.S. in marketing and works in offseason as a stockbroker... In high school, lost a county hurdles race against Renaldo Nehemiah... 1988 salary: $400,000 ... Born Dec. 19, 1962, in Kingston, Jamaica.

ALONZO HIGHSMITH 24 6-1 234   Fullback

When he gets momentum, piles move... Known as one of NFL's top blocking backs, a necessity for team stocked with game-breaking tailbacks... Averaged 5.2 yards per carry... Former Miami Hurricane's pro career got off to rocky start as he held out rookie year until Week 9, then had knee surgery after season ... Planned to play linebacker and defensive end at Miami... Instead, Howard Schnellenberger moved him as freshman and he became school's No. 2 all-time rusher with 1,873 yards... Earned B.S. in business management... Father

Walter is offensive coordinator at Florida A&M . . . Played high-school ball with Mike Shula, now a Tampa Bay assistant . . . 1989 salary: $400,000. . . . Born Feb. 26, 1965, in Bartow, Fla.

COACH JERRY GLANVILLE:  Winning year spoiled by heavy criticism and front-office turmoil . . . Many feel Oilers aren't living up to their awesome collection of talent . . . Rumors persist that Glanville must make it to AFC title game to keep job . . . Noted Elvis fan has helped Oilers build reputation as aggressive, hard-hitting group of bad guys . . . Club doesn't seem to mind being known as dirty . . . Aside from leaving tickets for Elvis at will-call windows across the country, he gained notoriety in 1987 when Steelers' Chuck Noll ripped into him during postgame "handshake" . . . Has brought Houston to playoffs two years in a row after club's six-year absence . . . Joined Oilers in 1984 as defensive coordinator and replaced Hugh Campbell as head coach for final two games of '85 . . . Former Northern Michigan linebacker was an assistant with Lions, Falcons and Bills . . . Born Oct. 14, 1941, in Detroit.

GREATEST COACH

Since 1963, only one Houston Oilers' coach has turned in a winning record. He is Bum Phillips, whose trademark cowboy boots and down-home Texas personality might have overshadowed his 55-35 record and the way he turned around a struggling franchise.

The Oilers of 1972 and '73 won just one game each. Phillips became the team's defensive coordinator in 1974 and helped Houston to a 7-7 record. He took over as head coach the next year and pointed the Oilers toward the playoffs.

The Oilers reached the postseason in each of his last three years at Houston, but lost each time to the Super Bowl winner—Pittsburgh, 1978 and 1979; Oakland, 1980.

Phillips was gone after the '80 season. He became coach of the New Orleans Saints.

INDIVIDUAL OILER RECORDS

Rushing

Most Yards Game:	216	Billy Cannon, vs N.Y. Jets, 1961	
Season:	1,934	Earl Campbell, 1980	
Career:	8,574	Earl Campbell, 1978-84	

Passing

Most TD Passes Game:	7	George Blanda, vs N.Y. Jets, 1961
Season:	36	George Blanda, 1961
Career:	165	George Blanda, 1960-66

Receiving

Most TD Passes Game:	3	Bill Groman, vs N.Y. Jets, 1960
	3	Bill Groman, vs N.Y. Jets, 1961
	3	Billy Cannon, vs N.Y. Jets, 1961
	3	Charlie Hennigan, vs San Diego, 1961
	3	Charlie Hennigan, vs Buffalo, 1963
	3	Charles Frazier, vs Denver, 1966 (twice)
	3	Dave Casper, vs Pittsburgh, 1981
	3	Drew Hill, vs Washington, 1988
Season:	17	Bill Groman, 1961
Career:	51	Charlie Hennigan, 1960-66

Scoring

Most Points Game:	30	Billy Cannon, vs N.Y. Jets, 1961
Season:	115	George Blanda, 1960
Career:	596	George Blanda, 1960-66
Most TDs Game:	5	Billy Cannon, vs N.Y. Jets, 1961
Season:	19	Earl Campbell, 1979
Career:	73	Earl Campbell, 1978-84

INDIANAPOLIS COLTS

TEAM DIRECTORY: Pres./Tres.: Robert Irsay; VP/GM: Jim Irsay; VP/Gen. Counsel: Michael Chernoff; Dir. Player Personnel: Jack Bushofsky; Dir. Pub. Rel.: Craig Kelley; Head Coach: Ron Meyer. Home field: Hoosier Dome (60,127). Colors: Royal blue and white.

SCOUTING REPORT

OFFENSE: As much as Colt coaches try to prevent it from happening, the Indianapolis offense is Eric Dickerson. The Franchise ran for 1,659 yards last year and showed no signs of wear and tear.

The Colts (9-7) would like to give Dickerson some more help up front. The offensive line was banged up and failed to live up to its hype.

Eric Dickerson romped for fourth NFL rushing title.

Quarterback Chris Chandler has Colt followers thinking they finally have found a winner. Chandler was the starter for all nine victories last year and showed he can scramble. He will battle Jack Trudeau, who is coming off knee surgery.

Outside of Bill Brooks, Colt receivers were inconsistent. Coach Ron Meyer looks for first-rounder Andre Rison and free-agent acquisition Clarence Weathers to help the passing game.

DEFENSE: This is to be the year of the new-look Colts on defense. Meyer has taken over the defense and will install a more aggressive style to replace the team's old bend-but-don't-break strategy. The Colts signed free-agent safety Keith Bostic (Oilers) and linebacker Sam Clancy (Browns) to go along with the youngsters in place.

Linebackers are the Colts' strength. Veteran Fredd Young and youngster Jeff Herrod are inside with Duane Bickett and surprising O'Brien Alston outside.

The Colts' new defense probably will use several different looks up front to make up for lack of a superstar on the line. Indy, which had just 30 sacks last year, needs to pressure opposing quarterbacks more. Eugene Daniel is the Colts' top cover man, and Mike Prior adds toughness at safety.

The Colts allowed just 3.8 yards per carry, but opposing quarterbacks completed 60 percent of their passes. Meyer wants a few big plays to put the Colts ahead and let Dickerson run out the clock.

KICKING GAME: Punter Rohn Stark's 43.5-yard average ranked fourth in the NFL, but the Colts allowed opponents 11.3 yards per return. Kicker Dean Biasucci made 25 of 32 field-goal tries. Clarence Verdin can break a game open with his punt returns. He returned one for a 73-yard touchdown against Cleveland.

THE ROOKIES: Meyer and his staff were thrilled when wide receiver Rison somehow slipped past 21 other teams. The Michigan State standout gives the Colts the outside speed they need. He is a great athlete who makes spectacular catches. Indy will try to fill a hole at nose tackle with 294-pound Mitchell Benson of TCU.

OUTLOOK: The Colts are not far off from winning a weak division. They won eight of their final 10 games last year but couldn't erase a 1-5 start. Meyer may bring the Colts closer.

COLTS VETERAN ROSTER

HEAD COACH—Ron Meyer. Assistant Coaches—Greg Briner, Leon Burtnett, George Catavolos, Milt Jackson, Larry Kennan, Bill Muir, Dante Scarnecchia, Brad Seely, Rick Venturi, Tom Zupancic.

No.	Name	Pos.	Ht.	Wt.	NFL Exp.	College
97	Alston, O'Brien	LB	6-6	246	2	Maryland
79	Armstrong, Harvey	NT	6-3	268	7	Southern Methodist
62	Baldinger, Brian	G	6-4	268	7	Duke
31	Ball, Michael	CB-S	6-0	211	2	Southern University
86	Banks, Roy	WR	5-10	193	2	Eastern Illinois
81	Beach, Pat	TE	6-4	252	7	Washington State
20	Bentley, Albert	RB	5-11	214	5	Miami
4	Biasucci, Dean	K	6-0	191	5	Western Carolina
50	Bickett, Duane	LB	6-5	243	5	Southern California
25	Bostic, Keith	S	6-1	223	7	Michigan
85	Bouza, Matt	WR	6-3	212	8	California
84	Boyer, Mark	TE	6-4	242	5	Southern California
88	Brandes, John	TE	6-2	237	3	Cameron University
80	Brooks, Bill	WR	6-0	191	4	Boston University
71	Call, Kevin	T	6-7	302	6	Colorado State
17	Chandler, Chris	QB	6-4	210	2	Washington
76	Clancy, Sam	DE	6-7	275	6	Pittsburgh
40	Clinkscales, Joey	WR	6-2	198	3	Tennessee
38	Daniel, Eugene	CB	5-11	178	6	Louisiana State
48	Dee, Donnie	TE	6-4	235	2	Tulsa
29	Dickerson, Eric	RB	6-3	217	7	Southern Methodist
69	Dixon, Randy	G	6-3	293	3	Pittsburgh
53	Donaldson, Ray	C	6-3	288	10	Georgia
74	Ehin, Chuck	NT	6-5	275	6	Brigham Young
67	Elsenhooth, Stan	T-G	6-5	275	2	Towson State
37	Goode, Chris	CB	6-0	193	3	Alabama
78	Hand, Jon	DE	6-7	298	4	Alabama
61	Hendley, Jim	C	6-4	265	2	Florida State
54	Herrod, Jeff	LB	6-0	237	2	Mississippi
75	Hinton, Chris	T	6-4	295	7	Northwestern
21	Holt, John	CB	5-10	179	9	West Texas State
90	Johnson, Ezra	DE	6-4	250	13	Morris Brown
63	Knight, Steve	T-G	6-4	295	2	Tennessee
51	Kraynak, Rich	LB	6-1	225	6	Pittsburgh
60	McQuaid, Dan	T-G	6-7	278	4	Nevada-Las Vegas
28	Miller, Chuckle	CB-S	5-10	180	2	UCLA
41	Morrison, Tim	CB-S	6-1	200	3	North Carolina
93	Odom, Cliff	LB	6-2	245	9	Texas-Arlington
23	Plummer, Bruce	CB-S	6-1	197	3	Mississippi State
39	Prior, Mike	CB-S	6-0	200	4	Illinois State
49	Pruitt, James	WR	6-3	198	4	Cal State-Fullerton
72	Puzzuoli, Dave	NT	6-3	230	6	Pittsburgh
14	Ramsey, Tom	QB	6-1	185	5	UCLA
47	Robinson, Freddie	CB-S	6-1	191	3	Alabama
33	Rockins, Chris	CB-S	6-1	200	5	Oklahoma State
3	Stark, Rohn	P	6-3	204	8	Florida State
26	Swoope, Craig	CB-S	6-1	200	4	Illinois
27	Taylor, Keith	CB-S	5-11	193	2	Illinois
99	Thompson, Donnell	DE	6-4	275	9	North Carolina
10	Trudeau, Jack	QB	6-3	213	4	Illinois
12	Turner, Ricky	QB	6-0	190	2	Washington State
64	Utt, Ben	G	6-6	286	8	Georgia Tech
83	Verdin, Clarence	WR	5-8	160	4	SW Louisiana
57	Washington, Ronnie	LB	6-1	240	2	Northeast Louisiana
87	Weathers, Clarence	WR	5-9	172	7	Delaware State
98	Willis, Mitch	DT-DE	6-8	285	5	Southern Methodist
34	Wonsley, George	RB	5-10	219	6	Mississippi State
56	Young, Fredd	LB	6-1	233	6	New Mexico State

TOP DRAFT CHOICES

Rd.	Name	Sel. No.	Pos.	Ht.	Wt.	College
1	Rison, Andre	22	WR	5-10	185	Michigan State
3	Benson, Mitchell	72	DT	6-3	294	TCU
4	Tomberlin, Pat	107	T	6-3	310	Florida State
6	McDonald, Quintus	155	LB	6-3	241	Penn State
7	Hunter, Ivy Joe	182	RB	6-0	237	Kentucky

COLT PROFILES

ERIC DICKERSON 28 6-3 217   Running Back

Some consider him the franchise... Became fourth back in NFL history to lead league in rushing four times... Gained 1,659 yards to become first Colt since Alan Ameche (1955) to lead league... Only back in NFL history to rush for 1,000 yards in each of his first six seasons... Earned fifth Pro Bowl start... Ran for 14 TDs and caught a pass for one... NFL's No. 7 all-time rusher with 9,915 yards... Came to Colts via trade from Rams in '87. Colts gave up a No. 1 pick, two No. 2 picks, Owen Gill and turned over their rights to Cornelius Bennett to Buffalo... Holder of single-season NFL rushing record of 2,105 yards... Was All-American at SMU, where he was coached for three years by present coach Ron Meyer... 1989 salary: $1.4 million... Born Sept. 2, 1960, in Sealy, Tex.

CHRIS HINTON 28 6-4 295   Tackle

Made fifth Pro Bowl start... Went to Pro Bowl as a guard in 1983, then moved to important left tackle position... Was first rookie offensive lineman in NFL history to make Pro Bowl... Obtained in '83 in deal that gave Denver draft rights to John Elway... Played linebacker and tight end at Northwestern before switching to tackle in senior year and making All-Big Ten... Caught 19 passes for 265 yards as junior... Went from 218 pounds to 272 in college while maintaining 4.8 speed in 40... 1989 salary: $525,000... Born July 31, 1961, in Chicago.

RAY DONALDSON 31 6-3 288   Center

Dependable nine-year veteran has started 177 consecutive non-strike games since 1981... Made third straight Pro Bowl, second straight as a starter... Has emerged as AFC's premier center due to injury to Miami's Dwight Stephenson... "Ray Donaldson is, without a doubt, the best center in the NFL," said Colt coach Ron Meyer. "He is our most valuable player."... Needed arrival of Dickerson to gain much-deserved attention . . . Has never missed a game due to injury . . . Former Georgia Bulldog switched from linebacker to center as a sophomore . . . 1989 salary: $500,000 . . . Born May 18, 1958, in Rome, Ga.

DUANE BICKETT 26 6-5 243   Linebacker

Started every game but failed to match '87 award-filled season . . . Made 126 tackles to lead Colts for second straight year . . . Second on team with 3½ sacks and three interceptions . . . Had 10 tackles, an interception and fumble recovery Nov. 27 vs. New England to earn AFC Defensive Player of Week honors . . . Had superb 1987 season, leading team with 113 tackles, eight sacks and 10 QB pressures . . . Was Pro Bowl starter in '87 and NFL Defensive Rookie of Year in '85 . . . Has started all 60 games he has played in since being a No. 1 pick out of USC in '85 . . . 1988 salary: $330,000 . . . Born Dec. 1, 1962, in Los Angeles.

CHRIS CHANDLER 23 6-4 210   Quarterback

Rookie finished on top of Colts' QB derby, starting final 13 games, including all nine Indy victories . . . Ranked 10th among AFC QBs with 67.2 rating . . . Completed 129 of 233 passes for 1,619 yards and eight TDs. Threw 12 interceptions . . . Top game was 20-for-33 for 246 yards vs. Tampa Bay Oct. 16 . . . Threw two TDs in a game just once . . . Was knocked out of four games by injury . . . Third-round draft choice out of Washington, where he was a two-year starter . . . Threw for 4,161 yards in college, fourth-best in school history . . . Had 10 career 200-yard passing games . . . 1988 salary: $330,000 . . . Born Oct. 12, 1965, in Everett, Wash.

DEAN BIASUCCI 27 6-0 191   Kicker

Finished fifth in NFL kick-scoring with 114 points . . . Made 25 of 32 field goals and 39 of 40 PATs . . . Missed extra point vs. Jets Dec. 10, snapping string of 77 straight . . . His six field goals from 50 yards or more in '88 was an NFL record . . . Hit career-long 53-yarder Sept. 11 vs. Chicago . . . Hit crossbar from 57 yards Sept. 7 vs. Houston . . . Made 28 straight field goals from inside 45 yards before missing from 39 on Oct. 31 vs. Denver... Second-team All-Pro... Has top career success rate (.730) in club history... Made 24 of 27 in '87... Had been cut by Colts in '85 and by Falcons in '84... Performs in Indiana Repertory Theatre in offseason... Finished college career at Western Carolina as leading scorer in Southern Conference history with 280 points... 1988 salary: $235,000... Born July 25, 1962, in Niagara Falls, N.Y.

BILL BROOKS 25 6-0 191   Wide Receiver

Deep threat led Colts in receiving for second straight year... Caught 54 passes for 867 yards and three TDs... Was 14th in AFC in receptions... Caught passes in 38 straight games before being shut out Nov. 13 vs. Green Bay... Had two 100-yard games. No other Colt had one... Fourth-round pick out of Boston University in 1986, he caught 65 passes as rookie and 51 in '87... Made several All-Rookie teams in '86 and was the NFL Players Association Offensive Rookie of the Year... Finished college career with 228 receptions for 3,579 yards and 32 TDs... 1989 salary: $132,000... Born April 6, 1964, in Boston.

ALBERT BENTLEY 29 5-11 214   Running Back

Versatility is his key, as he is often used as a surprise when defenses key on Eric Dickerson... Was second in rushing with 230 yards, fourth in receiving with 26 for 252 and led Colt kickoff returners with 39 for 775 yards... His rushing yardage was a career low, as was his kickoff average of 19.9... Led AFC with 1,578 all-purpose yards in '87 but dropped to 1,257 last year... Was starting halfback before Dickerson's arrival, averaging 92 yards per game... Picked in second round of '84 supplemental draft after two years in USFL... Three-year letterman at Miami who scored winning TD in '84 national championship win over Nebraska... 1989 salary: $260,000... Born Aug. 15, 1960, in Imokalee, Fla.

FREDD YOUNG 27 6-1 233   Linebacker

Came to Colts in trade with Seahawks and started 12 games—two at left outside linebacker and 10 at left inside...Colts gave up two No. 1 picks (1988 and '89) for him... Finished sixth in tackles with 93, including 12 vs. Miami Dec. 4...Led Colts with five forced fumbles...In 1987, he led Seattle with 101 tackles and was second with nine sacks ...Is the only Seattle linebacker to be voted to Pro Bowl. He went in each of his first four seasons...Former special-teams standout had a blocked punt, a forced fumble and four tackles inside the 20 in first pro game...Third-round draft choice out of New Mexico State in '84...1988 salary: $890,000...Born Nov. 14, 1961, in Dallas.

O'BRIEN ALSTON 23 6-6 246   Linebacker

Rangy rookie finished ninth on team with 63 tackles and was third with three sacks... Started 11 games at left outside linebacker... Had season-high nine tackles Dec. 10 vs. Jets...Tenth-round draft pick out of Maryland, he started in second week of season... Runs 40-yard dash in 4.8 seconds...Named to *Pro Football Weekly* All-Rookie team... Was first-team All-ACC after making 99 tackles and four sacks as a senior...Had 16 tackles and three sacks in a victory over Duke...Finished career with 188 tackles...1988 salary: $81,000...Born Dec. 21, 1965, in New Haven, Conn.

COACH RON MEYER:

Has quickly turned Colts into contenders...Is 21-14 in two-plus years at Indy...Took a team that had won just two division games in two years to an AFC East title in 1987...His Colts have defeated each AFC East opponent each of his first two years. The last time a Colt team did so was in 1977 ...Was a winning coach at Nevada-Las Vegas, SMU and with the New England Patriots, where he became the first NFL coach to be fired during a winning season . . . He was 5-3 in 1984 when he was dismissed. While he was with the Pats, dissension spread among veterans unhappy with his strict discipline . . . Was 18-15 with the Patriots, including a playoff berth in 1982—just one year after New England was 2-14 . . . Was a walk-on defensive back at Purdue, then worked his way up the coaching ladder from the high school ranks . . . Has also been a scout and player agent . . . Born Feb. 17, 1941, in Westerville, Ohio.

GREATEST COACH

In the Colts' storied history, Don Shula's six-year record of 73-26-4 stands above all. At 33, Shula was the youngest head coach in NFL history when Baltimore picked him to succeed Weeb Ewbank in 1963. The former Detroit defensive coordinator brought the Colts to the NFL title game in 1964 and '68 after 12-2 and 13-1 seasons.

Shula is still remembered in Baltimore for the Colts' overtime loss at Green Bay in the 1965 playoffs. Because of injuries to Johnny Unitas and Gary Cuozzo, halfback Tom Matte played quarterback and nearly led the Colts to victory.

The 1968 Colts were stunned in perhaps the most famous Super Bowl of all, a 16-7 upset loss to Joe Namath and the New York Jets. The coach of the Jets was Ewbank, who nearly matches Shula's prominence in Colt record books. In nine years at Baltimore, Ewbank compiled a 61-52-1 mark that included consecutive NFL championships in 1958 and '59.

Ewbank's best regular-season record with the Colts was 9-3 and after winning his second title he did no better than 8-6.

INDIVIDUAL COLT RECORDS
Rushing

Most Yards Game:	198	Norm Bulaich, vs N.Y. Jets, 1971
Season:	1,659	Eric Dickerson, 1988
Career:	5,487	Lydell Mitchell, 1972-77

Passing

Most TD Passes Game:		5	Gary Cuozzo, vs Minnesota, 1965
		5	Gary Hogeboom, vs Buffalo, 1987
	Season:	32	John Unitas, 1959
	Career:	287	John Unitas, 1956-72

Receiving

Most TD Passes Game:		3	Jim Mutscheller, vs Green Bay, 1957
		3	Raymond Berry, vs Dallas, 1960
		3	Raymond Berry, vs Green Bay, 1960
		3	Jimmy Orr, vs Washington, 1962
		3	Jimmy Orr, vs Los Angeles, 1964
		3	Roger Carr, vs Cincinnati, 1976
	Season:	14	Raymond Berry, 1959
	Career:	68	Raymond Berry, 1955-67

Scoring

Most Points Game:		24	Lenny Moore, vs Chicago, 1958
		24	Lenny Moore, vs Los Angeles, 1960
		24	Lenny Moore, vs Minnesota, 1961
		24	Lydell Mitchell, vs Buffalo, 1975
		24	Eric Dickerson, vs Denver, 1988
	Season:	120	Lenny Moore, 1964
	Career:	678	Lenny Moore, 1956-67
Most TDs Game:		4	Lenny Moore, vs Chicago, 1958
		4	Lenny Moore, vs Los Angeles, 1960
		4	Lenny Moore, vs Minnesota, 1961
		4	Lydell Mitchell, vs Buffalo, 1975
		4	Eric Dickerson, vs Denver, 1988
	Season:	20	Lenny Moore, 1964
	Career:	113	Lenny Moore, 1956-67

KANSAS CITY CHIEFS

TEAM DIRECTORY: Owner: Lamar Hunt; Pres./CEO/GM: Carl Peterson; Exec. VP-Adm.: Tim Connolly; Player Personnel Dir.: Whitey Dovell; Dir. Pub. Rel.: Gary Heise; Head Coach: Marty Schottenheimer. Home field: Arrowhead Stadium (78,094). Colors: Red and gold.

SCOUTING REPORT:

OFFENSE: Bill Kenney, the starting quarterback at the outset last season, is out of the Chiefs' plans. Well-traveled veteran Steve DeBerg started 11 times, throwing for 2,935 yards and going 4-6-1. The Chiefs' running game was a mess. Talented second-year fullback Christian Okoye missed seven games with injuries, but still led the team with 473 yards. Kansas City's eight rushing TDs was an NFL-low.

Up-to-date in Kansas City: Another Deron Cherry Pro Bowl.

Much of the problem was up front, where injuries prevented the Chiefs (4-11-1) from maintaining continuity on the line. Folks in K.C. believe that if tackles John Alt and Irv Eatman and guards Rich Baldinger and Mark Addickes stay healthy, the line can be outstanding. Gerry Feehery is the center, but ageless veteran Mike Webster comes from Pittsburgh to make things interesting.

Stephone Paige, who caught 61 passes for seven touchdowns, is a top-rate receiver. Paige may need some help soon because former Pro Bowl receiver Carlos Carson is 30.

DEFENSE: There are times statistics don't tell the truth, but this isn't one of them. The Chiefs' defense ranked No. 1 against the pass and No. 28 against the run last year.

The Chiefs were the only NFL team to allow more rushing yards than passing yards. Opponents piled up 4.3 yards per rush as injuries forced the Chiefs to start five different nose tackles. The Chiefs' primary need is help at linebacker and they now have it in the presence of Butkus Award winner Derrick Thomas, 11th pick in the draft. Dino Hackett made the Pro Bowl and Jack Del Rio is respectable. The Chiefs had just 23 sacks but expect Neil Smith, a No. 1 pick in '88, to better a rookie year in which he turned in just 2½ sacks.

Meanwhile, the defensive backfield continues to be outstanding. Safety Deron Cherry, who made seven interceptions, and cornerback Albert Lewis started in the Pro Bowl. The Chiefs allowed 12 TD passes, least in the NFL, so there is genuine hope on defense. The Chiefs held opponents to seven points or less three times, but lost all three games.

KICKING GAME: As usual, Nick Lowery was dependable, hitting 27 of 32 field-goal attempts. He hit 3-of-3 from 50-or-more yards and was 8-for-10 from 40-49 yards. You can't ask for much more than that. Punter Kelly Goodburn averaged 40.3 yards, but his 31.9 net average wasn't so hot.

Paul Palmer dropped from being the AFC leader in 1988 with a 24.3 kick-return average to 15.8 in 1989. As a team, the Chiefs' 16.5 average was worst in the league. Punt returns (6.7) were poor, too. Punt and kick coverage was weak.

THE ROOKIES: Linebacker Thomas has all the makings of a future superstar. He had 27 sacks as a senior and should help the Chiefs establish a pass rush. Alabama followers say Thomas was better in college than Cornelius Bennett. Wake Forest's Mike

CHIEFS VETERAN ROSTER

HEAD COACH—Marty Schottenheimer. Assistant Coaches—Bruce Arians, Russ Ball, Bill Cowher, Tony Dungy, Howard Mudd, Joe Pendry, Tom Pratt, Dave Redding, Al Saunders, Kurt Schottenheimer, Darvin Wallis.

No.	Name	Pos.	Ht.	Wt.	NFL Exp.	College
61	Adickes, Mark	B	6-4	273	4	Baylor
32	Agee, Tommie	RB	6-0	218	2	Auburn
76	Alt, John	T	6-7	290	6	Iowa
54	Ashley, Walker Lee	LB	6-0	230	6	Penn State
77	Baldinger, Rich	G-T	6-4	285	8	Wake Forest
80	Barnes, Lew	WR-KR	5-8	163	3	Oregon
99	Bell, Mike	DE	6-4	260	9	Colorado State
65	Bowyer, Walt	DE	6-4	260	5	Arizona-State
34	Burruss, Lloyd	S	6-0	205	9	Maryland
88	Carson, Carlos	WR	5-11	190	10	Louisiana State
20	Cherry, Deron	S	5-11	203	9	Rutgers
62	Chilton, Gene	C	6-3	271	3	Texas
51	Cooper, George	LB	6-2	225	2	Michigan State
55	Cooper, Louis	LB	6-2	245	5	Western Carolina
17	DeBerg, Steve	QB	6-3	210	13	San Jose State
50	Del Rio, Jack	LB	6-4	238	5	Southern California
65	DeGiacomo, Curt	G-C	6-4	265	3	Arizona
93	Dressel, Chris	TE	6-4	245	6	Stanford
75	Eatman, Irv	T	6-7	294	4	UCLA
64	Feehery, Gerry	C	6-2	270	7	Syracuse
91	Gaines, Greg	LB	6-3	229	8	Tennessee
22	Gamble, Kenny	RB	5-10	197	2	Colgate
2	Goodburn, Kelly	P	6-2	198	3	Emporia State
98	Griffin, Leonard	DE	6-4	270	4	Grambling
58	Griggs, Anthony	LB	6-3	230	8	Ohio State
81	Griggs, Billy	TE	6-3	230	5	Virginia
56	Hackett, Dino	LB	6-3	228	4	Appalachian State
86	Harry, Emile	WR	5-11	176	3	Stanford
85	Hayes, Jonathan	TE	6-5	239	5	Iowa
44	Heard, Herman	RB	5-10	190	6	Southern Colorado
23	Hill, Greg	CB	6-1	202	7	Oklahoma State
60	Ingram, Byron	G	6-2	295	2	Eastern Kentucky
7	Jaworski, Ron	QB	6-1	205	15	Youngstown State
73	Jozwiak, Brian	G	6-5	293	4	West Virginia
9	Kenney, Bill	QB	6-4	217	11	Northern Colorado
29	Lewis, Albert	CB	6-2	198	7	Grambling
38	Loveall, Calvin	CB-S	5-9	180	2	Idaho
8	Lowery, Nick	K	6-4	189	10	Dartmouth
59	Lowry, Orlando	LB	6-4	236	5	Ohio State
72	Lutz, David	T	6-6	290	7	Georgia Tech
63	Maas, Bill	NT	6-5	268	6	Pittsburgh
57	Martin, Chris	LB	6-2	231	7	Auburn
92	McCabe, Jerry	LB	6-1	225	3	Holy Cross
14	McManus, Danny	QB	6-0	200	2	Florida State
69	Meisner, Greg	NT	6-3	269	9	Pittsburgh
35	Okoye, Christian	RB	6-1	253	3	Azusa Pacific
26	Paige, Stephone	WR	6-2	185	7	Fresno State
26	Palmer, Paul	RB-KR	5-9	181	3	Temple
96	Pearson, Aaron	LB	6-0	240	4	Mississippi State
24	Pearson, Jayice	CB	5-11	190	4	Washington
27	Porter, Kevin	CB-S	5-10	215	2	Auburn
87	Roberts, Alfredo	TE	6-3	250	2	Miami
31	Ross, Kevin	CB	5-9	182	6	Temple
4	Runager, Max	P	6-1	189	11	South Carolina
97	Saleaumua, Dan	NT	6-0	285	3	Arizona State
70	Sally, Jerome	NT	6-3	270	8	Missouri
21	Saxon, James	RB	5-11	215	2	San Jose State
70	Smith, Dave	T	6-6	290	2	Southern Illinois
90	Smith, Neil	DE	6-4	270	2	Nebraska
52	Snipes, Angelo	LB	6-0	227	4	West Georgia
67	Stensrud, Mike	NT	6-5	280	11	Iowa State
94	Watts, Randy	DE	6-6	279	2	Catawba
53	Webster, Mike	C	6-2	260	16	Wisconsin

TOP DRAFT CHOICES

Rd.	Name	Sel. No.	Pos.	Ht.	Wt.	College
1	Thomas, Derrick		4	LB	6-3	230	Alabama
2	Elkins, Mike	32	QB	6-2	220	Wake Forest
3	Worthen, Nasrullen	60	WR	5-8	175	N.C. State
4	Petry, Stanley	88	DB	5-11	165	TCU
6	Thomas, Robb	143	WR	5-11	174	Oregon State

Elkins, a second-round pick, will get a chance to learn from some experienced quarterbacks.

OUTLOOK: New coach Marty Schottenheimer said his goal with the Chiefs is to win the Super Bowl this season. "I'm not interested in rebuilding programs," he said upon taking over an injury-hampered team that won just eight games over the last two seasons. The Chiefs won't win it all, but they may not be as far off as some think.

CHIEF PROFILES

ALBERT LEWIS 28 6-2 198   Cornerback

Overlooked early in his career, he is now getting deserved recognition . . . Named to second straight Pro Bowl, first as starter . . . Had just one interception each of last two seasons after making 20 in first four years, but 12 pass deflections in 1988 show he continues to smother receivers . . . Played just 14 games, with 12 starts . . . Missed one game due to father's death and missed three starts with ankle sprain . . . An expert at blocking punts . . . Was AFC Defensive Player of Week vs. Bengals, blocking a punt for a safety, recovering fumble to set up game-winning TD, deflecting two passes, and making four tackles . . . Made three interceptions in final three games of '85 to give him AFC-leading eight for year . . . Played nickel back as rookie, then stepped in as starter at left cornerback . . . Third-round draft pick out of Grambling in 1983 . . . 1988 salary: $325,000 . . . Born Oct. 6, 1960, in Mansfield, La.

DERON CHERRY 29 5-11 203   Safety

Former free-agent punter ranks as one of the best safeties ever . . . Named to sixth straight Pro Bowl after leading Chiefs with seven interceptions, 151 tackles and six fumble recoveries . . . Latter is a team record . . . Has at least 100 tackles and seven pickoffs in five of the last six seasons . . . Couldn't make it as an unsigned punter out of Rutgers in 1981. Switched to safety and was cut. Re-signed a few weeks later and played in 13 games . . . Became a starter in 1983 and started in Pro Bowl . . . Eight-year totals: 88 starts, 41 interceptions, 12 fumble recoveries, three TDs . . . Played safety and punter at

Rutgers and earned degree in biology . . . 1988 salary: $1.075 million . . . Born Sept. 12, 1959, in Palmyra, N.J.

DINO HACKETT 25 6-3 228   Linebacker

Missed final three games of season because of knee injury . . . Still, he was named to Pro Bowl for first time . . . Had five games in '88 with 10 or more tackles . . . Recorded career-high three sacks . . . Relentless player who has played hurt most of career . . . Has made over 100 tackles in each of his three NFL seasons . . . Led Chiefs in tackles in 1986-87 . . . Club's top rookie in '86 . . . Second-round pick out of Appalachian State, where he made 200 tackles in senior season . . . Brother Joey played tight end with Denver in '86 after three years in USFL . . . 1989 salary: $200,000 . . . Born June 28, 1964, in Greensboro, N.C.

NICK LOWERY 33 6-4 189   Kicker

Made career-high 27 field goals, including last-minute kicks that beat Cincinnati and Seattle in consecutive weeks . . . Produced all Chiefs' scoring in five different games . . . Made 27-of-32 field-goal attempts (84.3 percent), including 5-for-5 against Bengals . . . Tied with Jan Stenerud with NFL-record 17 field goals from 50 yards and out . . . Has six seasons with more than 100 points . . . His 172 straight PATs is a team record . . . Injury-free, he is Chiefs' only kicker since 1980, excluding three strike games in 1987 . . . Played in 1981 Pro Bowl . . . Tried to make eight different teams before landing on Chiefs' roster in 1980 . . . Graduated from Dartmouth in 1978 with degree in government . . . 1988 salary: $315,000 . . . Born May 27, 1956, in Munich, West Germany.

PAUL PALMER 24 5-9 181   Running Back

All-purpose player whose 1,063 yards from scrimmage were most for a Chief running back since Joe Delaney had 1,367 in 1981 . . . Team's second-leading rusher (452 yards) and receiver (52 for 611 yards) . . . Had three 100-yard receiving games in '88 . . . Team's busiest kick-returner (23 for a 15.8 average) . . . Played in 15 games, starting first 11 . . .

Coaches questioned his attitude late in season... Was first-round pick in 1987 but played mostly on special teams... Scored TDs of 95 and 92 yards on kickoff returns in 1987 and was on most All-Rookie teams... Was 19th selection overall after standout career at Temple... Was Heisman Trophy runner-up to Vinny Testaverde in 1986, when he led NCAA in rushing with 1,866 yards... 1988 salary: $200,000. 1989 salary: $250,000... Born Oct. 16, 1964, in Bethesda, Md.

CHRISTIAN OKOYE 28 6-1 253 Running Back

Spent much of season in trainer's room but still led team in rushing with 473 yards and three TDs... Missed four games with broken thumb, one with a back injury and two with broken hand... Ran for 102 yards vs. Cincinnati... How bad has Chiefs' rushing been in recent years? Okoye is first K.C. running back to have 100-yard games in consecutive years since 1978-79 (Tony Reed) and first to have two career 100-yard games since 1981 (Joe Delaney)... Led NFL rookies with 660 yards in 1987... Pro debut resulted in 105-yard effort vs. Chargers... Has played just five years in organized football... Went to Azusu Pacific in 1982 as track star, then turned to football... Second-round draft pick... Holds African discus record... Runs 40-yard dash in 4.46 seconds... 1989 salary: $215,000... Born Aug. 16, 1961, in Enugu, Nigeria.

STEPHONE PAIGE 27 6-2 185 Wide Receiver

Acrobatic big-play threat... Led Chiefs with career-high 61 receptions for 902 yards and seven TDs... Fourth on Chiefs' all-time TD list with 42... Only K.C. offensive player to start all 16 games... Has played in 92 straight... Had 10 TDs in 1985 and 11 in 1986... Led Chief receivers in 1986 with 52 catches for 829 yards in first year as full-time starter... Turned in best receiving day in NFL history in 1985 with 309 yards on eight receptions vs. Chargers... Signed in 1983 as undrafted free agent from Fresno State and responded with six TDs... Scouts must have been too busy watching college teammate Henry Ellard to notice Paige, a junior-college transfer... 1988 salary: $350,000... Born Oct. 15, 1961, in Slidell, La.

STEVE DeBERG 35 6-3 210   Quarterback

Old pro has been pushed to sidelines by Joe Montana, John Elway and Vinny Testaverde in his career, but he beat out Bill Kenney in K.C. . . . Traded from Tampa Bay in spring of 1987 . . . Started 11 games and team was 4-6-1 in those games . . . Threw for 2,935 yards, better than Len Dawson's best year . . . Yards, completions (224) and attempts (414) were second-most in Chief history . . . Named AFC Offensive Player of Week vs. Denver after throwing for 259 yards and two TDs . . . Has been shuffled around league but has 22,517 yards in 12-year career . . . Owns 14 300-yard passing games . . . A 10th-round pick out of San Jose State by Cowboys in 1977 . . . Was cut and signed by 49ers . . . 1988 salary: $605,000 . . . Born Jan. 19, 1954, in Oakland.

JACK DEL RIO 25 6-4 238   Linebacker

Came on strong at end of season, making 33 tackles over one three-game span . . . Started two games at outside linebacker, eight inside . . . Made career-high 77 tackles (sixth on team) before missing season finale with knee sprain . . . Had one sack . . . Joined Chiefs in 1987 training-camp trade with Saints, who received a fifth-round pick in return . . . Was All-Rookie performer in 1985 but playing time decreased the next year . . . All-American and four-year starter at Southern Cal . . . Was USC's starting catcher on baseball team . . . Drafted by Toronto Blue Jays out of high school in 1981 . . . 1988 salary: $151,300 . . . Born April 4, 1963, in Castro Valley, Cal.

CARLOS CARSON 30 5-11 190   Wide Receiver

Production dropped off after Pro Bowl season in 1987 . . . Had 46 receptions for 711 yards and three TDs . . . His 15.8-yard average was lowest since 1980 rookie season . . . Had 162-yard game vs. Jets, his 18th career 100-yard game . . . Has 32 TDs in nine years . . . Is 280 yards away from second place on team's all-time list . . . Best year was 1983, when he had 80 catches for 1,351 yards and seven TDs . . . Fifth-round draft choice out of LSU in 1980 . . . Set NCAA record in 1977 with six consecutive receptions for TDs, including five in one game . . .

988 salary: $665,000 . . . Born Dec. 28, 1958, in Lake Worth, Fla.

COACH MARTY SCHOTTENHEIMER: Left Cleveland after 1988 postseason dispute with Browns' owner Art Modell . . . Signed four-year contract to take over for Frank Gansz, who was 8-22-1 in two years . . . Put thoughts of rebuilding out of Kansas City fans' minds upon taking job, saying, "Our goal for 1988 is to become the champions of the National Football League" . . . First head coach to come to K.C. with previous NFL head-coaching experience . . . Went to playoffs in all four full seasons with Browns, winning three AFC Central titles and reaching AFC championship game twice . . . Was 32-15 the past three years . . . Replaced Sam Rutigliano midway through 1984 season, going 4-4 . . . Was AFC Coach of the Year in 1986 . . . Joined Browns as defensive coordinator in 1980 . . . Was an assistant with Giants and Lions after serving as linebacker coach for World Football League's Portland Storm in 1974 . . . An All-American linebacker at Pitt, he played six years in NFL . . . Born Sept. 23, 1943, in Canonsburg, Pa.

GREATEST COACH

The Chiefs' first coach was their best. In 15 seasons, Hank Stram compiled a lofty 124-76-10 record as well as three AFL titles and a Super Bowl victory.

Stram was hired off the campus of the University of Miami, where he was an assistant, to guide the expansion Dallas Texans in 1960. Two years later, the Texans defeated the Houston Oilers, 20-17, in six quarters for the AFL championship. The Texans moved to Kansas City in 1963, then returned to the limelight in 66 with a 31-7 AFL championship victory over Buffalo and a berth in Super Bowl I, where they were trounced, 35-10, by Green Bay.

Stram got his ring three years later when the Chiefs upset Minnesota, 23-7, in Super Bowl IV. He coached the Chiefs through 1964.

INDIVIDUAL CHIEF RECORDS

Rushing

Most Yards Game:	193	Joe Delaney, vs Houston, 1981
Season:	1,121	Joe Delaney, 1981
Career:	4,451	Ed Podolak, 1969-77

Passing

Most TD Passes Game:	6	Len Dawson, vs Denver, 1964
Season:	30	Len Dawson, 1964
Career:	237	Len Dawson, 1962-75

Receiving

Most TD Passes Game:	4	Frank Jackson, vs San Diego, 1964
Season:	12	Chris Burford, 1962
Career:	57	Otis Taylor, 1965-75

Scoring

Most Points Game:	30	Abner Haynes, vs Oakland, 1961
Season:	129	Jan Stenerud, 1968
Career:	1,231	Jan Stenerud, 1967-79
Most TDs Game:	5	Abner Haynes, vs Oakland, 1961
Season:	19	Abner Haynes, 1962
Career:	60	Otis Taylor, 1965-75

LOS ANGELES RAIDERS

TEAM DIRECTORY: Managing Gen. Partner: Al Davis; Exec. Asst.: Al LoCasale; Sr. Exec.: John Herrera; Sr. Administrators: Irv Kaze, Morris Bradshaw; Business Mgr.: Dave Houghton; Publications: Mike Taylor; Head Coach: Mike Shanahan. Home field: Los Angeles Memorial Coliseum (92,487). Colors: Silver and black.

SCOUTING REPORT

OFFENSE: The Raiders are proof that big names don't add up to big production. An offense that included Marcus Allen, Bo Jackson, Willie Gault, Tim Brown, James Lofton and Mervyn Fernandez finished in the bottom half of the league in scoring.

As usual, the Raiders (7-9) had quarterback problems. Jay Schroeder was acquired from the Redskins early in the season

Nobody came close to Tim Brown's kickoff-return totals.

and suffered from not knowing the Raider system. He and Steve Beuerlein split time, but Schroeder, with his big-play ability, is the future.

Allen keeps rolling along while the Raiders wait for Jackson to pick a sport. Brown, a rookie, was the team's best receiver at the end of the season, and Gault and Fernandez are capable of great things.

The offensive line is inexperienced and was bothered by injury last year. Raider quarterbacks were sacked 46 times, most in the AFC. The Raiders' first draft pick, guard Steve Wisniewski, should help.

DEFENSE: Injuries and inconsistent linebacker play hurt the Raider defense. One of those sidelined was rookie cornerback Terry McDaniel, a No. 1 pick who has the talent to be a star. He teams with Mike Haynes, who is good but aging at 36.

Only two AFC teams allowed more points than the Raiders. Part of the problem was the absence of end Howie Long, who missed the final 10 games with a calf injury. Greg Townsend picked up a lot of the slack with 11½ sacks, but that was twice as many as any of his teammates.

KICKING GAME: Brown is a game-breaker, leading the NFL in kickoff returns with a 26.8 average and turning in a good 9.1 mark on punts.

Chris Bahr was let go in the free-agent scramble after hitting just 18 of 29 field-goal attempts. He was 6-for-10 from 40-49 yards and 1-for-4 from further out. Punter Jeff Gossett had a good year with a gross average of 41.8 and a net of 35.7. He landed an AFC-high 27 punts inside the 20.

THE ROOKIES: The Raiders didn't make a draft choice until the sixth round, but traded for Penn State's Wisniewski, who was Dallas' second-round pick. Wisniewski is regarded as an over-achiever who can help the Raiders' jumbled offensive line. He weighs just 266 but bench-presses almost 500 pounds. L.A.'s first pick of its own was quarterback Jeff Francis, a three-year starter at Tennessee.

OUTLOOK: The Raiders lost four of their last five games, so coach Mike Shanahan shook up his staff. He is still left with a load of questions on the offensive line and on defense. The Raiders have the offensive firepower to sneak into contention, but the chemistry on both sides of the ball doesn't seem present for all those superstars to produce a Super Bowl title.

RAIDERS VETERAN ROSTER

HEAD COACH—Mike Shanahan. Assistant Coaches—Dave Adolph, Fred Biletnikoff, John Dunn, Alex Gibbs, Sam Gruiesen, Terry Robiskie, Pete Rodriquez, Joe Scanella, Art Shell, Jack Stanton, Bill Urbanik, Tom Walsh.

No.	Name	Pos.	Ht.	Wt.	NFL Exp.	College
44	Adams, Stefon	S	5-10	185	4	East Carolina
32	Allen, Marcus	RB	6-2	205	8	Southern California
33	Anderson, Eddie	S	6-1	195	4	Fort Valley State
99	Baldwin, Keith	DE	6-4	265	7	Texas A&M
54	Benson, Tom	LB	6-2	240	6	Oklahoma
7	Beuerlein, Steve	QB	6-2	205	2	Notre Dame
21	Birdsong, Craig	S	6-2	220	2	North Texas State
64	Brown, Ron	LB	6-4	235	3	Southern California
81	Brown, Tim	WR	6-0	195	2	Notre Dame
61	Caldwell, David	DT	6-2	265	2	Texas Christian
29	Carter, Russell	S	6-2	200	6	Southern Methodist
46	Christensen, Todd	TE	6-3	230	11	Brigham Young
94	Costello, Joe	LB	6-3	240	4	Central Connecticut
47	Davis, Jeff	LB	6-0	230	7	Clemson
70	Davis, Scott	DE	6-7	270	2	Illinois
11	Evans, Vince	QB	6-2	210	10	Southern California
86	Fernandez, Mervyn	WR	6-3	200	3	San Jose State
83	Gault, Willie	WR	6-0	180	7	Tennessee
63	Gesek, John	G-C	6-5	275	3	Cal State-Sacramento
95	Glover, Clyde	DE	6-6	285	2	Fresno State
79	Golic, Bob	DT	6-2	265	10	Notre Dame
6	Gossett, Jeff	P	6-2	195	8	Eastern Illinois
85	Graddy, Sam	WR	5-10	165	3	Tennessee
60	Graves, Rory	T	6-6	290	2	Ohio State
22	Haynes, Mike	CB	6-2	190	14	Arizona State
65	Hellestrae, Dale	G	6-5	285	4	Southern Methodist
88	Horton, Ethan	TE	6-4	235	3	North Carolina
34	Jackson, Bo	RB	6-1	225	3	Auburn
18	Jaeger, Jeff	K	5-11	185	2	Washington
73	Jordan, David	T	6-5	280	4	Auburn
87	Junkin, Trey	TE	6-2	230	7	Louisiana Tech
59	Kimmel, Jamie	LB	6-3	235	3	Syracuse
92	King, Emanuel	LB	6-4	250	5	Alabama
52	King, Linden	LB	6-4	245	12	Colorado State
74	Koch, Pete	DE	6-6	260	5	Maryland
69	Lee, Larry	G	6-2	270	9	UCLA
40	Lee, Zeph	S	6-3	205	3	Southern California
51	Lewis, Bill	C	6-7	275	4	Nebraska
56	Lija, George	C	6-4	285	7	Michigan
80	Lofton, James	WR	6-3	190	12	Stanford
75	Long, Howie	DE	6-5	265	9	Villanova
26	McElroy, Vann	S	6-2	195	8	Baylor
55	Millen, Matt	LB	6-2	245	10	Penn State
72	Mosebar, Don	C-T	6-6	275	7	Southern California
97	Mraz, Mark	DE	6-4	260	2	Utah State
42	Mueller, Vance	RB	6-0	215	4	Occidental
61	Pettitt, Duane	G	6-4	280	2	San Diego State
71	Pickel, Bill	DT	6-5	265	7	Rutgers
20	Price, Dennis	CB	6-1	175	2	UCLA
27	Richardson, Mike	CB	6-0	185	7	Arizona State
77	Riehm, Chris	G	6-5	280	3	Ohio State
57	Robinson, Jerry	LB	6-2	230	11	UCLA
13	Schroeder, Jay	QB	6-4	215	6	UCLA
53	Shields, Jon	G	6-5	285	2	Portland State
58	Shipp, Jackie	LB	6-2	240	6	Oklahoma
35	Smith, Steve	RB	6-1	235	3	Penn State
39	Strachan, Steve	RB	6-1	225	5	Boston College
96	Taylor, Malcolm	DT	6-6	280	6	Tennessee State
30	Toran, Stacey	S	6-3	200	6	Notre Dame
93	Townsend, Greg	LB-DE	6-3	250	7	Texas Christian
48	Washington, Lionel	CB	6-0	185	7	Tulane
68	Wilkerson, Bruce	G-T	6-5	285	3	Tennessee
50	Wilson, Otis	LB	6-2	225	9	Louisville
90	Wise, Mike	DE	6-7	270	3	California-Davis
66	Wright, Steve	T	6-6	275	7	Northern Iowa

TOP DRAFT CHOICES

Rd.	Name	Sel. No.	Pos.	Ht.	Wt.	College
2	Wisniewski, Steve	29	G	6-4	266	Penn State
6	Francis, Jeff	140	QB	6-4	215	Tennessee
6	Lloyd, Doug	156	RB	6-1	217	N. Dakota State
8	Gainer, Derrick	205	RB	5-10	215	Florida A&M
9	Gooden, Gary	235	DB	6-0	170	Indiana

RAIDER PROFILES

TIM BROWN 23 6-0 195   Wide Receiver

1987 Heisman Trophy winner was lone bright spot in disappointing Raider offense... Led NFL in kick returns with 1,098 yards and a 26.8 average... Also had most punt-return yards in AFC (444)... Pro Bowl and *The Sporting News* All-NFL kick returner... Took wide-receiver starting job from Willie Gault late in year and was Raiders' best wideout... Led team with 43 receptions, good for 725 yards and five TDs ... Set Notre Dame records in receiving yards (2,493), kickoff-return yards (1,613) and all-purpose yards (5,024)... Consensus All-American twice... Lettered one year as sprinter on Irish track team... 1988 salary: $1.2 million... Born July 22, 1966, in Dallas.

BO JACKSON 26 6-1 225   Running Back

Part-time football player who has Raiders wishing he'd give up career with baseball's Kansas City Royals... Missed season's first six weeks but still piled up 580 yards and three TDs in 136 carries... People are still talking about the Monday night in 1987 when he ran for 221 yards against Seattle... Gained 554 yards on 81 carries in '87, a 6.8 average... Won 1985 Heisman Trophy and was drafted by Tampa Bay. After a year in baseball, Bucs' rights expired and Raiders grabbed him in seventh round of 1986 draft... Had four 200-yard games as a senior at Auburn... Gained 1,786 yards as senior and 4,303 overall... Two-time semifinalist in NCAA 60-meters... 1989 salary: $1.356 million... Born Nov. 30, 1962, in Bessemer, Ala.

MARCUS ALLEN 29 6-2 205   Running Back

Glitter of younger players has taken attention off Allen, but he keeps rolling... Has led club in rushing in each of his seven pro seasons... Gained 831 yards on 223 carries and scored seven TDs in 1988... Also caught 34 passes for 303 yards and a TD... Has rushed more than 200 times in each of the last six seasons ... Put together three straight 1,000-yard seasons from 1983-85...Has made room for Bo Jackson without causing trouble...Has been named to five Pro Bowls...Once put together streak of 11 straight 100-yard games, an NFL record...MVP of 1984 Super Bowl with 191 yards rushing...First-round draft choice out of USC in 1982...Won Heisman Trophy in '81...1988 salary: $1 million...Born March 22, 1960, in San Diego.

JAY SCHROEDER 28 6-4 215   Quarterback

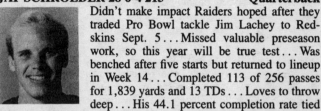

Didn't make impact Raiders hoped after they traded Pro Bowl tackle Jim Lachey to Redskins Sept. 5...Missed valuable preseason work, so this year will be true test...Was benched after five starts but returned to lineup in Week 14...Completed 113 of 256 passes for 1,839 yards and 13 TDs...Loves to throw deep...His 44.1 percent completion rate tied teammate Steve Beuerlein for lowest in AFC...Threw for over 300 yards twice, against Cincinnati and Seattle...At Washington, was pushed aside by Doug Williams' Super Bowl MVP performance after 1987 season...Best year was 1986, when he threw for a team-record 4,109 yards and 22 TDs and made Pro Bowl...Started just one game at UCLA and pursued baseball career for four years, then returned to football...Redskins picked him in third round in 1984...1989 salary: $1 million...Born June 28, 1961, in Milwaukee.

MERVYN FERNANDEZ 29 6-3 200   Wide Receiver

Turned out to be most explosive of Raiders' veteran receivers...Had four 100-yard games, including 155 vs. Saints...26.0-yards-per-catch average was highest in NFL...Finished with 31 receptions for 805 yards and four TDs...Came to Raiders in 1987 after five years in Canadian Football League...Started seven games in '87 before going on injured reserve...Was CFL MVP in 1985 with 95 receptions for 1,727 yards and 15 TDs...Played one year at San Jose State...1989 salary: $450,000...Born Dec. 29, 1959, in Merced, Cal.

HOWIE LONG 29 6-5 265 — Defensive End

Star-studded career took a pit stop in 1988 when a calf injury sidelined him for final 10 games . . . Had gone to five straight Pro Bowls . . . Had only four sacks in 1987 after recording 54½ in first six pro seasons . . . Still, the 1984 and '86 Defensive Lineman of the Year will continue to draw weekly double coverage . . . Had career-high 13 sacks in 1983, including five vs. Redskins . . . Starter since the middle of 1982 season . . . Second-round draft pick out of Villanova in 1981 . . . Was collegiate boxing champ . . . 1988 salary: $1 million . . . Born Jan. 6, 1960, in Sommerville, Mass.

WILLIE GAULT 28 6-0 180 — Wide Receiver

Another injury-related downer in Raiders' mysterious season . . . Caught 12 passes in first four games but only two in the next 11 . . . Suffered bruised shoulder at midseason and was sidelined . . . Served notice in finale that he will be back in full force, catching two passes for 108 yards . . . Finished season with 16 receptions for 392 yards and two TDs . . . Came to Raiders from Bears before 1988 season . . . Led Chicago in receiving yards and TDs four times . . . Formerly one of the world's top hurdlers, he went to the 1988 Olympics as member of U.S. bobsled team . . . Starred in college at Tennessee . . . 1988 salary: $700,000 . . . Born Sept. 5, 1960, in Griffin, Ga.

VANN McELROY 29 6-2 195 — Safety

Led Raiders in interceptions for third straight year . . . Had three, tying him with Mike Haynes . . . His 37 tackles ranked him 14th on team . . . Leader in interceptions among active Raiders with 29 in seven years . . . Was Pro Bowl selection in 1983 and 1984 . . . Shared AFC interception lead in '83 with eight, then added another in AFC championship game . . . Third-round pick out of Baylor in 1982 . . . Led nation with eight interceptions as a junior . . . Selected by Montreal Expos as a pitcher coming out of high school . . . 1988 salary: $500,000 . . . Born Jan. 13, 1960, in Birmingham, Ala.

BILL PICKEL 29 6-5 265   Defensive Tackle

Has 49½ sacks in six NFL seasons . . . One of five Raiders to start every game in 1988 . . . Finished fifth in tackles among Raiders with 78 and third in sacks with five, up from just one in '87 . . . Had 11½ sacks in 1986, 12½ in '85 and 12½ in '84 . . . Still, he never made it to Pro Bowl . . . Second-round draft pick out of Rutgers in 1983 . . . Had 15 sacks in four years there . . . 1988 salary: $375,000 . . . Born Nov. 5, 1959, in Queens, N.Y.

MATT MILLEN 31 6-2 245   Linebacker

Durable scrapper who led Raiders with 106 tackles . . . Hadn't led club since 1982 . . . Has started 133 straight non-strike games . . . Was named All-Pro in 1985 by *College and Pro Football News* . . . Second-round draft choice out of Penn State in 1980 . . . Started every game as a rookie, finishing third on team in tackles . . . Two-time All-American for Nittany Lions and Lombardi Award finalist in 1979 . . . Played final three college seasons at defensive tackle . . . 1988 salary: $375,000 . . . Born March 12, 1958, in Hokendauqua, Pa.

COACH MIKE SHANAHAN: NFL's youngest coach hit hard

times in rookie year . . . With all its talent, this Raider offense should take off under Shanahan, a former offensive coordinator at Denver who helped John Elway and Co. become one of football's most explosive teams . . . Succeeded Tom Flores . . . Experienced life as a Raider late last year as rumors of owner Al Davis' impatience began flying . . . Is just 37, but has been around . . . A former assistant at Florida, Minnesota, Eastern Illinois, Northern Arizona and Oklahoma . . . Overall records of teams for which he was an assistant: 126-49-4 . . . Went to Eastern Illinois as a quarterback, but injury ended aspirations as a player . . . Immediately began coaching career as graduate assistant . . . Born Aug. 22, 1952, in Oak Park, Ill.

GREATEST COACH

John Madden was a model of success and consistency in his 10 seasons as head coach of the Oakland Raiders. From 1969-78, Madden's teams were 103-32-7, winning seven division championships, an AFC title and a Super Bowl.

Madden didn't need to turn the franchise around. In his two seasons as linebacker coach under coach John Rauch, the Raiders had a regular-season record of 25-3. When Rauch left to coach the Buffalo Bills in '69, Madden took over.

In 1976, the Raiders avenged consecutive title-game losses to Pittsburgh, beating the Steelers, 24-7. Two weeks later, the Raiders topped the Vikings, 32-14, in Super Bowl XI.

Madden's postseason winning percentage of .563 (9-7) is second to Chuck Noll (15-7, .682) in NFL history among coaches with 15 or more playoff games.

Raiders hope Bo Jackson's Royals never make the playoffs.

INDIVIDUAL RAIDER RECORDS

Rushing

Most Yards Game:	221	Bo Jackson, vs Seattle, 1987	
Season:	1,759	Marcus Allen, 1985	
Career:	6,982	Marcus Allen, 1982-88	

Passing

Most TD Passes Game:	6	Tom Flores, vs Houston, 1963	
	6	Daryle Lamonica, vs Buffalo, 1969	
Season:	34	Daryle Lamonica, 1969	
Career:	150	Ken Stabler, 1970-79	

Receiving

Most TD Passes Game:	4	Art Powell, vs Houston, 1963	
Season:	16	Art Powell, 1963	
Career:	76	Fred Biletnikoff, 1965-78	

Scoring

Most Points Game:	24	Art Powell, vs Houston, 1963	
	24	Marcus Allen, vs San Diego, 1984	
Season:	117	George Blanda, 1968	
Career:	863	George Blanda, 1967-75	
Most TDs Game:	4	Art Powell, vs Houston, 1963	
	4	Marcus Allen, vs San Diego, 1984	
Season:	18	Marcus Allen, 1984	
Career:	77	Fred Biletnikoff, 1965-78	

MIAMI DOLPHINS

TEAM DIRECTORY: Pres.: Joseph Robbie; Head Coach: Don Shula; Dir. Pro Scouting: Charley Winner; Dir. Player Personnel: Chuck Connor; Dir. Media Relations: Harvey Greene. Home field: Joe Robbie Stadium (74,930). Colors: Aqua and orange.

SCOUTING REPORT

OFFENSE: Not long ago, the Dolphin offense was a sure thing. Now, however, Dan Marino and Mark Clayton appear to be the only consistencies. With Mark Duper coming off a poor year that ended with a drug suspension, and 1987 Rookie of the Year Troy Stradford trying to forget a miserable sophomore season, the Dolphins (6-10) have work to do to get back in gear.

What's more, they'll have to do it with some new faces. With David Shula gone to Dallas, the new offensive coordinator is Gary Stevens, formerly of the University of Miami. Also gone is backup QB Ron Jaworski, who beat out Don Strock, learned the Miami offense inside and out, then signed as a free agent with Kansas City.

The 1988 Dolphins were the NFL's best passing team and worst rushing team, with just 1,205 yards on the ground. Nine AFC teams scored more points than Miami. Coach Don Shula made Sammie Smith his top pick to give Stradford help and take the heat off Marino.

The offensive line protected Marino (no sacks in final 12 games) but gave runners little room to maneuver. Dwight Stephenson missed all of 1988 with a knee injury and may never play again. Although rookie guard Harry Galbreath was a pleasant surprise, the rest of the line is aging.

With all their problems, though, there is the promise of tight end Ferrell Edmunds. If he continues the development he made as a rookie, the Dolphins will be explosive once again.

DEFENSE: Incredibly, there was a five-game stretch early last season in which the Dolphin defense was carrying its offense. Then things returned to normal and Miami plummeted to its ranking as the No. 26 defense in the NFL.

The Dolphins' strength is inside linebacker with All-Pro John Offerdahl and Mark Brown, who put Jackie Shipp on the bench early last season. Everybody thought 1988 was the year of Hugh Green's comeback, but the former star outside linebacker was quiet most of the season. During the offseason, the Dolphins signed E.J. Junior.

Dan Marino will be aiming for his fifth 4,000-yard season.

The Dolphins did little last year to stop the run, as their opponents' 4.5-yard average indicates. In the finale, Pittsburgh rushed for a club-record 305 yards. Shula hopes defensive end John Bosa can return from a knee injury. First-round pick Eric Kumerow, also an end, started slowly but showed signs of being a decent pass-rusher.

The Dolphins feel they have a future star in hard-hitting safety Jarvis Williams, who started every game as a rookie and introduced a mean streak to the defensive backfield.

KICKING GAME: The Dolphins are solid with punter Reggie Roby (43-yard average), and they also would be strong in the kicking game if steady Fuad Reveiz could stay healthy. Reveiz hit 8 of 12 field-goal tries and won't get recognized until Marino loses his end-zone touch.

Scott Schwedes (9.6 average) improved his punt returns and didn't show the butterfingers he did as a rookie in '87. Veteran Joe Cribbs gave the kick-return game a life (21.0), but neither he nor Schwedes provided game-breaking plays. Miami's speedster on special-team coverage, Reyna Thompson, was signed by the Giants.

DOLPHINS VETERAN ROSTER

HEAD COACH—Don Shula. Assistant Coaches—George Hill, Tom Olivadotti, Mel Phillips, John Sandusky, Larry Seiple, Dan Sekanovich, Gary Stevens, Carl Taseff, Junior Wade, Mike Westoff.

No.	Name	Pos.	Ht.	Wt.	NFL Exp.	College
86	Banks, Fred	WR	5-10	180	4	Liberty
34	Bennett, Woody	RB	6-2	244	11	Miami
47	Blackwood, Glenn	S	6-0	193	10	Texas
97	Bosa, John	DE	6-4	273	3	Boston College
43	Brown, Bud	S	6-0	193	6	Southern Mississippi
51	Brown, Mark	LB	6-2	238	7	Purdue
59	Brudzinski, Bob	LB	6-4	235	13	Ohio State
35	Burse, Tony	RB	6-0	220	2	Middle Tenn. State
77	Cheek, Louis	T	6-6	295	2	Texas A&M
83	Clayton, Mark	WR	5-9	184	7	Louisville
98	Cline, Jackie	DE-NT	6-5	280	3	Alabama
67	Conlin, Chris	G-C	6-3	280	2	Penn State
20	Cribbs, Joe	RB	5-11	190	9	Auburn
91	Cross, Jeff	DE	6-4	270	2	Missouri
30	Davenport, Ron	RB	6-2	232	5	Louisville
65	Dellenbach, Jeff	C-T	6-5	280	5	Wisconsin
74	Dennis, Mark	T	6-6	290	3	Illinois
85	Duper, Mark	WR	5-9	190	8	NW Louisiana
80	Edmunds, Ferrell	TE	6-6	248	2	Maryland
61	Foster, Roy	G	6-4	275	8	Southern California
53	Frye, David	LB	6-2	227	7	Purdue
58	Furjanic, Tony	LB	6-1	228	4	Notre Dame
62	Galbreath, Harry	G-C	6-1	275	2	Tennessee
79	Giesler, Jon	T	6-5	272	11	Michigan
99	Graf, Rick	LB	6-5	249	3	Wisconsin
55	Green, Hugh	LB	6-2	228	9	Pittsburgh
27	Hampton, Lorenzo	RB	5-11	208	5	Florida
84	Hardy, Bruce	TE	6-4	234	11	Arizona State
92	Hill, Nate	DE	6-4	275	2	Auburn
29	Hobley, Liffort	S	6-0	202	4	Louisiana State
11	Jensen, Jim	WR-RB	6-4	220	9	Boston University
87	Johnson, Dan	TE	6-3	245	6	Iowa State
73	Johnson, Greg	G	6-4	295	2	Oklahoma
49	Judson, William	DB	6-1	192	8	South Carolina State
88	Kinchen, Brian	TE	6-2	238	2	Louisiana State
54	Kolic, Larry	LB	6-1	239	3	Ohio State
90	Kumerow, Eric	DE	6-7	260	2	Ohio State
69	Lambrecht, Mike	NT	6-1	274	3	St. Cloud State
44	Lankford, Paul	CB	6-1	190	8	Penn State
72	Lee, Ronnie	T	6-3	275	11	Baylor
13	Marino, Dan	QB	6-4	222	7	Pittsburgh
28	McNeal, Don	CB	6-0	193	9	Alabama
52	Nicolas, Scott	LB	6-3	230	7	Miami
56	Offerdahl, John	LB	6-3	237	4	Western Michigan
7	Reveiz, Fuad	K	5-11	220	5	Tennessee
4	Roby, Reggie	P	6-2	242	7	Iowa
81	Schwedes, Scott	WR-KR	6-0	182	3	Syracuse
68	Scott, Chris	DE	6-5	270	4	Purdue
70	Sochia, Brian	NT	6-3	275	7	NW Oklahoma
57	Stephenson, Dwight	C	6-2	264	9	Alabama
23	Stradford, Troy	RB	5-9	192	3	Boston College
82	Teal, Jimmy	WR	5-11	175	5	Texas A&M
45	Thomas, Rodney	CB	5-10	190	2	Brigham Young
76	Toth, Tom	G	6-5	282	4	Western Michigan
95	Turner, T.J.	DE	6-4	280	4	Houston
26	Williams, Jarvis	S	5-11	196	2	Florida

TOP DRAFT CHOICES

Rd.	Name	Sel. No.	Pos.	Ht.	Wt.	College
1	Smith, Sammie	9	RB	6-2	225	Florida State
1	Oliver, Louis	25	S	6-2	225	Florida
4	Holmes, David	92	DB	6-1	195	Syracuse
5	Uhlenhake, Jeff	121	C	6-3	275	Ohio State
6	Pritchett, Wes	147	LB	6-5	234	Notre Dame

THE ROOKIES: If Smith stays healthy—something he didn't do at Florida State—he can be the powerful, game-breaking tail-back the Dolphins have been looking for. Don Shula called Smith "a Dickerson-type back," and Miami had him rated higher than Tim Worley heading into the draft. Safety Louis Oliver should step in and start immediately alongside former Florida teammate Williams to form a hard-hitting safety tandem.

OUTLOOK: With Marino, anything is possible. But it is doubt-ful he can stay on his fast pace much longer without a running game. The Dolphins, once rulers of the AFC East, were a dismal 0-8 in division play last year. It may take one of Shula's best coaching jobs to reach the playoffs this year.

DOLPHIN PROFILES

DAN MARINO 27 6-4 222   Quarterback

Despite team's struggles, Marino keeps piling up the numbers...Led NFL in attempts (606), completions (354) and yards (4,434) and was second in TD passes (28)...Has thrown 196 TDs in six years, breaking Bob Griese's club record of 192, accomplished over 14 years...Had an off year by his stan-dards, finishing fifth in AFC passing...
Wasn't selected to Pro Bowl for first time in his career...In two games against the Jets, he threw for 874 yards and eight TDs. But Dolphins lost both...Has started 76 straight non-strike games ...Only QB in NFL history to have four 4,000-yard seasons... Pitt grad is one shy of Johnny Unitas' record of 17 four-TD games...1989 salary: $1.45 million...Born Sept. 15, 1961, in Pittsburgh.

MARK CLAYTON 28 5-9 184   Wide Receiver

Has been a picture of consistency for Miami ...Returned to Pro Bowl last year after miss-ing out in '87...Set team record with 86 catches, breaking his own mark of 73 set in '84...Led NFL in receiving touchdowns with 14...His 5,440 receiving yards are most in NFL in last five seasons...Stats are amazing in light of off year by Mark Duper at other receiver spot... Faced double coverage every week... Eighth-round draft pick out of Louisville is small but has 35-inch vertical leap... Held NFL record for touchdowns in a season (18) until 49ers' Jerry Rice scored 22 in '87... Avid Louisville basketball fan who leads Dolphins' hoop squad in scoring and dunks every year... 1989 salary: $511,500... Born April 8, 1961, in Indianapolis.

FERRELL EDMUNDS 24 6-6 248   Tight End

Potential of this third-round pick has Dolphin coaches drooling... Had 33 receptions in '88, 20 more than any previous Miami rookie tight end... Displayed 4.6 speed on 80-yard TD reception against Jets. Outran entire New York secondary on the play... Finished with 575 yards receiving for an average of 17.4 yards per catch... Scored three TDs... Had some problems with fumbles late in year... Former Dolphin QB Ron Jaworski compares him to Harold Carmichael... Four-year starter at Maryland who turned down offers to play for Terps' basketball team... Second on Maryland's all-time receiving list with 101 catches... 1989 salary: $155,000... Born April 16, 1965, in South Boston, Va.

JIM JENSEN 30 6-4 220   Wide Receiver

Perhaps most versatile player in NFL... Played receiver, running back, fullback, tight end and was special-teams standout. Also is emergency quarterback, holder and snapper on punts... Third down is his specialty. He touched ball 19 times on third down and picked up a first down 16 times... Gained first down on 44 of 68 (65 percent) times he touched ball... Had 58 catches in '88, second on team, after making just 45 in his previous seven seasons... His five TD receptions equaled previous career total... Drafted as a quarterback in 11th round in '81 out of Boston University, he finally abandoned aspirations of making it at that position last year... Has stuck on team with touch special-teams play which earned him nickname "Crash"... Presented engagement ring to Dolphin cheerleader during pregame introductions last year... 1989 salary: $276,000... Born Nov. 14, 1958, in Abington, Pa.

JOHN OFFERDAHL 25 6-3 237   Linebacker

Has been selected to Pro Bowl in each of his NFL seasons, the first Miami linebacker to make it three times... Led team in tackles with 117, 28 more than closest teammate... Makes up for small stature with toughness... Finished second on team in tackles in '87 despite missing three non-strike games... Led Dolphins with 135 tackles in '86 and was selected NFL Defensive Rookie of Year... May be most underpaid player in NFL. Made $175,000 in '88, making him Miami's sixth-highest paid linebacker... Second-round draft pick out of Western Michigan, where he started every game for four years ... Born Aug. 17, 1964, in Wisconsin Rapids, Wis.

TROY STRADFORD 24 5-9 192   Running Back

Had disappointing season after being named NFL's Offensive Rookie of the Year in '87... Rushed for 335 yards in 1988, down from 619 as a rookie... Finished second on team to Lorenzo Hampton's 414 yards... Was bothered by leg injuries throughout season, limiting his ability to use jitterbug moves... Best rushing game of '88 was 48 yards in Week 2... In '87, he led the Dolphins in both rushing and receiving ... Fourth-round draft pick out of Boston College, where he is the school's all-time leading rusher with 3,504 yards... Born Sept. 11, 1964, in Elizabeth, N.J.

MARK DUPER 30 5-9 190   Wide Receiver

Had most troublesome and controversial season of career in 1988... Missed much of training camp because of holdout and was suspended for final three games for violating NFL subtance-abuse policy... Had done work for Miami's "Say No to Drugs" program... Finished '88 with 39 receptions for 626 yards and just one TD. Previous lows in 16-game season were 51 catches, 1,003 yards, eight TDs... Went without a reception in two games... Had arthroscopic knee surgery to remove bone chips in December... 1988 was his second subpar year in a row... No. 4 receiver in team history... Holds team record for 100-yard receiving games with 22... Set Dolphin record with 217-yard game against Jets in '85 after missing eight games with thigh injury...Has 4.3 speed...Three-time Pro Bowl selection...Surprise second-round pick out of Northwestern State (La.) in '82...He legally changed full name to Mark Super Duper...Will make $650,000 this season...Born Jan. 25, 1959, in Pineville, La.

JARVIS WILLIAMS 25 5-11 196   Safety

Dolphins' best rookie of '88...His 89 tackles ranked second on team...Tied for lead in interceptions with four and fumble recoveries with three...Started every game at free safety...Made 11 tackles against Buffalo... Is a ferocious hitter...Second-round draft pick out of Florida, where he started four years and was All-SEC three times...Shifted from cornerback to safety his senior year...Credits Dolphin RB Lorenzo Hampton for convincing him not to quit school during redshirt freshman year...1989 salary: $168,000...Born May 16, 1964, in Palatka, Fla.

BRIAN SOCHIA 28 6-3 275   Nose Tackle

Was selected Pro Bowl alternate and played because of injury to Cincinnati's Tim Krumrie ...Team's No. 5 tackler with 72...Second to T.J. Turner with 4½ sacks, a career-high... Made nine tackles in a game twice...Blocked a kick at Chicago...Became a regular starter in '87 for first time since '83, when he was with Houston...Joined Dolphins in '86 after Oilers released him at end of holdout...Made *Pro Football Weekly's* All-Rookie team in '83...Signed by Houston as free agent after starting four years at Northwestern Oklahoma State ...1989 salary: $250,000...Born July 21, 1961, in Massena, N.Y.

MARK BROWN 28 6-2 238   Linebacker

Hard-hitting linebacker took job from former No. 1 pick Jackie Shipp in Week 2 last year ...Finished seventh in tackles with 66... Missed two games with an ankle injury and one after being suspended for a game because of a late hit to the head of Jet quarterback Ken O'Brien...Intensity seemed to lift Dolphin defense out of doldrums early in year...Made two interceptions in '88, equaling total for his previous five years... Has bounced from inside linebacker to outside his whole career, but seems to have found home at left inside next to John Offerdahl... Former Purdue star set a Big Ten record in '82 with 209 tackles... Sixth-round draft pick... 1988 salary: $247,500... Born July 18, 1961, in New Brunswick, N.J.

COACH DON SHULA: Suffered through what admittedly was his toughest year as a coach, but he has set lofty standards... Finished in fifth place for first time in his 26-year career... Lost five straight games for first time in his career, then had to deal with drug allegations thrown at his team... "We went into the season with a lot of goals, and we weren't able to achieve any of them," Shula said... Still is winningest active coach in NFL with a 261-111-6 (.698) regular-season record... In 1963, at age 33, he was youngest coach in NFL history when he took over the Baltimore Colts... Has taken six teams to Super Bowls and has won twice... Played running back at John Carroll and was a defensive back for seven years in the NFL with the Browns, Colts and Redskins... Son David is an assistant at Dallas and son Mike is an assistant at Tampa Bay. David was on the Dolphin staff from 1982-88... Born Jan. 4, 1930, in Grand River, Ohio.

GREATEST COACH

Don Shula thrives on challenges, and when he came to Miami from the Baltimore Colts in 1970 he faced a big one. In the Dolphins, Shula had a four-year-old franchise that had not won more than five games in a season.

So Shula went to the playoffs his first year, to the Super Bowl his second and registered a 17-0 record his third. For good measure, he won his second straight Super Bowl in '73.

Shula's three consecutive Super Bowl trips is a record, and the 17-0 mark in 1972 stands as the only perfect season in NFL history. He enters his 20th year with the Dolphins with a 204-98-2 (.671) record and 277-124-6 (.681) in his 26-year NFL career. He has taken a record six teams to the Super Bowl.

INDIVIDUAL DOLPHIN RECORDS

Rushing

Most Yards Game:	197	Mercury Morris, vs New England, 1973
Season:	1,258	Delvin Williams, 1978
Career:	6,737	Larry Csonka, 1968-74, 1979

Passing

Most TD Passes Game:	6	Bob Griese, vs St. Louis, 1977
	6	Dan Marino, vs N.Y. Jets, 1986
Season:	48	Dan Marino, 1984
Career:	196	Dan Marino, 1983-88

Receiving

Most TD Passes Game:	4	Paul Warfield, vs Detroit, 1973
Season:	18	Mark Clayton, 1984
Career:	74	Nat Moore, 1974-86

Scoring

Most Points Game:	24	Paul Warfield, vs Detroit, 1973
Season:	117	Garo Yepremian, 1971
Career:	830	Garo Yepremian, 1970-78
Most TDs Game:	4	Paul Warfield, vs Detroit, 1973
Season:	18	Mark Clayton, 1984
Career:	75	Nat Moore, 1974-86

NEW ENGLAND PATRIOTS

TEAM DIRECTORY: Chairman: Victor K. Kiam II; Vice Chairman: Francis W. Murray; Pres.: William Sullivan Jr.; VP: Bucko Kilroy; GM: Patrick J. Sullivan; Dir. Pub. Rel. and Sales: David J. Wintergrass; Dir. Publicity: Jim Greenidge; Head Coach: Raymond Berry. Home field: Sullivan Stadium (60,794). Colors: Red, white and blue.

SCOUTING REPORT

OFFENSE: You want a quarterback controversy? Check out New England, where little Doug Flutie led the Patriots into

NFL Offensive Rookie of Year John Stephens made Pro Bowl.

playoff contention, only to be benched in Week 15 in favor of Tony Eason. Eason will get first shot this year while Flutie, who doesn't do much except win, waits in the wings.

Actually, it was rookie running back John Stephens who did most of the work as the Pats (9-7) won six of eight down the stretch and fell a game short of the playoffs. Once the sure-handed Stephens got rolling, coach Raymond Berry dumped the passing game. Stephens had just 244 yards after seven games but finished with 1,168.

On the flip side, New England's passing game was the worst in the AFC, but Berry hopes the combination of Stephens and a healthy Eason will provide a dangerous balance. Wide receiver Hart Lee Dykes, the No. 1 pick, figures as a lethal weapon. Bruce Armstrong and Sean Farrell man a strong offensive line.

DEFENSE: While Flutie got all the praise last season, the Patriot defense quietly kept shutting opponents down. Despite injuries to linebackers Andre Tippett and Ed Williams and defensive ends Garin Veris and Ken Sims, the Pats allowed 10 points or less six times.

Tippett is always among the league's best. Johnny Rembert filled in superbly for retired linebacker Steve Nelson, and nose tackle Tim Goad could be solid for several years.

Pass defense is excellent. Ranked third in the NFL last year, the group of Raymond Clayborn and Ronnie Lippett at cornerback and Fred Marion and Roland James at safety allowed just 13 passing TDs.

KICKING GAME: Except for placekicking, the Patriots' special teams are indeed special. Teddy Garcia missed three field-goal attempts and an extra point in a 23-20 loss to Buffalo, then Jason Staurovsky missed two field goals in a 24-21 loss to the Colts. Staurovsky made seven of 11 tries, but none from more than 39 yards. Jeff Feagles blasted an NFL-high 74-yard punt, but finished with a 38.3-yard average. He did land 24 inside the 20, however.

Return men Irving Fryar and Sammy Martin are exciting. Fryar was sixth in the NFL (10.5) in punt returns while Martin was fifth (23.7) on kickoffs, including a 95-yard TD. New England held opponents to just 5.9 yards per punt return.

THE ROOKIES: Oklahoma State's Dykes is a big (6-3) target, has great hands and could start right away. Dykes is the Big Eight's all-time leading receiver with 224 catches, including 74 for 14 TDs last year. Wyoming's Eric Coleman will add depth

PATRIOTS VETERAN ROSTER

HEAD COACH—Raymond Berry. Assistant Coaches—Don Blackmon, Jimmy Carr, Bobby Grier, Ray Hamilton, Harold Jackson, Eddie Khayat, Guy Morriss, John Polonchek, Keith Rowen, Don Shinnick, Richard Wood.

No.	Name	Pos.	Ht.	Wt.	NFL Exp.	College
39	Allen, Marvin	RB-KR	5-10	215	2	Tulane
78	Armstrong, Bruce	T	6-4	284	3	Louisville
68	Baab, Mike	C	6-4	270	8	Texas
28	Bowman, Jim	S	6-2	210	5	Central Michigan
59	Brown, Vincent	LB	6-2	245	2	Miss. Valley State
26	Clayborn, Raymond	CB	6-1	186	13	Texas
5	Davis, Greg	K	5-11	197	3	Citadel
87	Dawson, Lin	TE	6-3	240	8	North Carolina State
67	Douglas, David	T	6-4	280	4	Tennessee
21	Dupard, Reggie	RB	5-11	205	4	Southern Methodist
11	Eason, Tony	QB	6-4	212	7	Illinois
66	Fairchild, Paul	G-C	6-4	270	6	Kansas
62	Farrell, Sean	G	6-3	260	8	Penn State
6	Feagles, Jeff	P	6-0	198	2	Miami
2	Flutie, Doug	QB	5-10	175	4	Boston College
81	Francis, Russ	TE	6-6	242	14	Oregon
80	Fryar, Irving	WR-KR	6-0	200	6	Nebraska
48	Gadbois, Dennis	WR	6-1	183	3	Boston University
72	Goad, Tim	NT	6-3	280	2	North Carolina
14	Grogan, Steve	QB	6-4	210	15	Kansas State
97	Hodge, Milford	NT-DE	6-3	278	4	Washington State
41	Holmes, Darryl	S	6-2	190	3	Fort Valley State
32	James, Craig	RB	6-0	215	5	Southern Methodist
39	James, Roland	S	6-2	191	10	Tennessee
99	Jeter, Gary	DE	6-4	260	13	Southern California
85	Johnson, Steve	TE	6-6	245	2	Virginia Tech
83	Jones, Cedric	WR	6-1	184	8	Duke
18	Jones, Mike	WR	5-11	183	6	Tennessee State
93	Jordan, Tim	LB	6-3	226	3	Wisconsin
42	Lippett, Ronnie	CB	5-11	180	7	Miami
31	Marion, Fred	S	6-2	191	8	Miami
82	Martin, Sammy	WR-KR	5-11	175	2	Louisiana State
64	Matich, Trevor	C	6-4	270	5	Brigham Young
50	McGrew, Lawrence	LB	6-5	233	9	Southern California
23	McSwain, Rod	CB	6-1	198	6	Clemson
86	Morgan, Stanley	WR	5-11	181	13	Tennessee
34	Perryman, Robert	RB	6-1	233	3	Michigan
76	Rehder, Tom	T	6-7	280	2	Notre Dame
52	Rembert, Johnny	LB	6-3	234	7	Clemson
95	Reynolds, Ed	LB	6-5	242	7	Virginia
88	Scott, Willie	TE	6-4	245	9	South Carolina
49	Sievers, Eric	TE	6-4	230	9	Maryland
77	Sims, Kenneth	DE	6-5	271	7	Texas
4	Staurovsky, Jason	K	5-9	170	3	Tulsa
44	Stephens, John	RB	6-1	220	2	N.W. Louisiana
30	Tatupu, Mosi	RB	6-0	227	12	Southern California
56	Tippett, Andre	LB	6-3	241	8	Iowa
60	Veris, Garin	DE	6-4	255	5	Stanford
73	Villa, Danny	T	6-5	305	3	Arizona State
94	Ward, David	LB	6-2	232	2	Southern Arkansas
96	Williams, Brent	DE	6-3	278	4	Toledo
54	Williams, Ed	LB	6-4	244	5	Texas
15	Wilson, Marc	QB	6-6	205	9	Brigham Young
61	Wooten, Ron	G	6-4	273	8	North Carolina

TOP DRAFT CHOICES

Rd.	Name	Sel. No.	Pos.	Ht.	Wt.	College
1	Dykes, Hart Lee	16	WR	6-3	220	Oklahoma State
2	Coleman, Eric	43	CB	5-11	185	Wyoming
3	Cook, Marv	63	TE	6-3	240	Iowa
3	Gannon, Chris	73	DE	6-5	255	SW Louisiana
4	Hurst, Maurice	96	DB	5-9	185	Southern

at cornerback. He played wide receiver in '85 and running back in '86 and was a track star. Iowa tight end Marv Cook is a smart player with good hands.

OUTLOOK: You can always count on the Pats' defense, so if Stephens keeps chugging and Berry settles on a quarterback, this team has the talent to battle the Bills for the AFC East title.

PATRIOT PROFILES

ANDRE TIPPETT 29 6-3 241   Linebacker

Selected to fifth straight Pro Bowl, fourth as a starter... Was second-team All-Pro... Missed four games because of groin injury... Finished eighth on team tackles with 50 (31 initial hits) and second in sacks with seven... Became Pats' all-time sack leader with 72½... Value was seen in Buffalo game Sept. 18 when Bills controlled ball for 10:20 of the final 15 minutes after he left game with injury... Was 1987 AFC Linebacker of the Year after coming back from injury-filled '86... All-American at Iowa, he was second-round pick in 1982... Holds second-degree black belt in karate... In second season of reported six-year, $4.5-million contract... Born Dec. 27, 1959, in Birmingham, Ala.

JOHN STEPHENS 23 6-1 220   Running Back

Voted NFL Offensive Rookie of the Year, beating out Philadelphia's Keith Jackson by one vote... Was second in AFC rushing and fifth in NFL with 1,168 yards... Was first Patriot rookie to make Pro Bowl since Mike Haynes in 1976... Had five 100-yard games and was first Patriot to break 100 in a non-strike game since 1985... Became a starter in Week 3 against Buffalo... His 297 carries were two shy of club record set by Jim Nance in 1966... Seventeenth player picked in draft, out of Northwestern (La.) State... Set school rushing mark with 3,057 yards... Can bench-press 445 pounds and run 4.38 40-yard dash... Was a guard in high school until senior year, when team's top rusher got hurt... 1988 salary: $565,000... Born Feb. 23, 1966, in Shreveport, La.

BRUCE ARMSTRONG 23 6-4 284   Tackle

Named All-AFC by UPI and second-team All-Pro by AP... Had shoulder surgery after '87 season but was reliable once again... Hasn't missed a game in his two years in league... Team's Rookie of the Year in '87... Finished third in voting for UPI Rookie of the Year behind Miami's Troy Stradford and the Raiders' Bo Jackson... Was first rookie offensive lineman to start for Patriots since John Hannah in 1973... First-round pick (23rd overall) out of Louisville... Was Cardinals' starting tight end before moving to tackle as a junior... 1988 salary: $165,000, 1989: $210,000... Born Sept. 7, 1965, in Miami.

SEAN FARRELL 29 6-3 260   Guard

Reliable veteran was honorable mention All-Pro... Started all but one game... Patriots acquired him from Tampa Bay for three draft picks (Nos. 2, 7, 9)... Has been NFL starter his entire career since being selected by Bucs out of Penn State in first round of 1982 draft... Nittany Lions were 28-8 in his three years as starter... Finished second to Nebraska's Dave Rimington in voting for 1981 Outland Trophy... Works in offseason as investment counselor for Prudential Bache... 1988 salary: $475,000... Born July 25, 1960, in Southampton, N.Y.

DOUG FLUTIE 26 5-10 175   Quarterback

Relieved Steve Grogan in Week 5 and helped Patriots turn season around... Rallied club to 21-15 win over Colts and became starter the next week... Pats won five of their last six games he started... Was benched in favor of Tony Eason for final two games... Completed just 92 passes as Pats relied heavily on running of John Stephens... Led Patriot QBs with eight TD passes... Was team's No. 3 rusher with 179 yards and a TD... Was 5-0 at Sulivan Stadium, making him 10-0 in his career, including college games... Came to New England in '87 in trade with Chicago and started a strike game. Didn't play rest of season... Won 1984 Heisman Trophy at Boston College before going to USFL's New Jersey Generals... 1988 salary: $150,000... Born Oct. 23, 1962, in Manchester, Md.

RAYMOND CLAYBORN 34 6-1 186   Cornerback

Came back from a 1987 knee injury to be one of just four Patriots to start all 16 games... Tied for team lead in interceptions (4)... Led club in interception yardage (65)... Owns Patriot career marks with 35 pickoffs for 555 yards... Honorable mention All-Pro... Made Pro Bowl in 1983, '85 and '86... Had career-high six interceptions in '85... Has been regular starter since 1978... Was an All-Pro kickoff returner as a rookie... Was 16th player taken overall in 1977 draft... Was two-sport (football, track) star at Texas... 1988 salary: $900,000... Born Jan. 2, 1955, in Fort Worth, Texas.

TONY EASON 29 6-4 212   Quarterback

Suffered through another injury-plagued season... Missed preseason with separated shoulder and didn't dress till Oct. 23... Started final two games, but suffered knee injury at start of fourth quarter in finale at Denver... Completed 28 of 43 passes for 249 yards and two interceptions... Led Pats to their first overtime victory in 11 tries, Dec. 11 over Tampa Bay... Played in just four games in '87 because of injuries... Set club record in completions (276) and percentage (61.6) while throwing for 3,328 yards in '86... Fifteenth player selected in 1983 draft... Set several Big Ten passing marks at Illinois... He and Jim McMahon are only QBs in NCAA history to pass for over 3,000 yards twice... 1988 salary: $962,500... Born Oct. 8, 1959, in Blythe, Cal.

IRVING FRYAR 26 6-0 200   Wide Receiver

Second on Patriots in receiving with 33 catches for 490 yards... His 14.8-yard average was career low... Led Patriots with five TD receptions... Third in AFC and fifth in NFL in punt returns with a 10.5-yard average ... Best season was 1986, when he caught 43 passes in 14 games for a 17.1-yard average ... Former Nebraska star was first overall draft pick in 1984... However, off-field problems have hampered him... Was consensus All-American in 1983... 1988 salary: $495,000... Born Sept. 28, 1962, in Mount Holly, N.J.

JOHNNY REMBERT 28 6-3 234   Linebacker

Starred at inside linebacker in his first year as a starter...Second among Patriots with 137 tackles (98 solo)...Led Pats with three fumble recoveries and 98 first-hit tackles...Was one of five Patriots to intercept a pass vs. Cincinnati Oct. 16...Made two interceptions and had 12 passes defensed...Pro Bowl alternate ...Had been solid contributor for five years, primarily as Steve Nelson's backup...Started 190 games in '86 and finished with 72 tackles, third on the team...Fourth-round draft pick in '83 out of Clemson...Was Tigers' No. 2 tackler behind safety Terry Kinard...1988 salary: $230,000...Born Jan. 19, 1961, in Hollandale, Miss.

STANLEY MORGAN 34 5-11 181   Wide Receiver

Twelve-year veteran showed he can still play, leading Patriots in receiving yards (502) and average (16.2)...Finished third on team with 31 catches, three shy of leader Reggie Dupard ...His 31 catches was lowest total since he had 28 in nine-game '82 season...His 506 career catches puts him into NFL all-time Top 20...In '88, set club career records for receptions, yardage (9,866) and TDs (65)...Led NFL in yards-per-catch average in '79 and '81 and in TDs in '79 and '85...Four-time Pro Bowl pick...Twenty-fifth player overall taken in '77 draft out of Tennessee...1989 salary: $600,000... Born Feb. 17, 1955, in Easley, S.C.

COACH RAYMOND BERRY:

Has 46-30 record in the only head coaching job he has ever held...Is only Patriot coach to take team to consecutive playoff berths...His .606 winning percentage is ninth among active coaches...Replaced Ron Meyer as head coach midway through the 1984 season...A real Mr. Nice Guy, he is popular with his players...Is 8-1, including seven straight wins, vs. Don Shula, his coach at Baltimore...One of the game's greatest receivers, he was inducted into Hall of Fame in 1973, the first year he was eligible

... Hooked up with Johnny Unitas on Colts and made it to five Pro Bowls... When he retired in 1967 after 13 years with the Colts, he was the NFL's leader in receptions and yards... Set championship-game records with 12 receptions for 178 yards in 1958 Colts' win over Giants... Signed five-year contract in 1986... Son Mark is a graduate assistant coach at Vanderbilt... Born Feb. 27, 1933, in Corpus Christi, Tex.

GREATEST COACH

Raymond Berry, a Hall of Fame receiver with the Baltimore Colts, had never been a head coach at any level when he took over the Pats' post for Ron Meyer midway through the 1984 season.

He went 4-4 and the next year the team was 11-5 and drove all the way from a wild-card spot to the Super Bowl. In 4½ seasons, Berry's record is 43-28 and he has brought New England to the playoffs twice and been eliminated in the final week of the season twice.

He has the best winning percentage in Patriot history (.606) and his two 11-win seasons are matched in New England annals only by Chuck Fairbanks, who compiled a .541 winning percentage (46-39) from 1973-78. Fairbanks' teams also reached the playoffs twice.

INDIVIDUAL PATRIOT RECORDS

Rushing

Most Yards Game:	212	Tony Collins, N.Y. Jets, 1983
Season:	1,458	Jim Nance, 1966
Career:	5,453	Sam Cunningham, 1973-79, 1981-82

Passing

Most TD Passes Game:	5	Babe Parilli, vs Buffalo, 1964
	5	Babe Parilli, vs Miami, 1967
	5	Steve Grogan, vs N.Y. Jets, 1979
Season:	31	Babe Parilli, 1964
Career:	169	Steve Grogan, 1975-88

Receiving

Most TD Passes Game:	3	Billy Lott, vs Buffalo, 1961
	3	Gino Cappelletti, vs Buffalo, 1964
	3	Jim Whalen, vs Miami, 1967
	3	Harold Jackson, vs N.Y. Jets, 1979
	3	Derrick Ramsey, vs Indianapolis, 1984
	3	Stanley Morgan, vs Seattle, 1986
Season:	12	Stanley Morgan, 1979
Career:	64	Stanley Morgan, 1977-88

Scoring

Most Points Game:	28	Gino Cappelletti, vs Houston, 1965
Season:	155	Gino Cappelletti, 1964
Career:	1,130	Gino Cappelletti, 1960-70
Most TDs Game:	3	Billy Lott, vs Buffalo, 1961
	3	Billy Lott, vs Oakland, 1961
	3	Larry Garron, vs Oakland, 1964
	3	Gino Cappelletti, vs Buffalo, 1964
	3	Larry Garron, vs San Diego, 1966
	3	Jim Whalen, vs Miami, 1967
	3	Sam Cunningham, vs Buffalo, 1974
	3	Mack Herron, vs Buffalo, 1974
	3	Sam Cunningham, vs Buffalo, 1975
	3	Harold Jackson, vs N.Y. Jets, 1979
	3	Tony Collins, vs N.Y. Jets, 1983
	3	Mosi Tatupu, vs L.A. Rams, 1983
	3	Derrick Ramsey, vs Indianapolis, 1984
	3	Stanley Morgan, vs Seattle, 1986
Season:	13	Steve Grogan, 1976
	13	Stanley Morgan, 1979
Career:	64	Stanley Morgan, 1977-88

NEW YORK JETS

TEAM DIRECTORY: Chairman: Leon Hess; Pres.: Steve Gutman; Dir. Player Personnel: Mike Hickey; Dir. Pro Personnel: Jim Royer; Dir. Pub. Rel.: Frank Ramos; Head Coach: Joe Walton. Home field: Giants Stadium (76,891). Colors: Kelly green and white.

SCOUTING REPORT

OFFENSE: The Jets showed once again that they can move the ball. Freeman McNeil, Johnny Hector and Roger Vick combined for 2,045 yards rushing and were the only three backs on the same AFC team to be among the top 20 rushers. The Jets (8-7-1) upped their average gain on the ground from 3.6 yards to 4.1 and finished third in scoring in the AFC.

Sure-handed Al Toon captured NFL receiving title.

The Jets' primary goal last year was to rebuild their offensive line, and they believe they've done so. Tackle Dave Cadigan, a No. 1 pick last year, missed the last 10 weeks with a foot injury but is expected to return strong. Guard Mike Haight is young, Jim Sweeney nearly made the Pro Bowl at center, and the right side is set with Reggie McElroy at tackle and Dan Alexander at guard. The Jets cut their sacks from 50 to 42.

Ken O'Brien signed a big contract during the offseason, but concern lingers about his sore shoulder. When healthy, he's prolific. Last year, O'Brien threw for 15 TDs and had just seven interceptions in 424 attempts. Pat Ryan is a great backup.

Receiver Al Toon is the star of the Jets. He led the NFL with 93 receptions and has caught at least three passes in 50 straight games. He and tight end Mickey Shuler went to the Pro Bowl. Wesley Walker, 34, returns, but Toon could use a speedy receiver across the field.

DEFENSE: The key to the Jet defense is how it adjusts to life without Bud Carson, who left his post as defensive coordinator to coach the Browns. The players called him "Magic Man" for his ingenuity, something New York still needs.

The Jets were saved last year by a surprising young secondary that helped the club lead the AFC with 24 interceptions. Rookie safety Erik McMillan had eight pickoffs and was the league's Defensive Rookie of the Year. Rookie cornerback James Hasty stepped right in and had five interceptions. The success came despite the fact that No. 2 pick Terry Williams, a cornerback, was slowed by a knee injury.

It was largely because of the secondary that the Jets registered 45 sacks, including eight in the finale. That total was achieved with good coverage. The Jets, who had no sacks in five of the seven games after Mark Gastineau retired, expect No 1 pick Jeff Lageman to be a formidable pass-rusher. Right end Marty Lyons is 32 and left end Paul Frase had just one sack. The Jets also hope the linebacking corps will be given a lift by free agent Tim Cofield, formerly of the Chiefs.

KICKING GAME: The Jets have dangerous return men in JoJo Townsell and Bobby Humphery. Townsell led AFC punt returners with an 11.7 average and added a 19.4 average on kickoffs. Humphery was fourth in the league on kickoffs with a 24.3 average. The Jets covered punts well, allowing 5.9 yards per return.

Pat Leahy hit 23 of 28 field goals and has made 52 of 54 inside 40 yards since 1985. Punter Joe Prokop (38.9) is average.

JETS VETERAN ROSTER

HEAD COACH—Joe Walton. Assistant Coaches—Zeke Bratkowski, Ray Callahan, Wally Chambers, Mike Faulkiner, Bobby Hammond, Ralph Hawkins, Rod Humenuik, Rich Kotite, Larry Pasquale, Jim Vechiarella.

No.	Name	Pos.	Ht.	Wt.	NFL Exp.	College
60	Alexander, Dan	G	6-4	274	13	Louisiana State
46	Andrews, Mitch	TE	6-2	229	2	Louisiana State
23	Banks, Chuck	RB	6-0	225	3	West Virginia Tech
31	Barber, Marion	RB	6-3	228	8	Minnesota
54	Benson, Troy	LB	6-2	235	4	Pittsburgh
64	Bingham, Guy	C-G	6-3	260	10	Montana
42	Booty, John	CB-S	6-0	179	2	Texas Christian
66	Cadigan, Dave	T-G	6-4	285	2	Southern California
59	Clifton, Kyle	LB	6-4	236	6	Texas Christian
56	Cofield, Tim	LB	6-2	242	4	Elizabeth City State
62	Collier, Steve	T	6-7	330	2	Bethune-Cookman
61	Criswell, Jeff	T-G	6-7	284	3	Graceland
63	Curns, Bob	LB	6-2	235	2	Savannah State
65	Dodge, Kirk	LB	6-1	233	4	Nevada-Las Vegas
80	Dunn, K.D.	TE	6-2	237	5	Clemson
30	Faaola, Nuu	RB	5-11	220	4	Hawaii
91	Frase, Paul	DE	6-5	273	2	Syracuse
55	Gordon, Alex	LB	6-5	246	3	Cincinnati
79	Haight, Mike	G-T	6-4	281	4	Iowa
84	Harper, Michael	WR-KR	5-10	180	4	Southern California
40	Hasty, James	CB	6-0	200	2	Washington State
34	Hector, Johnny	RB	5-11	202	7	Texas A&M
26	Holloway, Steve	TE	6-1	235	2	Tennessee State
28	Howard, Carl	CB-S	6-2	190	6	Rutgers
48	Humphery, Bobby	CB-KR	5-10	180	6	New Mexico State
44	Johnson, James	LB	6-2	240	2	San Diego State
23	Konecny, Mark	RB-KR	6-0	200	3	Alma College
5	Leahy, Pat	K	6-0	196	16	St. Louis
93	Lyons, Marty	DE-DT	6-5	269	11	Alabama
15	Mackey, Kyle	QB	6-3	216	3	East Texas State
57	McArthur, Kevin	LB	6-2	250	4	Lamar
68	McElroy, Reggie	T	6-6	276	7	West Texas State
22	McMillan, Erik	S	6-2	197	2	Missouri
24	McNeil, Freeman	RB	5-11	209	9	UCLA
94	Mersereau, Scott	DT-DE	6-3	273	3	Southern Connecticut
36	Miano, Rich	S	6-0	200	5	Hawaii
46	Mitchell, Michael	CB	5-9	192	2	Howard Payne
77	Nichols, Gerald	DT-DE	6-2	267	3	Florida State
7	O'Brien, Ken	QB	6-4	200	7	California-Davis
6	Prokop, Joe	P	6-2	224	4	Cal Poly-Pomona
25	Radachowsky, George	S	5-11	190	5	Boston College
92	Rose, Ken	LB	6-1	204	3	Nevada-Las Vegas
10	Ryan, Pat	QB	6-3	210	12	Tennessee
75	Schreiber, Adam	C-G	6-4	277	6	Texas
82	Shuler, Mickey	TE	6-3	231	12	Penn State
53	Sweeney, Jim	C-T-G	6-4	270	6	Pittsburgh
88	Toon, Al	WR	6-4	205	5	Wisconsin
83	Townsell, JoJo	WR-KR	5-9	180	5	UCLA
43	Vick, Roger	RB	6-3	228	3	Texas A&M
58	Walker, Jackie	LB	6-5	245	4	Jackson State
85	Walker, Wesley	WR	6-0	182	13	California
33	Williams, Terry	CB	5-11	197	2	Bethune-Cookman
76	Withycombe, Mike	G-T	6-5	295	2	Fresno State

TOP DRAFT CHOICES

Rd.	Name	Sel. No.	Pos.	Ht.	Wt.	College
1	Lageman, Jeff	14	LB	6-5	239	Virginia
2	Byrd, Dennis	42	DT	6-4	265	Tulsa
3	Mott, Joe	70	LB	6-3	240	Iowa
4	Stallworth, Ron	98	DT	6-4	260	Auburn
5	Martin, Tony	126	WR	6-0	175	Mesa

THE ROOKIES: The Jets pulled the shocker of the draft when they picked Virginia inside linebacker Lageman, then announced he will play right outside linebacker. Lageman doesn't have great speed, but he's big (6-5½, 239) and was productive in college. Tulsa defensive end Dennis Byrd, a second-round pick, is a fiery performer who might add intensity to the Jet pass rush.

OUTLOOK: Finally, the Jets are on the rise. And finally, they avoided a late-season collapse. The secondary and offensive line have bright futures and the offense can score, but the playoffs still are out of reach.

JET PROFILES

AL TOON 26 6-4 205   **Wide Receiver**

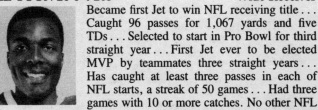

Became first Jet to win NFL receiving title... Caught 96 passes for 1,067 yards and five TDs... Selected to start in Pro Bowl for third straight year... First Jet ever to be elected MVP by teammates three straight years... Has caught at least three passes in each of NFL starts, a streak of 50 games... Had three games with 10 or more catches. No other NFL receiver had more than one... Missed one game with groin injury... Had four 100-yard games... Caught 14 passes for 181 yards against Dolphins... Average of 11.5 yards per reception was career low... First-round draft pick out of Wisconsin in 1985... Was All-American triple-jumper in college... 1988 salary: $375,000... Born April 30, 1963, in Newport News, Va.

ERIK McMILLAN 24 6-2 197   **Safety**

Rookie led AFC with eight interceptions... Went to Pro Bowl as a reserve... Had back-to-back games with TD returns vs. Buffalo and Miami, the first time that was accomplished in NFL since 1984... Intercepted Dan Marino three times in one game... Tied for team lead with 22 passes defensed... He and James Hasty give Jet defensive backfield a bright future... Third-round draft pick out of Missouri... Set Mizzou school record with 203 career solo tackles... Tied NCAA record as a senior with three interception returns for TDs

...Son of former St. Louis all-pro tackle Ernie McMillan...
1988 salary: $230,000...Born May 3, 1965, in St. Louis.

MICKEY SHULER 33 6-3 231   Tight End

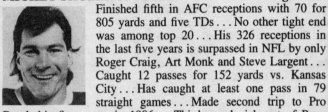

Finished fifth in AFC receptions with 70 for
805 yards and five TDs...No other tight end
was among top 20...His 326 receptions in
the last five years is surpassed in NFL by only
Roger Craig, Art Monk and Steve Largent...
Caught 12 passes for 152 yards vs. Kansas
City...Has caught at least one pass in 79
straight games...Made second trip to Pro
Bowl; his first came in 1986...Third-round pick out of Penn
State in 1978...Led Nittany Lions in receiving as junior and
senior...1988 salary: $484,000...Born Aug. 21, 1956, in Harrisburg, Pa.

KEN O'BRIEN 28 6-4 200   Quarterback

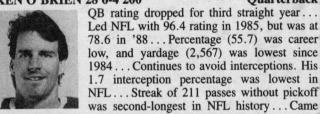

QB rating dropped for third straight year...
Led NFL with 96.4 rating in 1985, but was at
78.6 in '88...Percentage (55.7) was career
low, and yardage (2,567) was lowest since
1984...Continues to avoid interceptions. His
1.7 interception percentage was lowest in
NFL...Streak of 211 passes without pickoff
was second-longest in NFL history...Came
off bench to lead Jets to victory twice...Drafted in first round of
1983, the year of the quarterback. Was fifth of six QBs taken,
after John Elway, Todd Blackledge, Jim Kelly and Tony Eason.
Dan Marino was picked later in round...Division II All-American at Cal-Davis...Signed three-year contract in April for an
estimated $4.2 million...Born Nov. 27, 1960, in Brooklyn,
N.Y.

JIM SWEENEY 27 6-4 270   Center

Switched from left tackle to center and was
named alternate to Pro Bowl...Started all 16
games...Has played full seasons at guard,
tackle and center...Bench-presses 500
pounds...Has had shoulder surgery twice...
Was on Pro Football Writers All-Rookie team
as center in 1984...Second-round draft
choice out of Pittsburgh, where he played both

center and guard as a senior...Idolizes former Steeler center
Mike Webster...Serves as big brother for 24-year-old mentally
handicapped cousin Billy, who he calls "my best friend"...1988
salary: $400,000...Born Aug. 8, 1962, in Pittsburgh.

FREEMAN McNEIL 30 5-11 209   Running Back

Played in 16 games for first time in his career
...Gained 944 yards on 219 carries...Has
averaged 4.0 yards or better per carry for eight
straight years, the longest active streak in
NFL...Tied a career high with six rushing
TDs...Caught 34 passes for 288 yards...
Jets' leading rusher for eighth straight season,
despite nagging injury problems...Best year
was 1985, in which he ran for 1,331 yards...Led NFL in rushing (786 yards) and average (5.2) in 1982, the only time a Jet
ball-carrier has led the league...Named to Pro Bowl in 1982,
'84, '85...Set UCLA record for yards in a season (1,396)...
Third player chosen in 1981 draft...1989 salary: $905,000...
Born April 22, 1959, in Jackson, Miss.

JAMES HASTY 24 6-0 200   Cornerback

Showed mean streak as a rookie...Likes to
talk and hit on the field...Named to All-
Rookie teams after tying fellow-rookie Erik
McMillan for team-leading 22 passes
defensed...Had five interceptions, second on
club to McMillan...Missed one game with
hamstring injury...Third-round pick out of
Washington State who earned $225,000 last
season...Was a wide receiver at Central Washington for two
years before transferring...Born May 23, 1965, in Seattle.

MARTY LYONS 32 6-5 269   Defensive Lineman

Came back from subpar 1987 to lead team in
sacks for first time with 7½...Made 103
tackles, fourth-best on Jets...Kept going
strong at right end after Mark Gastineau left
team after seven games...Had three sacks vs.
Cincinnati and two vs. Giants...Played '88
season after having operation on both
shoulders for second straight year...Still
haunted by memories of late hit that may have ended career of

Miami's Dwight Stephenson, a former college teammate a
Alabama... Was 14th player picked in 1979 draft... Led Crim
son Tide to national title in 1978 with 119 tackles and 15 sack
... NFL's Man of the Year in 1985... 1988 salary
$467,000... Born Jan. 15, 1957, in Tokoma Park, Md.

ROGER VICK 25 6-3 228 Fullback

Third in Jet rushing behind Freeman McNei
and Johnny Hector... Gained 540 yards on
128 carries... Caught 19 passes for 120 yard:
... Both rushing and receiving stats are up
from rookie year... Good blocker... First
round pick in 1987 out of Texas A&M..
Considered Aggies' best fullback ever... Wa:
A&M's first player to lead Southwest Confer
ence in rushing since 1951 when he amassed 960 yards and 10
TDs as a senior... Was a 160-pound wide receiver in high
school... 1989 salary: $245,000.... Born Aug. 11, 1964, in
Conroe, Tex.

RICH MIANO 27 6-0 200 Safety

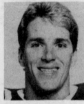

Hard-nosed strong safety finished third among
Jet tacklers with 112, including 80 solo..
Had two interceptions and 12 passes defensed
... Took over as starter in 1987 after injury to
Lester Lyles... Returned blocked field goa
67 yards for TD vs. Cincinnati in 1987..
Former special-teams standout... Drafted ou
of Hawaii in sixth round in 1985... Was a
diver at Hawaii who walked on to play football... Led team in
tackles as senior... Born Sept. 9, 1962, in Newton, Mass., and
moved to Honolulu during early high school years... 1988 sal
ary: $170,000.

COACH JOE WALTON:

Finally avoided end-of-season skid
that plagued his teams since 1983, going 3-1
in final four games... Struggled in middle of
year this time... Has 49-45-1 record in six
years and remains only Jet coach with a win
ning record... Has proved throughout career
he's not afraid to make controversial moves
... Took over from Walt Michaels after two
years as Jets' offensive coordinator... Was
Redskin assistant from 1974-81, helping the development of Joe

heismann . . . Tutored Fran Tarkenton while an assistant with
Giants . . . Played tight end with Redskins and Giants . . . Called
the best third-down receiver in the game, bar none," by Y.A.
'ittle . . . Was tried at left cornerback as a Redskin rookie (Don
hula was the right cornerback) before moving back to tight end
. . Was an All-American tight end at Pitt despite standing just
-10, 185 pounds . . . Father Frank was All-American at Pitt,
layed for Redskins and was a Steeler assistant . . . Born Dec. 15,
935, in Beaver Falls, Pa.

GREATEST COACH

Weeb Ewbank's winning percentage ranks just third among Jet
coaches, but he is responsible for the franchise's most memorable
moments.

In 11 seasons from 1963-73, Ewbank was 71-77-6 (.481). In
968, the Jets, behind flamboyant quarterback Joe Namath,

Jets' Ken O'Brien had NFL's lowest interception percentage.

stunned the football world with a Super Bowl victory over the favored Baltimore Colts, the team that released Ewbank six years before.

The Jets followed that up with another Eastern Division title in '69. Those two years represent the only first-place finishes in the Jets' 28-year history. Only one Jet coach has a winning record. Joe Walton is 49-45 (.516) in six seasons.

Ewbank came to New York after nine seasons in Baltimore, where he compiled a 61-52-1 mark and won consecutive NFL championships in 1958 and '59. The only coach to win championships in both the AFL and NFL, Ewbank was selected to the Pro Football Hall of Fame in 1978.

INDIVIDUAL JET RECORDS

Rushing

Most Yards Game:	192	Freeman McNeil, vs Buffalo, 1985
Season:	1,331	Freeman McNeil, 1985
Career:	6,794	Freeman McNeil, 1981-88

Passing

Most TD Passes Game:	6	Joe Namath, vs Baltimore, 1972
Season:	26	Al Dorow, 1960
	26	Joe Namath, 1967
Career:	170	Joe Namath, 1965-76

Receiving

Most TD Passes Game:	4	Wesley Walker, vs Miami, 1986
Season:	14	Art Powell, 1960
	14	Don Maynard, 1965
Career:	88	Don Maynard, 1960-72

Scoring

Most Points Game:	19	Jim Turner, vs Buffalo, 1968
	19	Pat Leahy, vs Cincinnati, 1984
Season:	145	Jim Turner, 1968
Career:	1,190	Pat Leahy, 1974-88
Most TDs Game:	4	Wesley Walker, vs Miami, 1986
Season:	14	Art Powell, 1960
	14	Don Maynard, 1965
	14	Emerson Boozer, 1972
Career:	88	Don Maynard, 1960-72

PITTSBURGH STEELERS

TEAM DIRECTORY: Pres.: Daniel Rooney; VP: John McGinley; VP: Art Rooney Jr.; Dir. Player Personnel: Dick Haley; Dir. Comm. and Business: Joe Gordon; Dir. Publicity: Dan Edwards; Head Coach: Chuck Noll. Home field: Three Rivers Stadium (59,000). Colors: Black and gold.

SCOUTING REPORT

OFFENSE: The Steelers were supposed to struggle offensively in 1988. They did, but not nearly as much as expected. Armed with a no-name cast, the Steelers had the No. 6 rushing attack in the NFL. Merril Hoge, a burly load from Idaho State, led the team in both rushing (705 yards) and receiving (50 catches). The

Given the chance, Merril Hoge carried the load.

Steelers' Rookie of the Year was running back Warren Williams, but they sought a game-breaker in the draft and believe they found one in Tim Worley, seventh pick.

Bubby Brister is the team's quarterback of the future, but he's still fairly raw. Brister completed just 47 percent of his passes last year, throwing 11 touchdowns and 14 interceptions, but with Mike Webster gone, he is the team's new leader. Until the Steelers (5-11) find quality speed on the outside, Louis Lipps (50 catches, 5 TDs in '88) will never have an easy time.

Tunch Ilkin is an All-Pro at right tackle and the drafting of Tom Ricketts (24th pick) should shore up left tackle, an area of concern. Coach Chuck Noll would like stability there so he can continue running the ball. Troubling to Noll has to be the fact that his club fumbled the ball an AFC-high 40 times last year. Luckily, they lost just 13 of those.

DEFENSE: 1988 was not a good year to be a Pittsburgh defensive back. Opposing quarterbacks had all the time in the world as the Steelers managed an NFL-low 19 sacks, just one more than Philadelphia's Reggie White. The team's top pass-rushers the past four years, Mike Merriweather and Keith Willis, sat out because of a holdout and injury, respectively. Willis is back, but Merriweather is gone—to Minnesota. Aaron Jones, a 1988 first-rounder drafted as a pass-rushing specialist, finished with just 1½ sacks.

The Steeler defensive backfield is decent. Rod Woodson could develop into an All-Pro.

KICKING GAME: As punter Harry Newsome gets better, his blocking gets worse. Newsome led the NFL in gross punting (45.4) but, through no fault of his own, set a league record with six blocks. Kicker Gary Anderson made 28 of 36 field goals and was second in AFC scoring. Super-athlete Woodson was sixth among NFL kick returners with a 23-yard average. But both punt- and kick-return teams gave up too much.

THE ROOKIES: Georgia's Worley brings explosiveness to the Pittsburgh running attack. As a senior, he averaged 6.4 yards per carry and rushed for 1,261 yards despite sharing the workload. Pitt's Ricketts could provide immediate help on the line. Carnell Lake went to UCLA as a running back, moved to linebacker and will be a pro safety.

OUTLOOK: Noll faces a tough rebuilding job. There are holes everywhere, and despite winning three of their last four games in

STEELERS VETERAN ROSTER

HEAD COACH—Chuck Noll. Assistant Coaches—Ron Blackledge, Dave Brazil, John Fox, Joe Greene, Dick Hoak, Jon Kolb, Tom Moore, Dwain Painter, Rod Rust, George Stewart.

No.	Name	Pos.	Ht.	Wt.	NFL Exp.	College
1	Anderson, Gary	K	5-11	170	8	Syracuse
14	Blackledge, Todd	QB	6-3	227	7	Penn State
60	Blankenship, Brian	G-C	6-1	275	3	Nebraska
6	Brister, Bubby	QB	6-3	210	4	Northeast Louisiana
91	Carr, Gregg	LB	6-2	222	5	Auburn
24	Carter, Rodney	RB	6-0	216	3	Purdue
40	Davis, Elgin	RB	5-10	192	3	Central Florida
63	Dawson, Dermontti	G-C	6-2	271	2	Kentucky
27	Everett, Thomas	S	5-9	179	3	Baylor
68	Freeman, Lorenzo	NT	6-5	298	3	Pittsburgh
92	Gary, Keith	DE	6-2	268	7	Oklahoma
86	Gothard, Preston	TE	6-4	235	4	Alabama
29	Gowdy, Cornell	S	6-1	202	4	Morgan State
22	Griffin, Larry	CB	6-0	200	4	North Carolina
35	Hall, Delton	S-CB	6-1	205	3	Clemson
53	Hinkle, Bryan	LB	6-2	222	8	Oregon
81	Hinnant, Mike	TE	6-3	258	2	Temple
33	Hoge, Merril	RB	6-2	231	3	Idaho State
62	Ilkin, Tunch	T	6-3	265	10	Indiana State
65	Jackson, John	T	6-6	282	2	Eastern Kentucky
88	Johnson, Jason	WR	5-11	180	2	Illinois State
78	Johnson, Tim	DE-NT	6-3	261	3	Penn State
85	Johnson, Troy	WR	6-0	185	4	Southern University
97	Jones, Aaron	DE-LB	6-5	257	2	Eastern Kentucky
55	Jordan, Darin	LB-DE	6-1	235	2	Northeastern
51	Lanza, Chuck	C	6-2	263	2	Notre Dame
21	Lee, Greg	CB	6-1	207	2	Arkansas State
83	Lipps, Louis	WR-KR	5-10	190	6	Southern Mississippi
50	Little, David	LB	6-1	230	9	Florida
95	Lloyd, Greg	LB	6-2	224	2	Fort Valley State
89	Lockett, Charles	WR	6-0	181	3	Long Beach State
74	Long, Terry	G	5-11	275	6	East Carolina
19	Martin, Tracy	WR	6-3	205	2	North Dakota
84	Mularkey, Mike	TE	6-4	238	7	Florida
18	Newsome, Harry	P	6-0	186	5	Wake Forest
54	Nickerson, Hardy	LB	6-2	225	3	California
76	Putzier, Rollin	NT	6-4	281	2	Oregon
64	Reese, Jerry	DE	6-2	267	2	Kentucky
23	Richard, Gary	CB-S	5-10	176	2	Pittsburgh
79	Reinstra, John	G	6-5	268	4	Temple
56	Smith, Vinson	LB	6-2	230	2	East Carolina
94	Stedman, Troy	LB	6-3	243	2	Washington
20	Stone, Dwight	RB-KR	6-0	188	3	Middle Tenn. State
90	Stowe, Tyronne	LB	6-1	236	3	Rutgers
43	Wallace, Ray	RB	6-0	230	3	Purdue
98	Williams, Gerald	NT	6-3	262	4	Auburn
42	Williams, Warren	RB	6-0	203	2	Miami
93	Willis, Keith	DE	6-1	263	7	Northeastern
73	Wolfley, Craig	T-G	6-1	269	10	Syracuse
49	Woodruff, Dwayne	CB	6-0	198	10	Louisville
26	Woodson, Rod	CB-KR	6-0	202	2	Purdue

TOP DRAFT CHOICES

Rd.	Name	Sel. No.	Pos.	Ht.	Wt.	College
1	Worley, Tim	7	RB	6-2	215	Georgia
1	Ricketts, Tom	24	OT	6-4	300	Pittsburgh
2	Lake, Carnell	34	S	6-0	205	UCLA
3	Hill, Derek	61	WR	6-1	190	Arizona
4	Williams, Jerrol	91	LB	6-4	240	Purdue

'88, the Steelers are years away from challenging in the loaded AFC Central.

STEELER PROFILES

TUNCH ILKIN 31 6-3 265   Tackle

Consistency finally was noticed in 1988 as this nine-year veteran was named to Pro Bowl for first time... Only Pittsburgh player selected, but kept alive streak of Steelers going every year since 1951... Starter since 1983, he rarely allows a sack... Sixth-round draft pick in 1980 who was cut rookie year and brought back when injuries hit team... Three-year starter at Indiana State, playing tackle and center... Born Sept. 23, 1957, in Istanbul, Turkey... Family moved to Illinois when he was two... Mother was Miss Turkey in 1950... Wife was Indiana State cheerleader... Full name is Tunch Ali Ilkin... 1989 salary: $258,000.

LOUIS LIPPS 27 5-10 190   Wide Receiver

Stayed healthy for first time in three years and showed deep-threat form that made him All-Pro his first two years in NFL... Caught 50 passes for 973 yards and five TDs... His 19.5 average was topped by only Eddie Brown among AFC's top receivers... Moved from 12th to seventh in Steeler career receptions (203) and from 10th to sixth in yards (3,721) ... The second Steeler to catch 200 passes in first five seasons. Buddy Dial was the other... Threw his first TD pass... Missed 14 games in 1986 and '87... Scored 13 TDs in 1985... NFL Rookie of the Year in '84... 1988 salary: $285,000... Born Aug. 9, 1962, in New Orleans.

BUBBY BRISTER 27 6-3 210   Quarterback

Physical tools were never questioned, but Steelers were thrilled to see him become a team leader in first year as starter... Said former Steeler center Mike Webster: "He's becoming the kind of quarterback you win with' ... Beat out Todd Blackledge convincingly for starting spot... His 2,634 passing yards were most by a Steeler since 1981, when Terry

Bradshaw racked up 2,887... Completed TD passes of 89, 80 (twice) and 72 yards... Fiery competitor who's not afraid to mix it up with opponents or officials... Third-round pick out of Northeast Louisiana in 1986... Transferred from Tulane in 1983 ... Originally signed with Alabama, but chose professional baseball instead... Detroit Tigers drafted him in the fourth round in 1981, but played just 39 games in Appalachian League as an outfielder and shortstop before quitting. Had a .180 batting average... 1989 salary: $187,000... Born Aug. 15, 1962, in Alexandria, La.

MERRIL HOGE 24 6-2 231   Running Back

Was team's offensive workhorse after year on bench... Led Steelers in rushing (705 yards) and tied Lipps with 50 receptions... First Steeler to lead team in both rushing and receiving since 1982, when Franco Harris did so... Bullish, straight-ahead runner who makes defenders pay... Scored six touchdowns (three run, three pass)... A 10th-round draft pick out of Idaho State in 1987... Top rusher in school history with 2,713 yards... Set Big Sky Conference record with 44 TDs... Led school in rushing and receiving three straight years... 1989 salary: $87,000... Born Jan. 26, 1965, in Pocatello, Idaho.

ROD WOODSON 24 6-0 202   Cornerback

Teammates voted him Steelers' MVP along with David Little... Tied Dwayne Woodruff for interception lead with four... Third-leading Steeler tackler with 61... Returned 33 punts for an 8.5-yard average... One of top athletes in NFL who has potential to play wide receiver and running back, too... Limited to nickel-back duties as rookie (1987) because of 94-day holdout that covered eight games... Was 10th player picked in draft after starting four years at Purdue... In final college game, played tailback, receiver, cornerback and kick returner. The numbers: 93 yards rushing, 67 receiving, 46 on kick returns, 30 on punt returns, 10 tackles, one forced fumble... Was All-American hurdler... 1989 salary: $325,000... Born March 10, 1965, in Fort Wayne, Ind.

WARREN WILLIAMS 24 6-0 203 Running Back

Surprise team Rookie of the Year... Started final seven games and finished as No. 2 rusher with 409 yards on 87 carries (4.7 average)... Yardage was most by a Pittsburgh rookie since Franco Harris' 1,055 in 1972... Former Miami Hurricane buried home-state Dolphins with 117 yards in season finale... Quiet type who was overshadowed by U. of Miami's high-profile players... Is ranked fourth on all-time 'Cane list with 1,734 yards rushing... Led team as senior with 673 yards ... Teamed with Melvin Bratton as senior and backed up Alonzo Highsmith as junior... 1988 salary: $107,500... Born July 29, 1965, in Fort Myers, Fla.

DAVID LITTLE 30 6-1 230 Linebacker

Brother of former NFL great Larry Little led Steelers in tackles for second straight season and for third time in four years... Made 107 stops, seven short of career high set in 1985 ... Named team MVP along with Rod Woodson. It marked third straight year a defender was team MVP... Asserted self as team leader in 1987... Has been starter since replacing Jack Lambert in 1984... Has never had more than $1\frac{1}{2}$ sacks in a season... Seventh-round pick out of Florida in 1981 ... Averaged 14.4 tackles in 33 Gator games for school-record 287 solo tackles and 475 total... 1988 salary: $335,000... Born Jan. 3, 1959, in Miami.

GARY ANDERSON 30 5-11 170 Kicker

Scored 118 points to move within five points of Roy Gerela's club record of 731... Set career club records in field goals (165), single-game field goals (six), single-game kicking points (21) and consecutive PATs (202)... However, he missed a PAT last year for first time since 1983... Made 28 of 36 field goals ... Missed one inside 40 yards but was just 6-for-12 from 40-49... Two-time Pro Bowler who was team MVP in 1983... Set NCAA record at Syracuse with 87.4-percent success rate... Roomed with Joe Morris in college... Father was pro soccer player in England... 1988 salary: $305,000... Born July 16, 1959, in Parys, South Africa, and moved to Downington, Pa., after high school.

HARRY NEWSOME 26 6-0 186 Punter

Everything this four-year veteran achieved in 1988 was on his own because he had no protection... He led the league with 45.4-yard average but set an NFL record with six blocked in the first 15 games... Average was best by a Steeler since 1961... His career average of 41.5 is third-best in team history ... Average has gone up each year... Had 62-yarder to come within two of career high... Eighth-round draft choice was team Rookie of the Year in 1985... Three-time All-ACC at Wake Forest... Was quarterback and backup punter in high school... Was backup because of presence of Dale Hatcher (Rams), who beat him out for All-ACC in '84... Has zero golf handicap... 1988 salary: $117,500... Born Jan. 25, 1963, in Cheraw, S.C.

HARRY NICKERSON 24 6-2 225 Linebacker

Second-leading tackler with 99 stops, finishing eight behind leader David Little... Second with $3\frac{1}{2}$ sacks and added six passes defensed and a fumble recovery... Was backup to Robin Cole in 1987 and made just 17 tackles ... Fifth-round draft choice in 1987... Known as "The Hardware Man" while becoming California's all-time leading tackler with 501... Was finalist for 1986 Butkus Award... High school team, Los Angeles Verbum Dei, won 25 straight games, including 13 shutouts... 1988 salary: $95,000... Born Sept. 1, 1965, in Los Angeles.

COACH CHUCK NOLL: Ended months of speculation in January when he announced he would return for

his 21st season as Steeler head coach... Club also announced he will "remain with the organization for the rest of his career"... That's fitting, for Noll is only NFL coach to win four Super Bowls... Won seven division titles between 1972-79... To cope with recent failures, he realigned his coaching staff... Hopes wins in three of final four games last year carries over to 1989 ... Has come a long way since being a 21st-round draft choice out of Dayton in 1953... Played guard seven years with

Cleveland . . . Was an assistant under Sid Gillman with Chargers and Don Shula with Colts . . . Took over Steelers in 1969 . . . Won first game but lost next 13 . . . Drafted Terry Bradshaw the next year and started to turn things around . . . The Hall of Fame awaits his retirement . . . Born Jan. 5, 1932, in Cleveland.

GREATEST COACH

It's hard to believe that the Chuck Noll of Steeler lore is the same one whom it seemed fashionable to criticize last year. Noll, who has the fifth-winningest record in NFL history, is the only coach to win four Super Bowls. Since taking over the Steelers in 1969, Noll has compiled a 183-132-1 record. A firm believer in building a team through the draft, Noll's first two No. 1 picks were Joe Greene in 1969 and Terry Bradshaw in '70. Noll took the once-woeful Steelers from a 1-13 record in 1969 to their first-ever division title in '72.

Pittsburgh reached the playoffs eight straight years, claiming Super Bowl victories after the 1974, '75, '78 and '79 seasons. Noll reached the AFC championship game again in 1984 but hasn't been to the playoffs since.

INDIVIDUAL STEELER RECORDS

Rushing

Most Yards Game:	218	John Fuqua, vs Philadelphia, 1970	
Season:	1,246	Franco Harris, 1975	
Career:	11,950	Franco Harris, 1972-83	

Passing

Most TD Passes Game:	5	Terry Bradshaw, vs Atlanta, 1981	
	5	Mark Malone, vs Indianapolis, 1985	
Season:	28	Terry Bradshaw, 1978	
Career:	210	Terry Bradshaw, 1970-82	

Receiving

Most TD Passes Game:	4	Roy Jefferson, vs Atlanta, 1968	
Season:	12	Buddy Dial, 1961	
	12	Louis Lipps, 1985	
Career:	63	John Stallworth, 1974-87	

Scoring

Most Points Game:	24	Ray Mathews, vs Cleveland, 1954
	24	Roy Jefferson, vs Atlanta, 1968
Season:	139	Gary Anderson, 1985
Career:	731	Roy Gerela, 1971-78
Most TDs Game:	4	Ray Mathews, vs Cleveland, 1954
	4	Roy Jefferson, vs Atlanta, 1968
Season:	14	Franco Harris, 1976
Career:	100	Franco Harris, 1972-83

Unsung vet Tunch Ilkin finally got to the Pro Bowl.

SAN DIEGO CHARGERS

TEAM DIRECTORY: Owner/Chairman of Board: Alex G. Spanos; Dir. of Administration: Jack Teele; Dir. Football Operations: Steve Ortmayer; Dir. Pub. Rel.: Rick Smith; Head Coach: Dan Henning. Home field: San Diego Jack Murphy Stadium (60,100). Colors: Blue, white and gold

SCOUTING REPORT

OFFENSE: Offensive problems continued in 1988 for the Chargers, once the most dangerous team in the league. Despite an improved running game, San Diego (6-10) finished 27th in scoring. Their 231 points were the franchise's worst ever in a 16-game season.

Naturally, the problems start at quarterback. Mark Vlasic took over for Mark Malone, won two games, then ripped up a knee. He expects to be back this year as the Chargers look for an air attack. They threw a league-low 11 TD passes despite the presence of a corps of burners at receiver. Last year's No. 1 pick Anthony Miller, Jamie Holland and Quinn Early give hope for the future, but they suffered along with Malone.

The Chargers averaged 4.6 yards per rush, well up from their 3.3 average of 1988. The leader was Gary Anderson, who finally silenced critics by finishing third among AFC rushers with 1,119 yards despite missing two games. Lionel James is versatile, but the Chargers need a big, strong back to complement Anderson. Tight end Rod Bernstine showed great potential last year before hurting a knee.

The Chargers are expected to overhaul their offensive line. A healthy return of John Clay, who is recovering from a neck injury, could help.

DEFENSE: Chip Banks' off-field woes left the Chargers' scrambling from the start, and they're still scrambling to find talent. After improving from 23rd to 15th in the NFL defensive standings in '87, they dropped back to 21st in '88.

The defensive line could be a strength this year. Lee Williams is coming off a Pro Bowl year and will be rejoined by Leslie O'Neal, who returned from a knee injury at midseason. Williams had 11 sacks, one-half behind AFC leader Greg Townsend of the Raiders. As a rookie in '87, O'Neal had 12½ sacks in 13 games before his injury. Now they've beefed up with the drafting of defensive end Burt Grossman (eighth pick).

Lee Williams revels in batting down passes and sacking QBs.

Williams wasn't the only bright spot of the defense. Cornerback Gil Byrd, who didn't have an interception in 1987, had seven last year and knocked down 15 passes. Linebacker Billy Ray Smith is the team's best all-around defender, but he broke a leg late in the year. The Chargers were hurt by lack of aggressiveness. Their minus-6 takeaway ratio was worst in the AFC.

KICKING GAME: For all their weaknesses, there's little doubt the Chargers can return kicks. They ranked first in the league in kickoff returns, with Holland (26.1) and Miller (25.9) finishing second and third, each with a touchdown. James was good for 9.9 yards per punt return.

Punter Ralf Mojsiejenko's 44.1 average was topped by only Harry Newsome of the Steelers. Kicker Vince Abbott hit eight of 12 field goals before hurting a knee.

CHARGERS VETERAN ROSTER

HEAD COACH—Dan Henning. Assistant Coaches—Larry Beightol, Gunther Cunningham, Mike Haluchak, Bobby Jackson, Charlie Joiner, Ron Lynn, Jim Mora, Joe Madden, Ted Tollner, Ed White.

No.	Name	Pos.	Ht.	Wt.	NFL Exp.	College
10	Abbott, Vince	K	5-11	206	3	Cal State-Fullerton
40	Anderson, Gary	RB	6-0	184	5	Arkansas
15	Archer, David	QB	6-2	208	6	Iowa State
3	Bahr, Chris	K	5-10	170	14	Penn State
44	Bayless, Martin	S	6-2	200	6	Bowling Green
61	Behning, Mark	T	6-6	285	2	Nebraska
32	Bennett, Roy	CB	6-2	200	2	Jackson State
82	Bernstine, Rod	TE	6-3	235	3	Texas A&M
58	Brandon, David	LB	6-4	225	3	Memphis State
73	Britz, Darrick	G-T	6-3	270	3	Oregon
57	Browner, Keith	DE	6-6	260	5	Southern California
22	Byrd, Gill	CB	5-11	198	7	San Jose State
95	Campbell, Joe	LB	6-3	242	2	New Mexico State
90	Caravello, Joe	TE	6-3	270	3	Tulane
71	Charles, Mike	NT	6-4	315	7	Syracuse
77	Clay, John	T	6-5	305	3	Missouri
31	Coleman, Leonard	S	6-2	233	5	Vanderbilt
96	Collins, Jim	LB	6-2	202	8	Tulane
88	Cox, Arthur	TE	6-2	260	7	Texas Southern
6	DeLine, Steve	K	5-11	185	2	Colorado State
87	Early, Quinn	WR	6-0	188	2	Iowa
53	Faucette, Chuck	LB	6-3	238	2	Maryland
51	Figaro, Cedric	LB	6-2	250	2	Notre Dame
70	Fitzpatrick, James	G-T	6-7	286	4	Southern California
31	Flutie, Darren	WR	5-10	185	2	Boston College
25	Glenn, Vencie	S	6-0	187	4	Indiana State
97	Hinkle, George	DE	6-5	269	2	Arizona
86	Holland, Jamie	WR	6-1	195	3	Ohio State
52	Jackson, Jeffery	LB	6-1	230	5	Auburn
26	James, Lionel	RB	5-6	170	6	Auburn
93	Keys, Tyrone	DE	6-7	275	7	Mississippi State
68	Kowalski, Gary	G-T	6-6	273	5	Boston College
24	Lyles, Lester	S	6-3	200	5	Virginia
62	Macek, Don	C	6-2	270	14	Boston College
16	Malone, Mark	QB	6-4	222	10	Arizona State
60	McKnight, Dennis	C-G	6-3	280	7	Drake
83	Miller, Anthony	WR	5-11	185	2	Tennessee
74	Miller, Brett	T	6-7	300	7	Iowa
69	Miller, Les	DE	6-7	285	2	Ft. Hays State
48	Miller, Pat	S	6-1	210	2	Florida
2	Mojsiejenko, Ralf	P	6-3	213	5	Michigan State
91	O'Neal, Leslie	DE	6-4	255	3	Oklahoma State
85	Parker, Andy	TE	6-5	245	6	Utah
78	Patten, Joel	T	6-7	307	4	Duke
34	Patterson, Elvis	CB	5-11	198	6	Kansas
75	Phillips, Joe	DE	6-5	275	4	Southern Methodist
50	Plummer, Gary	LB	6-2	240	4	California
20	Redden, Barry	RB	5-10	219	8	Richmond
65	Richards, David	T	6-4	301	2	UCLA
66	Rosado, Dan	G-T	6-3	280	3	Northern Illinois
30	Seale, Sam	CB	5-9	185	6	Western State, Colo.
54	Smith, Billy Ray	LB	6-3	236	7	Arkansas
36	Smith, Timmy	RB	5-11	222	3	Texas Tech
43	Spencer, Tim	RB	6-1	227	5	Ohio State
47	Thomas, Johnny	CB	5-9	185	2	Baylor
13	Thompson, Broderick	G-T	6-4	290	4	Kansas
76	Vlasic, Mark	QB	6-3	206	3	Iowa
67	Williams, Larry	G	6-5	290	4	Notre Dame
99	Williams, Lee	DE	6-5	271	6	Bethune-Cookman
72	Wilson, Karl	DE	6-4	268	3	Louisiana State
59	Woodard, Ken	LB	6-1	220	8	Tuskegee Institute

TOP DRAFT CHOICES

Rd.	Name	Sel. No.	Pos.	Ht.	Wt.	College
1	Grossman, Burt	8	DE	6-4	270	Pittsburgh
2	Hall, Courtney	37	C	6-1	269	Rice
3	Tolliver, Billy Joe	51	QB	6-0	215	Texas Tech
5	Smith, Elliot	120	DB	6-0	190	Alcorn State
7	Butts, Marion	183	RB	6-1	248	Florida State

THE ROOKIES: Grossman is a fast, aggressive pass-rusher who made 231 tackles the last three years at Pittsburgh. He was slowed by an ankle injury last season but was the top-rated defensive end in the '89 draft. Center Courtney Hall is small (6-1½, 269), but improved throughout his career at Rice. The Chargers' quarterback problems were addressed with the selection of Texas Tech's Billy Joe Tolliver in the second round.

OUTLOOK: New coach Dan Henning will need some offensive ingenuity to help his team rediscover the end zone. Despite being in a weak division, this year's club should be thrilled to break even.

CHARGER PROFILES

GARY ANDERSON 28 6-0 184   Running Back

Easy choice as team MVP . . . Silenced critics who had been saying he wasn't living up to hype and potential . . . AFC's third-leading rusher with 1,119 yards . . . Set Charger records with 34 attempts and 217 yards vs. Chiefs . . . That output was best in NFL in 1988 . . . Ran for 100 yards or more five times . . . Chargers are 5-1 in games in which he has gained over 100 . . . Averaged 5.0 yards per carry, up from previous career average of 3.5 . . . Ability to catch passes and run in open field makes him a game-breaker . . . Went to Chargers in 1985 after three USFL seasons . . . Was 20th player chosen in 1983 NFL draft . . . MVP in three bowl games while at Arkansas . . . 1988 salary: $400,000 . . . Born April 18, 1961, in Columbia, Mo.

LEE WILLIAMS 26 6-5½ 271   Defensive End

A sack machine, he recorded 11 in 1988 and has 43½ in 4½ NFL seasons . . . Had four sacks nullified by penalties in '88 . . . Only Charger in on every defensive play of the season . . . Had three sacks in two different games . . . Knocked down 10 passes at line of scrimmage . . . Started in Pro Bowl for first time . . . Third on Chargers' all-time sack list behind Gary Johnson (67) and Fred Dean (52½)... Has played in every Charger game since middle of 1984, when he arrived from USFL... Was fifth player selected in '84 supplemental draft... Four-year starter at Bethune-Cookman, where he had 27 sacks in last two seasons... 1988 salary: $275,000... Born Oct. 15, 1962, in Fort Lauderdale, Fla.

MARK MALONE 30 6-4 222   Quarterback

Had inconsistent year, but it had to be better than being booed every week in Pittsburgh... Tied personal best with 54.0 completion percentage... Completed 147 of 272 passes for 1,580 yards and six touchdowns... However, tossed 13 interceptions and had AFC-low quarterback rating of 58.8... Was 0-6 as a Charger starter before beating Steelers... Started eight games and played in 12... Came to Chargers in exchange for 1988 eighth-round pick and a conditional pick in '89 draft... Played at Arizona State and was first-round pick by Steelers in 1980... 1988 salary: $500,000 ... Born Nov. 22, 1958, in El Cajon, Cal.

BILLY RAY SMITH 28 6-3 236   Linebacker

Best all-around defender on team, but broke a leg late in season... Finished with 50 tackles and one sack... Failed to lead team in tackles for first time in four years... Was team's MVP in 1987 when he made 88 tackles and had team-high five interceptions... Played three NFL seasons at inside linebacker before switch to outside in 1986. Had 11 sacks that year, second only to Lawrence Taylor among NFL linebackers ... First defensive player selected in 1983 draft (fifth overall) has been starter since arrival... Two-time All-American defensive end at Arkansas... Father Billy Ray Sr. was All-Pro with Baltimore Colts... Has finance and banking degree... 1989 salary: $475,000... Born Aug. 10, 1961, in Fayetteville, Ark.

QUINN EARLY 24 6-0 188　　　　Wide Receiver

Third-round pick scored team-high four touchdowns on 29 receptions... Mainly a possession receiver... Gained 375 yards for a 12.9 average... Rushed seven times for 63 yards... While at Iowa, led Big Ten in receiving average as a senior (22.3)... 1986 Big Ten long-jump champ... Gifted artist whose illustrations of Hawkeye teammates appeared in 1987 football media guide... 1988 salary: $245,000... Born April 13, 1965, in West Hempstead, N.Y.

ANTHONY MILLER 24 5-11 185　　　Wide Receiver

Chargers plan to build their passing offense around Miller, another in a long line of speedsters from Tennessee... Finished second on team in receptions with 36 catches for 526 yards... Scored three touchdowns... Had 25.9-yard kickoff-return average, third in NFL behind Raiders' Tim Brown and Chargers' Jamie Holland... Ran kickoff back 93 yards for TD vs. Rams... Fifteenth player selected and rated fastest player in 1988 draft... Originally went to San Diego State on track scholarship... Played just one year of football in high school but was All-SEC as Tennessee senior... 1988 salary: $987,500... Born April 15, 1965, in Pasadena, Cal.

GIL BYRD 28 5-11 198　　　　　　Cornerback

Leader of San Diego secondary had best season of six-year career... Led team with seven interceptions after being shut out in 1987... Seven pickoffs was second in AFC and most by a Charger since 1983... Led club with 15 passes defensed and was third with 72 tackles... Voted Most Inspirational Player by teammates... Had five interceptions in 1986... First-round pick out of San Jose State... Was a college walk-on who started four years... Has worked as a financial analyst with a Palo Alto, Cal., aerospace firm... Also holds real-estate license... 1988 salary: $330,000... Born Feb. 20, 1961, in San Francisco.

JAMIE HOLLAND 25 6-1½ 195   Wide Receiver

Had a surprising season, overshadowing high draft picks Anthony Miller and Quinn Early . . . Led Chargers with 39 receptions and 536 yards after just six receptions for 138 yards in 1987 . . . Second among NFL kick-returners with 26.1-yard average . . . Had 94-yard return for TD in finale vs. Chiefs . . . Seventh-round draft choice out of Ohio State in 1987 . . . Was a backup for Cris Carter with Buckeyes and caught just eight passes as a senior . . . Ran track in college . . . 1988 salary: $94,000 . . . Born Feb. 1, 1964, in Raleigh, N.C.

RALF MOJSIEJENKO 26 6-3 213   Punter

Inefficient offense resulted in left-footed "Mojo" setting club record with 85 punts. Previous mark was 79 by Paul Maguire in 1962 . . . Second in NFL (behind Steelers' Harry Newsome) with 44.1 average, a career high . . . Landed 22 punts inside opponents' 20, also a career high . . . Went to Pro Bowl in 1987 with 42.9-yard average . . . Fourth-round pick out of Michigan State in 1985 . . . Had 43.8-yard average for Spartans and made 35 of 53 field-goal attempts . . . Made 61-yarder on first college field-goal attempt . . . Pitched for MSU baseball team, going 4-7 . . . 1989 salary: $175,000 . . . Born Jan. 28, 1963, in Salzgitter Lebenstadt, West Germany, and moved to Bridgeman, Mich., nine months later.

DENNIS McKNIGHT 29 6-3½ 280   Guard

The stabilizing force on the Charger line . . . Was only returning starter from 1987 . . . Has played 99 straight non-strike games, starting the last 76 . . . Has played everywhere on line but left tackle . . . Voted Pro Bowl alternate, team captain and player representative . . . Credits durability to rugged workout schedule that has earned him nickname "Conan" . . . Is Chargers' snapper on field-goal attempts . . . Signed with Chargers as free agent in 1982 . . . Signed with Cleveland in '81 but was cut in training camp...All-Missouri Conference line-man at Drake...1989 salary: $300,000...Born Sept. 12, 1959, in Dallas.

COACH DAN HENNING: Returns to head-coaching duties with five-year contract after two years as Redskins' offensive coordinator...Replaces Al Saunders, who was fired after two years of five-year contract...No-nonsense guy with dry sense of humor...Was 22-4-1 in his only other head-coaching role (Falcons, 1983-86) ...Made major contribution to Washington offense in 1987, which ended with Redskins' 42-10 Super Bowl victory over Denver...Began coaching career as a college assistant at Florida State, under Joe Gibbs, and Virginia Tech...Has also been an assistant with the Jets and Dolphins...An excellent handler of quarterbacks, he was a William & Mary quarterback who played briefly in the AFL (1966) ...Born June 21, 1942, in New York City.

GREATEST COACH

Sid Gillman got the Chargers off to a good start, bringing them to five AFL championship games in their first six years. His 51-10 walloping of Boston in the 1963 Eastern Division playoff represents the franchise's only championship.

Gillman was head coach of the Los Angeles Rams for five seasons before Barron Hilton formed the Chargers and put Gillman in charge. In each of their first two years (1960, 1961), the Chargers lost close games to Houston in the AFL title game. After an injury-filled 1962 season that saw San Diego drop to 4-10, the Chargers went 11-3 before capturing their lone championship. In all, Gillman won five Western Division titles.

Illness forced Gillman's resignation eight games into the 1969 season. He remained as general manager before returning as head coach in 1971. Ten games into that season, he resigned with an 87-57-6 (.580) record.

Another outstanding era in Charger history was engineered by Don Coryell. From 1978-86, Coryell was 75-65 (.536) in San Diego, with four playoff appearances that included two AFC championship-game appearances.

INDIVIDUAL CHARGER RECORDS

Rushing

Most Yards Game:	206	Keith Lincoln, vs Boston, 1964
Season:	1,179	Earnest Jackson, 1984
Career:	4,963	Paul Lowe, 1960-67

Passing

Most TD Passes Game:	6	Dan Fouts, vs Oakland, 1981
Season:	33	Dan Fouts, 1981
Career:	254	Dan Fouts, 1973-87

Receiving

Most TD Passes Game:	5	Kellen Winslow, vs Oakland, 1981
Season:	14	Lance Alworth, 1965
Career:	81	Lance Alworth, 1962-70

Scoring

Most Points Game:	30	Kellen Winslow, vs Oakland, 1981
Season:	118	Rolf Benirschke, 1980
Career:	766	Rolf Benirschke, 1977-86
Most TDs Game:	5	Kellen Winslow, vs Oakland, 1981
Season:	19	Chuck Muncie, 1981
Career:	83	Lance Alworth, 1962-70

SEATTLE SEAHAWKS

TEAM DIRECTORY: Pres./GM: Tom Flores; VP/Asst. GM: Chuck Allen; Dir. Player Personnel: Mike Allman; VP/Dir. Pub. Rel.: Gary Wright; Head Coach: Chuck Knox. Home field: Kingdome (64,757). Colors: Blue, green and silver.

SCOUTING REPORT

OFFENSE: The Seahawks have a new star in fullback John L. Williams, who rushed for 877 yards and led the team in receiving with 58 catches last year. When Williams didn't have the ball, he was blasting open holes for Curt Warner, who gained 1,025 yards.

The Seahawk passing game struggled, but coach Chuck Knox found out he has a future in Kelly Stouffer, who filled in admir-

John L. Williams: The emergence of a mighty all-around back.

ably when Dave Krieg missed seven weeks with a shoulder injury. When Krieg was healthy, he was effective; his 94.6 quarterback rating was second in the NFL.

Future Hall of Famer Steve Largent finally slowed down, but rookie Brian Blades showed great promise with eight touchdowns. The Seahawks (9-7) are caught short at tight end because starter Mike Tice and backup John Spagnola were lost in the free-agent pool.

The offensive line is stable despite the loss of center Blair Bush, who signed with Green Bay. Guard Bryan Millard is probably the best of the bunch. The Seahawks lost seven offensive players to free agency and they expect to fill part of the gap with tackle Andy Heck (No. 15 in the draft).

DEFENSE: As their playoff loss to the Bengals showed, the Seahawks were unable to stop the run. The front line of Jacob Green, Joe Nash and Jeff Bryant averages 30 years of age and is considered too light to be effective. The Seahawks allowed 352 yards per game and were outgained both on the ground and in the air.

Seattle needs Brian Bosworth to live up to the hype he created. The Boz underwent midseason shoulder surgery in 1988 and will be watched closely this year. In the absence of Bosworth and Fredd Young, who was traded before the season, David Wyman played well and Tony Woods had five sacks.

KICKING GAME: The Seahawks always are among the best on special teams, but this year there is a void. Return specialist Bobby Joe Edmonds, who averaged 22.5 yards on kickoffs and 9.7 on punts in '88, signed with Detroit, creating an immediate need.

The Seahawks' kicking game was solid all around, and the team had a rookie Pro Bowl selection in Rufus Porter, who made 16 special-team tackles. Seattle allowed an NFL-low 5.6 yards per punt return and blocked four field goals. Ruben Rodriguez averaged 40.8 yards per punt, and the team's net average of 36.8 was second in the league. Norm Johnson hit 22 of 28 field goals.

THE ROOKIES: For the second year in a row, the Seahawks concentrated on offense in the draft. Heck was a Notre Dame tight end for three years before moving to tackle. He is a good athlete who is expected to develop into an outstanding lineman. Center Joe Tofflemire of Arizona was taken in the second round after the Seahawks lost two centers to free agency.

SEAHAWKS VETERAN ROSTER

HEAD COACH—Chuck Knox. Assistant Coaches—John Becker, Tom Catlin, George Dyer, Chick Harris, Ken Meyer, Rod Perry, Russ Purnell, Kent Stephenson, Rusty Tillman, Joe Vitt.

No.	Name	Pos.	Ht.	Wt.	NFL Exp.	College
65	Bailey, Edwin	G	6-4	273	9	South Carolina State
62	Barbay, Roland	NT	6-4	270	2	Louisiana State
89	Blades, Brian	WR	5-11	182	2	Miami
55	Bosworth, Brian	LB	6-2	248	3	Oklahoma
77	Bryant, Jeff	DE	6-5	268	8	Clemson
35	Burse, Tony	RB	6-0	220	2	Middle Tenn.State
84	Clark, Louis	WR	6-0	193	3	Mississippi State
67	Clarke, Ken	NT	6-1	271	12	Syracuse
53	Comeaux, Darren	LB	6-1	227	8	Arizona State
85	Embree, Jon	TE	6-3	230	2	Colorado
54	Feasel, Grant	C	6-7	277	5	Abilene Christian
22	Glasgow, Nesby	S	5-10	187	11	Washington
60	Godfrey, Chris	G	6-3	265	7	Michigan
79	Green, Jacob	DE	6-3	254	10	Texas A&M
34	Harmon, Kevin	RB	6-0	190	2	Iowa
29	Harper, Dwayne	CB	5-11	165	2	South Carolina State
96	Henton, Anthony	LB	6-1	234	3	Troy State
25	Hollis, David	S	5-11	180	3	Nevada-Las Vegas
23	Hunter, Patrick	CB	5-11	185	4	Nevada-Reno
24	Jenkins, Melvin	CB	5-10	182	3	Cincinnati
26	Johnson, Johnnie	S	6-1	183	10	Texas
52	Johnson, M.L.	LB	6-3	229	3	Hawaii
9	Johnson, Norm	K	6-2	197	8	UCLA
81	Kane, Tommy	WR	5-11	180	2	Syracuse
15	Kemp, Jeff	QB	6-0	198	9	Dartmouth
17	Krieg, Dave	QB	6-1	192	10	Milton
80	Largent, Steve	WR	5-11	191	14	Tulsa
13	Mathison, Bruce	QB	6-3	205	5	Nebraska
70	Mattes, Ron	T	6-6	302	4	Virginia
30	McLemore, Chris	RB	6-1	230	3	Arizona
71	Millard, Bryan	G	6-5	281	6	Texas
91	Miller, Darrin	LB	6-1	227	2	Tennessee
61	Mitz, Alonzo	DE	6-3	271	4	Florida
21	Moyer, Paul	S	6-1	196	7	Arizona State
72	Nash, Joe	NT	6-2	269	8	Boston College
88	Pattison, Mark	WR	6-2	191	4	Washington
97	Porter, Rufus	LB	6-1	207	2	Southern University
41	Robinson, Eugene	S	6-0	183	5	Colgate
5	Rodriguez, Ruben	P	6-2	214	3	Arizona
58	Scholtz, Bruce	LB	6-6	241	8	Texas
82	Skansi, Paul	WR	5-11	184	7	Washington
11	Stouffer, Kelly	QB	6-3	210	2	Colorado State
20	Taylor, Terry	CB	5-10	181	6	Southern Illinois
64	Thomas, Kevin	C	6-2	268	2	Arizona State
66	Traynowicz, Mark	C	6-5	280	5	Nebraska
28	Warner, Curt	RB	5-11	205	6	Penn State
98	Wilburn, Steve	DE	6-4	266	2	Illinois State
68	Williams, Doug	T	6-6	295	3	Texas A&M
32	Williams, John L.	RB	5-11	226	4	Florida
75	Wilson, Mike	T	6-5	274	12	Georgia
57	Woods, Tony	LB	6-4	244	3	Pittsburgh
92	Wyman, David	LB	6-2	234	3	Stanford

TOP DRAFT CHOICES

Rd.	Name	Sel. No.	Pos.	Ht.	Wt.	College
1	Heck, Andy	15	OT	6-5	270	Notre Dame
2	Tofflemire, Joe	44	C	6-2	270	Arizona
3	Harris, Elroy	71	RB	5-9	210	Eastern Kentucky
4	McNeal, Travis	101	TE	6-3	235	Tenn.-Chattanooga
4	Henry, James	103	DB	5-9	190	Southern Mississippi

OUTLOOK: The Seahawks have enough holes to make you wonder how they won the AFC West last year. The key to the success in Seattle is Knox, who constantly adjusts and constantly wins. He'll keep the Seahawks competitive, but it appears that much of the AFC West is ready to pass the Seahawks.

SEAHAWK PROFILES

CURT WARNER 28 5-11 205   Running Back

Six-year veteran keeps chugging along... Turned in fourth career 1,000-yard season with 1,025 yards on 266 carries to rank fifth in AFC... His 12 TDs were third-most in AFC ... Teamed with fullback John L. Williams to form powerful 1-2 punch... Had three 100-yard games... Best was 130 yards vs. Raiders... Average-per-carry dropped below 4.0 for first time since 1985... Led AFC in rushing in 1983 and 1986, the latter with team-record 1,481 yards... Was AFC Player of Year in 1983... Suffered severe knee injury in 1984 opener but battled back to start all 16 games in 1985... First-round pick out of Penn State, where he had 18 100-yard games ... 1989 salary: $1 million... Born March 18, 1961, in Wyoming, W.Va.

JOHN L. WILLIAMS 24 5-11 226   Fullback

Seahawks' best player last year... Much more than a fullback... Led team in receiving, was second in rushing and paved way for Curt Warner's 1,025-yard season... Rushed for 877 yards and four TDs on 4.6-yard average ... Was second in receiving yards by NFL running backs with 651... His 11.2 yard-per-catch average also was second-best among NFL backs... Had 180 receiving yards vs. Raiders... His 239 total yards that game was NFL high in 1988... Along with Warner, accounted with 53.8 percent of Seattle offense... Had three 100-yard rushing days... First-round pick out of Florida rarely fumbles or misses a blocking assignment... First player in Gator history to have over 2,000 yards rushing and 800 receiving... 1989 salary: $375,000... Born Nov. 23, 1964, in Palatka, Fla.

BRIAN BOSWORTH 24 6-2 248   Linebacker

It sounds unbelievable, but Bosworth had a quiet season... Sidelined by midseason shoulder surgery and finished with 82 tackles, third on club... Didn't have a sack... Look for him to come back angry and controversial, as usual... Started 12 games in impressive 1987 rookie season, making 81 tackles, four sacks and getting bowled over by Bo Jackson in a confrontation for the ages... Had 17 tackles in '87 wild-card game... First pick in 1987 supplemental draft out of Oklahoma ... Butkus Award winner in 1986... First Oklahoma player to start 36 straight games... Will make $500,000 this season, with salary escalating to $1.4 million in 1996... Born March 9, 1965, in Oklahoma City, Okla.

BRIAN BLADES 24 5-11 182   Wide Receiver

Adjusted quickly to pro game, but that shouldn't be surprising considering he played at Miami... Led NFL rookie receivers with eight TD receptions... Only the Raiders' Tim Brown had more catches than Blades among AFC rookies... Finished with 40 catches for 682 yards... Had 145-yard game vs. Saints and 123-yard effort vs. Raiders... Didn't get much publicity at Miami due to presence of Michael Irvin (Cowboys)... Second behind Irvin on Hurricanes' TD reception list with 15. Irvin had 26... Had 394 yards and three two-point conversions as a senior... Brother Bennie was Lions' first-round choice last year... 1988 salary: $280,000... Born July 24, 1965, in Fort Lauderdale, Fla.

DAVE KRIEG 30 6-1 192   Quarterback

Missed seven weeks with shoulder separation ... Still, only Dan Marino and Boomer Esiason in AFC threw more TD passes than his 18... 1988 stats: 134 of 228 for 1,741 yards ... Ranked second in NFL behind Boomer Esiason with 94.6 quarterback rating... Remained fourth all-time rated passer (85.5) behind Joe Montana, Marino and Esiason... Named to 1984 Pro Bowl after throwing for 3,671 yards and 32 TDs, both team records... Followed that with 3,602 yards, 27

TDs in 1985...Signed in 1980 as free agent out of now-defunct Milton College...1989 salary: $850,000...Born Oct. 20, 1958, in Iola, Wis.

STEVE LARGENT 34 5-11 191   Wide Receiver

Hall of Fame is next stop for this 13-year veteran...Had 39 receptions for 645 yards and two TDs, lowest output since 1982 strike-shortened season...Needed five TD receptions to become NFL's all-time leader, but didn't catch first one until Week 13...NFL's all-time leader in pass receptions (791), receiving yards (12,686), 1,000-yard seasons (eight) and consecutive games with a pass reception (167 and counting)...Seven-time Pro Bowl selection who played at Tulsa ...Oilers gave him to Seahawks in 1976 for eighth-round pick ...1988 salary: $1.1 million...Born Sept. 28, 1954, in Tulsa, Okla.

BRYAN MILLARD 28 6-5 281   Guard

Getting better with age...Was named honorable mention All-Pro...In 1987, he was first offensive lineman in team history to be named first-team All-NFL (by NFL Films)...Came to Seahawks in 1984 as free agent after two seasons with USFL New Jersey Generals ...Two-year starter at Texas who was All-Southwest Conference as a senior...Bench-presses over 560 pounds...Texas state shot-put champ in high school...Has played country and western guitar in Seattle area ...1988 salary: $285,000...Born Dec. 2, 1960, in Sioux City, Iowa.

JACOB GREEN 32 6-3 254   Defensive End

Sack artist whose ability to hunt down passers hasn't dropped over the years...Led team with nine sacks, his lowest number since 1982...Remains NFL's third all-time leading sacker with 76 since 1982, when the league began keeping the statistic...Trails Lawrence Taylor (89) and Dexter Manley (82)... Seahawks credit him with 94½ in nine-year career...Has had 12 or more sacks five times...Made Pro

Bowl in 1986-87... Ninth on team in tackles in 1988 with 55 ... Tenth pick overall in 1980 draft out of Texas A&M... Had 20 sacks as senior... Owns a landscaping business in Houston ... 1988 salary: $725,000... Born Jan. 21, 1957, in Pasadena, Tex.

DAVID WYMAN 25 6-2 234   Linebacker

Came into his own after shoulder injury slowed Brian Bosworth... Many considered him Seahawks' 1988 defensive MVP... Finished second in tackles with 97... Added 2½ sacks and two fumble recoveries... Played in just four games as a rookie in 1987, as a reserve linebacker and special-teams performer, making three tackles... Second-round pick out of Stanford... All-American as senior... Made 27 tackles vs. Southern Cal as a senior... Won Nevada state shot-put title in high school... 1989 salary: $255,000... Born March 31, 1964, in San Diego, Cal.

EUGENE ROBINSON 26 6-0 183   Safety

Former free agent led Seahawks in tackles with 114... Starter at free safety the past three years... Made 99 tackles in 1986 (second on team) and 69 in '87 (third)... Was one of just two free agents to make 1985 Seahawk roster ... Two-year starter at Colgate... Had 52 tackles and two interceptions as senior... Has degree in computer science and has worked for a computer research and development company during offseason ... 1988 salary: $185,000... Born May 28, 1963, in Hartford, Conn.

NORM JOHNSON 29 6-2 197   Kicker

Became Seahawks' all-time leading scorer in 1988 with 636 career points... Made 22 of 28 field-goal attempts and all 39 PAT attempts ... Only player in team history to surpass 100 points in four different seasons... Has made 129 consecutive regular-season PATs, but missed one in 1988 playoffs... Best year was 1984, when he went to Pro Bowl after scoring career-high 110 points on 20-of-24 kicking... Made 50 of 51

PATs that year...Signed with Seattle as free agent after 1982 draft...Led UCLA in scoring as senior...Played tight end in high school...1988 salary: $265,000...Born May 31, 1960, in Inglewood, Cal.

COACH CHUCK KNOX: Has been a winner everywhere he's been, but still needs a Super Bowl berth... Only coach to win division titles with three different franchises (Rams, Bills, Seahawks)...Team has been to playoffs four of his six Seahawk seasons...Ranks fourth among active coaches with a 148-89-1 record...Has gone to playoffs 11 times in 16 seasons as head coach, including seven division titles... Has been NFL Coach of the Year four times...In Los Angeles from 1973-77, he won five straight division titles before going to Buffalo for five years...NFL assistant for 10 years with Jets and Lions...Also was assistant at Wake Forest and Kentucky... Holds degree in history from Juniata College, where he played tackle...Born April 27, 1932, in Sewickley, Pa.

GREATEST COACH

In its 13-year history the Seahawks have reached the playoffs four times, all in the last six seasons under Chuck Knox.

The third coach in Seattle history, Knox has made the Seahawks perennial contenders in the AFC West. The former Rams' and Bills' mentor brought the success-starved franchise to the AFC championship game in his first season, 1983. Knox's 1984 club set a franchise record with 12 victories. Seattle won its first division title last year.

Knox had been tagged "Ground Chuck" for his use of the running game over the years, but since he took over at Seattle only two NFL teams have scored a higher percentage of their offensive touchdowns by passing than the Seahawks.

Knox has a 57-38 regular-season record at Seattle (60-42 overall), and three of his Seahawks' playoff losses were to eventual AFC champions.

INDIVIDUAL SEAHAWK RECORDS

Rushing

Most Yards Game:	207	Curt Warner, vs Kansas City, 1983
Season:	1,481	Curt Warner, 1986
Career:	6,074	Curt Warner, 1983-88

Passing

Most TD Passes Game:	5	Dave Krieg, vs Detroit, 1984
	5	Dave Krieg, vs San Diego, 1985
	5	Dave Krieg, vs LA Raiders, 1988
Season:	32	Dave Krieg, 1984
Career:	148	Dave Krieg, 1980-88

Receiving

Most TD Passes Game:	4	Daryl Turner, vs San Diego, 1985
Season:	13	Daryl Turner, 1985
Career:	97	Steve Largent, 1976-88

Scoring

Most Points Game:	24	Daryl Turner, vs San Diego, 1985
	24	Curt Warner, vs Denver, 1988
Season:	110	Norm Johnson, 1984
Career:	689	Steve Largent, 1976-88
Most TDs Game:	4	Daryl Turner, vs San Diego, 1985
	4	Curt Warner, vs Denver, 1988
Season:	15	David Sims, 1978
	15	Sherman Smith, 1979
Career:	98	Steve Largent, 1976-88

OFFICIAL 1988 NFL STATISTICS

(Compiled by Elias Sports Bureau)

RUSHING

TOP TEN RUSHERS

	Att	Yards	Avg	Long	TD
Dickerson, Eric, Ind.	388	1659	4.3	t41	14
Walker, Herschel, Dall.	361	1514	4.2	38	5
Craig, Roger, S.F.	310	1502	4.8	t46	9
Bell, Greg, Rams	288	1212	4.2	44	16
Stephens, John, N.E.	297	1168	3.9	52	4
Anderson, Gary, S.D.	225	1119	5.0	36	3
Anderson, Neal, Chi.	249	1106	4.4	80	12
Morris, Joe, Giants	307	1083	3.5	27	5
Woods, Ickey, Cin.	203	1066	5.3	56	15
Warner, Curt, Sea.	266	1025	3.9	29	10

NFC — INDIVIDUAL RUSHERS

	Att	Yards	Avg	Long	TD
Walker, Herschel, Dall.	361	1514	4.2	38	5
Craig, Roger, S.F.	310	1502	4.8	t46	9
Bell, Greg, Rams	288	1212	4.2	44	16
Anderson, Neal, Chi.	249	1106	4.4	t80	12
Morris, Joe, Giants	307	1083	3.5	27	5
Settle, John, Atl.	232	1024	4.4	62	7
Ferrell, Earl, Phoe.	202	924	4.6	47	7
Hilliard, Dalton, N.O.	204	823	4.0	36	5
Mitchell, Stump, Phoe.	164	726	4.4	47	4
Mayes, Rueben, N.O.	170	628	3.7	21	3
Cunningham, Randall, Phil. .	93	624	6.7	t33	6
James, Garry, Det.	182	552	3.0	35	5
Byars, Keith, Phil.	152	517	3.4	52	6
Toney, Anthony, Phil.	139	502	3.6	20	4
Bryant, Kelvin, Wash.	108	498	4.6	25	1
Riggs, Gerald, Atl.	113	488	4.3	34	1
Fullwood, Brent, G.B.	101	483	4.8	t33	7

t = Touchdown
Leader based on most yards gained

	Att	Yards	Avg	Long	TD
Smith, Timmy, Wash.	155	470	3.0	29	3
Cate, Lars, T.B.	122	467	3.8	t47	7
Howard, William, T.B.	115	452	3.9	t29	1
Morris, Jamie, Wash.	126	437	3.5	t27	2
Rathman, Tom, S.F.	102	427	4.2	26	2
Nelson, Darrin, Minn.	112	380	3.4	27	1
Heyward, Craig, N.O.	74	355	4.8	t73	1
Wilder, James, T.B.	86	343	4.0	19	1
Sanders, Thomas, Chi.	95	332	3.5	t20	3
White, Charles, Rams	88	323	3.7	13	0
Rice, Allen, Minn.	110	322	2.9	24	6
Jones, James, Det.	96	314	3.3	13	0
Pelluer, Steve, Dall.	51	314	6.2	27	2
Anderson, Alfred, Minn.	87	300	3.4	18	7
Fenney, Rick, Minn.	55	271	4.9	28	3
Suhey, Matt, Chi.	87	253	2.9	19	2
Goode, Kerry, T.B.	63	231	3.7	22	0
Majkowski, Don, G.B.	47	225	4.8	24	1
Anderson, Ottis, Giants	65	208	3.2	11	8
Paige, Tony, Det.	52	207	4.0	20	0
Muster, Brad, Chi.	44	197	4.5	15	0
Woodside, Keith, G.B.	83	195	2.3	10	3
Mason, Larry, G.B.	48	194	4.0	17	0
Lang, Gene, Atl.	53	191	3.6	19	0
Haddix, Michael, Phil.	57	185	3.2	15	0
Young, Steve, S.F.	27	184	6.8	t49	1
Dozier, D.J., Minn.	42	167	4.0	t19	2
Jordan, Tony, Phoe.	61	160	2.6	12	3
Simms, Phil, Giants	33	152	4.6	17	0
Harris, Darryl, Minn.	34	151	4.4	34	1
Delpino, Robert, Rams	34	147	4.3	13	0
Carthon, Maurice, Giants ...	46	146	3.2	8	2
Miller, Chris, Atl.	31	138	4.5	29	1
Testaverde, Vinny, T.B.	28	138	4.9	24	1
Wilson, Wade, Minn.	36	136	3.8	15	2
Montana, Joe, S.F.	38	132	3.5	15	3
Davis, Kenneth, G.B.	39	121	3.1	27	1
Green, Gaston, Rams	35	117	3.3	13	0
DuBose, Doug, S.F.	24	116	4.8	t37	2
Jordan, Buford, N.O.	19	115	6.1	44	0
Carruth, Paul Ott, G.B.	49	114	2.3	14	0
Harbaugh, Jim, Chi.	19	110	5.8	19	1
Rice, Jerry, S.F.	13	107	8.2	29	1
Everett, Jim, Rams	34	104	3.1	19	0
McMahon, Jim, Chi.	26	104	4.0	16	4
Primus, James, Atl.	35	95	2.7	t29	1
Smith, Jeff, T.B.	20	87	4.4	23	0

	Att	Yards	Avg	Long	TD
Gentry, Dennis, Chi.	7	86	12.3	t58	1
Hebert, Bobby, N.O.	37	79	2.1	16	0
Adams, George, Giants	29	76	2.6	15	0
Newsome, Tim, Dall.	32	75	2.3	8	3
Dixon, Floyd, Atl.	7	69	9.9	24	0
McGee, Buford, Rams	22	69	3.1	12	0
Stoudt, Cliff, Phoe.	14	57	4.1	14	0
Lomax, Neil, Phoe.	17	55	3.2	13	1
Clack, Darryl, Dall.	11	54	4.9	17	0
Sydney, Harry, S.F.	9	50	5.6	13	0
Monk, Art, Wash.	7	46	6.6	23	0
Smith, Don, T.B.	13	46	3.5	15	1
Mandley, Pete, Det.	6	44	7.3	t21	0
Wolfley, Ron, Phoe.	9	43	4.8	20	0
Wright, Randy, G.B.	8	43	5.4	19	2
Painter, Carl, Det.	17	42	2.5	13	0
Carter, Anthony, Minn.	4	41	10.3	21	0
Morris, Ron, Chi.	3	40	13.3	21	0
Tomczak, Mike, Chi.	13	40	3.1	17	1
Hoage, Terry, Phil.	1	38	38.0	t38	1
Teltschik, John, Phil.	2	36	18.0	23	0
Sweeney, Kevin, Dall.	6	34	5.7	10	0
Rypien, Mark, Wash.	9	31	3.4	t19	1
Oliphant, Mike, Wash.	8	30	3.8	20	0
Gannon, Rich, Minn.	4	29	7.3	15	0
Tautalatasi, Junior, Phil.	14	28	2.0	9	0
Hilger, Rusty, Det.	18	27	1.5	11	0
Manuel, Lionel, Giants	4	27	6.8	14	0
McKinnon, Dennis, Chi.	3	25	8.3	12	1
Brown, Ron, Rams	3	24	8.0	13	0
Griffin, Keith, Wash.	6	23	3.8	9	0
Long, Chuck, Det.	7	22	3.1	11	0
Williams, Scott, Det.	9	22	2.4	5	1
Horne, Greg, Phoe.	3	20	6.7	20	0
Perriman, Brett, N.O.	3	17	5.7	17	0
Smith, J.T., Phoe.	1	15	15.0	15	0
Abercrombie, Walter, Phil.	5	14	2.8	5	0
Sanders, Ricky, Wash.	2	14	7.0	7	0
Martin, Eric, N.O.	2	12	6.0	9	0
Hansen, Brian, N.O.	1	10	10.0	10	0
Novacek, Jay, Phoe.	1	10	10.0	10	0
Del Greco, Al, Phoe.	1	8	8.0	8	0
Jeffery, Tony, Phoe.	3	8	2.7	9	0
Kramer, Tommy, Minn.	14	8	0.6	5	0
Ellard, Henry, Rams	1	7	7.0	7	0
Hill, Lonzell, N.O.	2	7	3.5	5	0
Jones, Hassan, Minn.	1	7	7.0	7	0

	Att	Yards	Avg	Long	TD
Millen, Hugh, Atl.	1	7	7.0	7	0
Clark, Gary, Wash.	2	6	3.0	4	0
Fowler, Todd, Dall.	3	6	2.0	4	0
Flagler, Terrence, S.F. ...	3	5	1.7	4	0
Hipple, Eric, Det.	1	5	5.0	5	0
Bland, Carl, Det.	1	4	4.0	4	0
Woolfolk, Butch, Det.	1	4	4.0	4	0
Davis, Wendell, Chi.	1	3	3.0	3	0
Hester, Jessie, Atl.	1	3	3.0	3	0
Kozlowski, Glen, Chi.	1	3	3.0	3	0
Matthews, Aubrey, G.B.	3	3	1.0	4	0
Collins, Patrick, G.B.	2	2	1.0	2	0
Irvin, Michael, Dall.	1	2	2.0	2	0
Archer, David, Wash.	3	1	0.3	4	0
Carter, Cris, Phil.	1	1	1.0	1	0
Dils, Steve, Atl.	2	1	0.5	t1	1
Green, Roy, Phoe.	4	1	0.3	18	0
Guman, Mike, Rams	1	1	1.0	1	0
Rouson, Lee, Giants	1	1	1.0	1	0
Stanley, Walter, G.B.	1	1	1.0	1	0
Criswell, Ray, T.B.	2	0	0.0	0	0
Ferguson, Joe, T.B.	1	0	0.0	0	0
Helton, Barry, S.F.	1	0	0.0	0	0
Scribner, Bucky, Minn.	1	0	0.0	0	0
Stamps, Sylvester, Atl. ...	3	0	0.0	3	0
Wagner, Bryan, Chi.	2	0	0.0	0	0
Williams, Doug, Wash.	9	0	0.0	4	1
Witkowski, John, Det.	1	0	0.0	0	0
Herrmann, Mark, Rams	1	-1	-1.0	-1	0
Rutledge, Jeff, Giants	3	-1	-0.3	0	0
Sharpe, Sterling, G.B.	4	-2	-0.5	5	0
Hostetler, Jeff, Giants ...	5	-3	-0.6	0	0
Martin, Kelvin, Dall.	4	-4	-1.0	11	0
Mularkey, Mike, Minn.	1	-6	-6.0	-6	0
Hill, Bruce, T.B.	2	-11	-5.5	3	0
Coleman, Greg, Wash.	2	-13	-6.5	0	0

AFC - INDIVIDUAL RUSHERS

Dickerson, Eric, Ind.	388	1659	4.3	t41	14
Stephens, John, N.E.	297	1168	3.9	52	4
Anderson, Gary, S.D.	225	1119	5.0	36	3
Woods, Ickey, Cin.	203	1066	5.3	56	15
Warner, Curt, Sea.	266	1025	3.9	29	10

	Att	Yards	Avg	Long	TD
Rozier, Mike, Hou.	251	1002	4.0	28	10
McNeil, Freeman, Jets	219	944	4.3	28	6
Brooks, James, Cin.	182	931	5.1	t51	8
Thomas, Thurman, Buff.	207	881	4.3	t37	2
Williams, John L., Sea. ...	189	877	4.6	t44	4
Allen, Marcus, Raiders	223	831	3.7	32	7
Hoge, Merril, Pitt.	170	705	4.1	20	3
Dorsett, Tony, Den.	181	703	3.9	26	5
Jackson, Bo, Raiders	136	580	4.3	25	3
Byner, Earnest, Clev.	157	576	3.7	t27	3
Hector, Johnny, Jets	137	561	4.1	19	10
Winder, Sammy, Den.	149	543	3.6	35	4
Vick, Roger, Jets	128	540	4.2	17	3
Pinkett, Allen, Hou.	122	513	4.2	27	7
Mack, Kevin, Clev.	123	485	3.9	65	3
Okoye, Christian, K.C.	105	473	4.5	48	3
Highsmith, Alonzo, Hou. ...	94	466	5.0	42	2
Palmer, Paul, K.C.	134	452	3.4	t26	2
Perryman, Bob, N.E.	146	448	3.1	16	6
Heard, Herman, K.C.	106	438	4.1	20	0
Riddick, Robb, Buff.	111	438	3.9	21	12
Hampton, Lorenzo, Mia.	117	414	3.5	33	9
Williams, Warren, Pitt. ...	87	409	4.7	33	0
Wilson, Stanley, Cin.	112	398	3.6	19	2
Manoa, Tim, Clev.	99	389	3.9	34	2
Stradford, Troy, Mia.	95	335	3.5	18	2
Jackson, Earnest, Pitt. ...	74	315	4.3	t29	3
Mueller, Jamie, Buff.	81	296	3.7	20	0
Davenport, Ron, Mia.	55	273	5.0	64	0
Esiason, Boomer, Cin.	43	248	5.8	24	1
Saxon, James, K.C.	60	236	3.9	14	2
Elway, John, Den.	54	234	4.3	26	1
Bentley, Albert, Ind.	45	230	5.1	20	2
Carter, Rodney, Pitt.	36	216	6.0	t64	3
Spencer, Tim, S.D.	44	215	4.9	24	0
Harmon, Ronnie, Buff.	57	212	3.7	32	1
Brister, Bubby, Pitt.	45	209	4.6	20	6
Flutie, Doug, N.E.	38	179	4.7	16	1
Malone, Mark, S.D.	37	169	4.6	t36	4
Smith, Steve, Raiders	38	162	4.3	21	3
Kelly, Jim, Buff.	35	154	4.4	20	0
Dupard, Reggie, N.E.	52	151	2.9	15	2
Adams, Curtis, S.D.	38	149	3.9	14	1
Chandler, Chris., Ind.	46	139	3.0	t29	3
Sewell, Steve, Den.	32	135	4.2	26	1
Lipps, Louis, Pitt.	6	129	21.5	t39	1
Stone, Dwight, Pitt.	40	127	3.2	11	0

	Att	Yards	Avg	Long	TD
aufenberg, Babe, S.D.	31	120	3.9	23	0
ennett, Woody, Mia.	31	115	3.7	12	0
hite, Lorenzo, Hou.	31	115	3.7	16	0
chroeder, Jay, Raiders ...	29	109	3.8	12	1
ames, Lionel, S.D.	23	105	4.6	23	0
ollard, Frank, Pitt.	31	93	3.0	7	0
yrum, Carl, Buff.	28	91	3.3	11	0
oon, Warren, Hou.	33	88	2.7	14	5
ontenot, Herman, Clev. ...	28	87	3.1	17	0
erdin, Clarence, Ind.	8	77	9.6	44	0
atupu, Mosi, N.E.	22	75	3.4	22	2
ensen, Jim, Mia.	10	68	6.8	23	0
ubiak, Gary, Den.	17	65	3.8	15	0
rieg, Dave, Sea.	24	64	2.7	17	0
eed, Andre, Buff.	6	64	10.7	36	0
arly, Quinn, S.D.	7	63	9.0	37	0
rooks, Bill, Ind.	5	62	12.4	38	0
oriarty, Larry, K.C.	20	62	3.1	9	0
ueller, Vance, Raiders ...	17	60	3.5	13	0
emp, Jeff, Sea.	6	51	8.5	21	0
attiel, Ricky, Den.	5	51	10.2	29	0
rown, Tim, Raiders	14	50	3.6	12	1
onsley, George, Ind.	26	48	1.8	4	1
ennings, Stanford, Cin. ..	17	47	2.8	9	1
iller, Anthony, S.D.	7	45	6.4	20	0
urner, Ricky, Ind.	16	42	2.6	14	2
llen, Marvin, N.E.	7	40	5.7	12	0
illhite, Gerald, Den.	13	39	3.0	7	2
ell, Ken, Den.	9	36	4.0	6	0
arlson, Cody, Hou.	12	36	3.0	10	1
euerlein, Steve, Raiders .	30	35	1.2	20	0
eBerg, Steve, K.C.	18	30	1.7	13	1
edden, Barry, S.D.	19	30	1.6	t5	3
touffer, Kelly, Sea.	19	27	1.4	17	0
ivins, Ernest, Hou.	4	26	6.5	10	0
anghorne, Reggie, Clev. ..	2	26	13.0	t20	1
lackledge, Todd, Pitt. ...	8	25	3.1	10	1
'Brien, Ken, Jets	21	25	1.2	17	0
lades, Brian, Sea.	5	24	4.8	12	0
yan, Pat, Jets	5	22	4.4	15	0
ribbs, Joe, Mia.	5	21	4.2	11	0
homas, Calvin, Chi.-Den. .	6	20	3.3	8	0
aker, Tony, Clev.	3	19	6.3	13	0
olland, Jamie, S.D.	3	19	6.3	10	0
ason, Tony, N.E.	5	18	3.6	10	0
oodburn, Kelly, K.C.	1	15	15.0	15	0
ames, Craig, N.E.	4	15	3.8	t8	1

	Att	Yards	Avg	Long	TD
Faaola, Nuu, Jets	1	13	13.0	13	0
Harmon, Kevin, Sea.	2	13	6.5	8	0
Fryar, Irving, N.E.	6	12	2.0	6	0
Grogan, Steve, N.E.	6	12	2.0	6	1
Strachan, Steve, Raiders ..	4	12	3.0	5	0
Walker, Wesley, Jets	1	12	12.0	12	0
Leahy, Pat, Jets	1	10	10.0	10	0
Logan, Marc, Cin.	2	10	5.0	9	0
Schonert, Turk, Cin.	2	10	5.0	7	0
Fernandez, Mervyn, Raiders	1	9	9.0	9	0
Ramsey, Tom, N.E.	3	8	2.7	9	0
Bernstine, Rod, S.D.	2	7	3.5	5	0
Morris, Randall, Sea.	3	6	2.0	5	0
Jackson, Mark, Den.	1	5	5.0	5	0
Norseth, Mike, Cin.	1	5	5.0	5	0
Tillman, Spencer, Hou.	3	5	1.7	2	0
Toon, Al, Jets	1	5	5.0	5	0
Clayton, Mark, Mia.	1	4	4.0	4	0
Gault, Willie, Raiders	1	4	4.0	4	0
Kenney, Bill, K.C.	2	4	2.0	2	0
Danielson, Gary, Clev.	4	3	0.8	5	0
Johnson, Jason, Den.	1	3	3.0	3	0
Agee, Tommie, Sea.	1	2	2.0	2	0
Taylor, Kitrick, K.C.	1	2	2.0	2	0
Carson, Carlos, K.C.	1	1	1.0	1	0
Johnson, Vance, Den.	1	1	1.0	1	0
Pagel, Mike, Clev.	4	1	0.3	5	0
Feagles, Jeff, N.E.	1	0	0.0	0	0
Newsome, Harry, Pitt.	2	0	0.0	0	0
Rodriguez, Ruben, Sea.	1	0	0.0	0	0
Runager, Max, Clev.	1	0	0.0	0	0
Vlasic, Mark, S.D.	2	0	0.0	0	0
Kosar, Bernie, Clev.	12	−1	−0.1	13	1
Pease, Brent, Hou.	8	−2	−0.3	t4	1
Strock, Don, Clev.	6	−2	−0.3	5	0
Largent, Steve, Sea.	1	−3	−3.0	−3	0
Reich, Frank, Buff.	3	−3	−1.0	−1	0
Brown, Eddie, Cin.	1	−5	−5.0	−5	0
Morgan, Stanley, N.E.	1	−6	−6.0	−6	0
Bahr, Matt, Clev.	1	−8	−8.0	−8	0
Edmunds, Ferrell, Mia.	1	−8	−8.0	−8	0
Hogeboom, Gary, Ind.	11	−8	−0.7	6	1
Marino, Dan, Mia.	20	−17	−0.9	6	0

Cowboys' Herschel Walker was NFC's No. 1 ground-gainer.

PASSING

TOP TEN PASSERS

	Att	Comp	Pct Comp	Yds
Esiason, Boomer, Cin.	388	223	57.5	3572
Krieg, Dave, Sea.	228	134	58.8	1741
Wilson, Wade, Minn.	332	204	61.4	2746
Everett, Jim, Rams	517	308	59.6	3964
Moon, Warren, Hou.	294	160	54.4	2327
Montana, Joe, S.F.	397	238	59.9	2981
Lomax, Neil, Phoe.	443	255	57.6	3395
Kosar, Bernie, Clev.	259	156	60.2	1890
Simms, Phil, Giants	479	263	54.9	3359
Marino, Dan, Mia.	606	354	58.4	4434

NFC - INDIVIDUAL PASSERS

	Att	Comp	Pct Comp	Yds
Wilson, Wade, Minn.	332	204	61.4	2746
Everett, Jim, Rams	517	308	59.6	3964
Montana, Joe, S.F.	397	238	59.9	2981
Lomax, Neil, Phoe.	443	255	57.6	3395
Simms, Phil, Giants	479	263	54.9	3359
Hebert, Bobby, N.O.	478	280	58.6	3156
Cunningham, Randall, Phil. ...	560	301	53.8	3808
Williams, Doug, Wash.	380	213	56.1	2609
Pelluer, Steve, Dall.	435	245	56.3	3139
Majkowski, Don, G.B.	336	178	53.0	2119
Miller, Chris, Atl.	351	184	52.4	2133
Wright, Randy, G.B.	244	141	57.8	1490
Hilger, Rusty, Det.	306	126	41.2	1558
Testaverde, Vinny, T.B.	466	222	47.6	3240

(Nonqualifiers)

	Att	Comp	Pct Comp	Yds
Ferguson, Joe, T.B.	46	31	67.4	368
Rypien, Mark, Wash.	208	114	54.8	1730
McMahon, Jim, Chi.	192	114	59.4	1346
Tomczak, Mike, Chi.	170	86	50.6	1310
Young, Steve, S.F.	101	54	53.5	680
Long, Chuck, Det.	141	75	53.2	856

t = Touchdown
Leader based on rating points, minimum 224 attempts

Avg Gain	TD	Pct TD	Long	Int	Pct Int	Sack	Yds Lost	Rating Points
9.21	28	7.2	t86	14	3.6	30	245	97.4
7.64	18	7.9	t75	8	3.5	12	92	94.6
8.27	15	4.5	t68	9	2.7	33	227	91.5
7.67	31	6.0	t69	18	3.5	28	197	89.2
7.91	17	5.8	t57	8	2.7	12	120	88.4
7.51	18	4.5	t96	10	2.5	34	223	87.9
7.66	20	4.5	t93	11	2.5	46	315	86.7
7.30	10	3.9	t77	7	2.7	25	172	84.3
7.01	21	4.4	t62	11	2.3	53	405	82.1
7.32	28	4.6	t80	23	3.8	6	31	80.8

Avg Gain	TD	Pct TD	Long	Int	Pct Int	Sack	Yds Lost	Rating Points
8.27	15	4.5	t68	9	2.7	33	227	91.5
7.67	31	6.0	t69	18	3.5	28	197	89.2
7.51	18	4.5	t96	10	2.5	34	223	87.9
7.66	20	4.5	t93	11	2.5	46	315	86.7
7.01	21	4.4	t62	11	2.3	53	405	82.1
6.60	20	4.2	t40	15	3.1	24	171	79.3
6.80	24	4.3	t80	16	2.9	57	442	77.6
6.87	15	3.9	58	12	3.2	10	88	77.4
7.22	17	3.9	t61	19	4.4	21	112	73.9
6.31	9	2.7	56	11	3.3	31	176	67.8
6.08	11	3.1	t68	12	3.4	24	207	67.3
6.11	4	1.6	51	13	5.3	20	148	58.9
5.09	7	2.3	56	12	3.9	31	251	48.9
6.95	13	2.8	t59	35	7.5	33	292	48.8

Avg Gain	TD	Pct TD	Long	Int	Pct Int	Sack	Yds Lost	Rating Points
8.00	3	6.5	34	1	2.2	1	8	104.3
8.32	18	8.7	t60	13	6.3	14	115	85.2
7.01	6	3.1	t63	7	3.6	13	79	76.0
7.71	7	4.1	t76	6	3.5	5	47	75.4
6.73	3	3.0	t73	3	3.0	13	75	72.2
6.07	6	4.3	40	6	4.3	18	134	68.2

	Att	Comp	Pct Comp	Yds
Gannon, Rich, Minn.	15	7	46.7	90
Hostetler, Jeff, Giants	29	16	55.2	244
White, Danny, Dall.	42	29	69.0	274
Stoudt, Cliff, Phoe.	113	63	55.8	747
Hipple, Eric, Det.	27	12	44.4	158
Kramer, Tommy, Minn.	173	83	48.0	1264
Cavanaugh, Matt, Phil.	16	7	43.8	101
Rutledge, Jeff, Giants	17	11	64.7	113
Harbaugh, Jim, Chi.	97	47	48.5	514
Dils, Steve, Atl.	99	49	49.5	566
Millen, Hugh, Atl.	31	17	54.8	215
Sweeney, Kevin, Dall.	78	33	42.3	314
Wilson, Dave, N.O.	16	5	31.3	73
(Fewer than 10 attempts)				
Anderson, Neal, Chi.	1	0	0.0	0
Archer, David, Wash.	2	0	0.0	0
Arnold, Jim, Det.	1	0	0.0	0
Byars, Keith, Phil.	2	0	0.0	0
Carruth, Paul Ott, G.B.	2	0	0.0	0
Coleman, Greg, Wash.	1	0	0.0	0
Fourcade, John, N.O.	1	0	0.0	0
Herrmann, Mark, Rams	5	4	80.0	38
Hill, Lonzell, N.O.	1	0	0.0	0
Hilliard, Dalton, N.O.	2	1	50.0	27
Jones, James, Det.	1	0	0.0	0
Monk, Art, Wash.	1	0	0.0	0
Rice, Jerry, S.F.	3	1	33.3	14
Sydney, Harry, S.F.	1	0	0.0	0
Teltschik, John, Phil.	3	1	33.3	18
Tupa, Tom, Phoe.	6	4	66.7	49
Wagner, Bryan, Chi.	1	1	100.0	3
Witkowski, John, Det.	1	0	0.0	0

AFC - INDIVIDUAL PASSERS

	Att	Comp	Pct Comp	Yds
Esiason, Boomer, Cin.	388	223	57.5	3572
Krieg, Dave, Sea.	228	134	58.8	1741
Moon, Warren, Hou.	294	160	54.4	2327
Kosar, Bernie, Clev.	259	156	60.2	1890
Marino, Dan, Mia.	606	354	58.4	4434
O'Brien, Ken, Jets	424	236	55.7	2567
Kelly, Jim, Buff.	452	269	59.5	3380
DeBerg, Steve, K.C.	414	224	54.1	2935
Elway, John, Den.	496	274	55.2	3309
Chandler, Chris, Ind.	233	129	55.4	1619

Avg Gain	TD	Pct TD	Long	Int	Pct Int	Sack	Yds Lost	Rating Points
6.00	0	0.0	19	0	0.0	3	22	66.0
8.41	1	3.4	t85	2	6.9	5	31	65.9
6.52	1	2.4	24	3	7.1	5	47	65.0
6.61	6	5.3	t52	8	7.1	13	85	64.3
5.85	0	0.0	31	0	0.0	3	25	63.5
7.31	5	2.9	47	9	5.2	11	62	60.5
6.31	1	6.3	42	1	6.3	0	0	59.6
6.65	0	0.0	33	1	5.9	2	14	59.2
5.30	0	0.0	56	2	2.1	6	49	55.9
5.72	2	2.0	50	5	5.1	15	112	52.8
6.94	0	0.0	38	2	6.5	4	29	49.8
4.03	3	3.8	28	5	6.4	9	80	40.2
4.56	0	0.0	25	1	6.3	0	0	21.1
0.00	0	0.0	—	0	0.0	0	0	39.6
0.00	0	0.0	—	0	0.0	0	0	39.6
0.00	0	0.0	—	0	0.0	0	0	39.6
0.00	0	0.0	—	0	0.0	0	0	39.6
0.00	0	0.0	—	0	0.0	0	0	39.6
0.00	0	0.0	—	0	0.0	0	0	39.6
0.00	0	0.0	—	0	0.0	0	0	39.6
7.60	0	0.0	15	0	0.0	0	0	98.3
0.00	0	0.0	—	0	0.0	0	0	39.6
13.50	1	50.0	t27	0	0.0	0	0	135.4
0.00	0	0.0	—	0	0.0	0	0	39.6
0.00	0	0.0	—	0	0.0	0	0	39.6
4.67	0	0.0	14	1	33.3	0	0	9.7
0.00	0	0.0	—	0	0.0	0	0	39.6
6.00	0	0.0	18	0	0.0	0	0	54.9
8.17	0	0.0	22	0	0.0	1	11	91.7
3.00	0	0.0	3	0	0.0	0	0	79.2
0.00	0	0.0	—	0	0.0	0	0	39.6
9.21	28	7.2	t86	14	3.6	30	245	97.4
7.64	18	7.9	t75	8	3.5	12	92	94.6
7.91	17	5.8	t57	8	2.7	12	120	88.4
7.30	10	3.9	t77	7	2.7	25	172	84.3
7.32	28	4.6	t80	23	3.8	6	31	80.8
6.05	15	3.5	t50	7	1.7	37	267	78.6
7.48	15	3.3	t66	17	3.8	30	229	78.2
7.09	16	3.9	t80	16	3.9	30	246	73.5
6.67	17	3.4	86	19	3.8	30	237	71.4
6.95	8	3.4	54	12	5.2	18	128	67.2

	Att	Comp	Pct Comp	Yds
Beuerlein, Steve, Raiders	238	105	44.1	1643
Brister, Bubby, Pitt.	370	175	47.3	2634
Schroeder, Jay, Raiders	256	113	44.1	1839
Malone, Mark, S.D.	272	147	54.0	1580

(Nonqualifiers)

	Att	Comp	Pct Comp	Yds
Jaworski, Ron, Mia.	14	9	64.3	123
Karcher, Ken, Den.	12	6	50.0	128
Kubiak, Gary, Den.	69	43	62.3	497
Strock, Don, Clev.	91	55	60.4	736
Ryan, Pat, Jets	113	63	55.8	807
Hogeboom, Gary, Ind.	131	76	58.0	996
Danielson, Gary, Clev.	52	31	59.6	324
Stouffer, Kelly, Sea.	173	98	56.6	1106
Pagel, Mike, Clev.	134	71	53.0	736
Flutie, Doug, N.E.	179	92	51.4	1150
Eason, Tony, N.E.	43	28	65.1	249
Blackledge, Todd, Pitt.	79	38	48.1	494
Laufenberg, Babe, S.D.	144	69	47.9	778
Carlson, Cody, Hou.	112	52	46.4	775
Vlasic, Mark, S.D.	52	25	48.1	270
Kenney, Bill, K.C.	114	58	50.9	549
Grogan, Steve, N.E.	140	67	47.9	834
Bono, Steve, Pitt.	35	10	28.6	110
Trudeau, Jack, Ind.	34	14	41.2	158
Ramsey, Tom, N.E.	27	12	44.4	100
Kemp, Jeff, Sea.	35	13	37.1	132
Pease, Brent, Hou.	22	6	27.3	64
(Fewer than 10 attempts)				
Agee, Tommie, Sea.	1	0	0.0	0
Allen, Marcus, Raiders	2	1	50.0	21
Bentley, Albert, Ind.	1	0	0.0	0
Blades, Brian, Sea.	0	0	----	0
Carter, Rodney, Pitt.	3	2	66.7	56
Dorsett, Tony, Den.	2	1	50.0	7
Fontenot, Herman, Clev.	1	0	0.0	0
Hector, Johnny, Jets	1	0	0.0	0
James, Lionel, S.D.	0	0	----	0
Lipps, Louis, Pitt.	2	1	50.0	13
Nattiel, Ricky, Den.	1	0	0.0	0
Riddick, Robb, Buff.	2	2	100.0	31
Schonert, Turk, Cin.	4	2	50.0	20
Sewell, Steve, Den.	1	0	0.0	0
Stradford, Troy, Mia.	1	0	0.0	0
Turner, Ricky, Ind.	4	3	75.0	92

Avg Gain	TD	Pct TD	Long	Int	Pct Int	Sack	Yds Lost	Rating Points
6.90	8	3.4	57	7	2.9	26	215	66.6
7.12	11	3.0	t89	14	3.8	36	292	65.3
7.18	13	5.1	t85	13	5.1	19	178	64.6
5.81	6	2.2	59	13	4.8	9	45	58.8
8.79	1	7.1	22	0	0.0	1	10	116.1
10.67	1	8.3	t74	0	0.0	0	0	116.0
7.20	5	7.2	t68	3	4.3	2	13	90.1
8.09	6	6.6	41	5	5.5	4	26	85.2
7.14	5	4.4	t42	4	3.5	5	24	78.3
7.60	7	5.3	58	7	5.3	12	88	77.7
6.23	0	0.0	26	1	1.9	6	43	69.7
6.39	4	2.3	53	6	3.5	13	110	69.2
5.49	3	2.2	28	4	3.0	1	9	64.1
6.42	8	4.5	t80	10	5.6	11	65	63.3
5.79	0	0.0	26	2	4.7	2	12	61.1
6.25	2	2.5	34	3	3.8	4	25	60.8
5.40	4	2.8	t47	5	3.5	18	155	59.3
6.92	4	3.6	t51	6	5.4	10	72	59.2
5.19	1	1.9	57	2	3.8	3	32	54.2
4.82	0	0.0	25	5	4.4	13	107	46.3
5.96	4	2.9	t41	13	9.3	8	77	37.6
3.14	1	2.9	15	2	5.7	1	8	25.9
4.65	0	0.0	48	3	8.8	2	13	19.0
3.70	0	0.0	23	3	11.1	2	6	15.0
3.77	0	0.0	19	5	14.3	3	21	9.2
2.91	0	0.0	21	4	18.2	2	18	0.0
0.00	0	0.0	—	1	100.0	0	0	0.0
10.50	0	0.0	21	0	0.0	1	1	87.5
0.00	0	0.0	—	0	0.0	0	0	39.6
----	0	---	—	0	----	1	0	0.0
18.67	0	0.0	40	0	0.0	0	0	109.7
3.50	1	50.0	t7	0	0.0	0	0	97.9
0.00	0	0.0	—	0	0.0	0	0	39.6
0.00	0	0.0	—	0	0.0	0	0	39.6
----	0	---	—	0	----	1	8	0.0
6.50	1	50.0	t13	1	50.0	1	6	70.8
0.00	0	0.0	—	0	0.0	0	0	39.6
15.50	0	0.0	26	0	0.0	0	0	118.8
5.00	0	0.0	17	0	0.0	0	0	64.6
0.00	0	0.0	—	0	0.0	0	0	39.6
0.00	0	0.0	—	0	0.0	0	0	39.6
23.00	0	0.0	37	0	0.0	2	15	116.7

Vikings' Wade Wilson topped NFL in completion percentage.

Rams' Greg Bell rushed for an NFC-leading 16 TDs.

TOP TEN PASS RECEIVERS

	No	Yards	Avg	Long	TD
Toon, Al, Jets	93	1067	11.5	42	5
Ellard, Henry, Rams	86	1414	16.4	68	10
Clayton, Mark, Mia.	86	1129	13.1	t45	14
Martin, Eric, N.O.	85	1083	12.7	t40	7
Smith, J.T., Phoe.	83	986	11.9	29	5
Jackson, Keith, Phil.	81	869	10.7	41	6
Craig, Roger, S.F.	76	534	7.0	22	1
Sanders, Ricky, Wash.	73	1148	15.7	t55	12
Carter, Anthony, Minn.	72	1225	17.0	t67	6
Hill, Drew, Hou.	72	1141	15.8	t57	10
Monk, Art, Wash.	72	946	13.1	t46	5
Byars, Keith, Phil.	72	705	9.8	t37	4

TOP TEN RECEIVERS BY YARDS

	Yards	No	Avg	Long	TD
Ellard, Henry, Rams	1414	86	16.4	68	10
Rice, Jerry, S.F.	1306	64	20.4	t96	9
Brown, Eddie, Cin.	1273	53	24.0	t86	9
Carter, Anthony, Minn.	1225	72	17.0	t67	6
Sanders, Ricky, Wash.	1148	73	15.7	t55	12
Hill, Drew, Hou.	1141	72	15.8	t57	10
Clayton, Mark, Mia.	1129	86	13.1	t45	14
Green, Roy, Phoe.	1097	68	16.1	52	7
Martin, Eric, N.O.	1083	85	12.7	t40	7
Toon, Al, Jets	1067	93	11.5	42	5

TOP TEN INTERCEPTORS

	No	Yards	Avg	Long	TD
Case, Scott, Atl.	10	47	4.7	12	0
McMillan, Erik, Jets	8	168	21.0	t55	2
Lee, Carl, Minn.	8	118	14.8	t58	2
Hoage, Terry, Phil.	8	116	14.5	38	0
Jackson, Vestee, Chi.	8	94	11.8	46	0
Kelso, Mark, Buff.	7	180	25.7	t78	1
Byrd, Gill, S.D.	7	82	11.7	42	0
Thomas, Eric, Cin.	7	61	8.7	37	0
Cherry, Deron, K.C.	7	51	7.3	24	0
McKyer, Tim, S.F.	7	11	1.6	7	0

TOP TEN KICKOFF RETURNERS

	No	Yards	Avg	Long	TD
Brown, Tim, Raiders	41	1098	26.8	t97	1
Holland, Jamie, S.D.	31	810	26.1	t94	1
Miller, Anthony, S.D.	25	648	25.9	t93	1
Humphery, Bobby, Jets	21	510	24.3	48	0
Martin, Sammy, N.E.	31	735	23.7	t95	1
Woodson, Rod, Pitt.	37	850	23.0	t92	1
Elder, Donnie, T.B.	34	772	22.7	51	0
Edmonds, Bobby Joe, Sea.	40	900	22.5	65	0
Burbage, Cornell, Dall.	20	448	22.4	53	0
Young, Glen, Clev.	29	635	21.9	34	0

TOP TEN PUNT RETURNERS

	No	FC	Yards	Avg	Long	TD
Taylor, John, S.F.	44	7	556	12.6	t95	2
Gray, Mel, N.O.	25	8	305	12.2	t66	1
Townsell, JoJo, Jets	35	9	409	11.7	t59	1
Verdin, Clarence, Ind.	22	7	239	10.9	t73	1
Futrell, Bobby, T.B.	27	10	283	10.5	40	0
Fryar, Irving, N.E.	38	8	398	10.5	30	0
Sikahema, Vai, Phoe.	33	8	341	10.3	28	0
James, Lionel, S.D.	28	11	278	9.9	24	0
Edmonds, Bobby Joe, Sea.	35	8	340	9.7	41	0
Nattiel, Ricky, Den.	23	0	223	9.7	24	0

TOP TEN LEADERS - SACKS

White, Reggie, Phil.	18.0
Greene, Kevin, Rams	16.5
Taylor, Lawrence, Giants	15.5
Nunn, Freddie Joe, Phoe.	14.0
Harris, Timothy, G.B.	13.5
Cofer, Mike, Det.	12.0
Haley, Charles, S.F.	11.5
Jeter, Gary, Rams	11.5
McMichael, Steve, Chi.	11.5
Townsend, Greg, Raiders	11.5

TOP TEN PUNTERS

	No	Yards	Long	Avg
Newsome, Harry, Pitt.	65	2950	62	45.4
Mojsiejenko, Ralf, S.D.	85	3745	62	44.1
Horan, Mike, Den.	65	2861	70	44.0
Stark, Rohn, Ind.	64	2784	65	43.5
Roby, Reggie, Mia.	64	2754	64	43.0
Arnold, Jim, Det.	97	4110	69	42.4
Gossett, Jeff, Raiders	91	3804	58	41.8
Wagner, Bryan, Chi.	79	3282	70	41.5
Buford, Maury, Giants	73	3012	66	41.3
Saxon, Mike, Dall.	80	3271	55	40.9

TOP TEN SCORERS - KICKERS

	XP	XPA	FG	FGA	PTS
Norwood, Scott, Buff.	33	33	32	37	129
Cofer, Mike, S.F.	40	41	27	38	121
Anderson, Gary, Pitt.	34	35	28	36	118
Lansford, Mike, Rams	45	48	24	32	117
Biasucci, Dean, Ind.	39	40	25	32	114
Zendejas, Tony, Hou.	48	50	22	34	114
Leahy, Pat, Jets	43	43	23	28	112
Andersen, Morten, N.O.	32	33	26	36	110
Nelson, Chuck, Minn.	48	49	20	25	108
Johnson, Norm, Sea.	39	39	22	28	105
Karlis, Rich, Den.	36	37	23	36	105

Total Punts	TB	Blk	Opp Ret	Ret Yds	In 20	Net Avg
71	10	6	40	418	9	32.8
86	11	1	56	558	22	34.5
65	2	0	33	364	19	37.8
64	8	0	37	418	15	34.5
64	9	0	35	318	18	35.3
97	7	0	57	483	22	35.9
91	8	0	47	397	27	35.7
79	10	0	40	447	18	33.4
75	10	2	36	296	13	33.5
80	15	0	37	239	24	34.2

TOP TEN SCORERS – NONKICKERS

	TD	TDR	TDP	TDM	PTS
Bell, Greg, Rams	18	16	2	0	108
Dickerson, Eric, Ind.	15	14	1	0	90
Woods, Ickey, Cin.	15	15	0	0	90
Brooks, James, Cin.	14	8	6	0	84
Clayton, Mark, Mia.	14	0	14	0	84
Riddick, Robb, Buff.	14	12	1	1	84
Anderson, Neal, Chi.	12	12	0	0	72
Hampton, Lorenzo, Mia.	12	9	3	0	72
Sanders, Ricky, Wash.	12	0	12	0	72
Warner, Curt, Sea.	12	10	2	0	72

NFL STANDINGS
1921-1988

1921

	W	L	T	Pct.
Chicago Staleys	10	1	1	.909
Buffalo All-Americans	9	1	2	.900
Akron, Ohio, Pros	7	2	1	.778
Green Bay Packers	6	2	2	.750
Canton, Ohio, Bulldogs	4	3	3	.571
Dayton Triangles	4	3	1	.571
Rock Island Independents	5	4	1	.556
Chicago Cardinals	2	3	2	.400
Cleveland Indians	2	6	0	.250
Rochester Jeffersons	2	6	0	.250
Detroit Heralds	1	7	1	.125
Columbus Panhandles	0	6	0	.000
Cincinnati Celts	0	8	0	.000

1922

	W	L	T	Pct.
Canton, Ohio, Bulldogs	10	0	2	1.000
Chicago Bears	9	3	0	.750
Chicago Cardinals	8	3	0	.727
Toledo Maroons	5	2	2	.714
Rock Island Independents	4	2	1	.667
Dayton Triangles	4	3	1	.571
Green Bay Packers	4	3	3	.571
Racine, Wis., Legion	5	4	1	.556
Akron, Ohio, Pros	3	4	2	.429
Buffalo All-Americans	3	4	1	.429
Milwaukee Badgers	2	4	3	.333
Marion, O., Oorang Indians	2	6	0	.250
Minneapolis Marines	1	3	0	.250
Evansville Crimson Giants	0	2	0	.000
Louisville Brecks	0	3	0	.000
Rochester Jeffersons	0	3	1	.000
Hammond, Ind., Pros	0	4	1	.000
Columbus Panhandles	0	7	0	.000

1923

	W	L	T	Pct.
Canton, Ohio, Bulldogs	11	0	1	1.000
Chicago Bears	9	2	1	.818
Green Bay Packers	7	2	1	.778
Milwaukee Badgers	7	2	3	.778
Cleveland Indians	3	1	3	.750
Chicago Cardinals	8	4	0	.667
Duluth Kelleys	4	3	0	.571
Buffalo All-Americans	5	4	3	.556
Columbus Tigers	5	4	1	.556
Racine, Wis., Legion	4	4	2	.500
Toledo Maroons	2	3	2	.400
Rock Island Independents	2	3	3	.400

(continued)

	W	L	T	Pct.
Minneapolis Marines	2	5	2	.286
St. Louis All-Stars	1	4	2	.200
Hammond, Ind., Pros	1	5	1	.167
Dayton Triangles	1	6	1	.143
Akron, Ohio, Indians	1	6	0	.143
Marion, O., Oorang Indians	1	10	0	.091
Rochester Jeffersons	0	2	0	.000
Louisville Brecks	0	3	0	.000

1924

	W	L	T	Pct.
Cleveland Bulldogs	7	1	1	.875
Chicago Bears	6	1	4	.857
Frankford Yellowjackets	11	2	1	.846
Duluth Kelleys	5	1	0	.833
Rock Island Independents	6	2	2	.750
Green Bay Packers	8	4	0	.667
Buffalo Bisons	6	4	0	.600
Racine, Wis., Legion	4	3	3	.571
Chicago Cardinals	5	4	1	.556
Columbus Tigers	4	4	0	.500
Hammond, Ind., Pros	2	2	1	.500
Milwaukee Badgers	5	8	0	.385
Dayton Triangles	2	7	0	.222
Kansas City Cowboys	2	7	0	.222
Akron, Ohio, Indians	1	6	0	.143
Kenosha, Wis., Maroons	0	5	1	.000
Minneapolis Marines	0	6	0	.000
Rochester Jeffersons	0	7	0	.000

1925

	W	L	T	Pct.
Chicago Cardinals	11	2	1	.846
Pottsville, Pa., Maroons	10	2	0	.833
Detroit Panthers	8	2	2	.800
New York Giants	8	4	0	.667
Akron, Ohio, Indians	4	2	2	.667
Frankford Yellowjackets	13	7	0	.650
Chicago Bears	9	5	3	.643
Rock Island Independents	5	3	3	.625
Green Bay Packers	8	5	0	.615
Providence Steamroller	6	5	1	.545
Canton, Ohio, Bulldogs	4	4	0	.500
Cleveland Bulldogs	5	8	1	.385
Kansas City Cowboys	2	5	1	.286
Hammond, Ind., Pros	1	3	0	.250
Buffalo Bisons	1	6	2	.143
Duluth Kelleys	0	3	0	.000
Rochester Jeffersons	0	6	1	.000
Milwaukee Badgers	0	6	0	.000
Dayton Triangles	0	7	1	.000
Columbus Tigers	0	9	0	.000

1926

	W	L	T	Pct.
Frankford Yellowjackets	14	1	1	.933
Chicago Bears	12	1	3	.923
Pottsville, Pa., Maroons	10	2	1	.833
Kansas City Cowboys	8	3	1	.727
Green Bay Packers	7	3	3	.700
Los Angeles Buccaneers	6	3	1	.667
New York Giants	8	4	1	.667
Duluth Eskimos	6	5	2	.545
Buffalo Rangers	4	4	2	.500
Chicago Cardinals	5	6	1	.455
Providence Steamroller	5	7	0	.417
Detroit Panthers	4	6	2	.400
Hartford Blues	3	7	0	.300
Brooklyn Lions	3	8	0	.273
Milwaukee Badgers	2	7	0	.222
Akron, Ohio, Indians	1	4	3	.200
Dayton Triangles	1	4	1	.200
Racine, Wis., Legion	1	4	0	.200
Columbus Tigers	1	6	0	.143
Canton, Ohio, Bulldogs	1	9	3	.100
Hammond, Ind., Pros	0	4	0	.000
Louisville Colonels	0	4	0	.000

1927

	W	L	T	Pct.
New York Giants	11	1	1	.917
Green Bay Packers	7	2	1	.778
Chicago Bears	9	3	2	.750
Cleveland Bulldogs	8	4	1	.667
Providence Steamroller	8	5	1	.615
New York Yankees	7	8	1	.467
Frankford Yellowjackets	6	9	3	.400
Pottsville, Pa., Maroons	5	8	0	.385
Chicago Cardinals	3	7	1	.300
Dayton Triangles	1	6	1	.143
Duluth Eskimos	1	8	0	.111
Buffalo Bisons	0	5	0	.000

1928

	W	L	T	Pct.
Providence Steamroller	8	1	2	.889
Frankford Yellowjackets	11	3	2	.786
Detroit Wolverines	7	2	1	.778
Green Bay Packers	6	4	3	.600
Chicago Bears	7	5	1	.583
New York Giants	4	7	2	.364
New York Yankees	4	8	1	.333
Pottsville, Pa., Maroons	2	8	0	.200
Chicago Cardinals	1	5	0	.167
Dayton Triangles	0	7	0	.000

1929

	W	L	T	Pct.
Green Bay Packers	12	0	1	1.000
New York Giants	13	1	1	.929
Frankford Yellowjackets	9	4	5	.692
Chicago Cardinals	6	6	1	.500
Boston Bulldogs	4	4	0	.500
Orange, N.J., Tornadoes	3	4	4	.429
Stapleton Stapes	3	4	3	.429
Providence Steamroller	4	6	2	.400
Chicago Bears	4	9	2	.308
Buffalo Bisons	1	7	1	.125
Minneapolis Red Jackets	1	9	0	.100
Dayton Triangles	0	6	0	.000

1930

	W	L	T	Pct.
Green Bay Packers	10	3	1	.769
New York Giants	13	4	0	.765
Chicago Bears	9	4	1	.692
Brooklyn Dodgers	7	4	1	.636
Providence Steamroller	6	4	1	.600
Stapleton Stapes	5	5	2	.500
Chicago Cardinals	5	6	2	.455
Portsmouth, O., Spartans	5	6	3	.455
Frankford Yellowjackets	4	14	1	.222
Minneapolis Red Jackets	1	7	1	.125
Newark Tornadoes	1	10	1	.091

1931

	W	L	T	Pct.
Green Bay Packers	12	2	0	.857
Portsmouth, O., Spartans	11	3	0	.786
Chicago Bears	8	5	0	.615
Chicago Cardinals	5	4	0	.556
New York Giants	7	6	1	.538
Providence Steamroller	4	4	3	.500
Stapleton Stapes	4	6	1	.400
Cleveland Indians	2	8	0	.200
Brooklyn Dodgers	2	12	0	.143
Frankford Yellowjackets	1	6	1	.143

1932

	W	L	T	Pct.
Chicago Bears	7	1	6	.875
Green Bay Packers	10	3	1	.769
Portsmouth, O., Spartans	6	2	4	.750
Boston Braves	4	4	2	.500
New York Giants	4	6	2	.400
Brooklyn Dodgers	3	9	0	.250
Chicago Cardinals	2	6	2	.250
Stapleton Stapes	2	7	3	.222

1933

EASTERN DIVISION

	W	L	T	Pct.	Pts.	OP
N.Y. Giants	11	3	0	.786	244	101
Brooklyn	5	4	1	.556	93	54
Boston	5	5	2	.500	103	97
Philadelphia	3	5	1	.375	77	158
Pittsburgh	3	6	2	.333	67	208

WESTERN DIVISION

	W	L	T	Pct.	Pts.	OP
Chi. Bears	10	2	1	.833	133	82
Portsmouth	6	5	0	.545	128	87
Green Bay	5	7	1	.417	170	107
Cincinnati	3	6	1	.333	38	110
Chi. Cardinals	1	9	1	.100	52	101

NFL Championship: Chicago Bears 23, N.Y. Giants 21

1934

EASTERN DIVISION	W	L	T	Pct.	Pts.	OP
N.Y. Giants	8	5	0	.615	147	107
Boston	6	6	0	.500	107	94
Brooklyn	4	7	0	.364	61	153
Philadelphia	4	7	0	.364	127	85
Pittsburgh	2	10	0	.167	51	206

WESTERN DIVISION	W	L	T	Pct.	Pts.	OP
Chi. Bears	13	0	0	1.000	286	86
Detroit	10	3	0	.769	238	59
Green Bay	7	6	0	.538	156	112
Chi. Cardinals	5	6	0	.455	80	84
St. Louis	1	2	0	.333	27	61
Cincinnati	0	8	0	.000	10	243

NFL Championship: N.Y. Giants 30, Chicago Bears 13

1935

EASTERN DIVISION	W	L	T	Pct.	Pts.	OP
N.Y. Giants	9	3	0	.750	180	96
Brooklyn	5	6	1	.455	90	141
Pittsburgh	4	8	0	.333	100	209
Boston	2	8	1	.200	65	123
Philadelphia	2	9	0	.182	60	179

WESTERN DIVISION	W	L	T	Pct.	Pts.	OP
Detroit	7	3	2	.700	191	111
Green Bay	8	4	0	.667	181	96
Chi. Bears	6	4	2	.600	192	106
Chi. Cardinals	6	4	2	.600	99	97

NFL Championship: Detroit 26, N.Y. Giants 7
One game between Boston and Philadelphia was canceled.

1936

EASTERN DIVISION	W	L	T	Pct.	Pts.	OP
Boston	7	5	0	.583	149	110
Pittsburgh	6	6	0	.500	98	187
N.Y. Giants	5	6	1	.455	115	163
Brooklyn	3	8	1	.273	92	161
Philadelphia	1	11	0	.083	51	206

WESTERN DIVISION	W	L	T	Pct.	Pts.	OP
Green Bay	10	1	1	.909	248	118
Chi. Bears	9	3	0	.750	222	94
Detroit	8	4	0	.667	235	102
Chi. Cardinals	3	8	1	.273	74	143

NFL Championship: Green Bay 21, Boston 6

1937

EASTERN DIVISION	W	L	T	Pct.	Pts.	OP
Washington	8	3	0	.727	195	120
N.Y. Giants	6	3	2	.667	128	109
Pittsburgh	4	7	0	.364	122	145
Brooklyn	3	7	1	.300	82	174
Philadelphia	2	8	1	.200	86	177

WESTERN DIVISION	W	L	T	Pct.	Pts.	OP
Chi. Bears	9	1	1	.900	201	100
Green Bay	7	4	0	.636	220	122
Detroit	7	4	0	.636	180	105
Chi. Cardinals	5	5	1	.500	135	165
Cleveland	1	10	0	.091	75	207

NFL Championship: Washington 28, Chicago Bears 21

1938

EASTERN DIVISION	W	L	T	Pct.	Pts.	OP
N.Y Giants	8	2	1	.800	194	79
Washington	6	3	2	.667	148	154
Brooklyn	4	4	3	.500	131	161
Philadelphia	5	6	0	.455	154	164
Pittsburgh	2	9	0	.182	79	169

WESTERN DIVISION	W	L	T	Pct.	Pts.	OP
Green Bay	8	3	0	.727	223	118
Detroit	7	4	0	.636	119	108
Chi. Bears	6	5	0	.545	194	148
Cleveland	4	7	0	.364	131	215
Chi. Cardinals	2	9	0	.182	111	168

NFL Championship: N.Y. Giants 23, Green Bay 17

1939

EASTERN DIVISION	W	L	T	Pct.	Pts.	OP
N.Y. Giants	9	1	1	.900	168	85
Washington	8	2	1	.800	242	94
Brooklyn	4	6	1	.400	108	219
Philadelphia	1	9	1	.100	105	200
Pittsburgh	1	9	1	.100	114	216

WESTERN DIVISION	W	L	T	Pct.	Pts.	OP
Green Bay	9	2	0	.818	233	153
Chi. Bears	8	3	0	.727	298	157
Detroit	6	5	0	.545	145	150
Cleveland	5	5	1	.500	195	164
Chi. Cardinals	1	10	0	.091	84	254

NFL Championship: Green Bay 27, N.Y. Giants 0

1940

EASTERN DIVISION	W	L	T	Pct.	Pts.	OP		WESTERN DIVISION	W	L	T	Pct.	Pts.	OP
Washington	9	2	0	.818	245	142		Chi. Bears	8	3	0	.727	238	152
Brooklyn	8	3	0	.727	186	120		Green Bay	6	4	1	.600	238	155
N.Y. Giants	6	4	1	.600	131	133		Detroit	5	5	1	.500	138	153
Pittsburgh	2	7	2	.222	60	178		Cleveland	4	6	1	.400	171	191
Philadelphia	1	10	0	.091	111	211		Chi. Cardinals	2	7	2	.222	139	222

NFL Championship: Chicago Bears 73, Washington 0

1941

EASTERN DIVISION	W	L	T	Pct.	Pts.	OP		WESTERN DIVISION	W	L	T	Pct.	Pts.	OP
N.Y. Giants	8	3	0	.727	238	114		Chi. Bears	10	1	0	.909	396	147
Brooklyn	7	4	0	.636	158	127		Green Bay	10	1	0	.909	258	120
Washington	6	5	0	.545	176	174		Detroit	4	6	1	.400	121	195
Philadelphia	2	8	1	.200	119	218		Chi. Cardinals	3	7	1	.300	127	197
Pittsburgh	1	9	1	.100	103	276		Cleveland	2	9	0	.182	116	244

Western Division playoff: Chicago Bears 33, Green Bay 14
NFL Championship: Chicago Bears 37, N.Y. Giants 9

1942

EASTERN DIVISION	W	L	T	Pct.	Pts.	OP		WESTERN DIVISION	W	L	T	Pct.	Pts.	OP
Washington	10	1	0	.909	227	102		Chi. Bears	11	0	0	1.000	376	84
Pittsburgh	7	4	0	.636	167	119		Green Bay	8	2	1	.800	300	215
N.Y. Giants	5	5	0	.500	155	139		Cleveland	5	6	0	.455	150	207
Brooklyn	3	8	0	.273	100	168		Chi. Cardinals	3	8	0	.273	98	209
Philadelphia	2	9	0	.182	134	239		Detroit	0	11	0	.000	38	263

NFL Championship: Washington 14, Chicago Bears 6

1943

EASTERN DIVISION	W	L	T	Pct.	Pts.	OP		WESTERN DIVISION	W	L	T	Pct.	Pts.	OP
Washington	6	3	1	.667	229	137		Chi. Bears	8	1	1	.889	303	157
N.Y. Giants	6	3	1	.667	197	170		Green Bay	7	2	1	.778	264	172
Phil-Pitt	5	4	1	.556	225	230		Detroit	3	6	1	.333	178	218
Brooklyn	2	8	0	.200	65	234		Chi. Cardinals	0	10	0	.000	95	238

Eastern Division playoff: Washington 28, N.Y. Giants 0
NFL Championship: Chicago Bears 41, Washington 21

1944

EASTERN DIVISION	W	L	T	Pct.	Pts.	OP		WESTERN DIVISION	W	L	T	Pct.	Pts.	OP
N.Y. Giants	8	1	1	.889	206	75		Green Bay	8	2	0	.800	238	141
Philadelphia	7	1	2	.875	267	131		Chi. Bears	6	3	1	.667	258	172
Washington	6	3	1	.667	169	180		Detroit	6	3	1	.667	216	151
Boston	2	8	0	.200	82	233		Cleveland	4	6	0	.400	188	224
Brooklyn	0	10	0	.000	69	166		Card-Pitt	0	10	0	.000	108	328

NFL Championship: Green Bay 14, N.Y. Giants 7

1945

EASTERN DIVISION	W	L	T	Pct.	Pts.	OP		WESTERN DIVISION	W	L	T	Pct.	Pts.	OP
Washington	8	2	0	.800	209	121		Cleveland	9	1	0	.900	244	136
Philadelphia	7	3	0	.700	272	133		Detroit	7	3	0	.700	195	194
N.Y. Giants	3	6	1	.333	179	198		Green Bay	6	4	0	.600	258	173
Boston	3	6	1	.333	123	211		Chi. Bears	3	7	0	.300	192	235
Pittsburgh	2	8	0	.200	79	220		Chi. Cardinals	1	9	0	.100	98	228

NFL Championship: Cleveland 15, Washington 14

1946

EASTERN DIVISION	W	L	T	Pct.	Pts.	OP
N.Y. Giants	7	3	1	.700	236	162
Philadelphia	6	5	0	.545	231	220
Washington	5	5	1	.500	171	191
Pittsburgh	5	5	1	.500	136	117
Boston	2	8	1	.200	189	273

WESTERN DIVISION	W	L	T	Pct.	Pts.	OP
Chi. Bears	8	2	1	.800	289	193
Los Angeles	6	4	1	.600	277	257
Green Bay	6	5	0	.545	148	158
Chi. Cardinals	6	5	0	.545	260	198
Detroit	1	10	0	.091	142	310

NFL Championship: Chicago Bears 24, N.Y. Giants 14

1947

EASTERN DIVISION	W	L	T	Pct.	Pts.	OP
Philadelphia	8	4	0	.667	308	242
Pittsburgh	8	4	0	.667	240	259
Boston	4	7	1	.364	168	256
Washington	4	8	0	.333	295	367
N.Y. Giants	2	8	2	.200	190	309

WESTERN DIVISION	W	L	T	Pct.	Pts.	OP
Chi. Cardinals	9	3	0	.750	306	231
Chi. Bears	8	4	0	.667	363	241
Green Bay	6	5	1	.545	274	210
Los Angeles	6	6	0	.500	259	214
Detroit	3	9	0	.250	231	305

Eastern Division playoff: Philadelphia 21, Pittsburgh 0
NFL Championship: Chicago Cardinals 28, Philadelphia 21

1948

EASTERN DIVISION	W	L	T	Pct.	Pts.	OP
Philadelphia	9	2	1	.818	376	156
Washington	7	5	0	.583	291	287
N.Y. Giants	4	8	0	.333	297	388
Pittsburgh	4	8	0	.333	200	243
Boston	3	9	0	.250	174	372

WESTERN DIVISION	W	L	T	Pct.	Pts.	OP
Chi. Cardinals	11	1	0	.917	395	226
Chi. Bears	10	2	0	.833	375	151
Los Angeles	6	5	1	.545	327	269
Green Bay	3	9	0	.250	154	290
Detroit	2	10	0	.167	200	407

NFL Championship: Philadelphia 7, Chicago Cardinals 0

1949

EASTERN DIVISION	W	L	T	Pct.	Pts.	OP
Philadelphia	11	1	0	.917	364	134
Pittsburgh	6	5	1	.545	224	214
N.Y. Giants	6	6	0	.500	287	298
Washington	4	7	1	.364	268	339
N.Y. Bulldogs	1	10	1	.091	153	368

WESTERN DIVISION	W	L	T	Pct.	Pts.	OP
Los Angeles	8	2	2	.800	360	239
Chi. Bears	9	3	0	.750	332	218
Chi. Cardinals	6	5	1	.545	360	301
Detroit	4	8	0	.333	237	259
Green Bay	2	10	0	.167	114	329

NFL Championship: Philadelphia 14, Los Angeles 0

1950

AMERICAN CONFERENCE	W	L	T	Pct.	Pts.	OP
Cleveland	10	2	0	.833	310	144
N.Y. Giants	10	2	0	.833	268	150
Philadelphia	6	6	0	.500	254	141
Pittsburgh	6	6	0	.500	180	195
Chi. Cardinals	5	7	0	.417	233	287
Washington	3	9	0	.250	232	326

NATIONAL CONFERENCE	W	L	T	Pct.	Pts.	OP
Los Angeles	9	3	0	.750	466	309
Chi. Bears	9	3	0	.750	279	207
N.Y. Yanks	7	5	0	.583	366	367
Detroit	6	6	0	.500	321	285
Green Bay	3	9	0	.250	244	406
San Francisco	3	9	0	.250	213	300
Baltimore	1	11	0	.083	213	462

American Conference playoff: Cleveland 8, N.Y. Giants 3
National Conference playoff: Los Angeles 24, Chicago Bears 14
NFL Championship: Cleveland 30, Los Angeles 28

1951

AMERICAN CONFERENCE	W	L	T	Pct.	Pts.	OP
Cleveland	11	1	0	.917	331	152
N.Y. Giants	9	2	1	.818	254	161
Washington	5	7	0	.417	183	296
Pittsburgh	4	7	1	.364	183	235
Philadelphia	4	8	0	.333	234	264
Chi. Cardinals	3	9	0	.250	210	287

NATIONAL CONFERENCE	W	L	T	Pct.	Pts.	OP
Los Angeles	8	4	0	.667	392	261
Detroit	7	4	1	.636	336	259
San Francisco	7	4	1	.636	255	205
Chi. Bears	7	5	0	.583	286	282
Green Bay	3	9	0	.250	254	375
N.Y. Yanks	1	9	2	.100	241	382

NFL Championship: Los Angeles 24, Cleveland 17

1952

AMERICAN CONFERENCE	W	L	T	Pct.	Pts.	OP	NATIONAL CONFERENCE	W	L	T	Pct.	Pts.	OP
Cleveland	8	4	0	.667	310	213	Detroit	9	3	0	.750	344	192
N.Y. Giants	7	5	0	.583	234	231	Los Angeles	9	3	0	.750	349	234
Philadelphia	7	5	0	.583	252	271	San Francisco	7	5	0	.583	285	221
Pittsburgh	5	7	0	.417	300	273	Green Bay	6	6	0	.500	295	312
Chi. Cardinals	4	8	0	.333	172	221	Chi. Bears	5	7	0	.417	245	326
Washington	4	8	0	.333	240	287	Dallas	1	11	0	.083	182	427

National Conference playoff: Detroit 31, Los Angeles 21

NFL Championship: Detroit 17, Cleveland 7

1953

EASTERN CONFERENCE	W	L	T	Pct.	Pts.	OP	WESTERN CONFERENCE	W	L	T	Pct.	Pts.	OP
Cleveland	11	1	0	.917	348	162	Detroit	10	2	0	.833	271	205
Philadelphia	7	4	1	.636	352	215	San Francisco	9	3	0	.750	372	237
Washington	6	5	1	.545	208	215	Los Angeles	8	3	1	.727	366	236
Pittsburgh	6	6	0	.500	211	263	Chi. Bears	3	8	1	.273	218	262
N.Y. Giants	3	9	0	.250	179	277	Baltimore	3	9	0	.250	182	350
Chi. Cardinals	1	10	1	.091	190	337	Green Bay	2	9	1	.182	200	338

NFL Championship: Detroit 17, Cleveland 16

1954

EASTERN CONFERENCE	W	L	T	Pct.	Pts.	OP	WESTERN CONFERENCE	W	L	T	Pct.	Pts.	OP
Cleveland	9	3	0	.750	336	162	Detroit	9	2	1	.818	337	189
Philadelphia	7	4	1	.636	284	230	Chi. Bears	8	4	0	.667	301	279
N.Y. Giants	7	5	0	.583	293	184	San Francisco	7	4	1	.636	313	251
Pittsburgh	5	7	0	.417	219	263	Los Angeles	6	5	1	.545	314	285
Washington	3	9	0	.250	207	432	Green Bay	4	8	0	.333	234	251
Chi. Cardinals	2	10	0	.167	183	347	Baltimore	3	9	0	.250	131	279

NFL Championship: Cleveland 56, Detroit 10

1955

EASTERN CONFERENCE	W	L	T	Pct.	Pts.	OP	WESTERN CONFERENCE	W	L	T	Pct.	Pts.	OP
Cleveland	9	2	1	.818	349	218	Los Angeles	8	3	1	.727	260	231
Washington	8	4	0	.667	246	222	Chi. Bears	8	4	0	.667	294	251
N.Y. Giants	6	5	1	.545	267	223	Green Bay	6	6	0	.500	258	276
Chi. Cardinals	4	7	1	.364	224	252	Baltimore	5	6	1	.455	214	239
Philadelphia	4	7	1	.364	248	231	San Francisco	4	8	0	.333	216	298
Pittsburgh	4	8	0	.333	195	285	Detroit	3	9	0	.250	230	275

NFL Championship: Cleveland 38, Los Angeles 14

1956

EASTERN CONFERENCE	W	L	T	Pct.	Pts.	OP	WESTERN CONFERENCE	W	L	T	Pct.	Pts.	OP
N.Y. Giants	8	3	1	.727	264	197	Chi. Bears	9	2	1	.818	363	246
Chi. Cardinals	7	5	0	.583	240	182	Detroit	9	3	0	.750	300	188
Washington	6	6	0	.500	183	225	San Francisco	5	6	1	.455	233	284
Cleveland	5	7	0	.417	167	177	Los Angeles	5	7	0	.417	270	322
Pittsburgh	5	7	0	.417	217	250	Green Bay	4	8	0	.333	264	342
Philadelphia	3	8	1	.273	143	215	Los Angeles	4	8	0	.333	291	307

NFL Championship: N.Y. Giants 47, Chicago Bears 7

1957

EASTERN CONFERENCE

	W	L	T	Pct.	Pts.	OP
Cleveland	9	2	1	.818	269	172
N.Y. Giants	7	5	0	.583	254	211
Pittsburgh	6	6	0	.500	161	178
Washington	5	6	1	.455	251	230
Philadelphia	4	8	0	.333	173	230
Chi. Cardinals	3	9	0	.250	200	299

WESTERN CONFERENCE

	W	L	T	Pct.	Pts.	OP
Detroit	8	4	0	.667	251	231
San Francisco	8	4	0	.667	260	264
Baltimore	7	5	0	.583	303	235
Los Angeles	6	6	0	.500	307	278
Chi. Bears	5	7	0	.417	203	211
Green Bay	3	9	0	.250	218	311

Western Conference playoff: Detroit 31, San Francisco 27
NFL Championship: Detroit 59, Cleveland 14

1958

EASTERN CONFERENCE

	W	L	T	Pct.	Pts.	OP
N.Y. Giants	9	3	0	.750	246	183
Cleveland	9	3	0	.750	302	217
Pittsburgh	7	4	1	.636	261	230
Washington	4	7	1	.364	214	268
Chi. Cardinals	2	9	1	.182	261	356
Philadelphia	2	9	1	.182	235	306

WESTERN CONFERENCE

	W	L	T	Pct.	Pts.	OP
Baltimore	9	3	0	.750	381	203
Chi. Bears	8	4	0	.667	298	230
Los Angeles	8	4	0	.667	344	278
San Francisco	6	6	0	.500	257	324
Detroit	4	7	1	.364	261	276
Green Bay	1	10	1	.091	193	382

Eastern Conference playoff: N.Y. Giants 10, Cleveland 0
NFL Championship: Baltimore 23, N.Y. Giants 17, sudden-death overtime

1959

EASTERN CONFERENCE

	W	L	T	Pct.	Pts.	OP
N.Y. Giants	10	2	0	.833	284	170
Cleveland	7	5	0	.583	270	214
Philadelphia	7	5	0	.583	268	278
Pittsburgh	6	5	1	.545	257	216
Washington	3	9	0	.250	185	350
Chi. Cardinals	2	10	0	.167	234	324

WESTERN CONFERENCE

	W	L	T	Pct.	Pts.	OP
Baltimore	9	3	0	.750	374	251
Chi. Bears	8	4	0	.667	252	196
Green Bay	7	5	0	.583	248	246
San Francisco	7	5	0	.583	255	237
Detroit	3	8	1	.273	203	275
Los Angeles	2	10	0	.167	242	315

NFL Championship: Baltimore 31, N.Y. Giants 16

1960 AFL

EASTERN DIVISION

	W	L	T	Pct.	Pts.	OP
Houston	10	4	0	.714	379	285
N.Y. Titans	7	7	0	.500	382	399
Buffalo	5	8	1	.385	296	303
Boston	5	9	0	.357	286	349

WESTERN DIVISION

	W	L	T	Pct.	Pts.	OP
L.A. Chargers	10	4	0	.714	373	336
Dall. Texans	8	6	0	.571	362	253
Oakland	6	8	0	.429	319	388
Denver	4	9	1	.308	309	393

AFL Championship: Houston 24, L.A. Chargers 16

1960 NFL

EASTERN CONFERENCE

	W	L	T	Pct.	Pts.	OP
Philadelphia	10	2	0	.833	321	246
Cleveland	8	3	1	.727	362	217
N.Y. Giants	6	4	2	.600	271	261
St. Louis	6	5	1	.545	288	230
Pittsburgh	5	6	1	.455	240	275
Washington	1	9	2	.100	178	309

WESTERN CONFERENCE

	W	L	T	Pct.	Pts.	OP
Green Bay	8	4	0	.667	332	209
Detroit	7	5	0	.583	239	212
San Francisco	7	5	0	.583	208	205
Baltimore	6	6	0	.500	288	234
Chicago	5	6	1	.455	194	299
L.A. Rams	4	7	1	.364	265	297
Dall. Cowboys	0	11	1	.000	177	369

NFL Championship: Philadelphia 17, Green Bay 13

1961 AFL

EASTERN DIVISION	W	L	T	Pct.	Pts.	OP	WESTERN DIVISION	W	L	T	Pct.	Pts.	OP
Houston	10	3	1	.769	513	242	San Diego	12	2	0	.857	396	219
Boston	9	4	1	.692	413	313	Dall. Texans	6	8	0	.429	334	343
N.Y. Titans	7	7	0	.500	301	390	Denver	3	11	0	.214	251	432
Buffalo	6	8	0	.429	294	342	Oakland	2	12	0	.143	237	458

AFL Championship: Houston 10, San Diego 3

1961 NFL

EASTERN CONFERENCE	W	L	T	Pct.	Pts.	OP	WESTERN CONFERENCE	W	L	T	Pct.	Pts.	OP
N.Y. Giants	10	3	1	.769	368	220	Green Bay	11	3	0	.786	391	223
Philadelphia	10	4	0	.714	361	297	Detroit	8	5	1	.615	270	258
Cleveland	8	5	1	.615	319	270	Baltimore	8	6	0	.571	302	307
St. Louis	7	7	0	.500	279	267	Chicago	8	6	0	.571	326	302
Pittsburgh	6	8	0	.429	295	287	San Francisco	7	6	1	.538	346	272
Dall. Cowboys	4	9	1	.308	236	380	Los Angeles	4	10	0	.286	263	333
Washington	1	12	1	.077	174	392	Minnesota	3	11	0	.214	285	407

NFL Championship: Green Bay 37, N.Y. Giants 0

1962 AFL

EASTERN DIVISION	W	L	T	Pct.	Pts.	OP	WESTERN DIVISION	W	L	T	Pct.	Pts.	OP
Houston	11	3	0	.786	387	270	Dall. Texans	11	3	0	.786	389	233
Boston	9	4	1	.692	346	295	Denver	7	7	0	.500	353	334
Buffalo	7	6	1	.538	309	272	San Diego	4	10	0	.286	314	392
N.Y. Titans	5	9	0	.357	278	423	Oakland	1	13	0	.071	213	370

AFL Championship: Dallas Texans 20, Houston 17, sudden-death overtime

1962 NFL

EASTERN CONFERENCE	W	L	T	Pct.	Pts.	OP	WESTERN CONFERENCE	W	L	T	Pct.	Pts.	OP
N.Y. Giants	12	2	0	.857	398	283	Green Bay	13	1	0	.929	415	148
Pittsburgh	9	5	0	.643	312	363	Detroit	11	3	0	.786	315	177
Cleveland	7	6	1	.538	291	257	Chicago	9	5	0	.643	321	287
Washington	5	7	2	.417	305	376	Baltimore	7	7	0	.500	293	288
Dall. Cowboys	5	8	1	.385	398	402	San Francisco	6	8	0	.429	282	331
St. Louis	4	9	1	.308	287	361	Minnesota	2	11	1	.154	254	410
Philadelphia	3	10	1	.231	282	356	Los Angeles	1	12	1	.077	220	334

NFL Championship: Green Bay 16, N.Y. Giants 7

1963 AFL

EASTERN DIVISION	W	L	T	Pct.	Pts.	OP	WESTERN DIVISION	W	L	T	Pct.	Pts.	OP
Boston	7	6	1	.538	317	257	San Diego	11	3	0	.786	399	255
Buffalo	7	6	1	.538	304	291	Oakland	10	4	0	.714	363	282
Houston	6	8	0	.429	302	372	Kansas City	5	7	2	.417	347	263
N.Y. Jets	5	8	1	.385	249	399	Denver	2	11	1	.154	301	473

Eastern Division playoff: Boston 26, Buffalo 8
AFL Championship: San Diego 51, Boston 10

1963 NFL

EASTERN CONFERENCE	W	L	T	Pct.	Pts.	OP	WESTERN CONFERENCE	W	L	T	Pct.	Pts.	OP
N.Y. Giants	11	3	0	.786	448	280	Chicago	11	1	2	.917	301	144
Cleveland	10	4	0	.714	343	262	Green Bay	11	2	1	.846	369	206
St. Louis	9	5	0	.643	341	283	Baltimore	8	6	0	.571	316	285
Pittsburgh	7	4	3	.636	321	295	Detroit	5	8	1	.385	326	265
Dallas	4	10	0	.286	305	378	Minnesota	5	8	1	.385	309	390
Washington	3	11	0	.214	279	398	Los Angeles	5	9	0	.357	210	350
Philadelphia	2	10	2	.167	242	381	San Francisco	2	12	0	.143	198	391

NFL Championship: Chicago 14, N.Y. Giants 10

1964 AFL

EASTERN DIVISION	W	L	T	Pct.	Pts.	OP	WESTERN DIVISION	W	L	T	Pct.	Pts.	OP
Buffalo	12	2	0	.857	400	242	San Diego	8	5	1	.615	341	300
Boston	10	3	1	.769	365	297	Kansas City	7	7	0	.500	366	306
N.Y. Jets	5	8	1	.385	278	315	Oakland	5	7	2	.417	303	350
Houston	4	10	0	.286	310	355	Denver	2	11	1	.154	240	438

AFL Championship: Buffalo 20, San Diego 7

1964 NFL

EASTERN CONFERENCE	W	L	T	Pct.	Pts.	OP	WESTERN CONFERENCE	W	L	T	Pct.	Pts.	OP
Cleveland	10	3	1	.769	415	293	Baltimore	12	2	0	.857	428	225
St. Louis	9	3	2	.750	357	331	Green Bay	8	5	1	.615	342	245
Philadelphia	6	8	0	.429	312	313	Minnesota	8	5	1	.615	355	296
Washington	6	8	0	.429	307	305	Detroit	7	5	2	.583	280	260
Dallas	5	8	1	.385	250	289	Los Angeles	5	7	2	.417	283	339
Pittsburgh	5	9	0	.357	253	315	Chicago	5	9	0	.357	260	379
N.Y. Giants	2	10	2	.167	241	399	San Francisco	4	10	0	.286	236	330

NFL Championship: Cleveland 27, Baltimore 0

1965 AFL

EASTERN DIVISION	W	L	T	Pct.	Pts.	OP	WESTERN DIVISION	W	L	T	Pct.	Pts.	OP
Buffalo	10	3	1	.769	313	226	San Diego	9	2	3	.818	340	227
N.Y. Jets	5	8	1	.385	285	303	Oakland	8	5	1	.615	298	239
Boston	4	8	2	.333	244	302	Kansas City	7	5	2	.583	322	285
Houston	4	10	0	.286	298	429	Denver	4	10	0	.286	303	392

AFL Championship: Buffalo 23, San Diego 0

1965 NFL

EASTERN CONFERENCE	W	L	T	Pct.	Pts.	OP	WESTERN CONFERENCE	W	L	T	Pct.	Pts.	OP
Cleveland	11	3	0	.786	363	325	Green Bay	10	3	1	.769	316	224
Dallas	7	7	0	.500	325	280	Baltimore	10	3	1	.769	389	284
N.Y. Giants	7	7	0	.500	270	338	Chicago	9	5	0	.643	409	275
Washington	6	8	0	.429	257	301	San Francisco	7	6	1	.538	421	402
Philadelphia	5	9	0	.357	363	359	Minnesota	7	7	0	.500	383	403
St. Louis	5	9	0	.357	296	309	Detroit	6	7	1	.462	257	295
Pittsburgh	2	12	0	.143	202	397	Los Angeles	4	10	0	.286	269	328

Western Conference playoff: Green Bay 13, Baltimore 10, sudden-death overtime
NFL Championship: Green Bay 23, Cleveland 12

1966 AFL

EASTERN DIVISION	W	L	T	Pct.	Pts.	OP	WESTERN DIVISION	W	L	T	Pct.	Pts.	OP
Buffalo	9	4	1	.692	358	255	Kansas City	11	2	1	.846	448	276
Boston	8	4	2	.667	315	283	Oakland	8	5	1	.615	315	288
N.Y. Jets	6	6	2	.500	322	312	San Diego	7	6	1	.538	335	284
Houston	3	11	0	.214	335	396	Denver	4	10	0	.286	196	381
Miami	3	11	0	.214	213	362							

AFL Championship: Kansas City 31, Buffalo 7

1966 NFL

EASTERN CONFERENCE	W	L	T	Pct.	Pts.	OP	WESTERN CONFERENCE	W	L	T	Pct.	Pts.	OP
Dallas	10	3	1	.769	445	239	Green Bay	12	2	0	.857	335	163
Cleveland	9	5	0	.643	403	259	Baltimore	9	5	0	.643	314	226
Philadelphia	9	5	0	.643	326	340	Los Angeles	8	6	0	.571	289	212
St. Louis	8	5	1	.615	264	265	San Francisco	6	6	2	.500	320	325
Washington	7	7	0	.500	351	355	Chicago	5	7	2	.417	234	272
Pittsburgh	5	8	1	.385	316	347	Detroit	4	9	1	.308	206	317
Atlanta	3	11	0	.214	204	437	Minnesota	4	9	1	.308	292	304
N.Y. Giants	1	12	1	.077	263	501							

NFL Championship: Green Bay 34, Dallas 27
Super Bowl I: Green Bay (NFL) 35, Kansas City (AFL) 10

1967 AFL

EASTERN DIVISION	W	L	T	Pct.	Pts.	OP	WESTERN DIVISION	W	L	T	Pct.	Pts.	OP
Houston	9	4	1	.692	258	199	Oakland	13	1	0	.929	468	238
N.Y. Jets	8	5	1	.615	371	329	Kansas City	9	5	0	.643	408	254
Buffalo	4	10	0	.286	237	285	San Diego	8	5	1	.615	360	352
Miami	4	10	0	.286	219	407	Denver	3	11	0	.214	256	409
Boston	3	10	1	.231	280	389							

AFL Championship: Oakland 40, Houston 7

1967 NFL

EASTERN CONFERENCE

Capitol Division

	W	L	T	Pct.	Pts.	OP	Coastal Division	W	L	T	Pct.	Pts.	OP
Dallas	9	5	0	.643	342	268	Los Angeles	11	1	2	.917	398	196
Philadelphia	6	7	1	.462	351	409	Baltimore	11	1	2	.917	394	198
Washington	5	6	3	.455	347	353	San Francisco	7	7	0	.500	273	337
New Orleans	3	11	0	.214	233	379	Atlanta	1	12	1	.077	175	422

WESTERN CONFERENCE

Century Division

	W	L	T	Pct.	Pts.	OP	Central Division	W	L	T	Pct.	Pts.	OP
Cleveland	9	5	0	.643	334	297	Green Bay	9	4	1	.692	332	209
N.Y. Giants	7	7	0	.500	369	379	Chicago	7	6	1	.538	239	218
St. Louis	6	7	1	.462	333	356	Detroit	5	7	2	.417	260	259
Pittsburgh	4	9	1	.308	281	320	Minnesota	3	8	3	.273	233	294

Conference Championships: Dallas 52, Cleveland 14; Green Bay 28, Los Angeles 7
NFL Championship: Green Bay 21, Dallas 17
Super Bowl II: Green Bay (NFL) 33, Oakland (AFL) 14

1968 AFL

EASTERN DIVISION	W	L	T	Pct.	Pts.	OP	WESTERN DIVISION	W	L	T	Pct.	Pts.	OP
N.Y. Jets	11	3	0	.786	419	280	Oakland	12	2	0	.857	453	233
Houston	7	7	0	.500	303	248	Kansas City	12	2	0	.857	371	170
Miami	5	8	1	.385	276	355	San Diego	9	5	0	.643	382	310
Boston	4	10	0	.286	229	406	Denver	5	9	0	.357	255	404
Buffalo	1	12	1	.077	199	367	Cincinnati	3	11	0	.214	215	329

Western Division playoff: Oakland 41, Kansas City 6
AFL Championship: N.Y. Jets 27, Oakland 23

1968 NFL

EASTERN CONFERENCE

Capitol Division

	W	L	T	Pct.	Pts.	OP	Coastal Division	W	L	T	Pct.	Pts.	OP
Dallas	12	2	0	.857	431	186	Baltimore	13	1	0	.929	402	144
N.Y. Giants	7	7	0	.500	294	325	Los Angeles	10	3	1	.769	312	200
Washington	5	9	0	.357	249	358	San Francisco	7	6	1	.538	303	310
Philadelphia	2	12	0	.143	202	351	Atlanta	2	12	0	.143	170	389

WESTERN CONFERENCE

Century Division

	W	L	T	Pct.	Pts.	OP	Central Division	W	L	T	Pct.	Pts.	OP
Cleveland	10	4	0	.714	394	273	Minnesota	8	6	0	.571	282	242
St. Louis	9	4	1	.692	325	289	Chicago	7	7	0	.500	250	333
New Orleans	4	9	1	.308	246	327	Green Bay	6	7	1	.462	281	227
Pittsburgh	2	11	1	.154	244	397	Detroit	4	8	2	.333	207	241

Conference Championships: Cleveland 31, Dallas 20; Baltimore 24, Minnesota 14
NFL Championship: Baltimore 34, Cleveland 0
Super Bowl III: N.Y. Jets (AFL) 16, Baltimore (NFL) 7

1969 AFL

EASTERN DIVISION	W	L	T	Pct.	Pts.	OP	WESTERN DIVISION	W	L	T	Pct.	Pts.	OP
N.Y. Jets	10	4	0	.714	353	269	Oakland	12	1	1	.923	377	242
Houston	6	6	2	.500	278	279	Kansas City	11	3	0	.786	359	177
Boston	4	10	0	.286	266	316	San Diego	8	6	0	.571	288	276
Buffalo	4	10	0	.286	230	359	Denver	5	8	1	.385	297	344
Miami	3	10	1	.231	233	332	Cincinnati	4	9	1	.308	280	367

Divisional playoffs: Kansas City 13, N.Y. Jets 6; Oakland 56, Houston 7
AFL Championship: Kansas City 17, Oakland 7

1969 NFL

EASTERN CONFERENCE

Capitol Division

	W	L	T	Pct.	Pts.	OP
Dallas	11	2	1	.846	369	223
Washington	7	5	2	.583	307	319
New Orleans	5	9	0	.357	311	393
Philadelphia	4	9	1	.308	279	377

Century Division

	W	L	T	Pct.	Pts.	OP
Cleveland	10	3	1	.769	351	300
N.Y. Giants	6	8	0	.429	264	298
St. Louis	4	9	1	.308	314	389
Pittsburgh	1	13	0	.071	218	404

WESTERN CONFERENCE

Coastal Division

	W	L	T	Pct.	Pts.	OP
Los Angeles	11	3	0	.786	320	243
Baltimore	8	5	1	.615	279	268
Atlanta	6	8	0	.429	276	268
San Francisco	4	8	2	.333	277	319

Central Division

	W	L	T	Pct.	Pts.	OP
Minnesota	12	2	0	.857	379	133
Detroit	9	4	1	.692	259	188
Green Bay	8	6	0	.571	269	221
Chicago	1	13	0	.071	210	339

Conference Championships: Cleveland 38, Dallas 14; Minnesota 23, Los Angeles 20
NFL Championship: Minnesota 27, Cleveland 7
Super Bowl IV: Kansas City (AFL) 23, Minnesota (NFL) 7

1970

AMERICAN CONFERENCE

Eastern Division

	W	L	T	Pct.	Pts.	OP
Baltimore	11	2	1	.846	321	234
Miami*	10	4	0	.714	297	228
N.Y. Jets	4	10	0	.286	255	286
Buffalo	3	10	1	.231	204	337
Boston	2	12	0	.143	149	361

Central Division

	W	L	T	Pct.	Pts.	OP
Cincinnati	8	6	0	.571	312	255
Cleveland	7	7	0	.500	286	265
Pittsburgh	5	9	0	.357	210	272
Houston	3	10	1	.231	217	352

Western Division

	W	L	T	Pct.	Pts.	OP
Oakland	8	4	2	.667	300	293
Kansas City	7	5	2	.583	272	244
San Diego	5	6	3	.455	282	278
Denver	5	8	1	.385	253	264

NATIONAL CONFERENCE

Eastern Division

	W	L	T	Pct.	Pts.	OP
Dallas	10	4	0	.714	299	221
N.Y. Giants	9	5	0	.643	301	270
St. Louis	8	5	1	.615	325	228
Washington	6	8	0	.429	297	314
Philadelphia	3	10	1	.231	241	332

Central Division

	W	L	T	Pct.	Pts.	OP
Minnesota	12	2	0	.857	335	143
Detroit*	10	4	0	.714	347	202
Chicago	6	8	0	.429	256	261
Green Bay	6	8	0	.429	196	293

Western Division

	W	L	T	Pct.	Pts.	OP
San Francisco	10	3	1	.769	352	267
Los Angeles	9	4	1	.692	325	202
Atlanta	4	8	2	.333	206	261
New Orleans	2	11	1	.154	172	347

*Wild Card qualifier for playoffs
Divisional playoffs: Baltimore 17, Cincinnati 0; Oakland 21, Miami 14
AFC Championship: Baltimore 27, Oakland 17
Divisional playoffs: Dallas 5, Detroit 0; San Francisco 17, Minnesota 14
NFC Championship: Dallas 17, San Francisco 10
Super Bowl V: Baltimore (AFC) 16, Dallas (NFC) 13

1971

AMERICAN CONFERENCE

Eastern Division

	W	L	T	Pct.	Pts.	OP
Miami	10	3	1	.769	315	174
Baltimore*	10	4	0	.714	313	140
New England	6	8	0	.429	238	325
N.Y. Jets	6	8	0	.429	212	299
Buffalo	1	13	0	.071	184	394

Central Division

	W	L	T	Pct.	Pts.	OP
Cleveland	9	5	0	.643	285	273
Pittsburgh	6	8	0	.429	246	292
Houston	4	9	1	.308	251	330
Cincinnati	4	10	0	.286	284	265

Western Division

	W	L	T	Pct.	Pts.	OP
Kansas City	10	3	1	.769	302	208
Oakland	8	4	2	.667	344	278
San Diego	6	8	0	.429	311	341
Denver	4	9	1	.308	203	275

NATIONAL CONFERENCE

Eastern Division

	W	L	T	Pct.	Pts.	OP
Dallas	11	3	0	.786	406	222
Washington*	9	4	1	.692	276	190
Philadelphia	6	7	1	.462	221	302
St. Louis	4	9	1	.308	231	279
N.Y. Giants	4	10	0	.286	228	362

Central Division

	W	L	T	Pct.	Pts.	OP
Minnesota	11	3	0	.786	245	139
Detroit	7	6	1	.538	341	286
Chicago	6	8	0	.429	185	276
Green Bay	4	8	2	.333	274	298

Western Division

	W	L	T	Pct.	Pts.	OP
San Francisco	9	5	0	.643	300	216
Los Angeles	8	5	1	.615	313	260
Atlanta	7	6	1	.538	274	277
New Orleans	4	8	2	.333	266	347

Wild Card qualifier for playoffs
Divisional playoffs: Miami 27, Kansas City 24, sudden-death overtime; Baltimore 20, Cleveland 3
AFC Championship: Miami 21, Baltimore 0
Divisional playoffs: Dallas 20, Minnesota 12; San Francisco 24, Washington 20
NFC Championship: Dallas 14, San Francisco 3
Super Bowl VI: Dallas (NFC) 24, Miami (AFC) 3

1972

AMERICAN CONFERENCE

Eastern Division

	W	L	T	Pct.	Pts.	OP
Miami	14	0	0	1.000	385	171
N.Y. Jets	7	7	0	.500	367	324
Baltimore	5	9	0	.357	235	252
Buffalo	4	9	1	.321	257	377
New England	3	11	0	.214	192	446

Central Division

	W	L	T	Pct.	Pts.	OP
Pittsburgh	11	3	0	.786	343	175
Cleveland*	10	4	0	.714	268	249
Cincinnati	8	6	0	.571	299	229
Houston	1	13	0	.071	164	380

Western Division

	W	L	T	Pct.	Pts.	OP
Oakland	10	3	1	.750	365	248
Kansas City	8	6	0	.571	287	254
Denver	5	9	0	.357	325	350
San Diego	4	9	1	.321	264	344

NATIONAL CONFERENCE

Eastern Division

	W	L	T	Pct.	Pts.	OP
Washington	11	3	0	.786	336	218
Dallas*	10	4	0	.714	319	240
N.Y. Giants	8	6	0	.571	331	247
St. Louis	4	9	1	.321	193	303
Philadelphia	2	11	1	.179	145	352

Central Division

	W	L	T	Pct.	Pts.	OP
Green Bay	10	4	0	.714	304	226
Detroit	8	5	1	.607	339	290
Minnesota	7	7	0	.500	301	252
Chicago	4	9	1	.321	225	275

Western Division

	W	L	T	Pct.	Pts.	OP
San Francisco	8	5	1	.607	353	249
Atlanta	7	7	0	.500	269	274
Los Angeles	6	7	1	.464	291	286
New Orleans	2	11	1	.179	215	361

Wild Card qualifier for playoffs
Divisional playoffs: Pittsburgh 13, Oakland 7; Miami 20, Cleveland 14
AFC Championship: Miami 21, Pittsburgh 17
Divisional playoffs: Dallas 30, San Francisco 28; Washington 16, Green Bay 3
NFC Championship: Washington 26, Dallas 3
Super Bowl VII: Miami (AFC) 14, Washington (NFC) 7

1973

AMERICAN CONFERENCE

Eastern Division

	W	L	T	Pct.	Pts.	OP
Miami	12	2	0	.857	343	150
Buffalo	9	5	0	.643	259	230
New England	5	9	0	.357	258	300
Baltimore	4	10	0	.286	226	341
N.Y. Jets	4	10	0	.286	240	306

Central Division

	W	L	T	Pct.	Pts.	OP
Cincinnati	10	4	0	.714	286	231
Pittsburgh*	10	4	0	.714	347	210
Cleveland	7	5	2	.571	234	255
Houston	1	13	0	.071	199	447

Western Division

	W	L	T	Pct.	Pts.	OP
Oakland	9	4	1	.679	292	175
Denver	7	5	2	.571	354	296
Kansas City	7	5	2	.571	231	192
San Diego	2	11	1	.179	188	386

NATIONAL CONFERENCE

Eastern Division

	W	L	T	Pct.	Pts.	OP
Dallas	10	4	0	.714	382	203
Washington*	10	4	0	.714	325	198
Philadelphia	5	8	1	.393	310	393
St. Louis	4	9	1	.321	286	365
N.Y. Giants	2	11	1	.179	226	362

Central Division

	W	L	T	Pct.	Pts.	OP
Minnesota	12	2	0	.857	296	168
Detroit	6	7	1	.464	271	247
Green Bay	5	7	2	.429	202	259
Chicago	3	11	0	.214	195	334

Western Division

	W	L	T	Pct.	Pts.	OP
Los Angeles	12	2	0	.857	388	178
Atlanta	9	5	0	.643	318	224
New Orleans	5	9	0	.357	163	312
San Francisco	5	9	0	.357	262	319

*Wild Card qualifier for playoffs
Divisional playoffs: Oakland 33, Pittsburgh 14; Miami 34, Cincinnati 16
AFC Championship: Miami 27, Oakland 10
Divisional playoffs: Minnesota 27, Washington 20; Dallas 27, Los Angeles 16
NFC Championship: Minnesota 27, Dallas 10
Super Bowl VIII: Miami (AFC) 24, Minnesota (NFC) 7

1974

AMERICAN CONFERENCE

Eastern Division

	W	L	T	Pct.	Pts.	OP
Miami	11	3	0	.786	327	216
Buffalo*	9	5	0	.643	264	244
New England	7	7	0	.500	348	289
N.Y. Jets	7	7	0	.500	279	300
Baltimore	2	12	0	.143	190	329

Central Division

	W	L	T	Pct.	Pts.	OP
Pittsburgh	10	3	1	.750	305	189
Cincinnati	7	7	0	.500	283	259
Houston	7	7	0	.500	236	282
Cleveland	4	10	0	.286	251	344

Western Division

	W	L	T	Pct.	Pts.	OP
Oakland	12	2	0	.857	355	228
Denver	7	6	1	.536	302	294
Kansas City	5	9	0	.357	233	293
San Diego	5	9	0	.357	212	285

NATIONAL CONFERENCE

Eastern Division

	W	L	T	Pct.	Pts.	OP
St. Louis	10	4	0	.714	285	218
Washington*	10	4	0	.714	320	196
Dallas	8	6	0	.571	297	235
Philadelphia	7	7	0	.500	242	217
N.Y. Giants	2	12	0	.143	195	299

Central Division

	W	L	T	Pct.	Pts.	OP
Minnesota	10	4	0	.714	310	195
Detroit	7	7	0	.500	256	270
Green Bay	6	8	0	.429	210	206
Chicago	4	10	0	.286	152	279

Western Division

	W	L	T	Pct.	Pts.	OP
Los Angeles	10	4	0	.714	263	181
San Francisco	6	8	0	.429	226	236
New Orleans	5	9	0	.357	166	263
Atlanta	3	11	0	.214	111	271

*Wild Card qualifier for playoffs
Divisional playoffs: Oakland 28, Miami 26; Pittsburgh 32, Buffalo 14
AFC Championship: Pittsburgh 24, Oakland 13
Divisional playoffs: Minnesota 30, St. Louis 14; Los Angeles 19, Washington 10
NFC Championship: Minnesota 14, Los Angeles 10
Super Bowl IX: Pittsburgh (AFC) 16, Minnesota (NFC) 6

1975

AMERICAN CONFERENCE

Eastern Division

	W	L	T	Pct.	Pts.	OP
Baltimore	10	4	0	.714	395	269
Miami	10	4	0	.714	357	222
Buffalo	8	6	0	.571	420	355
New England	3	11	0	.214	258	358
N.Y. Jets	3	11	0	.214	258	433

Central Division

	W	L	T	Pct.	Pts.	OP
Pittsburgh	12	2	0	.857	373	162
Cincinnati*	11	3	0	.786	340	246
Houston	10	4	0	.714	293	226
Cleveland	3	11	0	.214	218	372

Western Division

	W	L	T	Pct.	Pts.	OP
Oakland	11	3	0	.786	375	255
Denver	6	8	0	.429	254	307
Kansas City	5	9	0	.357	282	341
San Diego	2	12	0	.143	189	345

NATIONAL CONFERENCE

Eastern Division

	W	L	T	Pct.	Pts.	OP
St. Louis	11	3	0	.786	356	276
Dallas*	10	4	0	.714	350	268
Washington	8	6	0	.571	325	276
N.Y. Giants	5	9	0	.357	216	306
Philadelphia	4	10	0	.286	225	302

Central Division

	W	L	T	Pct.	Pts.	OP
Minnesota	12	2	0	.857	377	180
Detroit	7	7	0	.500	245	262
Chicago	4	10	0	.286	191	379
Green Bay	4	10	0	.286	226	285

Western Division

	W	L	T	Pct.	Pts.	OP
Los Angeles	12	2	0	.857	312	135
San Francisco	5	9	0	.357	255	286
Atlanta	4	10	0	.286	240	289
New Orleans	2	12	0	.143	165	360

Wild Card qualifier for playoffs
Divisional playoffs: Pittsburgh 28, Baltimore 10; Oakland 31, Cincinnati 28
AFC Championship: Pittsburgh 16, Oakland 10
Divisional playoffs: Los Angeles 35, St. Louis 23; Dallas 17, Minnesota 14
NFC Championship: Dallas 37, Los Angeles 7
Super Bowl X: Pittsburgh (AFC) 21, Dallas (NFC) 17

1976

AMERICAN CONFERENCE

Eastern Division

	W	L	T	Pct.	Pts.	OP
Baltimore	11	3	0	.786	417	246
New England*	11	3	0	.786	376	236
Miami	6	8	0	.429	263	264
N.Y. Jets	3	11	0	.214	169	383
Buffalo	2	12	0	.143	245	363

Central Division

	W	L	T	Pct.	Pts.	OP
Pittsburgh	10	4	0	.714	342	138
Cincinnati	10	4	0	.714	335	210
Cleveland	9	5	0	.643	267	287
Houston	5	9	0	.357	222	273

Western Division

	W	L	T	Pct.	Pts.	OP
Oakland	13	1	0	.929	350	237
Denver	9	5	0	.643	315	206
San Diego	6	8	0	.429	248	285
Kansas City	5	9	0	.357	290	376
Tampa Bay	0	14	0	.000	125	412

NATIONAL CONFERENCE

Eastern Division

	W	L	T	Pct.	Pts.	OP
Dallas	11	3	0	.786	296	194
Washington*	10	4	0	.714	291	217
St. Louis	10	4	0	.714	309	267
Philadelphia	4	10	0	.286	165	286
N.Y. Giants	3	11	0	.214	170	250

Central Division

	W	L	T	Pct.	Pts.	OP
Minnesota	11	2	1	.821	305	176
Chicago	7	7	0	.500	253	216
Detroit	6	8	0	.429	262	220
Green Bay	5	9	0	.357	218	299

Western Division

	W	L	T	Pct.	Pts.	OP
Los Angeles	10	3	1	.750	351	190
San Francisco	8	6	0	.571	270	190
Atlanta	4	10	0	.286	172	312
New Orleans	4	10	0	.286	253	346
Seattle	2	12	0	.143	229	429

Wild Card qualifier for playoffs
Divisional playoffs: Oakland 24, New England 21; Pittsburgh 40, Baltimore 14
AFC Championship: Oakland 24, Pittsburgh 7
Divisional playoffs: Minnesota 35, Washington 20; Los Angeles 14, Dallas 12
NFC Championship: Minnesota 24, Los Angeles 13
Super Bowl XI: Oakland (AFC) 32, Minnesota (NFC) 14

1977

AMERICAN CONFERENCE

Eastern Division

	W	L	T	Pct.	Pts.	OP
Baltimore	10	4	0	.714	295	221
Miami	10	4	0	.714	313	197
New England	9	5	0	.643	278	217
N.Y. Jets	3	11	0	.214	191	300
Buffalo	3	11	0	.214	160	313

Central Division

	W	L	T	Pct.	Pts.	OP
Pittsburgh	9	5	0	.643	283	243
Houston	8	6	0	.571	299	230
Cincinnati	8	6	0	.571	238	235
Cleveland	6	8	0	.429	269	267

Western Division

	W	L	T	Pct.	Pts.	OP
Denver	12	2	0	.857	274	148
Oakland*	11	3	0	.786	351	230
San Diego	7	7	0	.500	222	205
Seattle	5	9	0	.357	282	373
Kansas City	2	12	0	.143	225	349

NATIONAL CONFERENCE

Eastern Division

	W	L	T	Pct.	Pts.	OP
Dallas	12	2	0	.857	345	212
Washington	9	5	0	.643	196	189
St. Louis	7	7	0	.500	272	287
Philadelphia	5	9	0	.357	220	207
N.Y. Giants	5	9	0	.357	181	265

Central Division

	W	L	T	Pct.	Pts.	OP
Minnesota	9	5	0	.643	231	227
Chicago*	9	5	0	.643	255	253
Detroit	6	8	0	.429	183	252
Green Bay	4	10	0	.286	134	219
Tampa Bay	2	12	0	.143	103	223

Western Division

	W	L	T	Pct.	Pts.	OP
Los Angeles	10	4	0	.714	302	146
Atlanta	7	7	0	.500	179	129
San Francisco	5	9	0	.357	220	260
New Orleans	3	11	0	.214	232	336

Wild Card qualifier for playoffs

Divisional playoffs: Denver 34, Pittsburgh 21; Oakland 37, Baltimore 31, sudden-death overtime

AFC Championship: Denver 20, Oakland 17

Divisional playoffs: Dallas 37, Chicago 7; Minnesota 14, Los Angeles 7

NFC Championship: Dallas 23, Minnesota 6

Super Bowl XII: Dallas (NFC) 27, Denver (AFC) 10

1978

AMERICAN CONFERENCE

Eastern Division

	W	L	T	Pct.	Pts.	OP
New England	11	5	0	.688	358	286
Miami*	11	5	0	.688	372	254
N.Y. Jets	8	8	0	.500	359	364
Buffalo	5	11	0	.313	302	354
Baltimore	5	11	0	.313	239	421

Central Division

	W	L	T	Pct.	Pts.	OP
Pittsburgh	14	2	0	.875	356	195
Houston*	10	6	0	.625	283	298
Cleveland	8	8	0	.500	334	356
Cincinnati	4	12	0	.250	252	284

Western Division

	W	L	T	Pct.	Pts.	OP
Denver	10	6	0	.625	282	198
Oakland	9	7	0	.563	311	283
Seattle	9	7	0	.563	345	358
San Diego	9	7	0	.563	355	309
Kansas City	4	12	0	.250	243	327

NATIONAL CONFERENCE

Eastern Division

	W	L	T	Pct.	Pts.	OP
Dallas	12	4	0	.750	384	208
Philadelphia*	9	7	0	.563	270	250
Washington	8	8	0	.500	273	283
St. Louis	6	10	0	.375	248	296
N.Y. Giants	6	10	0	.375	264	298

Central Division

	W	L	T	Pct.	Pts.	OP
Minnesota	8	7	1	.531	294	306
Green Bay	8	7	1	.531	249	269
Detroit	7	9	0	.438	290	300
Chicago	7	9	0	.438	253	274
Tampa Bay	5	11	0	.313	241	259

Western Division

	W	L	T	Pct.	Pts.	OP
Los Angeles	12	4	0	.750	316	245
Atlanta*	9	7	0	.563	240	290
New Orleans	7	9	0	.438	281	298
San Francisco	2	14	0	.125	219	350

Wild Card qualifier for playoffs

First-round playoff: Houston 17, Miami 9

Divisional playoffs: Houston 31, New England 14; Pittsburgh 33, Denver 10

AFC Championship: Pittsburgh 34, Houston 5

First-round playoff: Atlanta 14, Philadelphia 13

Divisional playoffs: Dallas 27, Atlanta 20; Los Angeles 34, Minnesota 10

NFC Championship: Dallas 28, Los Angeles 0

Super Bowl XIII: Pittsburgh (AFC) 35, Dallas (NFC) 31

1979

AMERICAN CONFERENCE

Eastern Division

	W	L	T	Pct.	Pts.	OP
Miami	10	6	0	.625	341	257
New England	9	7	0	.563	411	326
N.Y. Jets	8	8	0	.500	337	383
Buffalo	7	9	0	.438	268	279
Baltimore	5	11	0	.313	271	351

Central Division

	W	L	T	Pct.	Pts.	OP
Pittsburgh	12	4	0	.750	416	262
Houston*	11	5	0	.688	362	331
Cleveland	9	7	0	.563	359	352
Cincinnati	4	12	0	.250	337	421

Western Division

	W	L	T	Pct.	Pts.	OP
San Diego	12	4	0	.750	411	246
Denver*	10	6	0	.625	289	262
Seattle	9	7	0	.563	378	372
Oakland	9	7	0	.563	365	337
Kansas City	7	9	0	.438	238	262

NATIONAL CONFERENCE

Eastern Division

	W	L	T	Pct.	Pts.	OP
Dallas	11	5	0	.688	371	313
Philadelphia*	11	5	0	.688	339	282
Washington	10	6	0	.625	348	295
N.Y. Giants	6	10	0	.375	237	323
St. Louis	5	11	0	.313	307	358

Central Division

	W	L	T	Pct.	Pts.	OP
Tampa Bay	10	6	0	.625	273	237
Chicago*	10	6	0	.625	306	249
Minnesota	7	9	0	.438	259	337
Green Bay	5	11	0	.313	246	316
Detroit	2	14	0	.125	219	365

Western Division

	W	L	T	Pct.	Pts.	OP
Los Angeles	9	7	0	.563	323	309
New Orleans	8	8	0	.500	370	360
Atlanta	6	10	0	.375	300	388
San Francisco	2	14	0	.125	308	416

Wild Card qualifier for playoffs

First-round playoff: Houston 13, Denver 7

Divisional playoffs: Houston 17, San Diego 14; Pittsburgh 34, Miami 14

AFC Championship: Pittsburgh 27, Houston 13

First-round playoff: Philadelphia 27, Chicago 17

Divisional playoffs: Tampa Bay 24, Philadelphia 17; Los Angeles 21, Dallas 19

NFC Championship: Los Angeles 9, Tampa Bay 0

Super Bowl XIV: Pittsburgh (AFC) 31, Los Angeles (NFC) 19

1980

AMERICAN CONFERENCE

Eastern Division

	W	L	T	Pct.	Pts.	OP
Buffalo	11	5	0	.688	320	260
New England	10	6	0	.625	441	325
Miami	8	8	0	.500	266	305
Baltimore	7	9	0	.438	355	387
N.Y. Jets	4	12	0	.250	302	395

Central Division

	W	L	T	Pct.	Pts.	OP
Cleveland	11	5	0	.688	357	310
Houston*	11	5	0	.688	295	251
Pittsburgh	9	7	0	.563	352	313
Cincinnati	6	10	0	.375	244	312

Western Division

	W	L	T	Pct.	Pts.	OP
San Diego	11	5	0	.688	418	327
Oakland*	11	5	0	.688	364	306
Kansas City	8	8	0	.500	319	336
Denver	8	8	0	.500	310	323
Seattle	4	12	0	.250	291	408

NATIONAL CONFERENCE

Eastern Division

	W	L	T	Pct.	Pts.	OP
Philadelphia	12	4	0	.750	384	222
Dallas*	12	4	0	.750	454	311
Washington	6	10	0	.375	261	293
St. Louis	5	11	0	.313	299	350
N.Y. Giants	4	12	0	.250	249	425

Central Division

	W	L	T	Pct.	Pts.	OP
Minnesota	9	7	0	.563	317	308
Detroit	9	7	0	.563	334	272
Chicago	7	9	0	.437	304	264
Tampa Bay	5	10	1	.343	271	341
Green Bay	5	10	1	.343	231	371

Western Division

	W	L	T	Pct.	Pts.	OP
Atlanta	12	4	0	.750	405	272
Los Angeles*	11	5	0	.688	424	289
San Francisco	6	10	0	.375	320	415
New Orleans	1	15	0	.063	291	487

Wild Card qualifier for playoffs

First-round playoff: Oakland 27, Houston 7

Divisional playoffs: San Diego 20, Buffalo 14; Oakland 14, Cleveland 12

AFC Championship: Oakland 34, San Diego 27

First-round playoff: Dallas 34, Los Angeles 13

Divisional playoffs: Philadelphia 31, Minnesota 16; Dallas 30, Atlanta 27

NFC Championship: Philadelphia 20, Dallas 7

Super Bowl XV: Oakland (AFC) 27, Philadelphia (NFC) 10

1981

AMERICAN CONFERENCE

Eastern Division

	W	L	T	Pct.	Pts.	OP
Miami	11	4	1	.719	345	275
N.Y. Jets*	10	5	1	.656	355	287
Buffalo*	10	6	0	.625	311	276
Baltimore	2	14	0	.125	259	533
New England	2	14	0	.125	322	370

Central Division

	W	L	T	Pct.	Pts.	OP
Cincinnati	12	4	0	.750	421	304
Pittsburgh	8	8	0	.500	356	297
Houston	7	9	0	.438	281	355
Cleveland	5	11	0	.313	276	375

Western Division

	W	L	T	Pct.	Pts.	OP
San Diego	10	6	0	.625	478	390
Denver	10	6	0	.625	321	289
Kansas City	9	7	0	.563	343	290
Oakland	7	9	0	.438	273	343
Seattle	6	10	0	.375	322	388

NATIONAL CONFERENCE

Eastern Division

	W	L	T	Pct.	Pts.	OP
Dallas	12	4	0	.750	367	277
Philadelphia*	10	6	0	.625	368	221
N.Y. Giants*	9	7	0	.563	295	257
Washington	8	8	0	.500	347	349
St. Louis	7	9	0	.438	315	408

Central Division

	W	L	T	Pct.	Pts.	OP
Tampa Bay	9	7	0	.563	315	268
Detroit	8	8	0	.500	397	322
Green Bay	8	8	0	.500	324	361
Minnesota	7	9	0	.438	325	369
Chicago	6	10	0	.375	253	324

Western Division

	W	L	T	Pct.	Pts.	OP
San Francisco	13	3	0	.813	357	250
Atlanta	7	9	0	.438	426	355
Los Angeles	6	10	0	.375	303	351
New Orleans	4	12	0	.250	207	378

Wild card qualifier for playoffs
First-round playoff: Buffalo 31, N.Y. Jets 27
Divisional playoffs: San Diego 41, Miami 38 (OT); Cincinnati 28, Buffalo 21
AFC Championship: Cincinnati 27, San Diego 7
First-round playoff: N.Y. Giants 27, Philadelphia 21
Divisional playoffs: Dallas 38, Tampa Bay 0; San Francisco 38, N.Y. Giants 24
NFC Championship: San Francisco 28, Dallas 27
Super Bowl XVI: San Francisco (NFC) 26, Cincinnati (AFC) 21

*1982

AMERICAN CONFERENCE

	W	L	T	Pct.	Pts.	OP
L.A. Raiders	8	1	0	.889	260	200
Miami	7	2	0	.778	198	131
Cincinnati	7	2	0	.778	232	177
Pittsburgh	6	3	0	.667	204	146
San Diego	6	3	0	.667	288	221
N.Y. Jets	6	3	0	.667	245	166
New England	5	4	0	.556	143	157
Cleveland	4	5	0	.444	140	182
Buffalo	4	5	0	.444	150	154
Seattle	4	5	0	.444	127	147
Kansas City	3	6	0	.333	176	184
Denver	2	7	0	.222	148	226
Houston	1	8	0	.111	136	245
Baltimore	0	8	1	.063	113	236

NATIONAL CONFERENCE

	W	L	T	Pct.	Pts.	OP
Washington	8	1	0	.889	190	128
Dallas	6	3	0	.667	226	145
Green Bay	5	3	1	.611	226	169
Minnesota	5	4	0	.556	187	198
Atlanta	5	4	0	.556	183	199
St. Louis	5	4	0	.556	135	170
Tampa Bay	5	4	0	.556	158	178
Detroit	4	5	0	.444	181	176
New Orleans	4	5	0	.444	129	160
N.Y. Giants	4	5	0	.444	164	160
San Francisco	3	6	0	.333	209	206
Chicago	3	6	0	.333	141	174
Philadelphia	3	6	0	.333	191	195
L.A. Rams	2	7	0	.222	200	250

Top eight teams in each Conference qualified for playoffs under format necessitated by strike-shortened season

First-round playoffs: Miami 28, New England 13; L.A. Raiders 27, Cleveland 10; N.Y. Jets 44, Cincinnati 17; San Diego 31, Pittsburgh 28
Second-round playoffs: N.Y. Jets 17, L.A. Raiders 14; Miami 34, San Diego 13
AFC Championship: Miami 14, N.Y. Jets 0
First-round playoffs: Green Bay 41, St. Louis 16; Washington 31, Detroit 7; Minnesota 30, Atlanta 24; Dallas 30, Tampa Bay 17
Second-round playoffs: Washington 21, Minnesota 7; Dallas 37, Green Bay 26
NFC Championship: Washington 31, Dallas 17
Super Bowl XVII: Washington 27, Miami 17

1983

AMERICAN CONFERENCE

Eastern Division

	W	L	T	Pct.	Pts.	OP
Miami	12	4	0	.750	389	250
New England	8	8	0	.500	274	289
Buffalo	8	8	0	.500	283	351
Baltimore	7	9	0	.438	264	354
N.Y. Jets	7	9	0	.438	313	331

Central Division

	W	L	T	Pct.	Pts.	OP
Pittsburgh	10	6	0	.625	355	303
Cleveland	9	7	0	.562	356	342
Cincinnati	7	9	0	.438	346	302
Houston	2	14	0	.125	288	460

Western Division

	W	L	T	Pct.	Pts.	OP
L.A. Raiders	12	4	0	.750	442	338
Seattle*	9	7	0	.562	403	397
Denver*	9	7	0	.562	302	327
San Diego	6	10	0	.375	358	462
Kansas City	6	10	0	.375	386	367

NATIONAL CONFERENCE

Eastern Division

	W	L	T	Pct.	Pts.	OP
Washington	14	2	0	.875	541	332
Dallas*	12	4	0	.750	479	360
St. Louis	8	7	1	.531	374	428
Philadelphia	5	11	0	.313	233	322
N.Y. Giants	3	12	1	.219	267	347

Central Division

	W	L	T	Pct.	Pts.	OP
Detroit	9	7	0	.562	347	286
Green Bay	8	8	0	.500	429	439
Chicago	8	8	0	.500	311	301
Minnesota	8	8	0	.500	316	348
Tampa Bay	2	14	0	.125	241	380

Western Division

	W	L	T	Pct.	Pts.	OP
San Francisco	10	6	0	.625	432	293
L.A. Rams*	9	7	0	.562	361	344
New Orleans	8	8	0	.500	319	337
Atlanta	7	9	0	.438	370	389

*Wild card qualifier for playoffs
First-round playoff: Seattle 31, Denver 7
Divisional playoffs: Seattle 27, Miami 20; L.A. Raiders 38, Pittsburgh 10
AFC Championship: L.A. Raiders 30, Seattle 14
First-round playoff: L.A. Rams 24, Dallas 17
Divisional playoffs: San Francisco 24, Detroit 23; Washington 51, L.A. Rams 7
NFC Championship: Washington 24, San Francisco 21
Super Bowl XVIII: L.A. Raiders 38, Washington 9

1984

NATIONAL CONFERENCE

Eastern Division

	W	L	T	Pct.	Pts.	OP
Washington	11	5	0	.688	426	310
N.Y. Giants*	9	7	0	.563	299	301
St. Louis	9	7	0	.563	423	345
Dallas	9	7	0	.563	308	308
Philadelphia	6	9	1	.406	278	320

Central Division

	W	L	T	Pct.	Pts.	OP
Chicago	10	6	0	.625	325	248
Green Bay	8	8	0	.500	390	309
Tampa Bay	6	10	0	.375	335	380
Detroit	4	11	1	.281	283	408
Minnesota	3	13	0	.188	276	484

Western Division

	W	L	T	Pct.	Pts.	OP
San Francisco	15	1	0	.939	475	227
L.A. Rams*	10	6	0	.625	346	316
New Orleans	7	9	0	.438	298	361
Atlanta	4	12	0	.250	281	382

AMERICAN CONFERENCE

Eastern Division

	W	L	T	Pct.	Pts.	OP
Miami	14	2	0	.875	513	298
New England	9	7	0	.563	362	352
N.Y. Jets	7	9	0	.438	332	364
Indianapolis	4	12	0	.250	239	414
Buffalo	2	14	0	.125	250	454

Central Division

	W	L	T	Pct.	Pts.	OP
Pittsburgh	9	7	0	.563	387	310
Cincinnati	8	8	0	.500	339	339
Cleveland	5	11	0	.313	250	297
Houston	3	13	0	.188	240	437

Western Division

	W	L	T	Pct.	Pts.	OP
Denver	13	3	0	.813	353	241
Seattle*	12	4	0	.750	418	282
L.A. Raiders*	11	5	0	.688	368	278
Kansas City	8	8	0	.500	314	324
San Diego	7	9	0	.438	394	413

*Wild card qualifier for playoffs
Wild Card Game: N.Y. Giants 16, L.A. Rams 13
NFC Divisional playoffs: San Francisco 21, N.Y. Giants 10; Chicago 23, Washington 19
NFC Championship: San Francisco 23, Chicago 0
Wild Card Game: Seattle 13, L.A. Raiders 7
AFC Divisional playoffs: Miami 31, Seattle 10; Pittsburgh 24, Denver 17
AFC Championship: Miami 45, Pittsburgh 28
Super Bowl XIX: San Francisco 38, Miami 16

1985

AMERICAN CONFERENCE

Eastern Division

	W	L	T	Pct.	Pts.	OP
Miami	12	4	0	.750	428	320
N.Y. Jets	11	5	0	.688	393	264
New England	11	5	0	.688	362	290
Indianapolis	5	11	0	.313	320	386
Buffalo	2	14	0	.125	200	381

CENTRAL DIVISION

	W	L	T	Pct.	Pts.	OP
Cleveland	8	8	0	.500	287	294
Cincinnati	7	9	0	.438	441	437
Pittsburgh	7	9	0	.438	379	355
Houston	5	11	0	.313	284	412

WESTERN DIVISION

	W	L	T	Pct.	Pts.	OP
L.A. Raiders	12	4	0	.750	354	308
Denver	11	5	0	.688	380	329
Seattle	8	8	0	.500	349	303
San Diego	8	8	0	.500	467	435
Kansas City	6	10	0	.375	327	360

NATIONAL CONFERENCE

Eastern Division

	W	L	T	Pct.	Pts.	OP
Dallas	10	6	0	.625	357	333
N.Y. Giants	10	6	0	.625	399	283
Washington	10	6	0	.625	298	313
Philadelphia	7	9	0	.438	286	310
St. Louis	5	11	0	.313	279	415

CENTRAL DIVISION

	W	L	T	Pct.	Pts.	OP
Chicago	15	1	0	.938	456	198
Green Bay	8	8	0	.500	337	355
Minnesota	7	9	0	.438	346	359
Detroit	7	9	0	.438	307	366
Tampa Bay	2	14	0	.125	294	448

WESTERN DIVISION

	W	L	T	Pct.	Pts.	OP
L.A. Rams	11	5	0	.688	340	287
San Francisco	10	6	0	.625	411	263
New Orleans	5	11	0	.313	294	401
Atlanta	4	12	0	.250	282	452

Wild Card Game: New England 26, N.Y. Jets 14
AFC Divisional playoffs: Miami 24, Cleveland 21; New England 27, L.A. Raiders 20
AFC Championship: New England 31, Miami 14
Wild Card Game: N.Y. Giants 17, San Francisco 3
NFC Divisional playoffs: L.A. Rams 20, Dallas 0; Chicago 21, N.Y. Giants 0
NFC Championship: Chicago 24, L.A. Rams 0
Super Bowl XX: Chicago 46, New England 10

1986

AMERICAN CONFERENCE

Eastern Division

	W	L	T	Pct.	Pts.	OP
N.Y. Giants	14	2	0	.875	371	236
Washington	12	4	0	.750	368	296
Dallas	7	9	0	.438	346	337
Philadelphia	5	10	1	.344	256	312
St. Louis	4	11	1	.281	218	351

Central Division

	W	L	T	Pct.	Pts.	OP
Chicago	14	2	0	.875	352	187
Minnesota	9	7	0	.563	398	273
Detroit	5	11	0	.313	277	326
Green Bay	4	12	0	.250	254	418
Tampa Bay	2	14	0	.125	239	473

Western Division

	W	L	T	Pct.	Pts.	OP
San Francisco	10	5	1	.656	374	247
L.A. Rams	10	6	0	.625	309	267
Atlanta	7	8	1	.469	280	280
New Orleans	7	9	0	.438	288	287

NATIONAL CONFERENCE

Eastern Division

	W	L	T	Pct.	Pts.	OP
New England	11	5	0	.688	412	307
N.Y. Jets	10	6	0	.625	364	386
Miami	8	8	0	.500	430	405
Buffalo	4	12	0	.250	287	348
Indianapolis	3	13	0	.188	229	400

Central Division

	W	L	T	Pct.	Pts.	OP
Cleveland	12	4	0	.750	391	310
Cincinnati	10	6	0	.625	409	394
Pittsburgh	6	10	0	.375	307	336
Houston	5	11	0	.313	274	329

Western Division

	W	L	T	Pct.	Pts.	OP
Denver	11	5	0	.688	378	327
Kansas City	10	6	0	.625	358	326
Seattle	10	6	0	.625	366	293
L.A. Raiders	8	8	0	.500	323	346
San Diego	4	12	0	.250	335	396

NFC Wild Card Game: Washington 19, L.A. Rams 7
NFC Divisional playoffs: Washington 27, Chicago 13; N.Y. Giants 49, San Francisco 3
NFC Championship: N.Y. Giants 17, Washington 0
AFC Wild Card Game: N.Y. Jets 35, Kansas City 15
AFC Divisional playoffs: Cleveland 23, N.Y. Jets 20 (2 OT); Denver 22, New England 17
AFC Championship: Denver 23, Cleveland 20 (OT)
Super Bowl XXI: N.Y. Giants 39, Denver 20

The down side of Super Bowl XXI for John Elway.

Skins' Ricky Sanders scores on pass in Super Bowl XXII.

1987

NATIONAL CONFERENCE

Eastern Division

	W	L	T	Pct.	Pts.	OP
Washington	11	4	0	.733	379	285
St. Louis	7	8	0	.467	362	368
Dallas	7	8	0	.467	340	348
Philadelphia	7	8	0	.467	337	380
N.Y. Giants	6	9	0	.400	280	312

Central Division

	W	L	T	Pct.	Pts.	OP
Chicago	11	4	0	.733	356	282
Minnesota	8	7	0	.533	336	335
Green Bay	5	9	1	.367	255	300
Tampa Bay	4	11	0	.267	286	360
Detroit	4	11	0	.267	269	384

Western Division

	W	L	T	Pct.	Pts.	OP
San Francisco	13	2	0	.867	459	253
New Orleans	12	3	0	.800	422	283
L.A. Rams	6	9	0	.400	317	361
Atlanta	3	12	0	.200	205	436

AMERICAN CONFERENCE

Eastern Division

	W	L	T	Pct.	Pts.	OP
Indianapolis	9	6	0	.600	300	238
New England	8	7	0	.533	320	293
Miami	8	7	0	.533	362	335
Buffalo	7	8	0	.467	270	305
N.Y. Jets	6	9	0	.400	334	360

Central Division

	W	L	T	Pct.	Pts.	OP
Cleveland	10	5	0	.667	390	239
Houston	9	6	0	.600	345	349
Pittsburgh	8	7	0	.533	285	299
Cincinnati	4	11	0	.267	285	370

Western Division

	W	L	T	Pct.	Pts.	OP
Denver	10	4	1	.700	379	288
Seattle	9	6	0	.600	371	314
San Diego	8	7	0	.533	253	317
L.A. Raiders	5	10	0	.333	301	289
Kansas City	4	11	0	.267	273	388

NFC Wild Card Game: Minnesota 44, New Orleans 10
NFC Divisional playoffs: Minnesota 36, San Francisco 24; Wash. 21, Chicago 17
NFC Championship: Washington 17, Minnesota 10
AFC Wild Card Game: Houston 23, Seattle 20 (OT)
AFC Divisional playoffs: Cleveland 38, Indianapolis 21; Denver 34, Houston 10
AFC Championship: Denver 38, Cleveland 33
Super Bowl XXII: Washington 42, Denver 10

1988

AMERICAN CONFERENCE

Eastern Division

	W	L	T	Pct.	Pts.	OP
Buffalo	12	4	0	.750	329	237
Indianapolis	9	7	0	.563	354	315
New England	9	7	0	.563	250	284
N.Y. Jets	8	7	1	.531	372	354
Miami	6	10	0	.375	319	380

Central Division

	W	L	T	Pct.	Pts.	OP
Cincinnati	12	4	0	.750	448	329
Cleveland	10	6	0	.625	304	288
Houston	10	6	0	.625	424	365
Pittsburgh	5	11	0	.313	336	421

Western Division

	W	L	T	Pct.	Pts.	OP
Seattle	9	7	0	.563	339	329
Denver	8	8	0	.500	327	352
L.A. Raiders	7	9	0	.438	325	369
San Diego	6	10	0	.375	231	332
Kansas City	4	11	1	.281	254	320

NATIONAL CONFERENCE

Eastern Division

	W	L	T	Pct.	Pts.	OP
Philadelphia	10	6	0	.625	379	319
N.Y. Giants	10	6	0	.625	359	304
Washington	7	9	0	.438	345	387
Phoenix	7	9	0	.438	344	398
Dallas	3	13	0	.188	265	381

Central Division

	W	L	T	Pct.	Pts.	OP
Chicago	12	4	0	.750	312	215
Minnesota	11	5	0	.688	406	233
Tampa Bay	5	11	0	.313	261	350
Detroit	4	12	0	.250	220	313
Green Bay	4	12	0	.250	240	315

Western Division

	W	L	T	Pct.	Pts.	OP
San Francisco	10	6	0	.625	369	294
L.A. Rams	10	6	0	.625	407	293
New Orleans	10	6	0	.625	312	283
Atlanta	5	11	0	.313	244	315

AFC Wild Card Game: Houston 24, Cleveland 23
AFC Divisional playoffs: Cincinnati 21, Seattle 13; Buffalo 17, Houston 10
AFC Championship: Cincinnati 21, Buffalo 10
NFC Wild Card Game: Minnesota 28, L.A. Rams 17
NFC Divisional playoffs: Chicago 20, Philadelphia 12; San Francisco 34, Minnesota 9
NFC Championship: San Francisco 28, Chicago 3
Super Bowl XXIII: San Francisco 20, Cincinnati 16

1989 NFL DRAFT

Player	Order No.	Pos.	College	Club	Round
Aeilts, Rick	214	TE	S.E. Missouri	Cleveland	8
Affholter, Erik	110	WR	Southern California	Washington	4
Aikman, Troy	1	QB	UCLA	Dallas	1
Andrews, Michael	137	DB	Alcorn State	Buffalo	5
Andrews, Ricky	260	LB	Washington	San Diego	10
Ankrom, Scott	308	WR	Texas Christian	Dallas	12
Armstrong, Trace	12	DE	Florida	Chicago	1
Arnold, David	118	DB	Michigan	Pittsburgh	5
Asbeck, Chris	201	NT	Cincinnati	Pittsburgh	8
Atwater, Steve	20	DB	Arkansas	Denver	1
Ball, Eirc	35	RB	UCLA	Cincinnati	2
Barber, Mike	112	WR	Marshall	San Francisco	4
Batiste, Dana	232	LB	Texas A&M	Miami	9
Baum, Mike	295	DE	Northwestern	Seattle	11
Bax, Carl	200	G	Missouri	Tampa Bay	8
Baxter, Brad	303	RB	Alabama State	Minnesota	11
Becker, Chris	261	P	Texas Christian	Phoenix	10
Beebe, Don	82	WR	Chadron, Neb.	Buffalo	3
Bell, Jim	289	RB	Boston College	San Francisco	11
Benson, Mitchell	72	DT	Texas Christian	Indianapolis	3
Bethune, George	188	LB	Alabama	Los Angeles Rams	7
Bob, Adam	265	LB	Texas A&M	New York Jets	10
Bowick, Tony	313	NT	Tenn.-Chattanooga	Atlanta	12
Bratton, Mel	180	RB	Miami	Denver	7
Braxton, David	52	LB	Wake Forest	Minnesota	2
Brinson, Dana	204	WR	Nebraska	San Diego	8
Brock, Matt	58	DE	Oregon	Green Bay	3
Brothers, Richard	189	DB	Arkansas	Chicago	7
Brown, Anthony	209	RB	West Virginia	New York Jets	8
Brown, J.B.	315	DB	Maryland	Miami	12
Brown, Marlon	328	LB	Memphis State	Cleveland	12
Buddenberg, John	274	T	Akron	Cleveland	10
Burch, John	207	RB	Tennese-Martin	Phoenix	8
Butts, Anthony	264	DT	Mississippi State	Denver	10
Butts, Marion	183	RB	Florida State	San Diego	7
Byrd, Dennis	42	DE	Tulsa	New York Jets	2
Cadore, Mike	327	WR	Eastern Kentucky	New Orleans	12
Carlson, Jeff	102	QB	Weber State	Los Angeles Rams	4
Carrington, Darren	134	DB	Northern Arizona	Denver	5
Carter, Rod	252	LB	Miami	Dallas	10
Cheattom, Carlo	276	DB	Auburn	Buffalo	10
Chenault, Chris	222	LB	Kentucky	Cincinnati	8
Childress, Freddie	55	G	Arkansas	Cincinnati	2
Chubb, Aaron	324	LB	Georgia	New England	12
Coleman, Eric	43	DB	Wyoming	New England	2
Collins, Shawn	27	WR	Northern Arizona	Atlanta	1
Cook, Marv	63	TE	Iowa	New England	3
Cribbs, James	309	DE	Memphis State	Detroit	12
Crockett, Ray	86	DB	Baylor	Detroit	4
Crockett, Willis	119	LB	Georgia Tech	Dallas	5
Cross, Howard	158	TE	Alabama	New York Giants	6

Oklahoma State RB Barry Sanders (No. 3) is a Lion.

Player	Order No.	Pos.	College	Club	Round
Darrington, Charles	233	TE	Kentucky	Washington	9
Davis, Pat	231	TE	Syracuse	San Diego	9
De Long, Keith	28	LB	Tennessee	San Francisco	1
Dilweg, Anthony	74	QB	Duke	Green Bay	3
Dixon, Titus	153	WR	Troy State	New York Jets	6
Doctor, Sean	164	RB	Marshall	Buffalo	6
Drummond, Robert	76	RB	Syracuse	Philadelphia	3
Du Bose, William	314	RB	South Carolina State	Indianapolis	12
Duncan, Herb	302	WR	Northern Arizona	Tampa Bay	11
Dunn, Chris	229	LB	Cal Poly-Obispo	Atlanta	9
Dykes, Hart Lee	16	WR	Oklahoma State	New England	1
Dyko, Chris	221	T	Washington State	Chicago	8
Edeen, David	128	DE	Wyoming	Phoenix	5
Egu, Patrick	230	RB	Nevada-Reno	Tampa Bay	9
Elkins, Mike	32	QB	Wake Forest	Kansas City	2
Fenner, Derrick	268	RB	North Carolina	Seattle	10
Florence, Anthony	90	DB	Bethune-Cookman	Tampa Bay	4
Floyd, Victor	287	RB	Florida State	San Diego	11
Foger, Charvez	196	RB	Nevada-Reno	Dallas	8
Fontenot, Jerry	65	G	Texas A&M	Chicago	3
Ford, John	30	WR	Virginia	Detroit	2
Francis, Jeff	140	QB	Tennessee	Los Angeles Raiders	6
Franks, David	238	G	Connecticut	Seattle	9

Player	Order No.	Pos.	College	Club	Round
Gainer, Derrick	205	RB	Florida A&M	Los Angeles Raiders	8
Gannon, Chris	73	DE	S.W. Louisiana	New England	3
Gary, Cleveland	26	RB	Miami	Los Angeles Rams	1
Gilbert, Greg	136	LB	Alabama	Chicago	5
Glover, Deval	259	WR	Syracuse	Miami	10
Gooden, Gary	235	DB	Indiana	Los Angeles Raiders	9
Goss, Antonio	319	LB	North Carolina	San Francisco	12
Graham, Jeff	87	QB	Cal State-Long Beach	Green Bay	4
Granger, Ty	257	T	Clemson	Tampa Bay	10
Graybill, Mike	187	T	Boston U.	Cleveland	7
Green, Mark	130	RB	Notre Dame	Chicago	5
Green, Paul	208	TE	Southern California	Denver	8
Greene, A.J.	245	DB	Wake Forest	New York Giants	9
Griffin, Willie	290	DE	Nebraska	Tampa Bay	11
Griggs, David	186	LB	Virginia	New Orleans	7
Grossman, Burt	8	DE	Pittsburgh	San Diego	1
Guyton, Myron	218	DB	Eastern Kentucky	New York Giants	8
Hadley, Fred	213	WR	Mississippi State	New Orleans	8
Hager, Britt	81	LB	Texas	Philadelphia	3
Hale, Chris	193	DB	Southern California	Buffalo	7
Hall, Courtney	37	C	Rice	San Diego	2
Hall, Mark	169	DE	S.W. Louisiana State	Green Bay	7
Hamilton, Darrell	69	T	North Carolina	Denver	3
Harmon, Rudy	251	LB	Louisiana State	San Francisco	9
Harper, LaSalle	243	LB	Arkansas	Chicago	9
Harris, Elroy	71	RB	Eastern Kentucky	Seattle	3
Harris, Rod	104	WR	Texas A&M	Houston	4
Hartlieb, Chuck	325	QB	Iowa	Houston	12
Harvey, Richard	305	LB	Tulane	Buffalo	11
Haselrig, Carlton	312	DE	Pittsburgh	Pittsburgh	12
Haverdink, Kevin	133	T	Western Michigan	New Orleans	5
Hawkins, Bill	21	DE	Miami	Los Angeles Rams	1
Heck, Andy	15	T	Notre Dame	Seattle	1
Henderson, Joe	273	RB	Iowa State	New Orleans	10
Henderson, Keith	84	RB	Georgia	San Francisco	3
Hendrickson, Steve	167	LB	California	San Francisco	6
Hendrix, Kevin	179	LB	South Carolina	Washington	7
Henke, Brad	105	NT	Arizona	New York Giants	4
Henley, Darryl	53	DB	UCLA	Los Angeles Rams	2
Henry, James	103	DB	So. Mississippi	Seattle	4
Hill, Derek	61	WR	Arizona	Pittsburgh	3
Hill, Eric	10	LB	Louisiana State	Phoenix	1
Hinz, Tony	294	RB	Harvard	New England	11
Holloway, Cornell	256	DB	Pittsburgh	Cincinnati	10
Holmes, Artie	293	DB	Washington State	New York Jets	11
Holmes, David	92	DB	Syracuse	Miami	4
Hunter, Ivy Joe	182	RB	Kentucky	Indianapolis	7
Hunter, Jeffrey	291	DE	Albany State	Phoenix	11
Hunter, John	80	T	Brigham Young	Minnesota	3
Hurst, Maurice	96	DB	Southern U.	New England	4
Ingram, Darryl	108	TE	California	Minnesota	4
Jacke, Chris	142	K	Texas-El Paso	Green Bay	6
Jackson, Alfred	135	WR	San Diego State	Los Angeles Rams	5
Jackson, Charles	262	DT	Jackson State	Los Angeles Raiders	10
Jackson, Greg	78	DB	Louisiana State	New York Giants	3
Jackson, Johnny	122	DB	Houston	San Francisco	5
Jackson, Tim	224	DB	Nebraska	Dallas	9
Javis, John	320	WR	Howard	Denver	12

Browns grabbed Texas RB Eric Metcalf as 13th choice.

Pats picked Oklahoma State WR Hart Lee Dykes (No. 16).

Clemson CB Donnell Woolford wound up a Bear (No. 11).

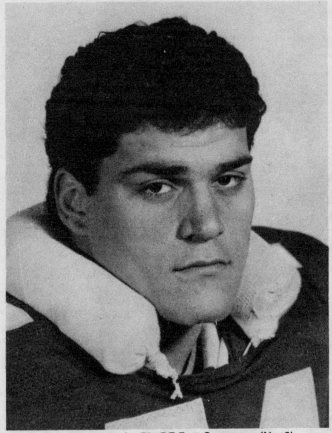

Chargers went for Pitt DE Burt Grossman (No. 8).

Player	Order No.	Pos.	College	Club	Round
Jean, Bob	278	QB	New Hampshire	Cincinnati	10
Jenkins, A.J.	228	DE	Cal State-Fullerton	Pittsburgh	9
Jennings, Keith	113	TE	Clemson	Dallas	5
Jessie, Ben	254	DB	S.W. Texas State	Green Bay	10
Johnson, A.J.	149	DB	S.W. Texas State	Washington	6
Johnson, David	174	DB	Kentucky	Pittsburgh	7
Johnson, Jimmy	316	TE	Howard	Washington	12
Johnson, Tracy	271	RB	Clemson	Houston	10
Johnson, Undra	172	RB	West Virginia	Atlanta	7
Johnson, Wayne	296	QB	Georgia	Indianapolis	11
Johnston, Daryl	39	RB	Syracuse	Dallas	2

Player	Order No.	Pos.	College	Club	Round
Joines, Vernon	116	WR	Maryland	Cleveland	5
Jones, Bill	311	RB	S.W. Texas State	Kansas City	12
Jones, Keith	62	RB	Illinois	Atlanta	3
Jones, Scott	334	T	Washington	Cincinnati	12
Jones, Terrence	195	QB	Tulane	San Diego	7
Jordan, Brian	173	DB	Richmond	Buffalo	7
Karpinski, Keith	282	LB	Penn State	Detroit	11
Kaumeyer, Thom	148	DB	Oregon	Los Angeles Rams	6
King, Thomas	198	DB	S.W. Louisiana	Green Bay	8
Kirby, Scott	225	T	Arizona State	Green Bay	9
Kirk, Vernon	242	TE	Pittsburgh	Los Angeles Rams	9
Kolesar, John	109	WR	Michigan	Buffalo	4
Kors, R.J.	322	DB	Cal State-Long Beach	Seattle	12
Kozak, Scott	50	LB	Oregon	Houston	2
Kramer, Kyle	114	DB	Bowling Green	Cleveland	5
Kratch, Bob	64	G	Iowa	New York Giants	3
Lageman, Jeff	14	LB	Virginia	New York Jets	1
Lake, Carnell	34	DB	UCLA	Pittsburgh	2
Larson, Kurt	212	LB	Michigan State	Indianapolis	8
Lawson, Jamie	117	RB	Nicholls State	Tampa Bay	5
Leggett, Jerry	246	LB	Cal State-Fullerton	New Orleans	9
Lindstrom, Eric	178	LB	Boston College	New England	7
Little, Derrick	154	LB	South Carolina	Tampa Bay	6
Lloyd, Doug	156	RB	North Dakota State	Los Angeles Raiders	6
Lowe, Rodney	272	DE	Mississippi	New York Giants	10
Mac Cready, Derek	226	DE	Ohio State	Detroit	9
Mackall, William	239	WR	Tennessee-Martin	Indianapolis	9
Mandarich, Tony	2	T	Michigan State	Green Bay	1
Marlatt, Pat	237	DT	West Virginia	New York Jets	9
Marshall, Derrell	332	T	Southern California	Buffalo	12
Martin, Tony	126	WR	Mesa (Colo.)	New York Jets	5
Martin, Wayne	19	DE	Arkansas	New Orleans	1
Massey, Robert	46	DB	N. Carolina Central	New Orleans	2
Mayes, Mike	106	DB	Louisiana State	New Orleans	4
Mays, Alvoid	217	DB	West Virginia	Houston	8
Mc Cullough, Richard	97	DE	Clemson	Denver	4
Mc Donald, Quintus	155	LB	Penn State	Indianapolis	6
Mc Dowell, Bubba	77	DB	Miami	Houston	3
Mc Gee, Norm	307	WR	North Dakota	San Francisco	11
Mc Govern, Rob	255	LB	Holy Cross	Kansas City	10
Mc Nair, Todd	220	RB	Temple	Kansas City	8
Mc Neal, Travis	101	TE	Tenn.-Chattanooga	Seattle	4
Mc Neil, Emanuel	267	DT	Tenn.-Martin	New England	10
Meggett, Dave	132	RB	Towson State	New York Giants	5
Messner, Mark	161	LB	Michigan	Los Angeles Rams	6
Metcalf, Eric	13	RB	Texas	Cleveland	1
Mickel, Jeff	163	T	Eastern Washington	Minnesota	6
Mickles, Joe	317	RB	Mississippi	Washington	12
Millikan, Todd	270	TE	Nebraska	Chicago	10
Mitchel, Eric	165	RB	Oklahoma	New England	6
Mohr, Chris	146	P	Alabama	Tampa Bay	6
Montgomery, Glenn	131	NT	Houston	Houston	5
Moore, Stevon	181	DB	Mississippi	New York Jets	7
Mott, Joe	70	LB	Iowa	New York Jets	3
Mounts, Rod	284	G	Texas A&I	Tampa Bay	11
Mrosko, Bob	244	TE	Penn State	Houston	9
Nelms, Joe	297	DT	California	Chicago	11
Nelson, Todd	318	G	Wisconsin	Phoenix	12

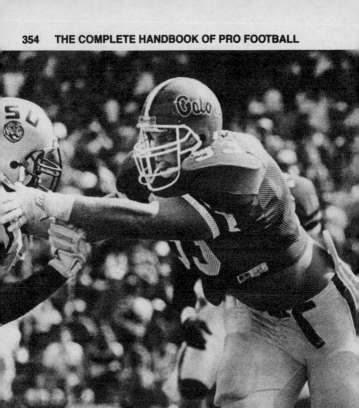

Florida DE Trace Armstrong is a Bear first-rounder.

Michigan State WR Andre Rison was Colts' first choice.

*Tom Ricketts, Pitt OT
Steelers (No. 24)*

*Brod Thomas, Nebraska LB
Buccaneers (No. 6)*

*Steve Atwater, Arkansas S
Broncos (No. 20)*

*Cleveland Gary, Miami RB
Rams (No. 26)*

*Derrick Thomas, Alabama LB
Chiefs (No. 4)*

*Wayne Martin, Arkansas DE
Saints (No. 19)*

Player	Order No.	Pos.	College	Club	Round
Nettles, Mike	184	DB	Memphis State	Seattle	7
Nicholson, Calvin	300	DB	Oregon State	New Orleans	11
Norris, Darron	240	RB	Texas	New England	9
Norwood, Ralph	38	T	Louisiana State	Atlanta	2
Oliver, Louis	25	DB	Florida	Miami	1
Olsavsky, Jerry	258	LB	Pittsburgh	Pittsburgh	10
Orlando, Bo	157	DB	West Virginia	Houston	6
Owens, Kerry	89	LB	Arkansas	Cincinnati	4
Parker, Chris	197	DT	West Virginia	Detroit	8
Paterra, Greg	286	RB	Slippery Rock	Atlanta	11
Paul, Markus	95	DB	Syracuse	Chicago	4
Peebles, Danny	33	WR	North Carolina State	Tampa Bay	2
Peete, Lawrence	115	DT	Nebraska	Detroit	5
Peete, Rodney	141	QB	Southern California	Detroit	6
Peterson, Kevin	168	LB	Northwestern	Dallas	7
Petry, Stanley	88	DB	Texas Christian	Kansas City	4
Phillips, Anthony	333	G	Oklahoma	Chicago	12
Phillips, Jack	227	DB	Alcorn State	Kansas City	9
Phillips, Jason	253	WR	Houston	Detroit	10
Phillips, Kim	79	DB	North Texas State	New Orleans	3
Plocki, Dan	301	K	Maryland	Cleveland	11
Popp, Dave	175	T	Eastern Illinois	New York Giants	7
Powers, Warren	47	DE	Maryland	Denver	2
Pritchett, Wes	147	LB	Notre Dame	Miami	6
Query, Jeff	124	WR	Millikin	Green Bay	5
Rabold, Pat	249	DT	Wyoming	Buffalo	9
Reeves, Walter	40	TE	Auburn	Phoenix	2
Rice, Rodney	210	DB	Brigham Young	New England	8
Ricketts, Tom	24	T	Pittsburgh	Pittsburgh	1
Rinehart, Jerome	299	LB	Tenn.-Martin	New York Giants	11
Rison, Andre	22	WR	Michigan State	Indianapolis	1
Robbins, Tracy	75	T	Michigan State	Los Angeles Rams	3
Robinson, Lybrant	139	DE	Delaware State	Washington	5
Rocker, Tracy	66	DT	Auburn	Washington	3
Rogers, Reggie	190	LB	Fresno State	Houston	7
Roland, Benji	191	DT	Auburn	Minnesota	7
Roper, John	36	LB	Texas A&M	Chicago	2
Ross, Everett	335	WR	Ohio State	Minnesota	12
Ross, Greg	275	NT	Memphis State	Miami	10
Roth, Jeff	125	DT	Florida	Dallas	5
Royal, Rickey	177	DB	Sam Houston State	Phoenix	7
Sadowski, Troy	145	TE	Georgia	Atlanta	6
Sancho, Ron	171	LB	Louisiana State	Kansas City	7
Sanders, Barry	3	RB	Oklahoma State	Detroit	1
Sanders, Byron	248	RB	Northwestern	Chicago	9
Sanders, Deion	5	DB	Florida State	Atlanta	1
Schlereth, Mark	263	C	Idaho	Washington	10
Shannon, Randy	280	LB	Miami	Dallas	11
Shelton, Richard	292	DB	Liberty	Denver	11
Sherman, Heath	162	RB	Texas A&I	Philadelphia	6
Shiver, Stan	310	DB	Florida State	Green Bay	12
Shulman, Brian	206	P	Auburn	Green Bay	8
Simpson, John	277	WR	Baylor	Chicago	10
Sinclair, Andy	279	C	Stanford	San Francisco	10
Singer, Paul	202	QB	Western Illinois	Atlanta	8
Slater, Brian	285	WR	Washington	Pittsburgh	11

Georgia RB Tim Worley (No. 7) is a Steeler.

Player	Order No.	Pos.	College	Club	Round
Small, Jessie	49	LB	Eastern Kentucky	Philadelphia	2
Smider, Brian	298	T	West Virginia	Houston	11
Smiley, Tim	129	DB	Arkansas State	Washington	5
Smith, Brian	48	LB	Auburn	Los Angeles Rams	2
Smith, Elliot	120	DB	Alcorn State	San Diego	5
Smith, Eric	326	LB	UCLA	New York Giants	12
Smith, Kendal	194	WR	Utah State	Cincinnati	7
Smith, Monte	236	G	North Dakota	Denver	9
Smith, Sammie	9	RB	Florida State	Miami	1
Snead, Willie	321	WR	Florida	New York Jets	12
Snyder, Brent	192	QB	Utah State	Chicago	7
Stafford, Anthony	152	WR	Oklahoma	Denver	6
Stallworth, Cedric	281	DB	Georgia Tech	Green Bay	11
Stallworth, Ron	98	DE	Auburn	New York Jets	4
Stams, Frank	45	LB	Notre Dame	Los Angeles Rams	2
Stephens, Richard	250	T	Tulsa	Cincinnati	9
Stepnoski, Mark	57	G	Pittsburgh	Dallas	3
Stewart, Alex	219	DE	Cal State-Fullerton	Minnesota	8
Stewart, Andrew	107	DE	Cincinnati	Cleveland	4
Stock, Mark	144	WR	Virginia Military	Pittsburgh	6
Stoyanovich, Pete	203	K	Indiana	Miami	8
Streeter, George	304	DB	Notre Dame	Chicago	11
Tardits, Richard	123	LB	Georgia	Phoenix	5
Taylor, Craig	166	RB	West Virginia	Cincinnati	6
Taylor, Jay	150	DB	San Jose State	Phoenix	6
Taylor, Steve	323	QB	Nebraska	Indianapolis	12
Thomas, Broderick	6	LB	Nebraska	Tampa Bay	1
Thomas, Derrick	4	LB	Alabama	Kansas City	1
Thomas, Robb	143	WR	Oregon State	Kansas City	6
Thompson, Jim	266	T	Auburn	Indianapolis	10
Tillman, Lawyer	31	WR	Auburn	Cleveland	2
Tillman, Lewis	93	RB	Jackson State	New York Giants	4
Timpson, Michael	100	WR	Penn State	New England	4
Tobey, Bryan	199	RB	Grambling	Kansas City	8
Tofflemire, Joe	44	C	Arizona	Seattle	2
Tolbert, Tony	85	DE	Texas-El Paso	Dallas	4
Tolliver, Billy Joe	51	QB	Texas Tech	San Diego	2
Tomberlin, Pat	99	G	Florida State	Indianapolis	4
Trainor, Kendall	234	K	Arkansas	Phoenix	9
Tuatagaloa, Natu	138	DT	California	Cincinnati	5
Turner, Floyd	159	WR	N.W. Louisiana	New Orleans	6
Turner, Marcus	283	DB	UCLA	Kansas City	11
Uhlenhake, Jeff	121	C	Ohio State	Miami	5
Utley, Mike	59	G	Washington State	Detroit	3
Wahler, Jim	94	DT	UCLA	Phoenix	4
Walls, Wesley	56	TE	Mississippi	San Francisco	2
Washington, Charles	185	DB	Cameron (Okla.)	Indianapolis	7
Washington, Marvin	151	DE	Idaho	New York Jets	6
Weidner, Bert	288	DT	Kent State	Miami	11
Wells, Dana	306	DT	Arizona	Cincinnati	11
Weston, Rhondy	68	DE	Florida	Dallas	3
Weygand, Freddy	330	WR	Auburn	Chicago	12
Wheat, Warren	215	T	Brigham Young	Los Angeles Rams	8
Widell, Doug	41	G	Boston College	Denver	2
Wilhelm, Erik	83	QB	Oregon State	Cincinnati	3
Wilkerson, Gary	160	DB	Penn State	Cleveland	6
Williams, Brian	18	G	Minnesota	New York Giants	1
Williams, David	23	T	Florida	Houston	1

Dolphins chose Florida S Louis Oliver (No. 25).

Player	Order No.	Pos.	College	Club	Round
Williams, Jerrol	91	LB	Purdue	Pittsburgh	4
Williams, Marlin	211	DE	Western Illinois	Seattle	8
Williams, Mike	269	WR	Northeastern	Los Angeles Rams	10
Williams, Wayne	241	RB	Florida	Denver	9
Wilson, Curtis	247	C	Missouri	New England	9
Wisniewski, Steve	29	G	Penn State	Dallas	2
Wolf, Joe	17	G	Boston College	Phoenix	1
Woods, Jerry	170	DB	Northern Michigan	Detroit	7

Player	Order No.	Pos.	College	Club	Round
Woods, Rob	111	T	Arizona	Cincinnati	4
Woods, Tony	216	DT	Oklahoma	Chicago	8
Woodson, Shawn	331	LB	James Madison	Minnesota	12
Woolford, Donnell	11	DB	Clemson	Chicago	1
Workman, Vince	127	RB	Ohio State	Green Bay	5
Worley, Tim	7	RB	Georgia	Pittsburgh	1
Worthen, Nasrallah	60	WR	North Carolina State	Kansas City	3
Young, Terry	329	DB	Georgia Southern	Tampa Bay	12
Zackery, Tony	223	DB	Washington	New England	8
Zandofsky, Mike	67	G	Washington	Phoenix	3
Zawatson, Dave	54	T	California	Chicago	2
Zdelar, Jim	176	T	Youngstown	Miami	7

Falcons made Florida State DB Deion Sanders top pick.

1989
NFL SCHEDULE

*NIGHT GAME

SUNDAY, SEPT. 10
Buffalo at Miami
Cincinnati at Chicago
Cleveland at Pittsburgh
Dallas at New Orleans
Houston at Minnesota
Kansas City at Denver
Los Angeles Rams at Atlanta
New England at New York Jets
Phoenix at Detroit
San Diego at Los Angeles Raiders
San Francisco at Indianapolis
Seattle at Philadelphia
Tampa Bay at Green Bay

MONDAY, SEPT. 11
*New York Giants at Washington

SUNDAY, SEPT. 17
Dallas at Atlanta
Detroit at New York Giants
Houston at San Diego
Indianapolis at Los Angeles Rams
Los Angeles Raiders at Kansas City
Miami at New England
Minnesota at Chicago
New Orleans at Green Bay
New York Jets at Cleveland
Philadelphia at Washington
Phoenix at Seattle
Pittsburgh at Cincinnati
San Francisco at Tampa Bay

MONDAY, SEPT. 18
*Denver at Buffalo

SUNDAY, SEPT. 24
Atlanta at Indianapolis
Buffalo at Houston
Chicago at Detroit
Green Bay at Los Angeles Rams
Kansas City at San Diego

Los Angeles Raiders at Denver
Minnesota at Pittsburgh
New Orleans at Tampa Bay
New York Jets at Miami
Phoenix at New York Giants
San Francisco at Philadelphia
Seattle at New England
Washington at Dallas

MONDAY, SEPT. 25
*Cleveland at Cincinnati

SUNDAY, OCT. 1
Atlanta vs. Green Bay at Milwaukee
Cincinnati at Kansas City
Denver at Cleveland
Indianapolis at New York Jets
Los Angeles Rams at San Francisco
Miami at Houston
New England at Buffalo
New York Giants at Dallas
Pittsburgh at Detroit
San Diego at Phoenix
Seattle at Los Angeles Raiders
Tampa Bay at Minnesota
Washington at New Orleans

MONDAY, OCT. 2
*Philadelphia at Chicago

SUNDAY, OCT. 8
Atlanta at Los Angeles Rams
Buffalo at Indianapolis
Chicago at Tampa Bay
Cincinnati at Pittsburgh
Cleveland at Miami
Dallas at Green Bay
Detroit at Minnesota
Houston at New England
Kansas City at Seattle
New Orleans at San Francisco
New York Giants at Philadelphia
Phoenix at Washington
San Diego at Denver

Seattle's Steve Largent: All-time NFL pass-catcher.

MONDAY, OCT. 9
*Los Angeles Raiders at N.Y. Jets

SUNDAY, OCT. 15
Detroit at Tampa Bay
Green Bay at Minnesota
Houston at Chicago
Indianapolis at Denver
Kansas City at Los Angeles Raiders
Miami at Cincinnati
New England at Atlanta
New York Jets at New Orleans
Philadelphia at Phoenix
Pittsburgh at Cleveland
San Francisco at Dallas
Seattle at San Diego
Washington at New York Giants

MONDAY, OCT. 16
*Los Angeles Rams at Buffalo

SUNDAY, OCT. 22
Atlanta at Phoenix
Dallas at Kansas City
Denver at Seattle
Green Bay at Miami
Indianapolis at Cincinnati
Los Angeles Raiders at Philadelphia
Minnesota at Detroit
New England at San Francisco
New Orleans at Los Angeles Rams
New York Giants at San Diego
New York Jets at Buffalo
Pittsburgh at Houston
Tampa Bay at Washington

MONDAY, OCT. 23
*Chicago at Cleveland

SUNDAY, OCT. 29
Atlanta at New Orleans
Detroit vs. Green Bay at Milwaukee
Houston at Cleveland
Kansas City at Pittsburgh
Los Angeles Rams at Chicago
Miami at Buffalo
New England at Indianapolis
Philadelphia at Denver
Phoenix at Dallas
San Diego at Seattle
San Francisco at New York Jets

Tampa Bay at Cincinnati
Washington at Los Angeles Raiders

MONDAY, OCT. 30
*Minnesota at New York Giants

SUNDAY, NOV. 5
Buffalo at Atlanta
Chicago at Green Bay
Cincinnati at Los Angeles Raiders
Cleveland at Tampa Bay
Detroit at Houston
Indianapolis at Miami
Los Angeles Rams at Minnesota
New York Giants at Phoenix
New York Jets at New England
Philadelphia at San Diego
Pittsburgh at Denver
Seattle at Kansas City
*Dallas at Washington

MONDAY, NOV. 6
*San Francisco at New Orleans

SUNDAY, NOV. 12
Atlanta at San Francisco
Chicago at Pittsburgh
Cleveland at Seattle
Dallas at Phoenix
Denver at Kansas City
Green Bay at Detroit
Indianapolis at Buffalo
Miami at New York Jets
Minnesota at Tampa Bay
New Orleans at New England
New York Giants at Los Angeles Rams
Washington at Philadelphia
*Los Angeles Raiders at San Diego

MONDAY, NOV. 13
*Cincinnati at Houston

SUNDAY, NOV. 19
Buffalo at New England
Detroit at Cincinnati
Green Bay at San Francisco
Kansas City at Cleveland
Los Angeles Raiders at Houston
Miami at Dallas
Minnesota at Philadelphia
New Orleans at Atlanta

Phoenix at Los Angeles Rams
San Diego at Pittsburgh
Seattle at New York Giants
Tampa Bay at Chicago
*New York Jets at Indianapolis

MONDAY, NOV. 20
*Denver at Washington

THURSDAY, NOV. 23
Cleveland at Detroit
Philadelphia at Dallas

SUNDAY, NOV. 26
Atlanta at New York Jets
Chicago at Washington
Cincinnati at Buffalo
Houston at Kansas City
Minnesota vs. Green Bay at Milwaukee
New England at Los Angeles Raiders
Pittsburgh at Miami
San Diego at Indianapolis
Seattle at Denver
Tampa Bay at Phoenix
*Los Angeles Rams at New Orleans

MONDAY, NOV. 27
*New York Giants at San Francisco

SUNDAY, DEC. 3
Cincinnati at Cleveland
Denver at Los Angeles Raiders
Green Bay at Tampa Bay
Houston at Pittsburgh
Indianapolis at New England
Los Angeles Rams at Dallas
Miami at Kansas City
New Orleans at Detroit
New York Jets at San Diego
Philadelphia at New York Giants
San Francisco at Atlanta
Washington at Phoenix
*Chicago at Minnesota

MONDAY, DEC. 4
*Buffalo at Seattle

SUNDAY, DEC. 10
Atlanta at Minnesota
Cleveland at Indianapolis
Dallas at Philadelphia

Detroit at Chicago
Kansas City at Green Bay
New Orleans at Buffalo
New York Giants at Denver
Phoenix at Los Angeles Raiders
Pittsburgh at New York Jets
San Diego at Washington
Seattle at Cincinnati
Tampa Bay at Houston
*New England at Miami

MONDAY, DEC. 11
*San Francisco at Los Angeles Rams

SATURDAY, DEC. 16
Dallas at New York Giants
Denver at Phoenix

SUNDAY, DEC. 17
Buffalo at San Francisco
Green Bay at Chicago
Houston at Cincinnati
Miami at Indianapolis
Minnesota at Cleveland
New England at Pittsburgh
New York Jets at Los Angeles Rams
San Diego at Kansas City
Tampa Bay at Detroit
Washington at Atlanta
*Los Angeles Raiders at Seattle

MONDAY, DEC. 18
*Philadelphia at New Orleans

SATURDAY, DEC. 23
Buffalo at New York Jets
Washington at Seattle
*Cleveland at Houston

SUNDAY, DEC. 24
Chicago at San Francisco
Denver at San Diego
Detroit at Atlanta
Green Bay at Dallas
Indianapolis at New Orleans
Kansas City at Miami
Los Angeles Raiders at N.Y. Giants
Los Angeles Rams at New England
Phoenix at Philadelphia
Pittsburgh at Tampa Bay

MONDAY, DEC. 25
*Cincinnati at Minnesota

Will this finally be the Year of the Bills and Jim Kelly?

Nationally Televised Games

(All games carried on CBS Radio Network)

REGULAR SEASON

Monday, Sept. 11–New York Giants at Washington (night, ABC)
Monday, Sept. 18–Denver at Buffalo (night, ABC)
Monday, Sept. 25–Cleveland at Cincinnati (night, ABC)
Monday, Oct. 2–Philadelphia at Chicago (night, ABC)
Monday, Oct. 9–Los Angeles Raiders at New York Jets (night, ABC)
Monday, Oct. 16–Los Angeles Rams at Buffalo (night, ABC)
Monday, Oct. 23–Chicago at Cleveland (night, ABC)
Monday, Oct. 30–Minnesota at New York Giants (night, ABC)
Sunday, Nov. 5–Dallas at Washington (night, ESPN)
Monday, Nov. 6–San Francisco at New Orleans (night, ABC)
Sunday, Nov. 12–Los Angeles Raiders at San Diego (night, ESPN)
Monday, Nov. 13–Cincinnati at Houston (night, ABC)
Sunday, Nov. 19–New York Jets at Indianapolis (night, ESPN)
Monday, Nov. 20–Denver at Washington (night, ABC)
Thursday, Nov. 23–Cleveland at Detroit (day, NBC)
     Philadelphia at Dallas (day, CBS)
Sunday, Nov. 26–Los Angeles Rams at New Orleans (night, ESPN)
Monday, Nov. 27–New York Giants at San Francisco (night, ABC)
Sunday, Dec. 3–Chicago at Minnesota (night, ESPN)
Monday, Dec. 4–Buffalo at Seattle (night, ABC)
Sunday, Dec. 10–New England at Miami (night, ESPN)
Monday, Dec. 11–San Francisco at Los Angeles Rams (night, ABC)
Saturday, Dec. 16–Dallas at New York Giants (day, CBS)
     Denver at Phoenix (day, NBC)
Sunday, Dec. 17–Los Angeles Raiders at Seattle (night, ESPN)
Monday, Dec. 18–Philadelphia at New Orleans (night, ABC)
Saturday, Dec. 23–Buffalo at New York Jets (day, NBC)
     Washington at Seattle (day, CBS)
     Cleveland at Houston (night, ESPN)
Monday, Dec. 25–Cincinnati at Minnesota (night, ABC)

POSTSEASON

Sunday, Dec. 31–AFC and NFC First-Round Playoffs (NBC and CBS)
Saturday, Jan. 6–AFC and NFC Divisional Playoffs (NBC and CBS)
Sunday, Jan. 7–AFC and NFC Divisional Playoffs (NBC and CBS)
Sunday, Jan. 14–AFC and NFC Championship Games (NBC and CBS)
Sunday, Jan. 28–Super Bowl XXIV, Louisiana Superdome,
 New Orleans, (CBS)
Sunday, Feb. 4–AFC-NFC Pro Bowl, Honolulu, Hawaii (ESPN)

Revised and updated with over 75 all
new sports records and photographs!

THE ILLUSTRATED
SPORTS RECORD BOOK
Zander Hollander and David Schulz

Here, in a single book, are more than 350
all-time sports records with stories and
photos so vivid it's like "being there." All the
sports classics are here: Babe Ruth, Wilt
Chamberlain, Muhammad Ali ... plus the
stories of such active stars as Dwight Gooden
and Wayne Gretzky. This is the authoritative
book on what the great records are, and
who set them—an engrossing, fun-filled
reference guide filled with anecdotes of
hundreds of renowned athletes whose
remarkable records remain as fresh as when
they were set.
